Planting
Growing
Churches
for the 21st Century

Other Books by Aubrey Malphurs

Advanced Strategic Planning
Being Leaders
Biblical Manhood and Womanhood
Building Leaders (coauthor)
Church Next (coauthor)
A Contemporary Handbook for Weddings, Funerals, and Other Occasions (coauthor)
Developing a Dynamic Mission for Your Ministry
Developing a Vision for Ministry in the Twenty-first Century
Doing Church
The Dynamics of Church Leadership
Maximizing Your Effectiveness
Ministry Nuts and Bolts
Pouring New Wine into Old Wineskins
Strategy 2000
Values-Driven Leadership
Vision America

Planting
Growing
Churches
for the 21st Century

*A Comprehensive Guide
for New Churches and
Those Desiring Renewal*

Third Edition

Aubrey Malphurs

BakerBooks

Grand Rapids, Michigan

© 2004 by Aubrey Malphurs

Published by Baker Books
a division of Baker Publishing Group
P.O. Box 6287, Grand Rapids, MI 49516-6287
www.bakerbooks.com

Printed in the United States of America

Library of Congress Cataloging-in-Publication Data
Malphurs, Aubrey.
    Planting growing churches for the 21st century : a comprehensive guide for
new churches and those desiring renewal / Aubrey Malphurs.—3rd ed.
        p.   cm.
    Includes bibliographical references and index.
    ISBN 10: 0-8010-6514-3 (pbk.)
    ISBN 978-0-8010-6514-9 (pbk.)
    1. Church development, New. I. Title.
BV652.24.M35 2004
254'.1—dc22   2004012909

10   11   12   13   14   15   16   11   10   9   8   7   6   5

To all of my students
who've caught the vision
and taken the risk

Contents

Foreword

This book invades enemy territory and challenges the strongholds of the adversary. These strongholds don't exist "out there." They are the ideas and thoughts that are satanically designed to siphon life and vitality out of the living organism we call the church. These mind-sets inform decisions and determine directions that are often contrary to divine intent and strategy.

It is the nature of a living organism to grow. If it is not growing, something is wrong. The church, a living organism, is not growing in the United States. In fact not a single country has experienced church growth in the past decade. Yet the Lord of the church declared that the gates of hell would not be able to withstand the attack of the church.

Something is wrong. Some thoughts have not been brought into captivity to Christ and his plan for the growth of his church.

Sometimes the roadblock is theological. More often the problem is cultural mind-sets that create invisible barriers to evangelism and church growth. By and large the old wineskins cannot contain the new wine of the Spirit. The letter kills, but the Spirit brings life.

According to Dr. Malphurs, the most effective and efficient way to reach the seeker is to plant new churches and, where possible, bring renewal to existing churches. Whatever route taken, growth is predicated on keeping that living organism healthy, biblically informed, and culturally relevant. Like a pediatrician, the author leads the reader through the church planting process of conception, birth, growth, maturation, and reproduction.

Those with a heart for church planting will find no better treatment of the subject than *Planting Growing Churches for the 21st Century*. We can be thankful for its breadth and depth, for its attention to detail and practicality. For those longing for church renewal the principles delineated in this book could be the key to the revitalization of the existing church.

This book will aid church planters in tearing down the strongholds of doubt and misbelief and raising up vital churches prepared for the challenges of the twenty-first century.

Joe Aldrich
Former president, Multnomah School of the Bible

Introduction

I must have been daydreaming because I missed my exit off the freeway. It was Sunday morning, and I was on my way to fill a pulpit in a church located in a suburb of affluent north Dallas. The next exit was only a mile farther, so I was not greatly inconvenienced. It would cost me five minutes at the most. Yet that five minutes proved to be interesting and informative. Not far from the exit, I drove past a family-oriented health club. I was amazed at all the cars and vans crowded into the parking lot. The attractive, well-kept facility was packed and it wasn't even 11:00 AM! A few minutes later I arrived at my destination. It was a small, rundown church with an unkempt lawn. As I pulled into the parking lot, I noted that there weren't many cars. I had my choice of parking places.

The last fifty years have proved increasingly difficult for the church in America, whether liberal or evangelical. Things have not progressed as planned. During the first half of the twentieth century, the future looked bright. The people who attended church were those born in the 1910–1930 era, people whom Lyle Schaller describes as "the most church-going generation in American history."[1] In general, America was a Judeo-Christian, churched culture. On Sunday mornings, most people were found in their denominationally loyal churches; it was the thing to do. In fact, if people weren't in church on Sunday morning, chances were good that they had stayed home and slept in—behavior that was frowned on. The 1940s and the 1950s were the heyday for the church. If this was any indication of things to come, then the future looked bright. Perhaps the church would win the world for Christ in the twentieth century.

The church situation in the latter half of the century (in particular the 1980s and 1990s) forms a stark contrast to that of the first half. Storm clouds moved in and darkened the bright horizon of American Christianity. Rather than sending missionaries out from America and winning the world for Christ, America itself became a mission field. In 1988 church growth expert Win Arn wrote: "Between 80 percent and 85 percent of all churches in America are either *plateaued* or are *declining*." Then he added the following information:

America: 240 million population
           96 million (40%) have no religious affiliation
           73 million (31%) are Christians in "name only"
           169 million (71%) of total U.S. population[2]

At around the same period of time, George Gallup published *The Unchurched American—10 Years Later*. This was a sequel to a similar study that the organization had completed in 1977. In the later work, he indicated that the number of unchurched Americans had increased. He noted:

> Trying to analyze the findings of *The Unchurched American—10 Years Later* is a little like trying to decide whether the glass is half-full or half-empty—there's evidence to support both views.
> For those who believe the glass is half-empty, the evidence is that the churches have not made any inroads into attracting the unchurched over the past decade: in 1978, 41 percent of all American adults (18 or older) were unchurched; in 1988, that figure rose to 44 percent. . . .
> The same evidence, however, also supports the contention that the glass is half-full. One might maintain that the churches have done well to keep slippage to a minimum in light of the continued high mobility among Americans during the last decade, the distractions of modern life and the apparent growing appeal of non-traditional religious movements.[3]

Regardless of whether the glass was viewed as half-empty or half-full, the future looked bleak in terms of reaching unchurched America. Gallup's research indicated that things were moving in the wrong direction. Many churches were plateaued or decreasing in numbers while the ranks of the unchurched were growing. In May 2004 George Barna notes that the number of unchurched adults has nearly doubled since 1991.[4]

In *Effective Church Leadership*, Kennon Callahan summarizes what had taken place in the second half of the twentieth century:

> Yet, on all sides, it is self-evident that we are no longer in the churched culture that existed in the late 1940s and the 1950s.
> Statistical research, analyses of this culture, and long-range projections all clearly indicate that ours is no longer a churched culture. Study after study and the steady decline of many mainline denominations confirm this fact. We are clearly and decisively entering the mission field of the 1990s.[5]

Early in the twenty-first century the situation hasn't changed for the better. Secularism seems to be winning the day, and America is now clearly a post-Christian culture—if it ever was a Judeo-Christian culture. I heard from one church planter in inner-city Houston, Texas, who said that many of the people he's attempting to reach don't even know who Jesus Christ is. And that is true elsewhere as well. Some have only heard the Savior's name used profanely, while others have never heard it used at all. We're experiencing a modern-day Judges 2:10: "After that whole generation had been gathered to their fathers, another generation grew up, who knew neither the LORD nor what he had done."

All of this "doom and gloom" information raises an obvious question about the future of the church. Like the patient who's just been diagnosed with cancer, we want to know what our chances are for survival. Actually we can be optimistic about the future of American Christianity. While there will be lots of church funerals and much grief, not only will the American church survive, but it will bounce back and thrive.

The reason we can be this optimistic lies in the inerrant, absolute truth of the Scriptures. While on the one hand, we need to be aware of the severe problems facing the American church, on the other hand, we can claim the promise found in Matthew 16:18. Jesus says to Peter and to us, "And I tell you that you are Peter, and on this rock I will build my church, and the gates of Hades will not overcome it." Regardless of one's interpretation of this passage—and there are many—Jesus is saying that his church will survive. It has survived in the annals of church history; it has survived tremendous oppression in other countries in the nineteenth and twentieth centuries; and it will survive in America in the twenty-first century.

But how can we reconcile Matthew 16:18 and the current state of the church in America? While the church has survived the twentieth century and will thrive again in the twenty-first century, the present form of the church will change. The early twenty-first century church does not look the same as the typical, traditional church of the twentieth century. What has worked in the past will not work in the future.

This is not necessarily bad. There's a difference between what a church believes and what it practices. The church's faith must not change, because it is based on the eternal, absolute truth of the Bible. The church's practices (how the church implements its faith), on the other hand, must change from generation to generation as well as from culture to culture if the church is to be relevant, that is, to communicate the gospel clearly to new generations so that they at least understand the message. If a church desires to reach its generation in its culture, it must adapt its practices (not its faith) to that culture. This is one of the important principles that the church of the twentieth century missed. And this is one of the reasons why it has fared so poorly at the end of the century and the beginning of the twenty-first century. If the culture rejects Christianity, it should be because it has refused to hear the message of Christ rather than that it turned its back on the church's outdated, culturally irrelevant methods (1 Cor. 1:23).

Another question that must be answered is where the churches that thrive in the twenty-first century will come from. A great number will be planted. In fact, at the end of the 1990s and into the twenty-first century, there has been an awakening of the church. Many are catching a vision for reaching lost, unchurched Americans through the planting of a number of dynamic, leading-edge twenty-first-century churches. The Southern Baptist Convention plans to start sixty thousand churches before 2020. And more than fifty thousand churches were planted in North America between 1980 and 2000.[6] As Peter Wagner says, *"The single most effective evangelistic methodology under heaven is planting new churches."*[7]

While some established churches will renew themselves and successfully make the transition, this will be too painful and too difficult for the bulk of them, and they'll not survive. In fact a large number of churches closed their doors in the 1990s. Consequently, church planting will be the future for the American church (as it was for the first-century church) because it's far easier to plant a new church than to renew a dying one.

What will some of these twenty-first-century thriving churches look like? That's not a hard question to answer. Actually there are some positive indications that an awakening has started. God has already begun to sprinkle a number of these leading-edge churches across America. There have been a number of pioneers in the recent past who have braved much criticism[8] and taken the risk to start innovative, culturally relevant, Great Commission churches, which are reaching many unchurched lost. Today there are a number of church planters who are catching the vision and spirit of these pioneers and are fanning out across America to reach the growing nonchurched population. What was merely a spark is becoming a flame in the early twenty-first century.

The church needs to equip a generation of Christians with a deep passion to plant biblically based, spiritually healthy, Great Commission churches. These in turn will commit themselves to the task of sowing churches to reach various generations (modern and postmodern) and the people groups at home and abroad. This is by no means a new vision; it is already present in the pages of the book of Acts!

My temptation is to focus this book primarily on planting churches to reach the younger, postmodern generations, because over time they're the future of the church in America and Western Europe. So far I've resisted, because *modernism is still very much alive and well and will continue to be in the twenty-first century. And it's my contention that we must plant churches to reach both moderns and postmoderns if we're to be biblical.* Granted, more information exists on how to plant churches to reach moderns. Consequently, *I will address how to plant churches to reach postmoderns as well (see appendix G in particular).*

The purpose of this book is to encourage and equip individuals and churches to take a risk and become a vital part of this vision—to start church-planting churches (churches that will in turn plant other churches). Encouragement is essential because church planting isn't easy, and there are many within evangelical Christianity who are casting and will continue to cast stones. Yet we need to give God a chance! Take the risk! Ask the question, "What can God accomplish through *me?"*

It is essential to equip individuals and churches, because not many have the vision to pursue, evangelize, and disciple lost, unchurched people. A significant number of those who have caught this vision are implementing it the wrong way and are experiencing failure and disillusionment. They're attempting to plant churches that are replicas of the excellent pioneer churches that were so successful at reaching the unchurched Baby Boomers for the Savior in the latter half of the twentieth century. Certainly, much can be learned from these churches, and some of what they did is transferable. However, rather than imitate others, this book is committed to equipping church planters to design tailor-made, biblically based churches that are compatible with who they are (their unique identity), where they are (their unique location), and whom they're trying to reach (their unique community). The key is to pursue a common, proven process, not to clone the ministry of others.

This book is divided into three parts. Part 1 concerns the preparation for church planting. Its purpose is to orient the prospective church planter to the topic. It consists of four chapters. The first chapter defines the topic. The second chapter presents some thought-provoking reasons for getting involved in church birthing. The third chapter addresses some of the means for planting churches, provides information for budgeting, and gives some practical tips on how to raise finances. The fourth chapter presents various assumptions that undergird this work, such as the proper emphasis on numerical growth, the principles versus practice debate, the place of faith, and how to handle failure.

Part 2 examines the personnel for church planting. It consists of two chapters. The first helps you answer the question, "Am I a church planter?" or "Where do I fit into the process of starting churches?" The second helps you to determine if you're the kind of strong leader that's required to be a point or lead church starter.

Part 3 examines the actual process of starting a church. It contains seven chapters that are designed to help church planters understand the six stages that a new church passes through and what essentially takes place in each. These six stages—conception, development, birth, growth, maturity, and reproduction—are analogous to birthing a child.

Rather than locate worksheets at the end of key chapters, I've placed them in a Church Planter's Workbook, located at the back of this book. Throughout the book I will invite you to turn to the workbook to implement the content of certain chapters in your unique ministry situation. I'll also refer to the rich source of information in the appendices on such topics as people mobilization, culture, authentic worship, evangelism, and small groups. Be sure not to miss them.

This book is not only for church planters but also for those who are already in a church and want to learn more about how growing churches function. I woke up to this reality when I noted that some students at Dallas Seminary were taking my church-planting course but desired to pastor an established church. When I questioned them about why they were in the course, they said that much of the material was relevant to leading and pastoring in any church context.

This is no small book! Yet there is so much more to say! Thus I've placed additional material on my website, www.malphursgroup.com, to help you further. Check it out at www.malphursgroup.com/ChurchPlanting and register to receive further information on leadership.

Part 1

The Preparation
for Church Planting

At a very young age, my son planted his first garden: carrots, lettuce, tomatoes, green beans, potatoes, and onions. Unfortunately, it didn't do very well. Only the beans came up, and they left much to be desired. We had visions of fresh vegetables at each meal, so we were disappointed. Later we discovered that the garden didn't grow because Mike had failed to prepare the soil before planting the seed!

Church planting has much in common with gardening. It's imperative that those involved prepare the soil by thinking through certain key issues before attempting to plant the seed. Once this is accomplished, the chances of a fruitful harvest are much more likely. Consequently, Part 1 of this book covers four "seed" issues that are foundational. They include the definition of, reasons for, means for, and assumptions of church planting.

1

What Are We Talking About?

The Definition of Church Planting

The terms *leader* and *leadership* have become buzzwords among most leading-edge churches and ministry organizations in today's world. However, I've noted that few have paused to define what these terms mean to them and how they're using them. My question is, If we don't define our terms, how can we be sure that we're even talking about the same thing? Further, if our passion is to develop leaders and we don't have a clear definition, how can we know what we're attempting to accomplish and whether or not we've arrived?

Consequently, to avoid the potential for misunderstanding and miscommunication, this book will begin with a definition of church planting. I define *church planting* as an exhausting but exciting venture of faith that involves the planned process of beginning and growing new local churches, based on Jesus' promise and in obedience to his Great Commission.

Church Planting Exhausts

Church planting is not easy. It's exhausting work! However, it's no different than any other ministry in that church planters "reap what they sow." If they work hard, the ministry grows; if they take it easy, the ministry plateaus and eventually dies. Church planting can be exhausting because church planters must be initiators and because the actual work of planting a church is hard.

Church Planters Are Initiators

Church planters are initiators not maintainers. They're characterized as proactive and intentional. Far too many churches in America aren't aware that the churched culture of the mid–twentieth century no longer exists and that America is now largely an unchurched, post-Christian culture. In a churched culture the thing to do is to attend church on Sunday, whereas the thing to do in an unchurched culture is anything *but* attend church on Sunday. People spend time with their families, go to a shopping center, take in a movie, go to a ballgame, watch their children play soccer, or go to the health club. Sunday may be their only day off. It's a day to relax and have fun. So why would anyone want to go to church? And that's the question you as a church planter must answer.

In a churched culture, pastors could be maintainers because people sought them out for ministry. In an unchurched culture, pastors must be initiators or watch their churches die. Church planters also have to be initiators when it comes to reaching people and building churches. They cannot sit in their studies and wait for people to come to them, because most people will not come. The days of maintenance ministry are over. Instead, leaders will have to develop strategies and lead their people in reaching the unchurched in their communities. Initiation takes far more mental, emotional, and physical effort than maintenance. The result is often exhaustion.

Church Planting Is Hard Work

Church planting is hard work. That's not to say that pastoring an established church isn't hard work. It is! But there's a difference. First, church planters spend less time in the study (at least initially) and more time in the field. This fieldwork consists of networking with core members and lost people. It involves countless hours of sharing a vision over coffee. It includes much time in the car driving to various appointments to meet with people who are interested in the new work or who are in places and positions to help it.

Another reason it's hard is that church-planting pastors are criticized more than are pastors of established churches. Because many established churches in America are still living and ministering with a twentieth-century mentality, they're convinced that what has worked in the past will continue to work in the future. Consequently, there's a tendency among some to be critical of anything that's contemporary and innovative. The real tragedy is that they simply don't understand what it is they're criticizing. Regardless, the rocks they throw are big and they hurt: "It's of the devil!" "It's Christian hedonism!" "It's just secular entertainment!"

Criticism can be very hard and emotionally exhausting for those innovative pioneers who dare to "color outside the lines." They will have to pay a price to do what is right, because many who belong to the Christian community will not understand.

Church Planting Excites

While church planting may be exhausting, this is balanced by the fact that it is most exciting. I have attended or visited numerous established churches that, quite frankly, were rather boring. Not much is happening in these churches. Every Sunday there are the same old faces, the same old sermons, and the same old hymns played on the same old organ by the same old organist. Everything is predictable. In fact, we begin to know which choir member will fall asleep first during the sermon and approximately when that will take place!

Boredom and routine are completely foreign to church planting. Starting a church is one of the most exciting spiritual ventures a group of Christians may ever undertake. In fact, if you're not excited about it, don't do it!

There are several factors behind this intense excitement. One is that church planting appeals to the pioneer spirit. The idea of starting something new and different appeals to a spirit of entrepreneurship that lies deep within the soul of church starters. They relish the idea of being on the leading edge of something new that God is doing!

Another factor is the sense of anticipation. As Christians, we know that God is capable of doing extraordinary things in and through our lives, such as building a great church. While we may never have experienced these things personally, we're aware that others have. But maybe it's our turn! Maybe God is about to do something extraordinary, and we're going to be part of it!

A third factor is expectation. Not only do we anticipate that God could do something special through the new church, but deep within our being we expect him to do so. We can feel it in our bones! We sense that the time is right; the time is now!

Life is too short, and we don't have many opportunities to be involved in something special for God. Consequently, let's step out in faith and be a part of a great new work for him. After all, how can we know what God intends to do until we've tried it?

Church Planting Requires Faith

Church planting is an exhausting but exciting venture of faith. Whenever people put on pioneer garb and ride off into the wilderness, they have entered the realm of faith. This means that they, like Abraham, will have to move outside their comfort zones of certainty and security and enter an unknown, somewhat frightening world. This involves taking risks, which is easier for some than for others. Yet faith and risk go hand in hand.

Anything of authentic spiritual significance is accomplished through faith. The writer of Hebrews affirms that "without faith it is impossible to please God" (Heb. 11:6). Those who enlist in launching new churches must be men and women of strong, stretching faith in God. This involves both believing and obeying God.

People Who Believe God

We must be willing to believe God as Noah did when he built the ark in spite of the fact that there was no sign there was going to be a flood (v. 7). There are numerous commands in Scripture that require Christians to believe God can do the impossible. For example, in Matthew 6:33 the Savior says that if we seek first his kingdom and his righteousness, God will provide for the basic necessities of our lives, such as food, drink, and clothing. We either believe him and act, or doubt and vacillate.

People Who Obey God

We must be willing not only to believe but to obey God, as Abraham did when he responded to God's call to leave Haran, even though God hadn't revealed where Abraham was going (Heb. 11:8). The command was simply "Go!" In a similar way, church planters must obey God and travel to locations that are new and foreign to them. It's important that they believe that God is sending them to a special place for a significant ministry and will provide for them along the way.

What kinds of things impress the Savior? In Matthew 8:5–13, a centurion had strong faith in Christ's ability to heal his servant. Jesus was astounded and said, "I tell you the truth, I have not found anyone in Israel with such great faith" (v. 10). In Matthew 15:21–28 a Gentile woman trusted deeply in Jesus' ability to heal her daughter. The Savior healed her daughter and said, "Woman, you have great faith." God is impressed not with our education or the degrees hanging on our walls but with men and women of faith who are willing to trust him for the impossible.

Church planters are men and women of intense, authentic faith. They believe and obey God as demonstrated in their willingness to step out and boldly bring unchurched communities the saving message of Christ. They're people with whom the Savior is impressed; he acknowledges, "Your faith is great!"

Church Planting Involves a Process

Church planting is an exhausting but exciting venture of faith that involves a process. It's dynamic. It's not a once and for all kind of thing. This process is twofold.

A Life Cycle

The planting of a church is a process. In 1 Corinthians 12 Paul compares the church to the human body. In many ways, birthing a church is comparable to birthing a child. The final section of this book, which concerns the process of church planting, will show church planters how to take the new work through a cycle, similar to the human life cycle. This cycle consists of six stages of development: conception, development, birth, growth, maturity, and reproduction. Successful church planting involves taking the church through this entire process from birthing the church to its birthing other churches. To stop at any one stage in the process is to risk either plateauing or promoting the untimely death of the new church.

Reproduction

Once the church is started, the process doesn't end there. We must not sit back and be satisfied with maintaining what God has done. Christ's Great Commission is to disciple the world for him, not simply to maintain new churches. Thus every planted church must not forget its roots. Each church owes its existence to some person or church of vision. So each planted church has an obligation to articulate the vision and start other churches. Reproduction, the final stage of the entire church planting process, provides churches with the potential to evangelize unchurched communities all across America and throughout the world.

The idea is that planted churches reproduce themselves and make disciples by planting other churches. This is a process that will continue until the Savior returns. In fact this is the true meaning of the Great Commission. If we desire to know how the early church understood Christ's commission, we can find the answer in the book of Acts. Acts is a church planting book because much of what takes place is done in the context of starting new churches. We are in the faith today because the early church (that no longer exists as in the first century) planted churches yesterday. Therefore it shouldn't surprise us when someone such as Peter Wagner says, *"The single most effective evangelistic methodology under heaven is planting new churches."*[1]

Church Planting Requires a Plan

The Problem of Ignorance

The problem is that in the past many people with pure motives have attempted to start a new work but have no idea what they're doing. Often the result of this kind of approach is either a failed church or a small, struggling one.

This was my experience when I planted a church in Miami, Florida. I began with a group of motivated, excited people. The only problem was that none of us knew what we were doing! We simply started an evangelistic Bible study in my apartment that developed into a church. God blessed this effort and people came to faith in Christ, but we constantly found ourselves guessing about what we should do next. Consequently, after a mushrooming start, we plateaued at under a hundred people due largely to our ignorance concerning how to start and grow a church.

The Solution Is Planning

Church planting that is intentional involves strategic planning. Unlike the time when I planted the Miami church in the early 1970s, today there's much more information available due to a growing body of church growth research. The field of church planting is becoming more sophisticated, and entrepreneurial church starters can get much help and direction so that they don't have to guess but can strategically plan what they're doing. In fact this book is written to provide this kind of help for the numerous people who will be planting biblically based, spiritually healthy churches in the twenty-first century.

Church Planting Involves Both Beginning and Growing Churches

Church planting is an exhausting but exciting venture of faith that involves the planned process of beginning and growing new local churches. This raises a question: What is a local church and how do you grow them?

Beginning the Church

It's imperative that before we start a church we know what we're starting. How can we know if we're a church if we don't know what a church is? This demands that the planter have a definition of a local church. I define a local church as a gathering of professing believers in Christ who, under leadership, have organized to observe the ordinances and obey Jesus' Great Commission. This definition has two basic ingredients: *being* and *doing*.

Being

First, the church is. My definition says that it *is* a gathering of professing believers in Christ who *are* under leadership. It exists as a gathering. It exists as a group that is "called out" (*ekklasia*) by God. This means that people—professing believers—have purposefully come together with the intent to be a church. I use the term *professing believers* because my teacher Dr. Charles Ryrie used to ask, "If unbelievers are present, does that mean it's not a church?" Whether we realize it or not, some lost people will likely be present. However, their presence does not negate the fact that it is a church.

The church exists under leadership. Scripture refers to these leaders primarily as elders and deacons (1 Timothy 3 and Titus 1). Though I don't believe that the titles matter, there is no such thing as a leaderless church. If there is no leadership, there is no church.

Doing

Second, the church does. My definition says that the church is organized *to do* two things. One is to observe the ordinances. They are the ordinances of baptism (Matt. 28:19; Acts 2:41) and the Lord's Supper (1 Cor. 11:23–25; Matt. 26:26–28). The church also obeys the Great Commission, which consists of two divinely ordained functions: evangelism and edification (Matt. 28:19–20). Evangelism involves bringing people to faith in Christ, and edification concerns helping them grow in Christ. The latter involves such concepts as learning Bible doctrine, fellowship, prayer, and worship (Acts 2:42–47). All that the church *does* can be summarized under these two functions.

Being and doing are vital to a local church. Legitimately, to call your ministry a church, you must intend to be a church, you must be under leadership, you must observe the ordinances, and you must pursue the lost and build up the saved. These functions are prescriptive. To fall short in any of these areas is to risk not being a New Testament church.

Growing the Church

There is more to planting churches than beginning churches. A major part of the process is starting churches that grow (Acts 2:41, 47; 4:4; and many other passages in Acts). This means that church planters must be familiar with biblical church growth principles, or they'll see their churches plateau and even begin to decline. It's this emphasis on church growth that is missing in most older works on church planting. While it's true that God grows the church (Matt. 16:18), he does so through his people.

This book explains a number of biblical church growth principles, mostly in chapter 11, which covers the growth stage of church planting, and in the appendices. For now, we'll briefly examine two assumptions of church growth.

A Numerical Balance

I've observed that a number of smaller, struggling evangelical churches have embraced a bias against large churches and church growth. Often this bias is expressed by such statements as, "We may not have quantity (lots of people), but we sure have quality (spiritual people), and that's what's really important to God."

While it's true that some churches overemphasize the importance of numbers, others often use this as an excuse to remain passive and not reach people. Quality churches with rare exceptions will become quantity churches because quality churches are actively involved in fulfilling Christ's Great Commission, which involves reaching and discipling lost people. This results in numerical growth in the majority of situations.

A Biblical Focus

A second assumption of church growth is that we must focus not only on what is pragmatic, that is, what works in growing churches, but on what is biblical. Our goal is to plant biblically based churches! The Church Growth Movement has had a positive effect on revitalizing and growing churches around the world. However, one of the accurate criticisms of this movement is that it has focused more on the pragmatic aspects of church growth than on the biblical or spiritual aspects. I would argue strongly that church starters seek biblical-theological training because church planting is a deeply theological enterprise.

Church Planting Rests on Jesus' Promise

Church planting is an exhausting but exciting venture of faith that involves the planned process of beginning and growing local churches, based on Jesus' promise in Matthew 16:18: "And I tell you that you are Peter, and on this rock I will build my church, and the gates of Hades will not overcome it." This promise makes clear that ultimately Jesus Christ is the builder of churches. He is the one who plants them, and he is the one who grows them.

The Problem

Currently, the church in America, evangelical as well as liberal, is in trouble.

A Changed Culture

According to one church growth expert, many of the churches in this country are either plateaued or in decline. At the same time, the number of unchurched Americans has grown to the point that the majority of people are unchurched. All of this has created a void that is being filled to some extent by a sudden growth in such major cults as Mormonism, the Jehovah's Witnesses, and other groups.

As mentioned earlier in this chapter, the America and the Europe of the early twenty-first century are no longer the America or Europe of the mid–twentieth century. Essentially, what was a churched, supposedly Christian culture has become an unchurched, post-Christian culture. People in our culture are not antichurch; they simply view the church as irrelevant to their lives.

An Unprepared Church

These are dark and difficult days for the church, and a big part of the problem is the fact that many churches aren't even aware that they're in trouble! They're like the proverbial ostrich with its head buried in the sand—completely oblivious to what is taking place all around yet dangerously exposed.

A large number of these churches, even those that survived the 1990s, are dying in the early twenty-first century. When Haddon Robinson was the president of Denver Seminary, he recognized that America was a post-Christian culture and advocated that the seminary prepare its students, who desire to minister in American churches, as foreign missionaries in an alien world. He was far ahead of his time. It's truly unfortunate that more seminaries haven't figured this out. With faculty who are out of touch, far too many seminaries are currently preparing their students for a world that no longer exists. When the average seminarian graduates and takes a church, it takes him several years to get over the culture shock of the church world compared to that of the seminary.

The Solution

We who make up the church must not throw up our hands in despair or assume a "gloom and doom" mentality. The Savior hasn't given up on his church.

An Old Promise

Although he made the promise in the first century, it still applies to the church today. Christ's promise is not to bury but to build the church. Not only will the church in America survive, it has a wonderful, exciting future ahead. If Christ has promised to build his church, then it will not become extinct. This means that something will have to change drastically in the next ten to twenty years.

While some existing churches will see the need to change, undergo a transition period, and renew themselves, the future lies with church planting. As someone once said, "It is easier to have babies than to raise the dead!" The point is that God has already begun to challenge thousands to plant new, vibrant, cutting-edge churches for the twenty-first century, as inspired by the ministries of Chuck Swindoll, Bill Hybels, E. K. Bailey, Rick Warren, Tony Evans, Chuck Smith, and many others. We are only at the very beginning of a groundswell that is about to sweep across America sometime in the first half of the twenty-first century.

A New Look

The churches of the twenty-first century will not look like the typical church of the twentieth century. A different culture calls for a different way in which we "do church." The biblical principles are eternal and will remain the same in the evangelical church, yet our methods for implementing and manifesting these principles will have to change so the church will be more relevant to and able to reach the present modern and postmodern generations and the cultures that are yet on the horizon.

Church Planting Responds to Jesus' Great Commission

Finally, intentional church planting starts churches that obey Christ's Great Commission. One of the critical problems in the typical church is that it has forgotten its mission. Somewhere in the process of "doing church," it has wandered away from Christ's original intent.

The Problem

It's critical that any church pause and ask an important question: Why are we doing what we're doing? Essentially, we need to ask, What is the mission of the church? What is it that Christ has left us here to do? The answer to this question is found in the Great Commission, which involves pursuing and then making and maturing believers at home and abroad for our Savior.

Apparently this isn't being accomplished by 80 to 85 percent of our churches. Indeed, George Barna in the 1990s wrote: "In the past seven years, the proportion of adults who have accepted Jesus Christ as their personal Savior (34 percent) has not increased."[2] Things haven't changed much since 1990. The problem is that far too many established American churches have missed their mission. This should make us wonder what they're doing.

The Solution

At the same time, there's a new wind that's blowing across American soil. God is currently in the process of seeding America with new churches that are teaching the rest of us how to do evangelism and win our contemporary culture to Christ in the local church. The ministries of a new generation of leaders have seen countless numbers of unchurched, lost postmoderns as well as moderns become "completely committed Christians."

Not only does this give us hope, but it creates vision and motivates the church of Jesus Christ to reaffirm its purpose and return to the Great

Commission mandate. Indeed, the criterion of successful churches in the future is not how much Bible knowledge their people have, how strong their pastors are in the pulpit, or their abilities to manifest the sign gifts. While content and pulpit expertise aren't to be minimized, the biblical measure of success is whether they're making disciples.

2

Do We Need Another Church?

The Reasons for Church Planting

Bill Smith has just completed seminary, and his excitement and personal sense of destiny are much stronger than when he began. In various ways God had made it clear to Bill that he should pursue professional ministry, pastoral ministry in particular, but first he needed some formal, theological preparation. Now that seminary is behind him, he plans to start a church.

Initially, this was not part of the plan. In fact both he and his wife, Betty, were just a little nervous about Bill quitting his job as an engineer, selling their house, and transporting the family halfway across the country to live off their savings and odd jobs for the years that Bill pursued seminary training. During Bill's first year at seminary, both he and his wife had anticipated that after graduation Bill would take an exciting, dynamic pastorate in an established church that had a first-class facility and a salary comparable to or better than what he had made as an engineer.

In Bill's second year, all that changed. The seminary required an elective in pastoral ministries, so he and a couple of friends decided to take a course in church planting. This proved to be the spark that ignited a flame that began to burn within his soul. The course, combined with an internship in a dynamic, recently planted church in the area, sealed his future ministry.

Of course, Betty was caught by surprise. At first, she was rather upset. This wasn't part of their original plan! "Church planting—what's that?" she exclaimed. "Why would you want to go and do a thing like that?" But God worked in her heart in such a way that through her involvement in Bill's internship, she eventually caught the vision and became a vital part of the team.

Given some of the reasons for pastoring an established church, such as an existing congregation with existing facilities and, in particular, a salary, why would anyone in their right mind want to plant a church? Betty's question is a good one and must be asked by all who desire to become involved in some way with starting a church. While numerous reasons exist, four stand out: the need for new churches, Jesus' promise, the Great Commission, and the advantages of church starts.

The Need for New Churches

To begin with, there is a tremendous need for more significant churches that can make a spiritual difference around the world in general and in America in particular.

Plateaued and Declining Churches

Studies reveal that many of the churches in North America are either plateaued or in decline. If they were to check into a hospital, the doctors would put them on life support.

How Are Churches in General Doing?

Win Arn, a researcher of church growth, contrasts the state of the church at the end of the twentieth century with the church of the 1950s. He writes, "In the years following World War II, thousands of new churches were established. Today, of the approximately 350,000 churches in America, four out of five are either plateaued or declining."[1]

When examining these figures, it's helpful to understand that all organizations pass through a life cycle that consists of the organization's birth, then a period of growth that's followed by eventual decline, which in turn leads to death (see illustration below). The churches of the first century went through this cycle, so we shouldn't be surprised that the same has occurred with churches throughout human history. Regardless, Arn's research reveals that "80–85 percent of the churches in America are on the down-side of the growth cycle."[2]

In one of the most comprehensive surveys that's ever been conducted on American faith communities, Carl Dudley and David Roozen write that more than one-half of all congregations predate World War II.[3] The problem, again, as Lyle Schaller observes, is that "66 percent to 75 percent

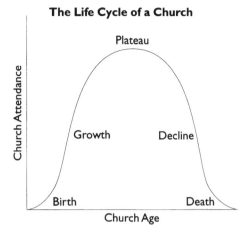

The Life Cycle of a Church

Church Attendance (vertical axis)

Plateau

Growth　　　　　Decline

Birth　　　　　　Death

Church Age

of all congregations founded before 1960 are either on a plateau in size or shrinking in numbers."[4]

How Are Mainline Churches Doing?

Arn's figures would include churches that are mainline and generally more liberal in their theology. Benton Johnson, Dean Hoge, and Donald Luidens write:

> America's so-called mainline Protestant churches aren't what they used to be. For generations on end, the Methodists, Presbyterians, Congregationalists, Episcopalians, and kindred denominations reported net annual membership gains. As recently as the 1950s their growth rate equaled or exceeded that of the United States as a whole.
>
> But in the early 1960s their growth slowed down, and after the middle of the decade they had begun to lose members. With very few exceptions, the decline has continued to this date. Never before had any large religious body in this country lost members steadily for so many years.[5]

How Are Evangelical Churches Doing?

Though some theologically conservative churches are growing, the majority aren't. Two conservative denominations serve as illustrations. First, the conservative Lutheran Church, Missouri Synod, has dropped from 2,788,536 people in 1970 to 2,582,440 in 2001.[6] Second, the conservative Southern Baptist denomination has traditionally seen a growth in members since 1926. However, in 1987 it reported a statistical stall in some denominational programs. When pollster George Gallup reviewed the statistics, he reported, "Southern Baptist statistics appear to represent a leveling out rather than a reversal or sudden turnaround."[7] Then in 1998 membership in Southern Baptist churches registered a decrease in church membership from 15,891,514 in 1997 to 15,729,356 in 1998 (1.02 percent). The number of Southern Baptist churches showed a decline from 40,887 in 1997 to 40,870 in 1998 (.04 percent). And the number of baptisms dropped from 412,027 in 1997 to 407,264 in 1998 (1.16 percent). However, the Sunday morning worship attendance increased by 3.33 percent.[8]

In my experience of traveling across America as a church consultant and working with these churches, I have found that many are in serious decline. In fact I rejoice when I hear of a church that is growing and reaching lost people, because I don't hear this very often. While some denominations deny the obvious, others have turned to a vigorous program of church planting, knowing that starting new churches will be the key to their survival.

According to data collected by *Faith Communities Today*, two growing conservative groups did report at least a 10 percent gain in regularly participating adults from 1995 to 2000. They are the megachurches and the Assemblies of God. A megachurch has at least two thousand people in attendance. According to Hartford Seminary researcher Scott Thumma, these large congregations developed rapidly during the last two decades (1980–2000) when attendance shot up an average of 90 percent.[9] However, less than 10 percent of the churches in America are megachurches.

The Assemblies of God have also experienced rapid growth, due in part to the denomination's strong emphasis on church planting.[10] In addition, in the past some researchers have noted that growth in conservative groups has been more the result of "a kind of circulation process by which evangelicals move from one conservative church to another."[11] Two researchers conclude "conservative churches do a better job of retaining those already familiar with evangelical culture—both transfers and children of members—than moderate and liberal churches do in retaining their members."[12]

The primary evidence for conservative church growth is the comparison of official church membership figures of conservative and mainline denominations. In 1972 Dean Kelley wrote the popular, controversial book *Why Conservative Churches Are Growing*, arguing this exact point.[13] However, Tom Smith questions this evidence, specifically that conservative churches are growing, and feels that it has been exaggerated for several reasons. First, the growth may focus on denominations that are growing but aren't typical of all conservative churches or denominations. Second, these figures may not be accurate due to exaggeration or unintentional over-counting by conservatives who place greater emphasis on growth and conversion. He supplies a number of other reasons along with these.[14]

Declining Numbers

While many mainline and conservative churches are plateaued or declining, the number of churched people in North America is also declining. This raises the questions, how many are churched, how accurate are the figures, and who isn't churched?

How Many Are Churched?

One primary way to examine American adult church attendance is to look at the polls. Two pollsters provide us with this information. The first is George Barna with the Barna Research Group. Figure 2 presents the statistics on American church attendance from his website[15] and updated in the *Dallas Morning News*.[16]

Barna describes the picture from the mid-eighties through the mid-nineties as that of a church on a roller coaster. In 1986, 42 percent of adults attended a church service during a typical week in January. The roller coaster reaches its highest peak of 49 percent in 1991. However, it plummets in 1996 to its lowest point of 37 percent. It rises to 40 percent in 2000 and to 42 percent in late July to mid-August, prior to the terrorist

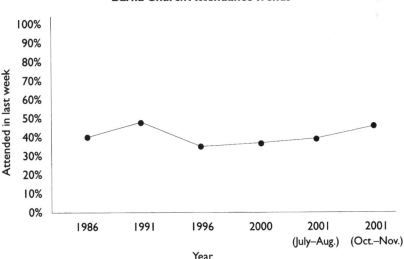

Barna Church Attendance Trends

assault on the World Trade Center in New York on September 11, 2001. In the months following the attack (late October to early November) attendance rises to its highest point since 1991 of 48 percent. However, the Barna material doesn't reflect a drop in attendance in November of 2001 that is reflected in the Gallup polls. Thus, during the mid-eighties through the mid-nineties, the average church attendance was 43 percent with a high of 49 percent and a low of 37 percent. Then, as we saw earlier, Barna writes that by May 2004 the number of unchurched adults has nearly doubled since 1991.[17]

The second pollster is George Gallup who heads up the Gallup Organization. Currently this group, which began to record American church attendance in 1939, provides the most comprehensive research. The Gallup pollsters ask the trend question: Did you happen to attend church or synagogue in the last seven days or not?

The average number of American adults who attended a church or synagogue between 1939 to the present is 42 percent. The roller coaster hit its peak between 1954 and 1962 with a high of 49 percent in 1954–55 and again in 1958. The average for this period was 48 percent. The church roller coaster hit its lowest point in 1996 at 38 percent.[18]

How Accurate Are the Figures?

How accurate are the polls? How much should we trust self-identification or self-report surveys that take respondents at their word? Is America secular or Christian? All of this statistical information assumes the accuracy of the polls. Commenting on one of his polls, Louis Harris admits, "It should be noted that church attendance is notoriously over reported as a socially desirable activity, so true attendance figures are surely lower than those reported here."[19] Barry Kosmin is the codirector of the 2001 American Religious Identification Survey (ARIS)—an ongoing study conducted by the Graduate Center of the City University of New York. He notes in an article in *USA Today*: "Leadership of all faiths exaggerate or manufacture their numbers."[20]

In 1994 a team of sociologists led by C. Kirk Hadaway challenged the view that approximately 40 percent of Americans were weekly church attenders. In their article "What the Polls Don't Show," using the same Gallup question, they reportedly found that only 20 percent of American Protestants and 28 percent of Roman Catholics show up on Sundays, in contrast to Gallup's figures that cite 45 percent of Protestants and 51 percent of Catholics attend church.[21] They suggest several explanations, one of which is that people like to see or present themselves as better than they are—what we might call a "halo effect." The same is true when people are polled about voting or charitable giving. The researchers suspect that the actual attendance rate has declined since World War II, in spite of the fact that surveys suggest it has basically remained stable.

However, this writer and many church pastors are not surprised at these findings. I've spent much of my life teaching at Dallas Seminary and consulting and ministering with churches in the Dallas–Fort Worth metroplex that is popularly viewed as not just the Bible Belt but the "buckle" on the Bible Belt. Even in this part of the country, where there seems to be a church on every street corner, most churches would be surprised to hear that as many as 40 percent or more of the people are attending church. Though we have more churches than most places in America, many are plateaued and in decline with a failing attendance. In fact one pastor cited a survey indicating that 74 percent of Plano residents do not belong to a church (Plano is a town just north of Dallas).[22] Another church in Arlington (just west of Dallas) estimates that 74 percent of the 270,000 Arlington residents don't attend church.[23]

Another issue with the polls is whether they reflect American population growth. The question is, do the polls take into account that the American population increases every year? This means that more people need to attend church to maintain the 40 percent figure. Hadaway, in a more recent article, "Did You Really Go to Church This Week?" expresses the belief that most people don't go to church.

> If the percentage of Americans attending church is stable, aggregate church membership should have increased as the American population grew. But after adding together denominational membership statistics (including estimates of membership for independent congregations) we found that the aggregate membership total has been virtually static since the late 1960s.[24]

Who Isn't Churched?

Pollster George Barna addresses the issue of who isn't churched in a survey conducted in 1999 (see table below).[25]

Generation	Percentage Attending Church
Builders (born before 1946)	51%
Boomers (1946–64)	41%
Busters (1965–1976)	34%
Bridgers (1977–1994)	29%

What is unmistakable is that the younger postmodern generations (the Busters and Bridgers) are increasingly unchurched. Barna indicates that only 34 percent of Busters and 29 percent of Bridgers report attending church. If these figures are overreported as sociologists such as Hadaway and Marler argue, then the real figures could indicate that even fewer Busters and Bridgers actually attend church. I predict that over time these generations will report their actual attendance, and the American church attendance figures will dip closer to reality. Regardless, the real concern here is over the nation's younger generations' lack of belief and interest in Christ's church.

Are these younger generations angry with the church? When asked why they didn't attend church more often, few expressed any deep animosity toward the church. Only 8 percent claimed that they disagreed with such things as policy and teaching. Many felt that they were either too busy or simply didn't believe that it was all that important.[26]

Growth of Cults and Non-Christian Faiths

A third reason why the church and thus Christianity in America is in decline is the growth of various cults and non-Christian faiths all across North America. The decline in the Christian church has created a spiritual vacuum that others have rushed to fill. It's both significant and alarming that several major cults have almost tripled in size from 1965 to 2001 and that other religious groups are prospering.

The Cults

One such group is the Mormons. According to the *Yearbook of American and Canadian Churches*, the Mormon Church has almost tripled in membership, from 1,789,175 in 1965 to 5,113,409 in 2001.[27] In 2002 the *Dallas Morning News* reported that, for the first time, the Church of Jesus Christ of Latter-day Saints was one of the five largest churches in the United States, according to the National Council of Churches' 2002 *Yearbook of American and Canadian Churches*. "This ranking represents a very brisk increase in membership for a church with a relatively brief history," said the Rev. Eileen W. Lindner, the yearbook's editor. The Latter-day Saints were organized in 1830.[28]

The *Yearbook of American and Canadian Churches* reports that by 2001 the Jehovah's Witnesses had grown from 330,358 in 1965 to 990,340.[29]

Non-Christian Faiths

One non-Christian faith with notable growth is Islam. According to a report from the Mosque Study Project, Muslim mosques are springing up in cities and suburbs across America. The report gives the following statistics:

> The number of mosques and mosque participants are experiencing tremendous growth. From 1994 to 2000 the number of mosques increased 25 percent and the total number of people associated per mosque increased 235 percent.[30]

A conclusion of this report suggests that currently Islam is one of the fastest growing religious groups in the United States and that American Muslims are most eager to become full and accepted participants in the mainstream of American cultural, political, and religious life.

According to the 2001 American Religious Identification (AMRI) survey, the Buddhist and Hindu faiths have also experienced significant growth this past decade. From 1990 to 2001, Buddhists have grown 109.5 percent, and Hindus have increased at 237.4 percent. Perhaps the greatest surprise is the growth of Wiccans. The AMRI reports that they've grown from 8,000 in 1990 to 134,000 self-proclaimed witches in 2001—a growth of an eyebrow-raising 1,575 percent.[31]

Many indicators signal that the American church is in deep trouble early in the twenty-first century. What all this means is that American Christianity is also in decline, for as the church goes, so goes Christianity.

The question is, does the typical American church understand what is taking place and what the implications are? Perhaps Thom Rainer says it best, "America is clearly becoming less Christian, less evangelized, and less churched. Yet too many of those in our churches seem oblivious to this reality."[32] One of the purposes of this book in general and this chapter in particular is to awaken Christian leaders and thus their churches to this alarming reality.

Jesus' Promise

America has entered a post-Christian era from which some believe that it will not recover. Indeed, the situation looks grim. Yet the question needs to be asked: How should Christians respond to all these events? At first our response might understandably be that of discouragement and even a growing pessimism. However, there's a much better response that is based not so much on what is taking place presently in America but on an eternal biblical promise. This promise provides the second reason why we must plant churches.

A Biblical Promise

In Matthew 16:18 the Savior says, "And I tell you that you are Peter, and on this rock I will build my church, and the gates of Hades will not overcome it." There are at least two promises in this passage. One is that Christ, not Christians, is ultimately the person who plants and grows churches. Second, Satan and all of his forces will not be able to prevail against the church.

The present situation would seem to contradict this second promise. However, there is in this passage much hope for the future of Christ's church. Since this passage was written, the history of the church has been that of numerical growth and decline. The point of the promise is that the church will continue to exist regardless of its size.

An Optimistic Future

Consequently, we can look to the twenty-first century with great hope and enthusiasm. Based on the current condition of the American church and the promises in Matthew 16:18, God has begun and will continue to plant a great number of biblically based, spiritually healthy churches in the twenty-first century. In fact there are already a number of individuals and organizations that are beginning to encourage church planting as a significant solution to the problem of church decline.

Church growth analyst Lyle Schaller sees church planting as the key to reaching the next generation. While speaking at the annual meeting of the Southern Baptist New Work Fellowship in Atlanta, Schaller said, "If you are interested in reaching new people, by far the most effective way to do this is through church planting." Later in the same message he addressed the issue of making established churches relevant as opposed to planting new churches: "Some think we need to make all our existing congregations vital before starting new churches. What's wrong with that is nobody knows how to do that . . . and nobody's young enough to live long enough to do it."[33]

Various groups have placed church planting among their top priorities. The Southern Baptist Convention plans to start sixty thousand churches before 2020. And more than fifty thousand churches were planted in North America between 1980 and 2000.[34]

Church growth expert Peter Wagner writes the following:

We live in a time when general interest in church planting is higher than it has been since the 1950s. While some denominations continued to plant new churches and thereby have grown during the last 40 years, others have virtually eliminated that ministry with the exception of a new church here and there or a cluster of ethnic minority churches. They have been paying the price.

Now the climate is changing. Denominational headquarters are adding church planting desks. Motivational material is appearing in denominational publications. Training programs for church planters are being developed.[35]

Later in the same work he writes, "I begin this book with a categorical statement that will seem bold and brash to some at first sight, even though it has been well substantiated by research over the past two or three decades: *The single most effective evangelistic methodology under heaven is planting new churches.*"[36]

The Great Commission

What Is the Great Commission?

The Great Commission, found in Matthew 28:19–20; Mark 16:15; Luke 24:46–48; and Acts 1:8, is the third reason for our giving birth to new works. An analysis of the biblical passages reveals various components that make up the commission. These are represented in the table below.

The Great Commission

Scripture	Who	What	To Whom	How	Where
Matthew 28:19–20	Eleven Disciples	"Go and make disciples."	All nations	Baptizing and teaching	—
Mark 16:15	Eleven Disciples	"Go . . . and preach the good news."	All creation	—	All the world
Luke 24:46–48	Eleven Disciples	"[Be] witnesses."	All nations	Preaching repentance and forgiveness of sins	Beginning at Jerusalem
Acts 1:8	Eleven Disciples	"Be my witnesses."	—	With power	Jerusalem, Judea, Samaria, and the uttermost parts of the world

I have several observations to make concerning the Great Commission. The first consists of the intentional pursuit of lost people. This is reflected in the word *go* found at the beginning of the commission as it is recorded in both Matthew 28:19 and Mark 16:15. The Savior clarifies what he means by this word in such passages as Luke 5:27–32; 15:1–10; and 19:1–10, where he develops the concept of proactively pursuing lost people, such as Levi the tax-gatherer and his friends, tax-gatherers and sinners in general, and Zacchaeus. As then, so the twenty-first-century church will have to take the initiative and pursue these lost people.

The second observation is that the Great Commission has essentially two components: evangelism and edification. In Mark 16:15, Christ says, "Go into all the world and preach the good news to all creation." A Great Commission church is one that places a high priority on evangelism. The church in general and the people in particular aren't simply talking about evangelism, but they're actively seeking and reaching lost people. In fact a church that isn't reaching lost people has lost its purpose! Also the emphasis in these passages is on evangelism more than on edification. Perhaps this was because the Savior knew that his church would be drawn more to edification than evangelism.

Once the church reaches lost people, it doesn't drop them but proceeds to enfold and disciple them. This is the process of edification, which involves bringing new believers to Christ-likeness (Eph. 4:11–16). This involves a personal commitment to Bible study, fellowship, communion, and prayer (Acts 2:42). Consequently, the local church provides a place where a new believer is discipled and mobilized for service.

The third observation is that while the commission is addressed to the disciples in particular, it extends to Christ's church in general. The book of Acts demonstrates that the early church and the disciples understood the commission to apply to the church reaching out to the world as they knew it in their day.

How Do We Implement the Great Commission?

Now that we know our commission, there is a second vital question: How do we implement it? Perhaps the best answer lies in a hermeneutic that examines how the early church implemented the commission. This information is found in the book of Acts, where the early church sought to put into practice the commission command of our Lord. A careful reading of Acts reveals that the early church implemented the Great Commission mandate primarily by planting churches. A study of the missionary journeys recorded in Acts reveals that they, in fact, were church planting forays into what was predominantly a pagan culture. As a result of these trips, Paul and others planted high-impact churches in key cities, such as Derbe, Lystra, Iconium, Antioch, Philippi, Thessalonica, Berea, Corinth, and Ephesus.

If the church is to obey its visionary Savior and implement his commission mandate, it's imperative that it start significant churches that are led by visionary leaders. Indeed, if our churches are to reach the great cities of America and the world, they can't do so by themselves. Instead, they must multiply themselves by starting a network of biblically based, spiritually healthy churches in their target area. Unfortunately, there aren't very many churches with this kind of vision. God is going to change this over the next several decades. It would be much more exciting and rewarding if churches could catch the vision now and not later!

The Advantages of Church Starts

The fourth reason that argues for starting churches is the various advantages that new churches have over established ones.

Faster Growth

The first advantage is the fact that new churches grow faster than older, established churches. Win Arn cites a study by the Southern Baptist Convention that demonstrates this advantage.[37] In this study, churches started between 1972 and 1981 were compared to those existing prior to 1971. These churches were examined according to their membership sizes, which included the categories of 1–50, 51–100, 101–200, 201–400, 401–600, 601–1000, and 1000+. The growth span on which the study was based was the percentage of growth of all these churches from 1981 to 1986. The result was that churches of all sizes that were started between 1972 and 1981 grew at a ratio of 60 percent to 80 percent. Those started prior to 1971 grew at a rate of 20 percent to 60 percent, with the older and larger churches coming closer to the 20 percent figure. Certainly, older churches shouldn't be overly discouraged by these figures. Instead, they should find in them a challenge to renewal and the planting of daughter churches.

Lyle Schaller also argues that new churches grow faster than long-established parishes.[38] The reason is the following:

> Perhaps the simplest explanation of this pattern is that new congregations are organized around evangelism and reaching people not actively involved in the life of any worshipping community. By contrast, powerful internal institutional pressures tend to encourage long-established churches to allocate most of their resources to the care of members.[39]

Better Evangelism

The second advantage of new churches is that they evangelize better than older, established churches. In a study that appeared in *Christianity Today*, Bruce McNicol writes that, among evangelical churches, those under three years old will win ten people to Christ per year for every one hundred members. Those churches from three to fifteen years old will win five people per year for every one hundred church members. Finally, after a church reaches age fifteen, the figure drops to three people per year for every one hundred members.[40]

Greater Leader Credibility

The third advantage of church planting is that church planters gain credibility as leaders faster than do people who become leaders of established churches.

Assuming the Leadership in Established Churches

Wayne Zunkel in *Growing the Small Church* writes: "Most pastorates proceed according to a pattern. They go from the minister as *chaplain to pastor to leader.*"[41] When new pastors take an established church, they proceed through these three stages on their way to becoming the leaders of their churches.

The chaplain stage. The first stage lasts from one to three years. During this time, people often refer to church leaders as "pastors." The leaders function much as chaplains, preaching and performing pastoral care but exercising little influence as leaders.

The pastor stage. The next stage may last from three to as few as five years at best, or it may last for the pastor's entire tenure at the church. In the latter situation the church will not let their pastor become a true leader. During the pastor stage, people often refer to the leader as "our pastor." What has taken place—and what moves pastors through the stage—is their increased credibility and the increased trust of the people. As pastors build credibility and trust, people are more likely to let them lead.

The leader stage. The final stage is that of leader. This is the point in the pattern when pastors can exercise great influence in their churches and are able to implement their visions.

The problem with the process is that it usually takes so long (if it happens at all) that most leaders leave for greener pastures before reaching this stage in their ministry. The median tenure for most pastors is three to four years.

Assuming the Leadership in Planted Churches

Planting pastors often become leaders without having to go through the first two stages described above. While pastors taking established churches have to build credibility and trust, church planters are granted this up front, and they either maintain that trust or lose it in the process of exercising leadership. Often this trust is granted because in planted churches, the people are most likely "joining the pastor," whereas in established churches, pastors are "joining the people."

More Flexible Congregation

A fourth advantage of planted churches is that those involved in church planting are more open to change than those in established, traditional churches. This relates to the difference between old and new wineskins.

The Problem of "Old Wineskins"

Over the years, established churches build up a number of practices and traditions that become set in concrete. This is because these practices have proved valuable and helpful in the past. In the present, however, they are "excess baggage," because times change and so must our practices and traditions. But in far too many of these churches, the need for change is never realized.

This is the problem of "old wineskins." It's not anything unique to the twenty-first century. In Matthew 9:16–17, the Savior says,

> No one sews a patch of unshrunk cloth on an old garment, for the patch will pull away from the garment, making the tear worse. Neither do men pour new wine into old wineskins. If they do, the skins will burst, the wine will run out and the wineskins will be ruined. No, they pour new wine into new wineskins, and both are preserved.

Jesus indicates that it's hard to change established traditions. Old skins don't stretch well! He's not evaluating those traditions or saying that one is better than the other. He's warning of the difficulties for those who attempt to bring change into situations where structures are already in place.

The Solution of "New Wineskins"

The advantage of church planting is that the people who are attracted come into a new situation in which they're open to jettisoning much of their old "baggage." No one is attempting to sew a new patch onto an old wineskin; rather, new wine is being poured into new skins. The result is that not only are those involved extremely excited about the new church—which, in turn, attracts other people—but they're open to change and are willing to try new and innovative ideas.

3

How Do You Make Ends Meet?

The Funds for Church Planting

Bill Smith has completed seminary and is enthusiastic about birthing a church. His wife, Betty, has caught the vision as well and now considers herself a part of the team, although she spends much of her time at home with their children. But that doesn't mean she's not without her doubts and questions about the ministry and their future.

Perhaps the most frightening aspect of church planting for Betty is the finances. Generally speaking, there's more financial security in established churches than in new churches. In an established church, there's usually some kind of salary package for the pastor. Betty understands this and often lies awake at night thinking about it. Bill, on the other hand, has become so caught up in the vision of starting a new church that he has not put a lot of thought into the finances of church planting. Betty knows this and it worries her, so she asks Bill, "How are we going to make ends meet?"

In this chapter we'll explore the personal and ministry finances that are necessary for church planters and their ministries to meet expenses. Whether we like it or not, money is necessary for ministry, and intentional church planters such as Bill Smith must think about how to provide for personal and ministry expenses. If certain finances aren't in place, the birthing process may not occur.

Financial Fact: God Provides!

Some people avoid missions in general and church planting in particular because of the issue of finances. To address this important issue, we must briefly examine one of the great promises in Scripture that deals with God's provision for his disciples' personal needs. Also we'll look at the condition and problems that surround this promise.

Jesus' Promise

The promise is found in Matthew 6:25–34. Jesus understands that while serving him, the disciples at times worry about meeting their basic needs—their need for food, drink, and clothing. In verses 26–30 he tells them that in his kingdom worrying about these things accomplishes nothing. Instead, they must understand that, just as God provides for the birds of the air and the lilies of the field, he will provide for his disciples.

Jesus' Condition

There is one condition to Jesus' promise, which is found in verse 33. Christ's disciples must "seek first his kingdom and his righteousness." When they do, he promises in return to take care of their personal needs. The word *needs* is very important. The Savior is promising that he will provide for our needs but not necessarily for our wants.

God is committed to supplying our needs. Whether or not he supplies our wants is optional and not part of the promise. When our children were small, they would come to me or my wife and say, "I need a bicycle!" or "I need a new doll!" To make sure they understood the difference between "needs" and "wants," we would ask, "Do you really need a doll or a bicycle, or do you just want one?" They understood the difference but usually insisted that their wants were truly needs. We did the very best we could to supply their needs, but we would attempt to provide for their wants only if that was best for them.

We may have certain problems meeting the condition of seeking first his kingdom and his righteousness.

The Problem of Our Faith

In verse 30 the Savior points to the real problem for most of his disciples—the problem of faith. Not to accept Jesus' teaching on his promised provision is a faith issue! The Savior has addressed the matter of our personal needs. As long as we put him first, he has promised to provide for us. We choose either to believe or to disbelieve him! Consequently, the first issue we must face in terms of our finances is the cold, hard fact of whether we believe the Savior when it comes to his provision for our basic needs.

The Problem of Our Feelings

The second problem area is our emotions and feelings. Most Americans in general, including Christians, have become used to a lifestyle that far surpasses that of the rest of the world in terms of material things. While it isn't necessarily wrong to have material things, we tend to take them for granted. This includes even basic material things, such as housing and clothing. We feel we have a right to these things; indeed, for many of us, being Americans means having and enjoying them. In *The Spirit of the Disciplines*, Dallas Willard writes:

> Contemporary Westerners are nurtured on the faith that everyone has a *right* to do what they want when they want, to pursue happiness in all ways possible, to feel good, and to lead a "productive and successful life," understood largely in terms of self-contentment and material well-being. This vision of life has come, in the popular mind, to be identified with "the good life," and even with civilized existence. It is taught through the popular media, political rhetoric, and the educational system as the *natural* way for life to be.[1]

The obvious problem is that this mind-set can subtly prevent us from seeking God's kingdom and righteousness *first.* Our lifestyle begins to determine what we're willing to do in service for Christ. To suggest that Christians might be avoiding a particular ministry or place of ministry because it poses a change in lifestyle when they've subtly grown accustomed to that lifestyle is a very emotional matter. Most often they become both frightened and very angry at the suggestion.

Consequently, those who desire to pursue ministry, whether church planting or some other form, must take the time to think through the implications of Christ's teachings on this issue. In Matthew 6:25–34, he promises to provide for our needs but not necessarily for our present lifestyle. This concept must be worked through not only cognitively but also emotionally. A hard, often guilt-producing question that must be asked is, "Are you pursuing a ministry or a lifestyle?" Not asking the question is to enter ministry with certain expectations that may prevent Christians from putting Christ first.

Financial Sources: Whom Might God Use?

While the Savior wants us to trust him to provide for our basic needs, he wants us also to plan our finances (Luke 14:28–30). He uses a combination of both our faith and planning in providing abundantly for us.[2] In planning for their finances, church planters should be aware of the various financial sources available to them.

Sponsoring Churches

The best source of financial support is a sponsoring church. When a church catches a vision for starting a new work, church planters commonly refer to it as the "mother church" and the new church as the "daughter church." Often it is churches that are from two to five years old that are more willing to aid financially, because they've just been through what the new church is experiencing. There could be several churches that serve as sponsors of one new church.

The Advantages

When a church has a vision for church planting, they are usually willing to give financial support; otherwise they wouldn't initiate the process. Most often, this vision includes the desire to help the new church as much as possible.

Another advantage is that the sponsoring church can hold the new church accountable for those finances. In the twenty-first century, financial accountability will remain a priority for any ministry. The mother church has a responsibility to its people and the new church to serve in this capacity.

The Methods

There are various ways in which a mother church can assist a daughter church in providing finances. This could involve a one-time gift to help the new church get started. Northwest Bible Church in the Dallas area encouraged the planting of several daughter churches and assisted them with a one-time financial gift.

Another approach is to include church planting in the missions budget. Just as funds are regularly budgeted and set aside for missions, so the same can be done for new church starts.

A third approach is to present the new church during a service or at a congregational meeting and encourage people to support it with their finances on an individual basis.

A Core Group

Another source of funding is the core group itself. Once a core group is established, the people involved must understand that they have a responsibility to support the new ministry as much as possible. The core group will provide some income for the church-planting team initially, and within one to three years, the new church should be able to assume much of the responsibility for all the team, depending on their personal finances and the church's rate of growth. Therefore, it's important that core groups discuss and commit to financial support before they begin the actual process of starting the church.

There are exceptions. There will be some churches that will never become totally self-supporting. Some examples would be those that target special people groups, such as the inner city or Muslim ministries.

Family, Friends, and Acquaintances

Interested family, friends, and acquaintances can also be sources of funding. In general, these people know the prospective church planter and, therefore, may be predisposed to help financially in some way. In particular, this would include those who have been influenced by any prior ministry of the church planter.

These are people who already believe in the planter and often prove to be some of the best contributors. This is a very important source because an individual's ability to raise support from former constituents is often an indicator of that person's ability to plant churches.

A Denomination or Organization

Another source of funding is a denomination or cooperating organization of churches. A healthy denomination or organization of churches should see at least 20 percent of their established churches beginning new churches annually. To do this they must support church planting financially. This source includes such groups as the Southern Baptists, the Nazarenes, the Assemblies of God, the Evangelical Free churches, the Christian Missionary and Alliance churches, and many others.

Funding among these organizations varies from group to group. Often the Southern Baptists help with the purchase of land, the services of consultants, and the provision of demographic and psychographic services. Sources of such funds can be the state convention, the North American Mission Board (NAM), the International Mission Board (IMB), and various local associations. Others provide only limited funding or refer potential planters to member churches in their areas that might be able to lend support.

Words of caution need to be offered at this point. First, it's unwise for any group to cover all the expenses of the new church, because it's important that the church itself assume some of that responsibility. Otherwise it will remain forever tied to the sponsoring organization. Most organizations are aware of this and will help only for a limited period of time. Second, whenever an organization helps financially, there are usually "strings" attached—that's to be expected. Find out what those "strings" are and determine if they will pose any problems.

Though this chapter emphasizes financial support, these various organizations and denominations can lend support in other ways in addition to finances. One that has proved most effective is good coaching, where a more experienced church planter comes alongside a new one and provides counsel based on his wisdom and experience. This can save the new planter-leader much time and spare him from making costly mistakes. I would recommend that every church planter seek out a ministry coach. Also you should be aware of Bob Logan's Coachnet ministry. This is an online program that you'll find most helpful. You can learn more about Coachnet by going to the website (www.coachnet.org).

Personal Employment

A fifth source of funding is through the personal employment of the church planter. Of all the options, this is the least preferable because it limits the time the planter can give to the new ministry. However, in a team context this may be unavoidable initially. Personal employment has several possibilities.

One is that of a "tentmaker." In this situation, church planters turn to a particular trade or profession only when there aren't enough funds available for their support. They may work one week and be off the next. The advantage is that they can determine when and how long they work. Paul is a good example of this. Periodically he used his talents as an actual tentmaker to provide for his personal needs. He was able to schedule work around his ministry. (This is how we got the term *tentmaker*.)

Another possibility is the bivocational minister. In this situation, church planters find regular employment that occupies a certain portion of their time every week. The disadvantage of a bivocational ministry is that the ministry has to be scheduled around the hours of the other job.

In many cases a spouse's employment provides the needed finances. A wife may work full-time to support her husband until the church can assume their support or until they start a family.

It should be stressed that except in unusual circumstances any outside employment on the part of the church planting team must be viewed as temporary. Like most other ministries, church planting is a full-time responsibility. Anything less will hinder the work of this ministry.

Sale of Existing Church Properties

I noted in chapter 2 that a number of churches across North America are plateaued and many are in decline. One major reason for this is that they are located in older, gospel-resistant neighborhoods. A growing number of these churches have sold their property and facilities and used the funds to position themselves or others in a new, growing area as a church plant. Older, struggling churches that find themselves in this or a similar position should strongly consider this alternative. This would likely be handled at a denominational level rather than an individual level. Nevertheless, it's a good source for church starting funds.

A Prayer Team

I would encourage the prospective church planter early in the process to recruit an interested team of people apart from the core group that will regularly pray for the church planter. It isn't unusual for these people to desire to support the planter financially as well as prayerfully. However, the original intent for this group is prayer and not finances.

A Director of Support

Paul Srch is a church planter who's been involved in planting Epic Church in Homestead, Florida. He completed the conception stage under my tutelage while a student at Dallas Seminary. A part of recruiting his planting team in the development or prenatal stage involved enlisting a director of support ministries. This person—man or woman—is responsible for raising funds for the church planter, the church, and, in time, any other church planters on the team. The planter would be wise to look for someone who knows him and believes in his ministry. This person could serve part-time or full-time.

Financial Principles: What Do I Need to Know?

There are several important, practical financial principles that will help church planters in their efforts to raise funds. Three of them are negative and focus on what distracts or even alienates some potential contributors. The last two are positive and aid in knowing what attracts potential givers.

Givers Don't Like to Pay the Bills

Most contributors don't like to give funds to pay the bills. For example, they're not moved by appeals to help pay salaries, the electricity bill, or the mortgage. The problem they have with paying salaries is that they sense the potential for their funds to be used for wants and not needs. Paying the electricity bill or the mortgage, though necessary, isn't very glamorous!

Contributors may be willing to help in other areas. For example, they like to give toward facilities where ministry takes place—church buildings or libraries. They'll also contribute toward things that can be used to accomplish ministry—Bibles, sound equipment, lighting.

Givers Don't Respond Well to Guilt or Negativism

Potential givers don't respond well, if at all, to guilt and negativism. While they may give once or even twice, intelligent people resent this kind of approach and will not give long term to ministries that use this tactic.

Actually, this is a wise, biblical response because Scripture warns against giving under these circumstances. In 2 Corinthians 9:7, Paul writes, "Each man should give what he has decided in his heart to give, not reluctantly or under compulsion, for God loves a cheerful giver." Appeals based on guilt or negativism often fall under compulsion and, consequently, are questionable at best.

Givers Don't Respond Well to Needs

Most contributors don't like to give to meet needs. This is because need motivates negatively. For many, the appeal to need is comparable to investing in businesses that are in the red. As someone once said, "If need motivated giving, then everyone would be givers."

Regardless, many Christian organizations aren't aware of this principle and continue to appeal for funds primarily on the basis of their needs. Most people like to hear good news, not constant negative reports that conclude with a strong appeal based on present needs.

Givers Respond to Visions

The key to giving is a dynamic vision. Most contributors don't give regularly to meet needs; they give regularly to significant, dynamic visions that meet needs. In general, people enjoy spending money and they're willing to spend it on something they feel is of significance. But what brings a sense of significance to a ministry? The answer is a well-cast vision.

In the early stages of starting a church, visionary church planters must spend a significant amount of time cultivating and communicating a dynamic, compelling vision of how God could impact a community with the gospel.[3] If the envisioning process is done well, it catches people's attention more than ministry needs, no matter how dire. Most often, the bigger the vision, the bigger the investment.

Givers Respond to Big Visions

The key to giving is a big, dynamic vision. The Savior cast a big vision in Matthew 28:19–20 when he commissioned his church to reach the entire world. In Ephesians 3:20 Paul gently admonishes the Ephesian church for not asking and thinking big enough.

For some reason, far too many Christians are low on vision. Perhaps some suffer from low self-esteem and feelings of insignificance. They feel that they're not worthy of anyone's support. They ask, *Why would anyone want to support me?* Others have a temperament that focuses more on present realities than future possibilities.

Church planters need to think big and cast big visions because they have a big God who wants to accomplish big things through them. He is a God "who is able to do immeasurably more than all we ask or imagine, according to his power that is at work within us" (Eph. 3:20). Most knowledgeable givers understand this and want to give to ministries that desire to have a significant impact for the Savior.

Financial Provision: How Might God Provide?

While fund-raising will not be necessary for all who go into church planting, it will affect many. Often the ability to raise funds for ministry is indicative of a past lifestyle of sacrificial ministry to people and is predictive of future success in church planting. People who have been ministered to by a servant of God are not quick to forget and usually are open to investing in his future ministry. Also, raising funds has the potential to free the church planter's time that might otherwise be occupied by full- or part-time employment outside the church.

Presently, there isn't a lot of information available to help in terms of how to raise funds for personal and/or ministry support. (I would highly recommend William Dillon's *People Raising: A Practical Guide for Raising Support* [Chicago: Moody Press, 1993] for the serious fund-raiser. You'll also find his website, www.peopleraising.com, to be very helpful, providing numerous tips and other information on fund-raising.) There are two areas that must be discussed in covering the topic of fund-raising—whether for ministry in general or church planting in particular.

The Problems of Fund-Raising

The Problem of Pride

Personal pride is a problem for most Americans for reasons that relate to the average American lifestyle and what we've come to expect as the way life should be.

A part of this is a sense of independence. There is great personal satisfaction in believing that we don't need anyone else because we can take care of ourselves. We're not used to asking others for help, especially in the area of finances. Actually, this attitude is often indicative of a sense of intense pride and a lack of dependence on God, which is sin! This problem area must be dealt with before commencing any work for the Savior.

The Problem of Fear

Another problem is fear. Some people aren't proud, but they are afraid to ask for support. Most don't like to be turned down for emotional reasons. They take this as personal rejection, which proves to be a very painful blow to self-worth.

This too is an area that needs to receive attention before starting a ministry, because it may indicate a deeper emotional problem. We must realize that we can feel good about ourselves regardless of whether others accept us or are able to support us financially. Our self-worth has already been established through the grace of God in Jesus Christ. We have worth and are valuable because God has created us in his image and has totally and eternally accepted us through Jesus Christ (Rom. 5:10). Consequently, we must not be afraid to ask God's people for money to support God's work.

The Practice of Fund-Raising

The Contacts

We don't know whom God will motivate to help us financially. Therefore, it's extremely important to have a large number of people to contact. This involves networking. The Savior developed a network (John 1:40, 43–45). Why shouldn't we? Many of us forget that over the years we have developed a large network of ministry friends and acquaintances. These people, in turn, also have a large number of Christian friends and acquaintances. Initially, all of these people can become our contacts for developing a support team.

The prospective church planter should begin to list all these names well in advance of starting the church and continue to add the names of new friends and acquaintances to that list. As the opportunity arises, planters should begin to cast their visions and meet with these people, for God may use such vision casting to gain their initial attention and interest. When the time comes to raise support, there will already be a broad potential base of support available to harvest for advancing the kingdom.

The Conversation

Eventually, visionary church planters will begin to contact potential supporters. Initially, this will be done by telephone, especially if the network is large. It is necessary to develop a phone message that will communicate the essential information pleasantly and concisely.[4] The following procedure is recommended:

1. *Determine the goal for the initial phone conversation.* This could include three things. One is to inform the person of your vision and the fact that you are starting a church to implement this vision. Another is to explain that you're developing a financial support team to help initially in accomplishing this ministry. The last is to ask for an appointment to give more information about the ministry and its costs.

   A possible variation of this format would be to write a letter in which you explain your vision and ministry and the fact that you'll be following up the letter shortly with a phone call to answer any questions. When you call, you would answer questions and explain that you're developing a support team to help start the church. Then you could ask for an appointment to give more information about the ministry and its costs.

2. *In the initial phone conversation, communicate the essential information that people need to know regarding why you want to meet with them.* Save most of the information about the church plant for the time when you're with them in person. Attempt to get as much personal time with them as possible. The better they know you, the greater the chance that they'll support you.

3. *Develop two phone conversations: one for people you know and another for people you don't know.* The following is a sample phone conversation designed by Dallas Seminary church planters for use with someone they don't know:

Hello, Mr./Mrs. _____. My name is _____. I'm a recent graduate of Dallas Seminary, and God has placed on my heart a significant vision to move to _____ and start a church for people who don't like church. Currently, I'm in the process of putting together a support team of people who might share this vision and desire to be a vital part of this ministry. _____ suggested that I call you because he/she thought you might be interested in what the Lord has put on my heart and learning more about a church designed to reach the nonchurched. I'm not asking you to make any kind of commitment now, only to get together with me at your convenience so that I can explain the ministry to you. Would that be possible? What would be a good time for you?

A phone conversation with someone you already know should be more personal. You should talk about whatever is appropriate, depending on the nature of your relationship. Include a brief discussion of your vision and how you came to adopt it. You may want to address the area of financial support in more detail than you would with someone you don't know. It's helpful to provide additional details and allow your friend to interact and ask more questions over the phone. Even if you know someone well, it adds a personal touch when you follow up and meet with him or her personally.

4. *Prepare an attractive, well-designed brochure.* Send the brochure to the people who desire to meet with you and to those who don't but show some interest in the church. In this brochure, demonstrate through research and demographics why you're planting the church. Identify your target group and their need for the gospel. Present your core values, mission, vision, and strategy to accomplish the mission and vision. (I cover these concepts in chapters 7–8.) Next, using mini-biographical statements, introduce your team and explain

their qualifications and what part they'll play in accomplishing the vision. Finally, include a brief but clear budget that presents your plans and financial needs. Make sure the document is visually attractive. If necessary, invest some time and sufficient funds in working with a professional to develop the document. If you're not able to develop a quality piece of material, then it would be best not to use anything at all.

When you send this brochure, include a personal handwritten note explaining that you're forming a financial support team, and you'll visit them in a week or so to see if they have any questions and would like to become involved.

5. *When you meet with interested people, make sure they understand the vision.* After some introductory greetings and small talk, you may want to answer any questions they may have. And you'll want to ask a few questions yourself that focus on the vision, to determine if they understand it. Most likely, people who catch the vision will want to help in some way.

One advantage American church planters often have over cross-cultural missionaries is that they're raising support for a limited period of time, not for their lifetime. If this is your situation, you should make this clear to those with whom you meet, because it allows them to make a short-term commitment, which is much more appealing than a long-term or lifetime commitment. The idea is that the core group will grow into the church and eventually the church will be self-supporting.

In many cases, the core group should be able to take over the financial responsibility for the church planter anywhere from one to four or five years depending on the financial abilities of the people who make up the core group and the number of people on the church planting team. I worked with one Baby Boomer core group consisting of nine couples. After they had caught a vision for reaching their unchurched friends, they committed to provide enough funds to cover the planter-leader's expenses to get the church started.

6. *Finally, once you've established a support team, it's critical that you communicate with them regularly.* There are several ways to accomplish this. You could send your contacts a monthly letter to keep them informed as to the progress of the ministry. You could do the same with a more elaborate newsletter. If they live in the area, give them a phone call. Should you decide to use a mailer, then consider including a self-addressed envelope. Remind them

periodically that by making their check payable to the new church, the Internal Revenue Service will allow this as a deduction at the end of the year.

Financial Expenses: God Provides for What?

What are some expenses that the planter-leader and the team may face? For what expenses will God provide the funds? The answer to both questions is personal and ministry expenses.

The following is a list of potential personal expenses: salary, housing allowance (mortgage/rent), utilities (electricity, gas, water, sewage, telephone, repairs, and maintenance), medical/life insurance, giving/tithing, automobile (payment(s) and expenses such as gas, maintenance, and repairs), clothing, food, continuing education (subscriptions, books, conferences/seminars, and classes), retirement, and a contingency fund.

The following is a list of potential ministry expenses: salaries (pastors/staff, secretarial, maintenance/custodial), office space (rent/lease), utilities, office equipment (phone, fax, computer, printer, Internet account, copier, tape reproduction), office furniture (desks, chairs, lamps), office supplies (including bulletins, stationery, and tapes), meeting facilities (rent/lease, utilities, insurance, storage), audio-visual equipment (microphones, projectors, screens, CD and DVD players, sound board and system), worship (music, instruments, communion and pulpit supplies), children and youth ministries, babysitting, missions/outreach, denominational/organizational support, travel and moving expenses, telemarketing (advertising, stationery, logo, postage, printing), and a contingency fund.

These personal and ministry expenses are included in the Church Planter's Workbook at the back of this book. You will find it most helpful to turn to that section and complete the Financial Worksheet that also helps you with fund-raising.

4

What You Don't Know Might Hurt You!

The Assumptions of Church Planting

At first, Bill Smith couldn't understand why one of his classmates from seminary reacted so negatively to his vision. Initially, this person had shown an interest in church planting and becoming a part of Bill's team. However, he quickly backed off when he heard Bill's vision for planting a large church. He didn't like big churches! Instead, he believed that the churches in the New Testament were small, and he wasn't comfortable with the idea of planting what could be a large church. Also he felt that Bill overemphasized the role of evangelism in church planting. He believed that there should be more emphasis on Bible knowledge. "What people need today is content!" he explained. Suddenly Bill realized the nature of the problem. They held different assumptions about church planting.

It's most important that those who make up a church-birthing team examine their assumptions as they consider starting a church. Anyone who begins a ministry does so with certain practical and theological assumptions that are either consciously or subconsciously in place. These assumptions are important because they affect the initial planting of the new church and its survival. The following six assumptions will undergird all that is said about church planting in the rest of this book. These assumptions are basic and important to the planting of biblically based, Great Commission churches.

The Importance of Evangelism

The first assumption is that evangelicals are going to have to take evangelism seriously if they're going to plant biblically based, spiritually healthy churches. This seems to be a rather strange statement because evangelical churches and organizations are, after all, supposed to be evangelistic.

Churches and Schools Are Weak in Evangelism

Studies indicate that little evangelism is taking place in most American evangelical churches. In 1990 George Barna wrote: "In the past seven years, the proportion of adults who have accepted Jesus Christ as their personal Savior (34%) has not increased."[1] This figure hasn't changed for the better in the twenty-first century. Also the fact that 80 percent to 85 percent of the churches are plateaued or declining signals a need for a greater emphasis on reaching lost people.

It's discouraging to examine the catalogs of some Christian colleges and evangelical seminaries for classes and field education work in the area of evangelism. Unfortunately, studies and fieldwork in this critical area are sadly lacking, especially in the seminaries.[2] The problem is that these institutions are training many of those who will assume key leadership positions in various church and parachurch ministries.

Those who teach in these institutions must constantly remind themselves that the three to five years that students spend in school are formative years during which they are developing the values that give shape to their future ministry. If a theoretical approach is valued over a practical approach during these formative years, the early ministry years will reflect this fact. The result is that pastors will spend much of their time in their study and little time with people. While schools are by nature academic institutions, they must strive to create more of a balance between the theoretical and the practical. The seminary professor would be wise to heed the words of Calvin Guy who asked: "Does his theology motivate men who go into all the world and make disciples?"[3]

Several larger evangelistic churches have observed this tendency and have responded by discouraging prospective pastors from attending seminary altogether. Instead, they bring the most promising people on staff and train them within the local church. While this has some advantages, it also has its disadvantages.[4] In these difficult days for both seminaries and churches, I believe that the answer lies in a revision of how we do theological education with a better balance between the two.

Evangelism Accomplishes Church Growth

Church growth people indicate that there are three ways that a local church can grow numerically. The first kind of growth is biological growth, which takes place when couples in the church have children who then become a part of their parents' church. These children grow up in the church and usually embrace Christ as their Savior as the result of the efforts of their parents and those in the church, such as Sunday school teachers, vacation Bible school workers, and others. Although many drop out of their churches after high school, it's hoped that they'll continue to make the church an important part of their lives throughout the adult years.

The second kind of growth is transfer growth, which takes place as the result of people moving from one church to another. An article in *Christianity Today* indicates that in the early 1990s "more than 80 percent of all the growth taking place in growing churches comes through transfer, not conversion."[5]

Barna observes:

> Perhaps it is not surprising, then, to report that our studies of the Protestant churches that are growing the fastest are expanding primarily by incorporating people from other, declining churches. This is growth by transfer, rather than by conversion. Thus, while many churches across the nation receive attention for their explosive growth, relatively few of those churches are attracting adults who are newcomers to the faith. Most frequently, they are simply enlisting individuals who have left their existing church home to be part of the "happening" church. This is such a common behavior that an estimated 90 million adults in America have been "church shopping."[6]

The same appears to have been true in America in the 1960s and 1970s. For example, one study indicates that conservative church growth came as the result of what its authors call "a kind of circulation process, by which evangelicals move from one conservative church to another."[7]

The third way churches grow numerically is through conversion growth. This takes place when the church corporately or through individuals reaches lost people with the gospel of Christ. While most churches are generally aware of whether or not this is taking place, there's an accurate way to determine this. A church can measure its conversion growth by determining how many of those joining the church have been won to Christ through the ministry of the church. Most believe that a conversion rate of 25 percent or higher is necessary if churches are going to make any impact in this world for the Savior.

Of the approximately 15 percent of evangelical churches that are experiencing growth today, much of it is biological or transfer growth. According to the figure cited above from *Christianity Today*, about 80 percent is this kind of growth. While these may be legitimate forms of growth, the Savior had more than this in mind when in Matthew 28:19 he said, "Go and make disciples of all nations." This describes and demands conversion growth.

While a number of evangelical churches aren't very evangelistic, and some schools are weak in the area of evangelism, it's most refreshing to observe that God is sowing American soil with a number of new, biblically based evangelical churches with a Great Commission vision.

Some denominations and organizations have also expressed a fresh interest in evangelism. A new criterion for success is evident in the Evangelical Free Church in America. Recently, they've announced that in the future, their success will be measured more along the lines of obedience to Christ's Great Commission. They desire to see their churches "make disciples"!

Early in the twenty-first century, America will see the starting of a number of new, biblically based, spiritually healthy churches that will measure their success not so much by how well their people know the Scriptures (as important as that is) or how many programs they have but by whether or not they're making disciples. This is not to say that Bible knowledge and programs aren't important, because they are. Bible knowledge is critical and programs are essential in any church. But far too many of our evangelical churches have majored in these areas to the exclusion of Christ's more comprehensive Great Commission mandate.

The Importance of Numerical Growth

The Forms of Biblical Growth

Three forms of growth are detailed in the book of Acts. The first is spiritual growth. This takes place throughout the book of Acts and requires evangelism, sound teaching, fellowship, the breaking of bread, and prayer (Acts 2:41–42). The results can be observed in the practices that are mentioned in verses 45–47, such as the common sharing of material possessions with the needy, meeting together for fellowship and meals, and worship.

The second kind of growth is geographical. The key passage is Acts 1:8, where shortly before his ascension the Savior announces, "But you will receive power when the Holy Spirit comes on you; and you will be my witnesses in Jerusalem, and in all Judea and Samaria, and to the ends of the earth."

Not only is this a Great Commission text, but it serves to outline the spread of Christianity from the coming of the Holy Spirit on the day of Pentecost to Paul's arrival in Rome. It provides a geographical outline of the spread of Christianity as recorded in the book of Acts. This growth begins in Jerusalem (1:1–8:3), spreads throughout Judea and Samaria (8:4–12:25), and then goes to the "ends of the earth"—Rome (13:1–28:31). This implies that the Great Commission had geographical implications.

The third kind of biblical growth is numerical growth. Luke is careful to record the physical growth of various churches (1:13–15; 2:41; 4:4; 5:14; 6:1; 9:31; 11:21, 24; 14:1, 21; 16:5; 17:4, 12; 18:8, 10; 19:26; 21:20).

The first church, located in Jerusalem, was very large because about three thousand people responded to Peter's sermon on Pentecost (2:41). Shortly thereafter, Acts 4:4 records that five thousand men responded, not including women and children. In fact a detailed study of the passages listed above indicates that the churches in Acts were large churches in terms of numbers, not small as many assume.

The Principles of Numerical Growth

All three kinds of growth were vital to the life of the first-century church and each influenced the other. Obviously, all three kinds of growth are still important to the twenty-first-century church and continue to interact with one another. From this we can learn two important principles regarding numerical growth.

Don't Overemphasize or Denigrate Numerical Growth

It's wrong to either overemphasize or denigrate numerical growth. On the one hand, some larger churches place an undue emphasis on their size. They're very proud of their numbers and use them to bolster their self-esteem as well as their pride. In effect, they're playing the "numbers game" in an attempt to proclaim themselves as "spiritual king of the mountain."

On the other hand, some small churches clearly have a bias against large churches. They argue that the best churches are small churches and tend to see themselves as some kind of spiritual remnant. They can often be overheard saying, "We may not have quantity (lots of people), but we have quality (spiritual people), and we'd prefer quality over quantity any day!" This leads to the next principle.

Quality Churches Become Quantity Churches

Quality churches don't stay small for very long. It's true that quality churches are spiritual churches. And because they're spiritual churches, they're obedient to the Great Commission and are winning lost people for Christ. The result of this kind of obedience is quantity or numerical growth. This was certainly the case in the early church.

Many small churches don't have quantity because they don't have quality. They're weak in evangelism and will remain small. There are also some big churches that have quantity but are beginning to see some numerical decline because they're starting to lose their quality and aren't as active in winning lost people.

There are also some churches that are exceptions to the rule. They are small churches that serve a particular ministry niche, such as the people in a small rural area or a spiritually resistant group like the Muslims in urban North America or in North Africa. However, the exceptions are rare, and many of our smaller churches need to re-examine their purpose for existence and initiate some kind of evangelistic thrust in their communities.

The Importance of Functions

The third assumption is that the functions of the church (evangelism, worship, and others) are more important than its forms (how it accomplishes these functions). This assumption is best understood by looking at an issue that is faced by every local church and the solution to that issue.

The Issue

The issue concerns whether today's evangelical churches should follow the forms as well as the functions of the New Testament church.

Functions Plus Forms

There are those in the church today who teach that the local church is bound to follow not only the biblical functions or principles of the early church but its forms (methods or patterns) as well. They argue that both the functions of the New Testament church and its forms related to those functions are obligatory and binding on local churches of all ages. Thus the church is instructed in both what to do and how to do it. They believe that "apostolic precept is apostolic practice" or "God's work done in God's way will receive God's blessing."

An example would be when the church meets. They would argue that the local church should meet on Sunday because of the significance of the first day of the week and because it was the practice of some apostolic churches (possibly Troas—Acts 20:7) to meet on the first day of every week. Most would argue that other meetings, such as Sunday school classes or a singles' fellowship, are permitted by Scripture as long as they don't interfere with the prescribed Sunday meeting of the church.

Functions without the Forms

There are others who believe that the church is bound to follow only the scriptural mandates of the early church but not its practices or patterns, for the latter are cultural and relative. For example, they would argue that when the church meets in terms of the day, time of day, or how long it meets aren't as important as its actually meeting and what happens when it meets. They would also cite Romans 14:5–12.

The Solution

The latter view is the best solution to this issue. The key here is hermeneutics. The twenty-first-century church is bound to follow the prescriptive passages of the Bible (commands, prohibitions, and so forth), not the descriptive passages (such as those found in Acts 20:7 or 1 Cor. 16:2).[8] This affects the local church in terms of its liberty and relevance.

The Emphasis Is Liberty

The Scriptures appear to grant Christians a great deal of liberty in terms of *how* they do *what* they do and *when* they do it. While the patterns and practices of the apostolic church may be instructive and helpful, Scripture doesn't teach that some or all of these patterns are binding on the church throughout the ages.

Certainly, Sunday has significance for the Christian, but the early church met at various times throughout the week in different contexts for different reasons. We find in Acts 2:46 and 5:42 that the Jerusalem church held daily meetings in such places as the temple or various homes. The church at Corinth was instructed to set aside certain funds on the first day of the week (1 Cor. 16:1–2). However, this doesn't mean that they were bound to have the meeting of the church at this time. Romans 14:5–6 teaches that the church is free to choose when it meets. Thus we can see that it's very difficult even to determine the practices of the early church (such as when they met), much less to attempt to hold twenty-first-century churches to them. Consequently, each new generation of Christians is free to be innovative and, most important, creative in the forms that the functions take. Indeed, it's likely that the most effective churches in the twenty-first century will have little resemblance to those of the twentieth century and earlier.

The Result Is Relevance

God's intent was probably to instruct us in *what* we're to do, but he also gives us much liberty in *how* and *when* we're to do it. This allows the church to remain relevant to its particular culture, whether it's the first century or the twenty-first century, whether it's located in North America, South America, or the Middle East. Otherwise, it finds itself, much like the Amish, attempting to limit its practices to a particular time and culture, such as the eighteenth century.

Scripture is delightfully refreshing when it comes to the forms (practices and patterns) of local churches. It gives each one the freedom to make itself relevant to its unique culture in terms of what it does. The reason is that it takes different kinds of churches to reach different kinds of people. Thus our churches must constantly evaluate what they're doing in light of the culture and times in which they live. (They are to contextualize the culture, not accommodate or isolate themselves from the culture.) I believe that every pastor and church must develop a biblically based theology of culture that will direct their response to culture.

Whether we realize it or not, each church has its own unique culture. This isn't necessarily bad. Culture, in general, is neutral. (Adam and Eve lived in and with culture before the fall. Also see what Paul says about an item of culture—food—in Rom. 14:14–18.) Culture may be used for good or bad (James 3:9–10). Many older churches reflect the culture that surrounded them some thirty or forty years ago and clearly aren't in touch with the culture around them now. The result is that the unchurched lost in our present culture see this and reject the biblical beliefs of these churches because they sense that they're out of touch with reality and what's taking place in the world. They know a dinosaur when they see one!

The Importance of Excellence in Ministry

The fourth assumption that undergirds this book is that church planters must pursue excellence, not mediocrity, in ministry.

The Problem of Mediocrity

Far too many churches today don't pay enough attention to how well they do what they do. Consequently, they are maintaining ministry mediocrity.

Mediocrity Affects Ministry

This problem applies to various important areas of the church. One example would be the worship service, which is often poorly planned and poorly executed, especially in small churches.

I recall in one such church that a young lady stood up to sing a special song with her guitar. However, she had to stop in the middle of the song to tune her guitar because she had not done so prior to the service. So we all sat and watched and listened as she tuned the guitar. Once this was accomplished, she completed the rest of the song—only it was off key!

Another example of mediocrity is the appearance of the church facilities where much ministry takes place. Many churches seem to forget that if they don't properly and regularly maintain their facilities, they'll deteriorate. It has to do with one of the laws of thermodynamics. As these facilities grow older, the problem becomes more acute. Consequently, leaks develop in the roof, the paint begins to peel, and the sink in one of the bathrooms is hopelessly stopped up.

Mediocrity Affects People

Mediocrity affects two particular groups of people: the members and the visitors. Over a period of time, many church members grow accustomed to the above practices and conditions and don't really notice them anymore. As far as they're concerned, everything is fine. While they don't exactly prefer this situation, many have given in to the fact that "that's just the way it is around here." Others are more aware of the problem. While they've learned to live with the problems, they're constantly aware of them and are too embarrassed to invite any of their friends to church—especially the young people.

Visitors to the church are also affected by mediocrity. In particular, the unchurched lost who live and work in a world that has come to expect nothing short of excellence will notice a lack of excellence. They work in facilities that are well maintained and attend events that are well designed and programmed because the competition in the marketplace is so intense. These are people who are not impressed with and will not respond to mediocrity! Consequently, they attend church one time and never return because they've been convinced through ministry mediocrity that Christianity is second-class. If it's not worthy of the best efforts of those who profess it, then it's not worthy of further consideration by those who are curious.

If we're ever to reach these people for the Savior, we must begin to recognize the fact that the conditions of our facilities do, in fact, say something about those who worship there. We must also become aware that what we do sends a loud message about the hearts and attitudes of those who perform in such a manner. It's time for a change!

The Solution to Mediocrity

The solution to mediocrity is excellence. God desires that his church excel in its ministries on his behalf. Whatever we do for the Savior must be done well because we do it for him and in his name. Mediocrity and Christianity must never be mentioned in the same breath. The two must never be associated.

Biblical Documentation

But is this biblical? Scripture clearly teaches a theology of excellence. Its principles are found in both the Old and New Testaments.

A theology of excellence is found in the Old Testament. God wanted his people to give only their best when they worshiped him. Thus Moses instructed Israel to bring the best animals as a sacrifice to God (Lev. 22:20–22; Num. 18:29–30). It's important to note that when their hearts began to wander away from the Lord, it was reflected in their worship. Thus, in Malachi 1:8, the prophet warns, "'When you bring blind animals for sacrifice, is that not wrong? When you sacrifice crippled or diseased animals, is that not wrong? Try offering them to your governor! Would he be pleased with you? Would he accept you?' says the LORD Almighty."

We find the pursuit of excellence in the New Testament as well. In Ephesians 6:5–8 and Colossians 3:23–24, Paul tells us that God expects us to give our best in our work and to do it as if we are working for him. We discover that even at the judgment seat of Christ we'll ultimately be judged according to the "quality" of our works (1 Cor. 3:13). The point is that our God gave his very best when he gave his Son for us. He doesn't expect mediocrity in return.

Need for Clarification

This doesn't mean that God expects Christians to be perfect and that there's no room for failure in any Christian endeavor. The key is to ask why we failed when we fail. If we try our very best but fail because of our less than perfect humanity, this is understandable. For example, if a soloist practices hard all week for a special song yet fails to perform well on Sunday morning, this is understandable. We all have bad days, no matter how hard we work! That's the nature of our humanity. However, it would not be acceptable if she doesn't bother to practice at all during the week and then fails to sing well on Sunday morning. This is ministry mediocrity; this is offering up crippled and diseased animals to God!

Importance of Evaluation

The key to the pursuit of excellence in ministry is constant evaluation. The most effective, relevant churches regularly and intensely evaluate how they "do church." The pastor's sermons are evaluated; the worship service is evaluated. This shows a healthy spiritual concern that Christ be honored in all the church does in his name before a lost but ruthlessly critical world. I'll say more about evaluation and how to accomplish it in the church in chapter 8.

The Importance of Strong Faith

God desires to minister through men and women of strong faith who are willing to trust him for big things.

Jesus Commends Strong Faith

If we were to ask what impressed the Savior when he walked the earth, we'd have to conclude that he was impressed by men and women of strong faith. Jesus constantly commended people for their faith (Matt. 8:10; 15:28) and even healed some according to their faith (9:2, 22, 29). His constant complaint regarding his disciples was their lack of faith. As we read of his ministry to them, the words "you of little faith" constantly ring in our ears (6:30; 8:26; 14:31; 16:8; Mark 9:14–29).

Examples of Faith

Hebrews 11 is instructive in terms of the importance of our faith. Repeatedly, the author encourages us with various cameo appearances of people of great faith. Initially, he warns in verse 6 that "without faith it is impossible to please God." Then he illustrates this point using the lives of Noah and Abraham in verses 7–8.

Noah's great faith is seen in the fact that he believed God to the extent that he was willing to build a huge ark, even though it hadn't ever rained.

We can only imagine what it must have been like trying to explain what he was doing to all of his neighbors!

Abraham's faith is demonstrated in the fact that he was willing to believe God to the extent that he packed his bags and moved his family, even though he had no idea where he was going. We can only imagine what it must have been like to attempt to explain his actions to his friends and family, including those who were believers in the Old Testament sense.

The Lesson of Faith

What church planters can learn from all this is that nothing of any spiritual significance is accomplished outside of faith. It's imperative that church planters be men and women of faith who are willing to trust God for big things in their lives and ministries. What Christ has commissioned his church to accomplish requires tremendous faith, for in Matthew 28:19–20 he has asked us to win the world!

The question we must ask is what can he accomplish through us? Perhaps an even better question is what can't he accomplish through men and women of faith who are willing to trust him to do big things? We've already seen that Paul warns the Ephesian church against asking and thinking too small (Eph. 3:20). Asking and thinking too small is a sign of a small faith. As we, the church of Jesus Christ, minister in the twenty-first century, we need to realize that our esteem and significance are found not in our accomplishments or relationships but in the grace of God through Jesus Christ. And, therefore, we will begin to push ourselves beyond our protective comfort zones to attempt big things for our big God.

The Importance of Courageous Christians

In ministry God uses courageous men and women who are willing to risk failure.

The Problem of Failure

What happens if you fail? What will you do if the church doesn't make it? The answer is we must be willing to fail in order to succeed. Yet far too many people who go into ministry are afraid of failure! They'll not attempt big things for God because they're afraid of what people will think about them if they fail. I'm convinced this was a part of Moses' problem in Exodus 3:11–14.

This is an alarming sign of a deep problem in the area of self-esteem and significance. However, as we understand better the grace of God in our lives through Jesus Christ, we'll learn to value ourselves properly and discover our infinite value in Christ.[9] Then we'll be able to develop a biblical understanding of failure.

The Solution to Failure

Quite simply, we must not be so afraid of failure. Of all God's prohibitions in the Bible, the Savior's words "fear not" seem to stand out the most.

The Response

The best response to failure is twofold. First, we must realize that risk and failure are inherent in any successful work for God. They go hand in hand. There is not a single successful church today that didn't take risks and experience failure along the way. Often people in ministry are afraid to take risks because they're afraid they may fail. However, not to take risks is to fail!

Second, it's important to realize that obeying God always involves an element of risk. In Acts 15:25–26 Luke notes that the Jerusalem Council sent out with Barnabas and Paul not just any men but "men who have risked their lives for the name of our Lord Jesus Christ." In the parable of the talents (Matt. 25:14–30), the Savior soundly condemns the one who is afraid to take risks and takes from him that which had been entrusted to him. Then he proceeds to honor and reward those who were willing to risk failure.

The Examples

Both the Scriptures and recent history provide numerous examples of people who took risks and endured failure to accomplish great things.

This was true of such biblical personalities as Abraham, Moses, David, and Peter. In Genesis 12 Abraham took a risk. Essentially, he obeyed God and stepped out in faith not knowing where he was going. Moses also took a risk when he defied the pharaoh and led Israel out of Egypt.

The same has been true of more contemporary personalities. For example, Babe Ruth is known in the baseball world for his record-setting number of home runs. The truth is that he struck out 1,330 times but hit 714 home runs in between. It has been reported that he once said, "Never let the fear of striking out keep you from taking a swing at the ball!" Thomas Edison experimented with numerous filaments before he found the right combination and invented the electric lightbulb. R. H. Macy failed in the retail business several times before he became a success.

The Lesson

We must not glamorize those who take foolish risks or habitually make the same mistakes throughout life. However, risk is not necessarily bad, as long as you know the risks and are willing to assume them. All good leaders, no matter what their profession, learn from their mistakes. The key is that leaders are always learning, and they learn from their mistakes as well as from their successes.

The problem is that just as there are people in ministry who are afraid to fail, so there are churches that don't tolerate failure. If ministers risk making a few mistakes, some established churches will begin to question their leadership credibility. This is another plus for planting churches. The key to starting a church is to create a culture where there's room for failure. According to Robert Metcalfe, chairperson of 3COM, innovation "requires gambling and risk taking. We tell our folks to make at least ten mistakes a day. If they're not making ten mistakes a day, they're not trying hard enough."[10]

It's imperative that church planters prepare the soil before they sow the seed. Thus we must know what it is we're doing and why we want to do it. We must also think through how we'll finance the venture and be aware of certain critical assumptions that will affect our ultimate success. Once this is accomplished, the next step is to make sure that God has designed us to start churches. This will involve us in the new and developing area of personal assessment, which the next section of this book discusses.

Turn now to the Church Planter's Workbook and complete the Assumptions Worksheet.

Part 2

The Personnel
of Church Planting

Not only must farmers know how to prepare the soil and plant their crops; they must also decide if they're farmers. (*Who* is as important as *how*.) Not everyone comes into this world with a green thumb. Those who do, grow great gardens and enjoy it. Those who don't, may grow great gardens but don't enjoy it. The latter need to discover the true color of their thumbs and involve themselves accordingly. Since his initial gardening experience in our backyard, my son has discovered that his thumb is not green.

In the same way, people who desire to be church planters must discover if that's who they really are. The fact that you have an interest in starting new churches may or may not indicate that you're a church planter. There are several ways to find out. The first is experimental. It involves making an attempt at planting a church. After a year or two, you'll know if you're a church planter. The question is whether the price you and others would pay is worth the experiment.

Another way to find out if you're a church planter is to determine the nature of your divine design. This involves assessment, which is done before you attempt to start a church and can save you and others lots of grief. The next two chapters will help you determine if God has "wired" you to plant churches and if you're to function in the lead position in the process.

5

Are You a Church Planter?

The Practice and Application of Assessment

It was more than Bill Smith's entrepreneurial past that led him to decide that starting churches was to be an important part of his future. He also discovered that his character and competencies were ideally suited for the ministry of church planting. Like a surgeon's rubber glove pulled tightly over his extended hand, it was a natural fit.

But what exactly was the process that Bill went through and what specifically did he discover about himself? This chapter is intended to help those whom God has attracted to church planting determine if they are actually church planter material. It will emphasize the characteristics of the point or lead church planter.

There are several fundamental questions that anyone who desires to plant a church must ask. An obvious one that's often missed is, *Am I a church planter?* or, more accurately, *Am I a lead church planter?* (Again, the focus is on the lone church starter or lead church planter of a team.) One of the best ways to answer the question is through assessment. In light of the fact that personal and ministry assessment is new to most Christians, whether laypersons or professionals, this chapter is intended to orient prospective church planters to this ministry. It will provide a window for them to look into their soul.[1] It will help them to answer the question, *Am I a church planter?* I have also written the book *Maximizing Your Effectiveness* (Baker Books, 1995), which focuses totally on the divine design concept for those who wish to explore this concept and their own designs more fully.

The Value of Assessment

There are three ways that assessment can benefit those who are either considering or are already involved in professional Christian ministry. When prospective church planters go through a good assessment program, they benefit in several ways.

Knowing Who We Are

One benefit is *discovering* who we are, which naturally results in *knowing* who we are. Some people are initially afraid of personal assessment because in the past they've taken psychological tests that are designed to uncover any psychological abnormality or dysfunctional behavior. This can be a frightening and disconcerting experience. While there's an analytical side to assessment that is often associated with the field of psychological counseling, there's a positive side as well. Not only can we discover what's wrong with us, but we can discover what's right with us. The former concerns our depravity; the latter, our dignity. And it's the latter that represents the positive side of knowing who we are.

This positive side involves probing how God has designed us—our "divine design." Secularists often argue that we come into this world like pieces of clay in terms of who we are and that our families and other forces in the environment act as potters to shape and mold our personalities. The problem with this view is that it strips us of personal responsibility. Consequently, when people habitually sin or even commit a heinous crime, it's not so much their fault as that of their parents or society in general.

At the time we're born, much of our divine design is already in place. Assessment helps us in knowing who we are by aiding in the discovery of this design. This is a very positive and exciting experience because we're probing God's sovereign and unique makeup of us as his special image bearers.

Liking Who We Are

A second personal benefit of *knowing* who we are is *liking* who we are. There are far too many Christians who struggle with poor self-esteem, because when they look in a mirror they don't like what they see or they continually evaluate themselves only in terms of the imprint of the flesh on their lives. The result is that they don't like themselves very much.

Yet, in such passages as Ephesians 5:28–29, 33, Scripture speaks of loving ourselves in a positive light. A vital key to loving ourselves biblically is liking ourselves, and liking ourselves is facilitated through assessment.

Again, probing God's makeup of us reveals in a very positive way certain gifts, talents, and abilities of which we may not have been aware. We begin to discover not what we're bad at, but what we're good at. We realize that there are some things we enjoy doing because we were designed to do them well.

Being Who We Are

A third personal benefit is that *liking* who we are results in *being* who we are. People who don't like who they are often attempt to be someone else. They put on masks and play roles so that others will not discover their real identity. They fear that if people know them as they really are, they'll not like them and will reject them. And the pain from this would be unbearable and must be avoided at all costs.

However, when we discover who we are in Christ and how God has individually designed us to contribute in a wonderful way to his kingdom work, we become authentic. We take off our masks and stop playing fictitious roles, because we're no longer ashamed of what God has made. And this, in time, gets better because we discover a new freedom and liberty in Christ that we may never have experienced or realized. In John 8:32 Christ says that truth has a freeing effect. The truth of knowing who Christ has made us to be frees us to be authentic as well as special persons.

The Purpose of Assessment

Why would we want to implement an assessment program in a church? Not only are there personal benefits, but there are specific purposes for doing so.

To Discover Our Divine Design

Personal assessment enables us to discover our divine design. The general concept of divine design was discussed in the previous section. Here, two factors in particular will be the focus: Everyone has a design from God, and everyone's design is unique.

Everyone Has a Design from God

God is the author and source of our makeup long before we're born into this world (Job 10:8–9; Ps. 139:15–16; Isa. 49:1, 5; Jer. 1:5; Luke 1:15; 1 Cor. 12:18; Gal. 1:15).

Our divine design includes such things as our temperaments and our natural gifts, talents, and abilities. When we accept Christ, God adds other things as well, including our spiritual gifts. All of this constitutes our divine design or makeup, our special "wiring" or "chemistry."

Each Design Is Unique

While Christians may have similar designs, no two Christians have the same design. One way to view this concept is to think of the divine design as a "divine thumbprint." This emphasizes both its source and uniqueness. The source of the design is from the Creator-Designer. The uniqueness of the design can be compared to a human thumbprint. While each of us has a thumbprint, and some prints are very close in appearance, none is exactly alike. And much the same is true of us as divine thumbprints. Realizing this can be very helpful when we're tempted to compare ourselves with other Christians and wish that we were like them.

To Discover Our Personal Ministry Direction

Personal assessment helps us develop a personal ministry direction or "ministry niche." Once we've discovered who we are (our design), the next step is to take that information and use it to determine what we can do or what God has designed us to do whether it's starting churches or some other ministry.

Some refer to this process as discovering God's will or "calling" for our lives. Often Christians agonize as they attempt to discover God's will in a particular situation or for the direction of their lives in general. Most often, God's will is found in his Word, the Scriptures. The same agonizing takes place in determining God's will for our lives in terms of future ministry.

Here, God's will or calling can be found both in his Word and in how he's designed us. In other words, God's call for our lives can to a great extent be detected by his design of our lives. If, for example, he's given us the gifts of leadership, faith, and evangelism coupled with an entrepreneurial spirit and a love for ministry in the local church, he may be directing or calling us to become church planters.

The Importance of Assessment

Assessment is important because it helps us know ourselves in terms of our strengths, limitations, and weaknesses. For example, church planting isn't for the faint of heart. You'll have to put it all on the line. You may have to go without certain personal comforts. You'll have to reach a high level of risk tolerance or else you won't last. And don't underestimate the effort that it will take to communicate the gospel to a lost, unchurched, dying generation. Is this who you are?

Strengths

In the past, unfortunately, there's been too much emphasis on people's weaknesses. This was probably due to the early development of the fields of psychology and psychiatry. For example, my first exposure to the field of ministry assessment was as a faculty member with a group of students. An assessor asked all of us certain questions privately. I can remember how nervous I felt. I didn't understand; I was thinking pathologically not positively. This was because one graduate school that I'd attended used the *MMPI* (*Minnesota Multiphasic Personality Inventory*) as a tool in the admissions process to help in discerning dysfunctional applicants. I assumed the ministry assessment was going to be a similar process. I thought that the assessor was going to "tell all," and I'd be horribly embarrassed. This didn't take place. Not only was I not embarrassed, but when he finished, I wanted him to go on! I felt good about my "chemistry" and how God had "wired" me.

It's helpful and healthy to know what's good about us, to identify our gifts, passions, and temperament and focus on them. This is more beneficial than trying to improve on our weaknesses.

Limitations

A Clarification

Our limitations are the gifts, talents, and abilities we *don't* have as a part of our ministry makeup.[2] Since God in his sovereignty has decided not to give us these "tools," we are limited when we attempt to accomplish ministry that calls for them.

This doesn't mean it's wrong to use them or that we should attempt to avoid them entirely. What it means is that we're going to be somewhat limited when we attempt to use them in ministry. This also means that most likely we'll not derive as much satisfaction from their use. For example, we may not have the gift of evangelism. However, God desires that we share the gospel anyway. We'll not do it as effectively and we may not enjoy it as much as someone who has that gift, but we share our faith regardless.

The Advantages

Knowing our limitations can help us in our ministry in two ways. First, we can avoid potential ministry burnout. If we should become involved in a ministry that primarily calls for a different mix of gifts or a different temperament than we have, over a period of time we will most likely experience burnout. We should spend at least 60 percent or more of our time in the areas of our strengths. When we spend less than 60 percent, the chances of burnout increase proportionately. Obviously spending 100 percent of our time in our areas of strength isn't possible because there's no perfect ministry, nor is it wise to attempt to do so because we would neglect some ministries that need to be done regardless of our gifting.

Knowing our limitations also helps us work toward maximizing our ministry effectiveness. By knowing what we don't do well, we can focus more on what we do well. This should help us know when to say no. For example, if a ministry was seeking a staff evangelist, and someone approached you about the position, you could say no, based on the fact that you're not gifted for the position. This doesn't mean you wouldn't continue to share your faith as much as possible. It does mean that your negative response would allow you to pursue your area of giftedness to maximize your ministry efforts.

Weaknesses

A final reason why assessment is important is that it will uncover weaknesses. The term *limitations* refers to certain gifts, abilities, and temperaments that are outside our divine makeup. The term *weaknesses* refers primarily to negative character traits that are present in all of our lives to some extent. If not discovered and dealt with, these "emotional splinters" will work their way to the surface and cause us much pain in relating to others in both our public ministries and our private lives. Most in the field of assessment are of the opinion that we can't change our designs nor should we want to. However, we can change our negative character qualities and should attempt to do so with God's help. This is what Romans 6–8 is all about.

While the primary intent of assessment is not to uncover character flaws, nevertheless this should be done. In the process of discovering our dignity, we must deal with our depravity. As we begin to probe and learn about our dark side, which Scripture refers to as the "flesh," we'll learn to deal with that aspect of our person and grow in Christlikeness as a result.

The Accuracy of Assessment

Several factors affect the accuracy of any program of assessment no matter how sophisticated the procedure may be. One factor is self-knowledge. Some people know themselves quite well, while others don't know themselves at all. The former find assessment easier and often more confirming than illuminating. The latter are in for an amazing learning process.

The reason why knowledge of ourselves is so important is because we are the ones, ultimately, who determine the accuracy of any assessment program. We can use such highly valid and sophisticated tools as the *Personal Profile System®* (DiSC®) or the *Myers-Briggs Type Indicator®* (MBTI®), but they only reflect the information that we supply. If that information is based on who we want to be or who someone else thinks we are, and not on who we *really* are, then it tells us nothing. Next to our omniscient God, we're the ones who know us best and are the final judges of any personal assessment. As we weigh the results of an assessment program in general or a tool in particular, it's our responsibility to determine its accuracy based on our self-knowledge.

Another factor that affects the accuracy of assessment is ministry experience. This is "seasoning." The more ministry experience people have, the more accurate will be their assessment of themselves. We know our leadership abilities best when we take advantage of opportunities to lead. The more we do this, the more "seasoned" we become and the better we're able to discern our strengths, limitations, and weaknesses. However, we face several problems in the area of ministry experience.

One obvious problem is that we're not able to gain experience in all the areas we desire. In fact new believers may have very little ministry experience to turn to for help in assessment. A potential solution to the problem of a seeming lack of experience is to examine our pre-Christian lives for experiences that can parallel those of ministry. Again, we don't have to be Christians to exercise and experience leadership, teaching, counseling, and other abilities.

Another problem is a reluctance on the part of some to become involved in ministry areas to gain vital ministry experience. This seems to be a problem particularly in the academic setting. Obviously, in an academic environment, people will value academic pursuits over practical pursuits. Students will prefer learning in the classroom over learning in a ministry situation. But the classroom or the library isn't the real world where most ministry takes place! That's why it's imperative that our Bible colleges and seminaries do a better job of encouraging the practical pursuit of ministry as well as academic pursuits.

The Areas for Assessment

Character

The number one criterion for any ministry is godly character. The general character qualities that pastors in general and church planters in particular must evidence are found in 1 Timothy 3:1–7 and Titus 1:6–9. They consist of the following: above reproach, the husband of one wife, temperate, sensible, respectable, hospitable, able to teach, not violent, not given to drunkenness, gentle, not quarrelsome, not a lover of money, one who manages his family well, not a recent convert, not overbearing, not quick-tempered, has a good reputation with outsiders, not pursuing dishonest gain, loves what is good, holds firmly to the faith, is upright, and is holy. Leader-planters who are characterized by these qualities have trained themselves to "be godly," as Paul mentions in 1 Timothy 4:7–8. I'll say more about character in the next chapter on the church planter as leader. I have also placed a character audit on my website (www.malphursgroup.com/ChurchPlanting) that will help you assess how you're progressing in your development of these character qualities.

Competence

The rest of this chapter will focus on spiritual gifts, passion, temperament, and family. These primary areas of assessment help us determine our basic general design. They provide us with the "big picture." We give these areas priority in assessment because they reveal so much about our church planting potential.

Spiritual Gifts

First, we should determine our spiritual gifts. A spiritual gift is a God-given ability for service.[3] The gifts are listed in Romans 12, 1 Corinthians 12–14, Ephesians 4, and possibly 1 Peter 4. (There are probably more gifts than those listed in the New Testament.) The spiritual gifts include teaching, helps, exhortation, giving, leading, administration, and pastoring. We should also include preaching as a gift in light of Paul's use of it in 2 Timothy 1:11. These spiritual gifts are important because our God-given gifts provide the special abilities or tools we need for ministry.

In addressing our spiritual gifts, we need to look for two areas. The first is our gift-mix.[4] This consists of the spiritual gifts that we commonly demonstrate in ministry. Most who are fairly experienced have three to five gifts. The first three are discernible while the fourth and fifth may not be as clear. The second area is our gift-cluster, which consists of our gift-mix, with one of the gifts appearing clearly dominant and supported by the others.[5]

We can examine the gifts to discover if we have an affinity for certain ones. While this can be most productive, it's also very subjective. A more objective approach is to take one of the many spiritual gifts inventories that are available. They're often divided into those that test for all the gifts, including the sign gifts such as the *Wagner Modified Houts Questionnaire*, and those that don't such as the *Houts Inventory of Spiritual Gifts*, the *Spiritual Gifts Analysis*, and my Spiritual Gifts Inventory found in the appendix (pages 199–208) of *Maximizing Your Effectiveness*.

Following are the gifts that have characterized successful church planters in the last few decades.

Apostleship (1 Cor. 12:28; Eph. 4:11). The gift of apostleship is included here not as the primary gift exercised by the twelve apostles who laid the foundation of the church and whose ministries were authenticated by certain sign gifts, but in a secondary sense as used by people such as Barnabas (Acts 14:3, 14), Silvanus and Timothy (1 Thess. 2:6), and Andronicus and Junias (Rom. 16:7). Essentially, this gift involves the capacity to adapt and minister cross-culturally (Eph. 3:7–9). It's important for those who decide to spend their lives planting churches and ministering in a cross-cultural context.

Evangelism (Eph. 4:11). Those with the gift of evangelism are compassionate toward lost people and are attracted to and enjoy spending time with them. This gift is the desire to communicate clearly the gospel of Jesus Christ to unbelievers either individually or in a group context with the result that a number respond and come to faith in Christ. Evangelists may also enjoy training others to do evangelism (Eph. 4:11–12).

Faith (1 Cor. 12:9). The gift of faith is the ability to envision what needs to be done and to trust God to accomplish it, even though it seems impossible to most people. It may cluster with the gift of leadership and is often found in visionary Christians who dream big dreams and attempt big things for the Savior.

Leading (Rom. 12:8). Leaders are influencers. The gift of leading is found in people who have a clear, significant vision and are able to communicate it in such a way that they influence others to pursue that vision. It's not to be confused with the gift of administration.

Preaching (1 Tim. 2:7; 2 Tim. 1:11). This gift isn't mentioned in the three common listings of gifts in the New Testament. However, it's associated with the gift of apostle in 1 Timothy 2:7 and the gifts of apostle and teacher in 2 Timothy 1:11. Preaching is the God-given ability to communicate God's Word with clarity and power in a culturally relevant way so that it applies to the specific situation of the hearers.

Teaching (Rom. 12:7; 1 Cor. 12:28; Eph. 4:11). The gift of teaching is the ability to understand and communicate the Scriptures clearly and with spiritual insight. Those with this gift know their Bible and delight in helping people to better understand the Scriptures.

Passion

Next, we should seek to determine our passion, because we can't approach church planting half way. We can't dabble at church planting, because it requires all the passion we can bring to it. We do it because we have a passion for it, and it's that passion that gets us through the times of uncertainty, doubt, and discouragement.

What is passion and why is it important? Passion is what we feel strongly and care deeply about. It touches our emotions and captivates our attention. It's what gets us out of bed in the morning. In ministry, we tend to drift toward our passions.

Passion is particularly important in assessment for two reasons. First, it provides the necessary direction for ministry in general and spiritual gifts in particular. For example, two people may have the gift of teaching. However, one may have a passion for poor and oppressed children, while the other may have a passion for college students or internationals. The other reason is that it provides the necessary motivation. Passion motivates or energizes; it pushes or compels us to take some definite action. It spurs us to activity, not inactivity.

There are several questions that will help us discover our passion. Carefully think about each of the following:

1. What or whom do you feel strongly about?
2. What or whom do you care deeply about?

3. In light of your spiritual gifts, how or with whom do you desire to use these gifts?
4. If God gave you one wish for ministry, what would it be?
5. In your quiet moments, what fire is God igniting in the deep recesses of your soul?
6. What do you really want to do for God with your life?

Once we have identified the passion that motivates and directs our spiritual gifts, how does this relate to church planting? Perhaps the answer lies in the example of Paul, who was a church planter par excellence.

In general, Paul's passion was for the Great Commission. Throughout the book of Acts and the Epistles, he and the other disciples are pursuing, evangelizing, and discipling lost people. While the focus is on Jewish lost people initially, the Gentiles are brought into the picture as well, according to the plan of God (Eph. 3:1–8).

In terms of church planters, those with a passion for the Great Commission make good leader-planters. A passion for church planting, evangelism, lost people in general, and unchurched lost people in particular is also important to leader-planters.

Some areas of passion could hamper the initial planting of the new church. For example, if a person has the gift of teaching and a passion for theology, then the chances are good that reaching lost people will not be of primary importance to this individual. This isn't to say that this person will not reach lost people, but a passion for the lost will not be a strong motivating factor for him or her. Consequently, this person might be better off teaching in a school where a passion for theology and for students is essential.

If there is a church planting team, however, the situation may be different. While it's critical that all members of a church planting team have the same vision, there's more room for variation in passion. It's the vision of the team that unites it and gives it direction as a whole. Everyone on the team knows the direction of the entire team, which is the Great Commission mandate. But there's room for different passions within that mandate. For example, one member of the team may have a passion for helping people worship and value God apart from the sermon. Another person could be a Christian education specialist with a passion for ministering to children. As long as both of these team members have caught a vision for reaching the lost, their individual passions will contribute to, not distract from, the overarching vision of the entire team. The important thing is that someone on the team, preferably the team leader, have a passion for the Great Commission.

Temperament

Once we have identified our spiritual gifts and passion, the next area is temperament. We can learn a great deal about ourselves and others when we explore the different temperament types.

In assessing temperament, we begin with the traditional four-temperament model—the personal profile—which focuses on understanding normal, needs-based behavior. This model has been somewhat popularized by Tim LaHaye, who used the terms *choleric, sanguine, phlegmatic,* and *melancholy,* based on the work of Hippocrates in the first century.

A useful tool for temperament assessment is the *Personal Profile System®*, which was developed by John G. Geier and Dorothy E. Downey as based on the earlier work of William Marston, who popularized the DiSC® model. DiSC is an acronym for the four behavioral temperaments: dominance, influence, steadiness, and compliance. This tool helps specifically to determine who are the point or lead people in ministry and who function best as support people.

I've developed my own version of the four-temperament model, which I call DIRT. It is similar to the DiSC model. Read the following descriptions and see if you can identify your temperament.

Doers attempt to control or overcome the environment to accomplish their vision. They're more task- than people-oriented. They're catalytic people who love a challenge and are not afraid to take risks. Doers make quick decisions and like immediate results. They love to challenge the status quo. In their environment, they need freedom from control and supervision and desire opportunity for individual accomplishments. They are up-front and out-front kinds of people and are usually *D*s on the *Personal Profile.*

Influencers attempt to convince people to accomplish the vision. They are more people- than task-oriented. They're persuaders, promoting their ideas to bring others into alliance with them. Influencers enjoy contact with people and desire to make a favorable impression. They are articulate, very motivational, and enthusiastic, and they too will challenge the status quo. To minister at maximum effectiveness, they need freedom from control and detail. Like doers, they are up-front and out-front people and are usually *I*'s on the *Personal Profile.*

Relaters cooperate with others to accomplish their vision. They're more people- than task-oriented and prefer the status quo unless given good reasons to change. Patient, loyal, and good listeners, they're very well liked and pleasant to be around. They minister best in a secure and somewhat safe environment, where they receive credit for their accomplishments along with sincere appreciation. They prefer remaining behind the scenes and are *Ss* on the *Personal Profile*.

Thinkers tend to be very diplomatic with people and comply with authority. They shape their environment by promoting high quality and accuracy in accomplishing the vision. Thinkers are more task- than people-oriented. They are critical thinkers who are analytical and focus on key details and accuracy. In their environment, they desire to work under known conditions and prefer the status quo. They usually minister behind the scenes and are often *Cs* on the *Personal Profile*.

Another temperament tool is the *Myers-Briggs Type Indicator®* (MBTI®). This tool takes a different approach to personality than the *Personal Profile* (DiSC) in that it helps us discern how we handle key functional areas of our lives. First, it seeks to determine preference for extroversion or introversion. This helps us know where we focus our attention (the inner or outer world) and what energizes us. Second, it helps us discover how we perceive or take in information. We tend to prefer either sensing, which involves taking in information through the five senses, or intuition, which gathers information intuitively or beyond the senses. (Intuitive people are visionaries; sensing people are the practical realists.) Third, it helps us discover how we use the information we take in or how we make decisions. This involves a preference for thinking or feeling. Those who prefer thinking make decisions based on logic and objective analysis. Those who prefer feeling make decisions based on personal values and judgments. Finally, the MBTI helps in determining the lifestyle we adopt for dealing with the outer world. This involves a preference for judging or perceiving. Those who prefer judging are not judgmental people but those who take a very planned, organized approach to life. They like closure and are usually quick decision makers. Those who prefer perceiving are people who are adaptable and take a spontaneous, flexible approach to life. They don't like closure, preferring to wait until all the facts are in before making decisions.

At this point, you would be wise to take the *Personal Profile* (DiSC) and the *Myers-Briggs Temperament Indicator* (MBTI) or the Keirsey Temperament Sorter (KTS), a shorter version of the MBTI.[6] Though the results will not be as accurate, shortened versions of these tools can be found on my website (www.malphursgroup.com/ChurchPlanting) for your convenience.

Once you've discovered your temperament, based on the descriptions above and/or by taking one of the profiles, the next step is to apply the results to church planting.

The Personal Profile (DiSC). Lone church planters need to be strong, visionary leaders. This proves most helpful in the early stages of starting churches when there is need for significant direction and numerical growth and there's a potential for much discouragement. Those who score as high *D*s or *I*s or a combination of either on the *Personal Profile*, or from the descriptions in DIRT are doers or influencers, are usually best suited for this position of leadership.

The Christian Churches/Churches of Christ performed a recent survey using the *Personal Profile* to correlate the personality types of sixty-six church planters with the growth of their churches. The survey revealed that the high *D* planters had an average attendance of 72 after the first year and 181 after an average of 5.2 years. The high *I*s had an average of 98 after the first year and an average of 174 after 3.6 years. The high *S*s had an average of 38 after the first year and 77 after 6.3 years, while the high *C*s had an average of 39 after one year and 71 after 4.3 years.[7]

The high *D* planter tends to be a strong, catalytic person who takes authority, makes quick decisions, and loves a challenge such as starting a church. The high *I* planter is a strong person who is exciting and enthusiastic and good at motivating people. Both the high *D* and the high *I* are best in the point position. The next best combination is either a primary high *D* or high *I* with a secondary *S* or *C* on the DiSC *Profile* (or *R* or *T* on the DIRT profile).

The MBTI or KTS. First, lone church planters who are extroverts function better than those who are introverts. In *Personality Type and Religious Leadership*, Roy Oswald and Otto Kroeger conclude, after a study of the functions of ministry normally expected of an ordained person, "that the parish ministry is primarily an Extroverted profession."[8] The majority of the pastoral functions involve up-front work with large numbers of people. This certainly characterizes church planting. Up-front work with people energizes extroverts but exhausts introverts. Introverts function best in the team context of starting churches.

Second, in the point or primary leadership position, the intuitive types are clearly stronger leaders in church planting than sensing types. This is because church planters need to be strong, visionary leaders who are good at planning and prefer change and innovation that encourage growth. This describes well the intuitive-type person, especially in combination with thinking. Sensing-type people aren't that enthusiastic about vision, innovation, and change. They're very practical people who view ministry as doing; therefore, they make great workers.[9] They, like introverts, function best by working with a church planting team rather than leading it.

Third, the feeling types seem to have a slight advantage over the thinking types in terms of leadership in church planting when combined with intuition. Oswald and Kroeger indicate: "Approximately 80% of what a pastor does on a day-to-day basis involves inter-personal relations," which favors feeling-type clergy.[10] They also point to the fact that many established churches predominantly consist of feeling-type cultures, which leaves thinking-type pastors at a disadvantage.[11] Therefore, feeling types can make good church planters.

Idealistically speaking, however, thinking-intuitive people have the edge for several reasons. First, the feeling types eventually stop exercising consistent, strong leadership, which could plateau a church in terms of numerical growth. This isn't true of thinking-intuitive clergy.[12] Thinking-intuitive clergy are strong leaders who are visionary and prefer change.[13] They press toward excellence, which is very important in church planting.[14] The fact that they are not as strong at interpersonal skills is a disadvantage that can be overcome by recognizing the problem and involving others in the core group to help offset it.

Fourth, the perceiving types have a slight advantage in church planting over the judging types. The judging types have the ability to make hard decisions, take a strong stand, and commit themselves to a clear course of action.[15] However, when combined with the sensing type, they can become very rigid and inflexible, preferring the status quo—a preference that spells death for Great Commission churches.[16] They're the originators of the famous seven last words of the church: "We've never done it that way before!" The perceiving types have an advantage in their openness to change, which brings both new options and a freshness to their ministries. They're also masters at handling the unplanned and unexpected, which constantly characterize church planting.[17]

Family

For a married church planter an essential ingredient to his ministry is the backing of his family. Without this support, especially from his wife, the ministry won't happen; the effort is doomed to failure. The family will be directly involved in the ministry and must be fully supportive of it. In fact the church planter's family must come before the ministry. If the family isn't behind the vision, then God is telling the prospective church planter that the time for planting a church isn't right.

Qualifications for the Family

Some of the qualifications for church planters, such as motives and character, will be covered in chapter 6, which concerns leadership. The focus there will be on 1 Thessalonians 2. But there are also family qualifications for men, their wives, and their children.

Men. The qualifications found in 1 Timothy 3:1–7 and Titus 1:5–9 deal primarily with character. These are qualifications for elders but are also essential for church planters.

One important qualification in terms of the family is found in 1 Timothy 3:4–5: "He must manage his own family well and see that his children obey him with proper respect. (If anyone does not know how to manage his own family, how can he take care of God's church?)" Those who go into ministry must be good managers of their family and have the obedience and respect of their children. If this isn't the case, then the prospective church planter is disqualified.

Wives. Wives, like their husbands, must be pursuing Christlikeness. This doesn't mean they've arrived, but they're in active pursuit of the goal. They shouldn't be in opposition to the church planting ministry but must instead be fully supportive of it. If the wife is opposed to it, the potential church planter should not pursue this ministry until or unless his wife changes her mind.

There are no qualifications listed for elders' wives in 1 Timothy 3. Verse 11 reads: "In the same way, their wives are to be women worthy of respect, not malicious talkers but temperate and trustworthy in everything." The question is, to whom is this passage referring? Some commentators think it's a reference to deacons' wives (since deacons are mentioned in the previous verse); others believe it refers to a group of women who served in the church as deaconesses.

For a successful ministry, church planters must have wives who are worthy of respect, not malicious talkers, but temperate and trustworthy people. A book that would prove helpful to leader-planters' wives is Arnell ArnTessoni's *Gentle Plantings*.[18]

Children. The children of those in ministry should obey and respect their father (1 Tim. 3:40). If this isn't the case, it puts into question whether the father is qualified for any professional ministry.

Expectations of the Family

Churches have certain expectations of pastors' wives and children. Congregation members may expect wives to be involved in such ministries as teaching children, leading women's Bible studies, entertaining people in their home, playing the piano or organ in a traditional church, or singing in the choir. These expectations may be either obvious or subtle. Some churches will demand these things up front. Others may not voice them but the expectations are real nonetheless. In some churches, the board may not have requirements for the wife, but the people in the church do.

Scripture places no expectations on pastors' wives in terms of ministry in the church. It does place certain family responsibilities on them as wives and mothers. These are found in Titus 2:4–5 and include such things as loving their husband and children and being busy at home. Consequently, the church should expect nothing more from the church planter's wife than being a good wife and mother. If she has the time and desires to become involved in ministry in the church, that's her decision, but this must not be a requirement or expectation because she is the church planter's wife.

Another issue is the career-oriented wife. Should a wife pursue a professional career while her husband pastors a church? If there are no children, there is no problem with this as long as she is able to love her husband, maintain the household, and encourage and support him in the ministry. In fact, in a planted church that targets Boomers or Busters, most of the wives in the church will be employed. However, once the ministering couple begin a family, the wife should be at home rearing the children.

Churches generally don't have ministry expectations of children, especially if they're young. Often, however, they do expect them to be examples in terms of their behavior. This is one of the reasons some pastors' families feel that they live in a fishbowl, and it puts unfair pressure on the children and added pressure on their parents. The church should understand that it's not realistic to expect the pastors' children to set the example for all the other children in terms of their behavior. They aren't and cannot be perfect!

Disadvantages for the Family

There are several disadvantages for families in church planting. First, church planters may not have a lot of time for their families. While their schedules are rather flexible, church planting is hard work, and there's always something that needs to be done. If church planters don't know how to handle their time, or if they're obsessive, they may fail to spend adequate time with their wives and children.

A church planting ministry can create special problems for a wife. For example, if meetings are constantly held in her house or apartment, she may find herself functioning as a permanent hostess. In addition, if she's a "neatnik," she may feel a lot of pressure to keep the house immaculate to set a good example. With lots of traffic, this will not be possible and will prove to be most frustrating.

There's a lot of risk involved in church planting. This is difficult for some wives to handle. They may prefer a more secure position in an established church or another form of ministry.

Advantages for the Family

Church planting can involve the entire family in a positive way in the ministry. In an interview in *Leadership*, church planter Victor Fry says, "We started our second mission congregation when our children were in sixth grade, second grade, and kindergarten. They were involved delivering fliers and even got the neighborhood kids to help, too. They were caught up in the excitement of starting a new church."[19] In the same interview, another church planter, Kaye Pattison, says, "It's been very positive for us. All of my daughters ended up teaching Sunday school and doing other things they couldn't have done in a large established church."[20] He indicates that this has resulted in their continued activity in ministry later in life after marriage and children.

A church-planting ministry often makes life easier on the pastor's wife. The expectations of the pastor's wife are minimal if any at all. Regarding this, Kaye Pattison says, "I've even found being a church planter is easier on one's spouse. It eliminates many of the rigors of being a 'pastor's wife.' If your spouse fears the limelight and always has to have every hair in place, church planting is a more relaxed alternative."[21]

Often, since they're responsible for their own schedule, church planters have more time for their family. If they aren't workaholics, they can set aside specific time to be home with their wife and children. Again, Kaye Pattison says, "Church planters also have more time for family. If you're in a church of five hundred, someone's always calling, and the kids think Daddy loves the congregation more than them. That's not a problem in the early stages of a church."[22]

Other Characteristics of Strong Church Planters

At the risk of overlap, especially with the information on temperament, the following are some other characteristics that I've observed in strong church planters over the years. They are entrepreneurial, visionary, self-starters, flexible and adaptable, risk-takers, resilient, focused, optimistic (not pessimistic), nontraditional, humble, inspirational, challenging, servants, team players, creative, strategic thinkers, wise, and good communicators. They attract people, have strong people skills and good self-esteem, and maintain a vital prayer life.

Those who are "wired" to plant a church in the lead position have a distinct advantage. The drive comes to them naturally. It's instinctive.

However, no one, even the point person, has all or must have all the qualities mentioned in this chapter to be involved in church planting. While I'll say more about this later, I advocate planting a church as a team and not as a lone ranger. Again, these are the qualities and characteristics of the lead person on the team. Church planting support people will be wired differently so that they can complement the lead person and not be just like him.

Turn to the Church Planter's Workbook and complete the Ministry Design Worksheet.

6

Leading with Sustained Excellence

A Strong Servant-Leadership

The last chapter asked what kind of person makes a good church planter. This chapter asks what kind of leader will it take to plant a church. The fact that 80 to 85 percent of the churches in North America are plateaued or in decline shows that we're facing a serious crisis in leadership that affects not only established churches but planted churches as well. Actually, the problem is a leadership vacuum in the church. It's my view that God hasn't "shorted" us on leaders—they're out there somewhere. The problem is that with the decline of the church and its resistance to needed change, many young leaders are throwing up their hands in dismay and pursuing directions other than ministry.

A Great Commission vision is vital to any planted church. From the outset, it provides a sense of direction for the church—everyone knows where the church is going. But it takes leadership excellence to implement this vision. It's easy to get excited about what God has in store for the twenty-first century. The challenge, however, is to recruit and prepare the new generations to lead with sustained excellence, especially in planting churches. To accomplish this we must know the kind of person who can do the job.

What's vital for today's church in general and church planting in particular is a strong servant-leader. This second chapter dealing with personnel is about strong servant-leadership. But exactly what is a strong servant-leader? How would we know one if we saw him?

A Leader

Christian leaders are godly persons (character) who know where they are going (direction) and have followers (influence).[1]

Character

Godly character is the foundation of any leadership. It's the essential element that qualifies Christians to lead others. It earns people's respect and produces trust—the most essential factor in all relationships. A leader must be trusted to be followed. Since character forms the very foundation for ministry, if something goes wrong here, then the entire ministry will suffer the consequences. But what is godly character, and how do we develop it?

Motives

In examining the area of character, we must focus first on motives. Paul, a first-century church planter par excellence, gives us his motives for planting churches in 1 Thessalonians 2:2–6.

Paul's first motive is to spread the gospel (v. 2). He had dared proclaim the gospel to the Thessalonians in spite of much opposition, and everywhere Paul went it was his goal to spread the gospel. In 1 Corinthians 9:16, he confesses, "Woe to me if I do not preach the gospel!" Church planters must have a strong desire to see lost people come to faith in the Savior as the result of their ministry.

The second motive is to please God (v. 4). It's God, not people, to whom we're ultimately accountable. We should minister in such a way that we look forward someday to hearing the words, "Well done, good and faithful servant!"

The third motive is to tell people what they need to hear (v. 5). Paul was careful to avoid telling people what they wanted to hear. Instead, he told them what they needed to hear. Prospective church planters must expect criticism and be prepared for it when they tell people what they need to hear.

The fourth motive for church planting is to serve God (v. 5). Church planting is not to be done for personal gain. At some point in ministry, church planters are tempted to ask Peter's question (Matt. 19:27): "What then will there be for us?" (my translation: What's in it for us?). The Savior's answer in the rest of chapter 19 and chapter 20 is that the Father is most pleased when we serve him without regard for personal reward. When this is the case, he blesses us beyond all expectation.

The last motive is the grace of God in Jesus Christ and what he has done on the cross (v. 6). Church planting is not done for personal praise. Praise feeds our self-esteem and gives us a feeling of significance. If we minister because we want to earn the praise of others, we're headed for a fall because our worth and significance rest on the grace of God, not on what we've done in planting churches.

Character Qualities

Not only does Paul list the church planter's motives, but he lists certain character qualities in 1 Thessalonians 2:2–8. In verse 2 Paul says that church planting takes courage. Church planting isn't easy even though it's very exciting. There will be times when church planters may be attacked and even insulted, so it takes men and women of courage who are not afraid to take risks and step out in faith in obedience to the Savior. It is spiritually refreshing to read Hebrews 11, which contains various faith cameos of courageous people who trusted God in difficult times.

Another quality Paul puts forward in verse 2 is endurance. Paul wasn't quick to quit. With all the persecution and the criticism, there were times when he experienced devastating discouragement. It would have been so much easier to quit! Yet he was determined to hang tough, knowing that his circumstances would change in time and that he would benefit spiritually by enduring them.

In verse 3 Paul lists three character qualities of a person who has integrity: truthfulness (freedom from error), purity of motive, and honesty. Paul was a man of integrity and authenticity. His character was like that of Jesus Christ. He realized that if there was a problem in any of these areas that the entire cause of Christ would suffer. Just as in the first century, so today we must be men and women who speak and live what we know to be the truth out of a spirit of purity and honesty. Christian ministry in the 1980s and 1990s was adversely affected by those who professed the Savior publicly but lacked personal truthfulness, purity of motive, and honesty.

The last two character qualities are gentleness and affection. In verse 7 Paul compares himself to a caring mother. This is important because he was able to balance his high *D* temperament, which tends to be more task-oriented than people-oriented, with a sensitivity to people. In verse 8 he tells his people of his love for them. Though he was a strong leader who got things done, he was a caring, loving leader who wanted his people to know how dear they were to him. It's amazing what people will accomplish when they know you love them!

How do we develop godly character? With all the problems Christian leaders have experienced in terms of their character, if church planters are not serious about developing their character, it would be best for them not to consider professional Christian ministry. There are several sources that may serve to help us in the development of our character.

In his book *Too Busy Not to Pray,*[2] Bill Hybels tells of his spiritual struggles and how God has helped him grow and mature as a Christian leader. He discusses several aspects of his quiet time with the Lord (adoration, confession, thanksgiving, and supplication). Since we're all unique individuals, you may want to vary this with that which is particularly helpful to you. For example, I've placed commitment between thanksgiving and supplication. I've found in my worship of God that after realizing all that I have to be thankful for, I'm often moved to commit my life afresh to him in terms of serving him.

Another helpful source in developing character is Dallas Willard's *The Spirit of the Disciplines.*[3] In light of Paul's challenge in 1 Timothy 4:7, this book is helpful in showing leaders how to discipline themselves for godly character. Willard is particularly helpful in two specific areas: abstinence (solitude, silence, and sacrifice) and engagement (confession, celebration, study, and submission).

Willard has done us a real service in that he's restored the disciplines to their proper place in our spiritual formation. In general, evangelical Christianity has overreacted to early monasticism and its excesses with the result that it has tossed out the proverbial baby with the bathwater. We read in church history of believers who abused themselves in all kinds of ways, such as living on top of a pillar for as long as twenty or thirty years in an attempt to be closer to God. Who wouldn't walk away from this kind of excess! Yet, when we look closer, we discover that the monastic movement in general has much to offer us in terms of our spiritual development. Willard has done much to help us recover this critical aspect of the movement.

Direction

When a leader has a clear idea of his direction, not only will he know where he's going, but he will also be motivated to get there. Direction consists of mission and vision.

Ministry Mission

A ministry mission is a broad, brief biblical statement that drives the church. It's broad in that all the ministry should fit under it. When this isn't the case, then the particular ministry that doesn't fit is questionable—the church shouldn't be pursuing it. A mission statement is brief in that it must pass what Peter Drucker refers to as the T-shirt Test—it must be short enough to fit on a T-shirt. The point is if it's short, chances are good that people will remember it. It must be biblical because the church's mission is found in the Scriptures—make disciples (Matt. 28:19). Finally, the mission drives or directs the church. Everyone knows that the church is all about making disciples. That's where it's going and what it's doing. Ultimately, the church's mission (make disciples) is the leader's mission as well, and the planted church is the vehicle through which he pursues it.

Ministry Vision

A ministry vision is a clear and challenging picture of the future of the church as it can and must be. Once leaders have determined the mission of the church, they turn to its vision. The vision must be clear in that everyone can see it. Second, it must be challenging. If it doesn't challenge the church, it's not a vision. Third, it's a picture of the future of the ministry. It paints a picture of what the church will look like over the next two, five, ten, or twenty years as it realizes its mission to make disciples. The vision "can be" in the sense that the leader must believe it's possible. Finally, it "must be" in that the leader is passionate about it. What the leader is passionate about gets accomplished.

Influence

A third important characteristic of leadership is influence, which is affected by the leader's character and direction.

The Importance of Influence

Most definitions of leadership, both secular and Christian, include the concept of influence. An example from the Christian sector is the definition of Chuck Swindoll, who writes, "At the risk of oversimplifying, I'm going to resist a long, drawn-out definition and settle on one word. It's the word *influence*. If you will allow me two words—*inspiring influence*."[4] Then he explains further: "Those who do the best job of management—those most successful as leaders—use their influence to inspire others to follow, to work harder, to sacrifice, if necessary."[5] Swindoll accurately underscores the importance of influence in leadership.

Good leaders exert a powerful influence on people. They are like magnets; they attract people. When they turn and look behind them, they see people. Those who insist that they are leaders but have no one following them are not leaders at all.

The Key to Influence

The keys to influence are character and a significant vision (both personal and institutional). Godliness has a great attraction. Take, for example, the early ministry of the Savior. In John 1 the disciples appear to have been especially attracted to him. For example, in verses 35–37 John the Baptist introduces Jesus to Peter and another disciple with the result that they follow him. In verse 38 Jesus turns around and finds them standing there, probably in awe. Then in verse 43, he simply instructs Philip, "Follow me," and Philip responds without question.

People who are able to communicate a clear, significant vision for both themselves and their ministry will draw people. There's something attractive about leaders who know where they're going. They seem to have grasped a purpose in life that is intriguing and draws those who aren't sure about their own direction.

When godliness and vision are combined in the same person, that individual is able to exert a great influence over people. This is what Swindoll refers to as inspiring influence. Should this be combined with other qualities, such as natural leadership abilities or the ability to communicate with clarity, the result is powerful, inspiring leadership.

A Strong Leader

Not only must church planters be leaders, they must also be strong leaders. One of the reasons so many American churches are struggling today is because pastors are not exercising strong leadership.

The Problem of Co-Leadership

A primary leadership problem facing many pastors is the struggle they have with their lay boards concerning who will lead the church. In most cases, the boards have won the battle, and the church is led by a consensus of the board members. The result is that in a large number of churches the pastor is regarded as just one more leader in the church, or worse, as an employee of the board who follows orders that have "come down from on high." This is a constant complaint on the part of many pastors.[6] But how did this situation develop and what has been the result?

The Historical Development

There are at least three factors that have influenced strong lay leadership of church boards. The first is a reaction on the part of most Americans

102 The Personnel of Church Planting

to the various totalitarian regimes that have suppressed and brutalized people from World War II up to the present. Some obvious examples are Adolph Hitler in Nazi Germany, Idi Amin in Uganda, the Ayatollah Khomeini in Iran, and Saddam Hussein in Iraq. Seeing the excesses of these leaders and the financial and sexual indulgences of church leaders in our country, such as Jim Bakker and Jimmy Swaggert, has created a somewhat popular anti-authoritarian mood across America, especially toward pastors. Consequently, the idea of following a single, primary leader in the church frightens many.

A pastoral model that became popular in a number of seminaries in the late 1970s and early 1980s was the enabler model. Peter Wagner notes that this model gained adherents because it emphasized the servant role of pastors and their need to train laypeople for ministry.[7] This sounds very biblical. Yet there was another side to this model that proved disastrous. Lyle Schaller, impersonating a dissatisfied church layperson, writes, "We called a self-identified enabler type minister and we got burned. We found the word enabler was a synonym for not being an initiator, not calling, not being aggressive, and not taking leadership responsibilities."[8] The enabler model continues to be taught in seminaries today.

A third factor that has influenced strong lay leadership is the Church Renewal Movement of the 1960s and 1970s, which emphasized lay involvement in the leadership, ministries, and worship of the local church. Again, who can argue with this in light of such clear passages as 1 Corinthians 12 and Ephesians 4:11–12? However, there emerged from this the idea that laypeople were to lead the church. Consequently, many pastors turned their leadership authority over to various lay elder or deacon boards and assumed positions alongside of or under them.

The Result

Someone has said, "The proof of the pudding is in the tasting." This certainly has proved to be the case in terms of lay control of church boards. Essentially, lay control of the church's leadership at the board level has resulted in power blocks that stifle good pastoral leadership.

The argument of the Church Renewal Movement that lay board leadership is critical to church renewal has proved incorrect. The majority of these churches are in decline with poor lay participation in ministries, other than in their control of the elder or deacon boards.

This is the case because in most situations pastors are the best qualified to lead, not because they are necessarily more spiritual or more intelligent than the laypeople on their boards, but because they have two critical factors in their favor. In *The Unity Factor*, Larry Osborne identifies these as time and training.

Essentially, pastors immerse themselves in the church's ministry on a full-time basis. A typical week consumes anywhere from fifty to sixty hours or more. What difference does this make?

> As a full-time pastor, I'm immersed in the day-to-day ministry of the church. Unlike any of my board members, I'm thinking about our problems and opportunities full-time. I have the time to plan, pray, consult, and solve problems.
>
> To lead, a person needs to know the organization inside out—how the parts fit together and how each will be affected by proposed changes. And that takes time, lots of it. In all but the smallest churches, it can't be done on a spare-time basis. In a church with multiple staff, Lyle Schaller claims, it takes between fifty and sixty hours a week.
>
> Not that our board members are incapable of leading an organization. That's what a number do for a living. But they do it on a full-time basis. None would think of trying to do it in his or her spare time. Yet that is exactly what happens in a church where the board or a powerful lay leader tries to take on the primary leadership role.[9]

Not only do pastors spend much of their time in ministry, but many have been specifically trained for what they do. This may range anywhere from basic on-the-job experience to advanced studies in seminary. Osborne explains the advantages of this:

> I also have a decided advantage when it comes to training. Like most pastors, my formal education and ongoing studies have equipped me specifically to lead a church. Add to that a network of fellow pastors and church leaders, and I have a wealth of information from which to draw. When a church faces a tough situation or golden opportunity, the pastor is the one most likely to have been exposed to a similar situation. If not, he'll usually know where to find out what the experts recommend.
>
> By contrast, most board members are limited in their exposure to other ministries. They don't have the time to read the literature. And their network of experts is usually limited to a previous pastor or two. Because the church is spiritually centered, volunteer run, and educationally focused, it's different from any other organization, and as a rule, the pastor has more training in how to lead it than anyone else. Are there exceptions? Certainly, but that's the point: they're *exceptions*. A friend tried to model his church after one with an incredibly strong and competent group of lay elders. In his model church, the pastor simply prayed, taught, and counseled, while the elders took care of everything else. There was no need for strong pastoral leadership, he told me, if you picked the right people and discipled them

properly. But he failed to notice that the key elders in his model church were self-employed and independently wealthy. They had all the time in the world, and they attended seminars and seminary classes and read in their spare time.

His elders, on the other hand, all had jobs that called for fifty to sixty hours a week. They had neither the time nor the training to take a strong leadership role. As long as my friend waited for the elders to take charge, the church floundered.[10]

Arguments for Primary Pastoral Leadership

Passive pastors need to step out and take the lead in churches. This doesn't mean that others won't be involved in leadership. It means that the pastor becomes the leader of leaders, the point person on the ministry team. There are three strong arguments for this view.

The Theological Argument

Where two or more people relate together functionally for any period of time, such as in a ministry or even a family context, one person must take the position as the leader or head of the team. Scripture provides us with several examples, especially in 1 Corinthians 11:3. Paul writes that "the head of every man is Christ." The point is that in the leadership and ministry of the local church, Christ assumes the position of head.

A second example is the relationship between the man and the woman. Again, in 1 Corinthians 11:3, Paul writes "and the head of the woman is man." The debate over this passage concerns the identity of the man and the woman. Are they husband and wife, or are they representative of the male-female relationship in the church? The context indicates that this passage is concerned with the practices of the church in the worship services. Paul addresses the subordination of the wife to the husband in other places, such as Ephesians 5:22–24. It's generally accepted that this functional subordination concerns their relationship in all areas of life, including the church. Thus there would be no need to relate this to the church in particular. Consequently, Paul is teaching that in the local church context, where men are worshiping and ministering with women, the men are to take the lead.

A third example is the relationship of the Godhead. Paul writes in 1 Corinthians 11:3 that "the head of Christ is God." This passage is talking about the relationship among the various members of the Trinity. Scripture teaches that in terms of their essence, the Father, Son, and Holy Spirit are all one and equally divine. Therefore, this passage must be discussing the functional relationship of the Godhead. While all three are equal in essence, one is the head in terms of function. Robert Gromacki describes it this way: "Thus, even though there was an equality of persons within the divine oneness, there was an order (a headship) to execute the divine counsel."[11] And in this functional relationship, one Person, the Father, was the head.

This should be most instructive theologically for the functioning of pastor–lay board relationships. If the most perfect relationship that exists (the Godhead) functions with a single head (the Father), what about our less than perfect lay elder and deacon boards in the church? Who should the leader be? In light of Osborne's two points concerning time and training, the obvious answer is the pastor.

The Biblical Argument

The Bible presents a number of examples where individuals exercised primary leadership in ministry contexts. The classic example is the ministry relationship of Christ and his disciples. There's little question that he was the primary leader of this band of men.

Another example is Peter. F. F. Bruce notes that in the lists of the apostles in the Gospels, Peter is always mentioned first.[12] Peter's name appears in the book of Acts no less than fifty-seven times in chapters 1–5, 8–12, and 15, while the other apostles are mentioned only twenty-five times. He's the chief spokesman and preacher in the book of Acts (1:15–22; 2:14–36; 3:12–26; 4:8–12; 10:34–43; 11:4–17; 15:7–11). Finally, Peter is singled out and placed in juxtaposition to the other apostles in such places as Acts 2:37 and 5:29. Thus it would appear that among the apostles Peter was the leader of leaders.

A third example is James and his position in the Jerusalem church. In Acts 12:17, it's interesting to note that Peter instructs a small group that had been praying for his freedom to go and tell "James and the brothers" about his miraculous deliverance. Why does Peter specifically name James and not the others? In Acts 15 the Jerusalem church had gathered with the elders and apostles to determine the relationship of the law to the gospel, and James is the one who issues a summary directive. Finally, in Acts 21:18 James is mentioned first and in juxtaposition to the elders of the church. It would seem evident from all this that he was the primary leader in the church. In fact F. F. Bruce refers to the elders as "a sort of Sanhedrin, with James as their president."[13]

If it's God's will that local churches be led by a group of men (co-leadership) without a single leader or leader of leaders, then how do we explain these biblical examples? They would certainly be setting a poor example if there's to be no leader of leaders. One could argue that the example of Christ and the disciples is an exception because he's God, but how do we explain Peter's obvious position of prominence? Again, one might want to argue that he was an exception because he was an apostle. But it is more difficult to explain James's position in the Jerusalem church; he wasn't an apostle but was the Lord's half brother.

The Practical Argument

All people aren't created equal in terms of their leadership abilities, knowledge, experience, reputation, training, and commitment. Some have the spiritual gift of leadership (Rom. 12:8), while others don't. Some are gifted naturally with leadership skills and abilities and others aren't.

To put a group of people together on a board and not recognize and give primary leadership to the one with the greater leadership gifts, abilities, and training doesn't make sense. This, in essence, is what true co-leadership attempts to do! Consequently, true co-leadership most often results in no leadership. The fact of the matter is that a group can't lead a church.

Of course, this assumes that the full-time pastor is fully qualified as a leader. This breaks down when a church selects a pastor who is not a leader. Some churches are looking primarily for a pastor who is primarily a teacher or a pastoral caregiver to lead them. When this happens, there may very well be laypeople on the board who are better at leading than the pastor. It makes better sense to look for a leader who has the other qualities and gifts as well, especially if this person is going to lead the church.

Arguments for Strong Pastoral Leadership

It's a basic fact of life that in every organization there have to be leaders who have the power and the necessary authority to exercise that power. Without these strong leaders, no organization can function properly. This is true in the church as well as the marketplace. However, the issue for the church concerns who has this power and authority to lead.

Scripture teaches that this power and the authority to exercise it rest in the elders of the church. Of course, Christ is the ultimate head of his church. Just as the Father is the head of the Trinity (1 Cor. 11:3), so the Son is the head of the church (Eph. 5:23). He has all power and the authority to exercise that headship.

Yet it would appear from the Scriptures that Christ has passed some power and authority on through the apostles to the elders of the church. Thus, while the apostles are no longer on the scene, the elders remain and are the leaders in the churches. Apparently, each church had several elders (Acts 11:30; 16:4; 20:17; 21:18). Passages such as 1 Thessalonians 5:12,

1 Timothy 5:17, and Hebrews 13:7, 17 indicate that these people had the power and authority to lead and direct the affairs of each local church.

The issue at hand concerns whether these elders were part-time laypeople, as found in many evangelical churches today, or full-time professionals. There are three biblical arguments that indicate the latter.

The Size of the New Testament Churches

Many if not all of the churches in the book of Acts were large churches requiring the leadership of a substantial number of full-time elders. There are several passages that indicate that the churches in Acts, unlike the majority of churches in America today,[14] were large (see 2:41, 47; 4:4; 5:14; 6:1, 7; 9:31, 35, 42; 11:21, 24, 26; 14:1, 21; 16:5; 17:4, 12; 18:8, 10; 19:26).

The Jerusalem church. The first example is the church at Jerusalem. It began with 120 people (Acts 1:13) but, as the result of Peter's two sermons, gained 3,000 people (Acts 2:41), and then an additional 5,000 men, not including women and children (Acts 4:4).[15] This growth continued, for Luke writes in Acts 5:14, "Nevertheless, more and more men and women believed in the Lord and were added to their number." Then in Acts 6:1 he writes, "In those days when the number of disciples was increasing . . ." And again in Acts 6:7: "The number of disciples in Jerusalem increased rapidly, and a large number of priests became obedient to the faith." Luke's use of numbers in describing the Jerusalem church is important hermeneutically because it helps us gain an understanding of what he means in terms of size later in Acts when he uses such qualifiers as "many" or "great" instead of exact numbers.

The church in Judea, Galilee, and Samaria. In Acts 9 Luke directs the reader's attention to the church in Judea, Galilee, and Samaria. Like the Jerusalem church, "it grew in numbers" (Acts 9:31). In verse 35 he comments on Lydda and Sharon: "All those who lived in Lydda and Sharon saw him and turned to the Lord." In verse 42 Luke notes: "This became known all over Joppa, and many people believed in the Lord."

The Antioch church. Luke gives evidence in Acts 11 that the church at Antioch was very large. In verse 21 he writes, "A great number of people believed and turned to the Lord." In verse 24 he adds, "A great number of people were brought to the Lord." Finally, in verse 26 he says that they "taught great numbers of people."

The churches of the first missionary journey. Paul's three missionary, church planting journeys also resulted in large planted churches. For example, during the first journey in Iconium, "a great number of Jews and Gentiles believed" (14:1). At Derbe they "won a large number of disciples" (v. 21). Then, in a final summary comment at the end of the first journey, Luke writes, "So the churches were strengthened in the faith and grew daily in numbers" (16:5).

The churches of the second missionary journey. The results of the second church planting journey were much the same. The Corinthian church consisted of "a large number of God-fearing Greeks and not a few prominent women" (17:4). In reference to the church at Berea, Luke writes in verse 12: "Many of the Jews believed, as did also a number of prominent Greek women and many Greek men." He returns to the Corinthian church in Acts 18:8 and writes, "Many of the Corinthians who heard him believed and were baptized." In verse 10 he concludes by quoting Jesus' words: "I have many people in this city."

The churches of the third missionary journey. The third church planting journey also resulted in the starting of a number of large churches. For example, in Acts 19:26 an enemy of the faith, Demetrius, says, "And you see and hear how this fellow Paul has convinced and led astray large numbers of people here in Ephesus and in practically the whole province of Asia."

The evidence indicates that many if not most of the New Testament churches were large. A very conservative estimate of the size of the Jerusalem church, using only Acts 2:41 and 4:4 and not counting the women and children, is eight thousand people. In his commentary on Acts, Lenski remarks, "It has been conservatively estimated that at this time the total number of disciples was between twenty and twenty-five thousand."[16]

The sheer size of these first-century megachurches would necessitate a significant number of full-time elders. If the early churches were led by part-time elders, how many would it have required to shepherd these large churches? Consider for a moment the Jerusalem church. If it had only eight thousand people, and a part-time lay elder could adequately shepherd five families, then this church would have had as many as sixteen hundred elders! It would not seem likely that these elders were part-time laypeople, as so many assume who advocate lay co-leadership today.

What we must understand is that the apostolic church functioned at two levels. One was the large city-church meeting addressed above. When Paul wrote to the churches at Rome, Corinth, and so on, he was writing to the city-church. The other level was the house-church meeting that gathered more frequently. That is where much of the ministry took place. Scripture refers to these in Acts 2:46; 12:12–17; Rom. 16:3–5, 14–15; 1 Cor. 16:19; and so on. (Paul's letters to the city-churches were likely circulated among the house-churches—Col. 4:16.) My point is that today's local congregation is a slightly larger version of a first century house-church that was pastored by a first-century elder. The city-churches had several elders, each of whom pastored house-churches.

The Ministry of the Elders

A second argument that the elders in the early church were full-time is based on their ministry in the church. Essentially, the elders were expected to oversee and minister by shepherding the flock. For example, in Acts 20:28 Paul instructs, "Keep watch over yourselves and all the flock of which the Holy Spirit has made you overseers. Be shepherds of the church of God, which he bought with his own blood." In 1 Peter 5:2 Peter writes, "Be shepherds of God's flock that is under your care." In light of what real shepherds did with a flock of sheep on a Palestinian hillside, this would probably involve leading, caring for, guiding, instructing, and protecting people in the church.

This ministry in itself would require a large amount of the elders' time. Good shepherding necessitates both a reasonable amount of preparation time (as in a teaching ministry) as well as actual ministry time.

Does the part-time person have adequate time to devote to a shepherding ministry? The majority of those who are elders are married and have children. They also work a lot of hours. For instance, a survey in *Leadership* revealed that "77% of all middle-level executives spend 50 or more hours per week on their jobs." And "26% of executives spend more than 60 hours per week."[17] It seems doubtful that an elder with a family and full-time employment would have enough time available to shepherd a flock. Indeed, in addition to employment, the responsibility of ministering to and rearing a family is a full-time job.

Another consideration is whether it's fair to expect a layperson to set aside the time necessary to shepherd a flock. If the person is single or married without children, it might be possible. But it would not be possible for a married person who has children. Such demands on a person's time seem unfair and could result in feelings of strong guilt and inadequacy when the person isn't able to deliver. In fact in many churches with lay elder boards, very little if any shepherding takes place. This is because in most cases, it's not possible for the elders to deliver. Instead, most meet approximately once a month and make important decisions regarding matters they know little about. In effect, most elder boards function in a decision-making rather than a shepherding capacity.

The Remuneration of the Elders

A third argument that the elders in the early churches were full-time is the fact that many, if not all, were remunerated. There's no specific mention as to whether the elders in the earlier churches in the book of Acts were remunerated, but they were probably among those who were helped through a mutual sharing of goods (Acts 2:44–45; 4:32, 34–35).

The strong evidence is found in the later churches according to 1 Timothy 5:17–18 and 1 Peter 5:2. In 1 Timothy 5:17–18, Paul tells Timothy, "The elders who direct the affairs of the church well are worthy of double honor, especially those whose work is preaching and teaching. For the Scripture says, 'Do not muzzle the ox while it is treading out the grain,' and 'The worker deserves his wages.'" It's obvious from verse 18 that "honor" is a reference to some kind of remuneration such as wages.

In 1 Peter 5:2 Peter addresses the motives of those who would be elders. In particular, he warns elders against shepherding the flock out of greediness for money. This would obviously imply that elders were remunerated for their ministry.

The Conclusion

The conclusion of all this is that the elders who were given power and the authority to exercise that power in the local churches were not part-time but full-time workers. Consequently, the present system of lay co-leadership that is practiced in so many churches across the land isn't based on Scripture as so many have been led to think.

This doesn't mean that part-time laypeople aren't involved in leadership and ministry in the local church. Actually, their involvement is necessary to the health and stability of the entire church according to 1 Corinthians 12 and other passages. Their leadership, however, should be in terms of directing and ministering in small groups, evangelism teams, and target group ministries, according to their time schedules.

Application

But how does all this apply to churches today? It seems evident that professional staff pastors, who are equivalent to the first-century elders, should lead new or established churches. These leaders are given the power and authority to lead and direct the ministries of the churches. They have the time and the training to do the job most effectively, as opposed to a group of part-time lay co-leaders. When they are given the proper power and authority, professionals are able to exert the strong pastoral leadership that is needed in so many of our floundering churches early in the twenty-first century. This is also critical to planting churches, especially in the early stages when strong leadership is key to the growth and survival of the new church.

Accountability

One important issue that must naturally be raised is that of accountability. It's imperative that churches do a better job of selecting pastors in the first place. Paul in 1 Timothy 5:22 warns believers about selecting these individuals too quickly.

Often when a pastor leaves a church, the congregation is not in any real hurry to find a new pastor, so they move too slowly. Finally, when they realize that the church is starting to lose a lot of people, they take the first person who comes along. When a pastor leaves, the church should begin to search for a new pastor immediately. The search process should focus on character (1 Tim. 3:1–7; Titus 1:5–9) and servanthood (Mark 10:42–45). References should be contacted and asked to respond to the following: "Tell me three positive character traits and two negative character traits about this person." This gives the references permission to tell the whole story. The problem is that far too many churches don't properly check out a potential candidate's character before they call the individual.

Primary leaders should be accountable not only to some lay board of co-leaders but to the entire church. The biblical teaching on accountability is that all of us are to be involved (Matt. 5:23–24; 18:15–20; Gal. 6:1). Thus the entire church is responsible to hold the pastor as well as one another accountable for character and conduct. This is to be done according to the guidelines found in 1 Timothy 5:19–20.

Those who are on the professional leadership team are especially responsible to hold one another accountable. A good example of this is Peter and Paul in Galatians 2:11–14. Wise leaders make themselves accountable to a group or to single individuals.

A Strong Servant-Leader

Not only must church planters be strong leaders, but it's also imperative that they be strong servant-leaders. In understanding this, it's helpful to view the different approaches to leadership in terms of a continuum.

At one end of the leadership continuum is absolute leadership. This is typical of professional despots or tyrants. These are people who rule with an iron fist and are accountable to no one. They're so authoritarian that whatever they want gets done and nothing takes place in their churches without their approval. In Mark 10:42 Christ called the disciples together and said, "You know that those who are regarded as rulers of the Gentiles lord it over them, and their high officials exercise authority over them." This is the Savior's evaluation of absolute leadership. He describes it as a characteristic of pagan not Christian leaders.

Most Christians have a strong dislike for this kind of authoritarian leader. This is the very picture that comes to mind whenever they hear or think of strong leadership. Consequently, they react most negatively: "We're Americans and we're free; nobody's going to tell us what to do!"

At the other end of the continuum from absolute leadership is co-leadership. Co-leadership is characteristic of church boards that are controlled and run by part-time laypeople. Leadership is by compromise. The full-time professionals are primarily involved in ministry not leadership. This is the form that seems prevalent in many of our churches today. In essence, it's an overreaction to absolute leadership. Having rejected the one extreme, many have simply moved to the other extreme. Co-leadership isn't characteristic of biblical leadership and most commonly results in no leadership.

Peter Wagner makes several important observations about the issue of co-leadership. The first is that "the plurality-of-elders structure is good for small churches and nongrowing churches. But as a church gains growth momentum and becomes larger, the system becomes more dysfunctional."[18] Co-leadership is probably the reason why these churches are small and aren't growing.

The second observation concerns who is actually leading in the larger plurality-of-elder churches. Wagner notes: "in almost all of the plurality-of-elder churches which are growing, a top leader has emerged even though one was not supposed to. Some of the strongest leaders I know say 'I don't lead' and go ahead and do it."[19] Those churches that grow do so not because of lay leadership but because of the leadership of the pastor.

Gene Getz acknowledged this. For example, in an interview in *Leadership*, he was asked, "How has your leadership style changed since your early days in the first Fellowship Bible Church?" He responded with the following:

> I think I've gained more self-awareness—more self-honesty, if I may coin the word. If you had asked me ten years ago, "What makes this church

work?" I would have said, "Humanly speaking, it's our multiple leadership, primarily the elders."

Today I'd answer that question by saying, "Our elders are key, but I'm the key to helping the elders function."

In the early days I overreacted to authoritarian leadership styles—which I still think are unfortunate—but I've always led. Now I feel I'm more honest with myself and others about the importance of a strong leader, particularly in a growing church, and yet developing a strong multiple leadership that *does* lead as a team.[20]

In the middle of the leadership continuum is the biblical form of servant-leadership. In Mark 10:45, the Savior says, "For even the Son of Man did not come to be served, but to serve, and to give his life as a ransom for many." But what does this mean?

The greatest example of a servant-leader is the Savior. He proved to be both a strong leader and a servant-leader. No one would question the fact that he was in charge. His entire ministry was characterized by a personal, spiritual strength.

Yet the Savior also displayed a servant's heart. This is clear from such passages as Mark 10:45 and Matthew 20:28 and is illustrated in John 13, when he assumes the posture of a servant and washes the disciples' feet. Not only did he lead the disciples strongly, but he loved them passionately and ultimately gave his life for them.

Strong servant-leaders are the kind of people who lead with sustained excellence. We desperately need these leaders to take the church of Jesus Christ into the twenty-first century. Just as important, we need strong servant-leaders to plant Great Commission churches that will win for Christ the unchurched lost people of the twenty-first century. (I cover biblical servant leadership more in-depth in my book *Being Leaders*.)

Conclusion

What does all of this have to do with leading planted churches? It's my recommendation that pastors who start churches should not have co-leadership or a governing board (whether elders, deacons, or trustees) early in the process. In 1 Timothy 5:22 Paul warns Timothy, "Do not be hasty in the laying on of hands, and do not share in the sins of others." The context is addressing the local church's elders. Far too many church planting pastors can tell the story of how they established a governing board too soon, only to have that board attempt to take over the leadership of the church and tell him how to lead.

Instead, I advise pastors to delay the establishment of a governing board. If they insist on some oversight other than that of a sponsoring church or a denomination, they should consider instituting an advisory board primarily to provide wisdom and accountability, but without the power to take over the leadership of the church. The time to establish a governing board is later in the process, most likely in the maturity stages (see my discussion of governing boards in chapter 12), when the pastor has had sufficient time to determine who agrees with the church's core identity (core values, mission, vision, and strategy) as well as who meets the rigorous character requirements of board leadership (1 Tim. 3:1–7).

Now turn to the Church Planter's Workbook and complete the Leadership Worksheet.

Part 3

The Process
of Church Planting

The novice farmer must not give in to the temptation simply to walk out into a field and broadcast seed in all directions. While that seems the most natural thing to do, it would spell disaster. There are several steps that must take place prior to the planting of the crop. First, the true farmer will prepare the soil. The rule is that you don't drop seed into soil that's not been well prepared ahead of time. Second, good farmers know that they're farmers. While farming is strenuous, often exacting work, most love the land and what they do with it and find that they're naturally attracted to the work. They may complain a lot about their conditions, but they would have it no other way. Third, astute farmers know what crops they want to plant. They are well aware of what they can plant, and when and where they can plant it.

Once all these decisions have been made and the soil prepared, it's time to begin the actual planting process. The seed is sown. As it begins to sprout and grow, it will be watered, fertilized, and protected from various insects. Eventually, it will be harvested, packed in some way, and taken to market where it will benefit many.

The actual planting of a church also involves a process. Once church planters have thought through certain key issues (part 1 of this book), know that they are, indeed, designed to be church planters who are strong leaders (part 2), the remaining task is to begin the process of church planting (part 3). Whereas, these other parts have focused on the why and who of church planting, this part concerns the how of church planting. It involves six stages, which are analogous to the human birth process: conception, development (prenatal stage), birth, growth, maturity, and reproduction. Part 3 will cover all of these stages but will focus primarily on the first three, because these early stages have proved to be where church planters need the most help. I suggest that as you work through this material, you develop a church planting prospectus. I have placed a sample of what this could look like on my website (www.malphursgroup.com/ChurchPlanting).

7

We Want to Have a Baby

The Conception Stage, Part 1

An essential question in church planting is where do you begin? The answer: at the same place where a couple planning a family begins—at conception.[1] The conception stage starts with the genesis of the idea of birthing a church. Just as a baby is conceived in its mother's womb, so the idea of starting a church is conceived in a person's mind. For a seminarian, such as Bill Smith, this should take place during seminary. Actually, it's possible that much of the conception stage could take place while a person is still in school or prior to the formation of a core group!

Regardless of one's circumstances, once the idea is conceived, what happens next? What steps should Bill and Betty or anyone else for that matter follow? What events need to take place?

The conception stage of church planting is where you begin to apply the information gained in the first two parts of this book, the appendices, and material on my website. It consists of seven steps: discovering the church's core values, developing a mission statement, conducting an environmental scan, developing a vision, developing a strategy, implementing that strategy, and evaluation.[2] In part one of the conception stage, we'll work through values, mission, the environmental scan, and vision. In part two—chapter 8—we'll work with strategy, implementation, and evaluation.

At least four of these steps involve a church's DNA. You may recall from a science course you've taken that your DNA is the genetic blueprint that guides the life and growth of all living organisms. Every church has its own fundamental DNA (its values, mission, vision, strategy, and so on) that guides its life and growth. This material will get at the very core identity of the new church that will affect whether it grows and what kind of spiritual life it will have. When something goes either right or wrong with a church, it can be traced back in some way to the ministry's DNA.

Before we look at the first step, we need to consider the place of prayer in starting a church. Actually the first step is prayer. Before we attempt to plant a church anywhere, it's imperative that we spend hours on our knees in prayer. In fact it would be wise for church planters to recruit personal intercessors to make up an intercessory prayer team who will pray for them, their teams, and the entire planting endeavor on a constant basis.[3] Church planters, however, should not regard intercessory prayer as the first step because that might influence them to emphasize it only at the beginning of the process. Instead, it must be encouraged *throughout* the process. We can't place enough emphasis on prayer! It is best to view the church as an infant who is constantly dependent on and surrounded by the air of prayer. Just as a person needs a constant supply of oxygen throughout life to survive, so the new church will need a constant supply of prayer throughout its life if it is to survive.

Discovering Values

The process of church planting and the conception stage begin with the discovery of the church's core organizational values, which essentially are the church planter's core values. It's natural for his values to become the church's core values, which make up a vital part of its core identity. Its values are a critical aspect of its ministry DNA.

We begin here because the ministry's values answer the basic, fundamental question, Why do we do what we do? If you want to understand why a church does or doesn't pursue certain biblical functions, discover and analyze its values. The Jerusalem church demonstrates that core values are a vital part of the essence of what makes a biblically based, spiritually healthy church (Acts 2:42–47). Ultimately these values will affect the accomplishment or outcome of all the other steps that make up the conception stage of church planting.[4]

The Importance of Core Values

Why is the discovery of the organization's core values so important? *First, values determine a church's ministry distinctives.* No two ministries are alike. All are different in some way. Some churches focus on teaching, while others focus on evangelism. The determining factor in any case is largely the values.

Second, values dictate people's personal involvement in the church. Thus church planters can spare themselves and their churches much grief by communicating their values to all who consider becoming a part of the church (staff and congregants) before they come on board. Encourage those with similar values to join the team and those with different values to look for another church more in tune with their values.

Third, core values communicate what's important. They signal your ministry's bottom line. They make it clear to all what you stand for—what you believe is God's heart for your church.

Fourth, the church's values help you embrace positive change. Change has become a constant all across North America, and change has had a great impact on churches, some of it for good and some for bad. The key question to ask is, does this change agree with or contradict the ministry's core values?

Fifth, the values affect the church's overall behavior. They shape the entire organization. They dictate every decision that you make and determine every dollar you spend. Values are foundational to your behavior, the bottom line for what you will and won't do.

Sixth, your values inspire people to action. The shared beliefs of both the leaders and the followers are the invisible motivators that energize people to take action.

Seventh, core beliefs enhance credible leadership. All leaders are values-driven, and the ministries they build reflect those values. Leaders with good values build ministries of high integrity.

Eighth, your values shape the ministry's character. They are the qualities that make up and establish an organization's character, and that character determines how the organization conducts its ministry.

Ninth, values contribute to ministry success. The organization's ingrained understanding of its core beliefs, more than its technical skills, allows its people to be successful in ministry.

Tenth, core values have everything to do with the church's culture. It's imperative to understand that church starters are creating congregational culture.

The Definition of Core Values

I define a planted church's primary values as its constant, passionate, biblical core beliefs that drive its ministry. This definition has five key elements.

First, values are constant. Values tend to be change-resistant. Once the church sets its beliefs, they won't change appreciably. This is why change is so difficult for churches. Thus a planted church must be careful to launch with the proper values in place.

Second, core values are passionate. Just as vision is a seeing word, so passion is a feeling word. A church's passion is what it cares deeply and feels strongly about. It touches people's emotions and catalyzes them to action. Therefore, it is passion that distinguishes a ministry's core values from its other values.

Third, values are biblical. The core values found in a Christian organization, such as a planted church, should be biblical. The true test of a credo or values statement is asking, Is it biblical? That doesn't mean that it has to be found in the Bible. It does mean, however, that it shouldn't contradict the Bible.

Fourth, values are core beliefs. People use various synonyms for values: *precepts, principles, tenets, standards,* or *assumptions.* A ministry's values address its beliefs because it is those beliefs that lie at the heart of a value. A study of core values concerns not just any beliefs but your primary or central beliefs. A belief is a conviction or opinion you hold to be true based on limited evidence or proof. It isn't a fact so much as it's a conviction that a number of people hold to be true.

Fifth, core values drive the ministry. Finally, it is your core values or core beliefs, not just any beliefs, that drive or direct your ministry. Your core values are those that move your people to act, because values translate into behavior. They are the deeply ingrained drivers behind all of the church's behavior.

This needs further clarification. Most healthy churches are on a journey toward a destination that is their mission-vision. The church's mission sets or determines the church's destination, and the vision provides a picture of what the destination will look like. The church's values *should* drive the church toward its desired destination (mission-vision). I say *should* because the church's values will drive it toward *some* destination, but it may not be the desired destination. If it's not the desired destination, then there is a values-alignment problem (the values aren't in line with the church's desired mission-vision). For example, if the church's mission is the Great Commission, but the church doesn't value evangelism, it is not likely to accomplish the Great Commission. The values will drive it toward some mission, but it will be another destination with little evangelism taking place. The solution to such a problem is to change values, or in this case to add evangelism as a value.

The Kinds of Values

We can further refine the above definition of core values by analyzing the different kinds of values that your planted church may hold. There are five.

Conscious versus unconscious values. The credo or values of your church exist at both a conscious and unconscious level. Most are probably the latter. Leaders must discover and articulate the church's primary values so that all may know why they're doing what they're doing whether good or bad.

Shared versus unshared values. I am convinced that the degree to which you will experience success or failure in your church planting endeavors depends on whether your core people and ministry team share the same values. Shared values foster high levels of loyalty and commitment, lead to consensus on key decisions, promote a strong work ethic, and reduce levels of stress, along with other benefits to the ministry.

Personal ministry versus organizational ministry values. Each church planter has a set of personal organizational values that guide his ministry. One of the assignments for my pastoral students at Dallas Seminary is to discover their organizational ministry values before they go into a ministry. Those who take an established church need to discover the church's credo and make sure that its values align with their own. Otherwise, the honeymoon for both will be short-lived, and one or the other will likely sue for divorce. Church planters, however, bring their personal ministry values to the planted church. Their values will become the church's values. That's one of the many advantages of church planting. You as a church planter will need to identify your core values set.

Actual versus aspirational values. Leaders and their churches have both actual and aspirational values. Actual values are the beliefs they own and act on regularly. Aspirational values are those the church planter or church doesn't presently own but desires to own. It's important that the leader distinguish between the two or risk losing credibility when drafting a values statement. For example, to state that the church values evangelism when no one has come to the faith through its ministry hurts the leader's integrity and results in confusion and misdirection.

Strong versus weak values. Strong values are those beliefs that the church or culture holds broadly across the congregation and deeply within the people. Weak values are neither. A characteristic of spiritually healthy churches is strong values—those in Acts 2:42–47 in particular.

The Discovery of Your Values

Since a church planter's values most often become his church's ministry values, you can discover and establish your church's values by discovering your own. Several techniques will aid you in your values discovery.

1. Now that you have a definition of a value, take a sheet of paper and brainstorm, writing down what you believe are your key ministry beliefs.
2. Collect and study various churches' values statements or credos. Those that catch your eye or seem to jump off the page at you are probably your values (that's the passion element having its effect on you). I have provided one church's credo at the end of this section to get you started and give you an idea of what a statement might look like.
3. Take the Core Values Audit in appendix F. Take great care in answering number 26: What will be truly unique about this church that will attract people and likely differentiate it from other churches in the community?

Once you've unearthed your core values, how can you know if they're spiritually vital values? One answer is to compare them to the values of a church that is spiritually healthy as well as biblically based. An example of such a ministry is the Jerusalem church, described in the book of Acts. While Luke gives us a number of snapshots of the church's values, an obvious listing is found in Acts 2:41–47. They are Scripture (Bible doctrine), fellowship, prayer (some would include prayer under worship), worship, and evangelism. Should an audit of your values reveal that you fall short in one of these, you might set it as an aspirational value that you regularly work at embracing in the future.

The Development and Communication of Your Core Values

Once you've discovered your values, it's time to develop them into a credo or statement. You should publish this credo and make it available to those who are or desire to be a part of your ministry, because it is a leadership statement that clarifies the ministry and direction of the church. Below is the credo of a healthy community church. Note that the church distinguished its actual from its aspirational values by placing an asterisk after the latter.

The creation of a values credo is only one way to communicate your core beliefs. Others include your life, your sermons, the stories you tell, the heroes you make, a brochure, and a newcomers' or a membership class. It is important to communicate your values so that your people will catch and incarnate them.

Sample Core Values Statement

The following presents eight sample core values of a healthy community church. We desire that they define and drive this ministry in the context of a warm and caring environment.

Scripture

We value the Bible as God's authoritative and accurate word for salvation and service (2 Tim. 3:16). Therefore, we will strive to teach God's Word with integrity and authority so that seekers find Christ and believers mature in him.

Authentic Worship

We value worship that is authentic and acceptable to God (Rom. 12:1–2). Therefore, we desire to acknowledge God's supreme value and worth in our personal lives and in the corporate, contemporary worship of our church.

Sense of Community

We value biblical community where people have opportunity to minister to and love one another (Acts 2:44–46). Therefore, we ask all our people to commit to and fully participate in small groups where they may exercise their gifts and experience community.

Grace Orientation

We value a grace orientation to life as opposed to a legal orientation (Rom. 6:14). Therefore, we encourage our people to serve Christ from hearts of love and gratitude rather than guilt and condemnation.

Cultural Relevance

We value ministry that effectively communicates biblical truth in ways that people understand it (1 Chron. 12:32). Therefore, we will constantly evaluate our forms and methods, seeking cultural relevance and maximum ministry effectiveness for Christ.

Lost People

We value lost people because God does (Luke 19:10). Therefore, we will use every available Christ-honoring means to pursue, win, and disciple unchurched, lost people.*

Mobilized Congregation
We value total congregational involvement in ministry (Eph. 4:11–13).
Therefore, we seek to equip all our uniquely designed and gifted people to
effectively accomplish the work of our ministry.*

Ministry Excellence
We value giving our best in service to God because he gave his best—the
Savior (Col. 3:23–24). Therefore, we will seek to honor him by maintaining
a high standard of excellence in all our ministries and activities.*

*Aspirational Values

Developing a Mission

Once the church planter or the church planting team has discovered
and clearly articulated the planted church's core values, the next step in
the conception stage is to develop a mission statement.[5]

The Importance of the Mission

The church must have a mission for several reasons.
First, the mission dictates the ministry's direction. It provides a compelling sense of direction and serves to focus the church's energy. Most
important, it answers the directional question, Where are we going?
Second, the mission focuses on the church's function. Here it serves
to answer the functional question, What are we supposed to be doing?
Imagine what the ministry could accomplish if everyone knew what you
were trying to do.
Third, it spells out the congregation's preferred future. Someone has
observed that the best way to predict the future is to create it. That's the
function of the mission statement.
Fourth, the mission provides a template for decision making. It is a
pattern or guide that defines what the church will and won't do.
Fifth, the mission inspires church unity. It gets everyone on the same
page; it serves as a point around which the people can rally for the cause.
Sixth, it shapes the church's strategy. The mission determines the strategy that will be used to accomplish ministry. A strategy makes no sense
without a mission.
Seventh, a good mission enhances ministry effectiveness. Someone once
said that all good performance starts with a clear direction.
Finally, the mission facilitates evaluation. The mission is the criterion
or standard by which one evaluates a ministry. If the church's mission is

to make disciples, then it can evaluate how it's doing by whether or not it's making disciples.

What Is the Mission?

You'll never accomplish ministry that matters until you define what matters. And what matters is the mission. The church's mission is a broad, brief, biblical statement of what it's supposed to be doing. It has five vital components.

Breadth. Unlike a church's vision, the mission is broad. It needs to be all-encompassing, overarching, and comprehensive. It includes all that the church is attempting to accomplish for the Savior.

Brevity. As I said earlier, Peter Drucker recommends that a mission be short enough to fit on a T-shirt, because more people will remember the statement if it's short. Thus your mission must pass the T-shirt test.

It's biblical. That is, it must agree with the Scriptures. For example, God's mission for Moses is found in Exodus 3:10: "So now, go. I am sending you to Pharaoh to bring my people the Israelites out of Egypt." Christ's mission for the church is the Great Commission (Matt. 28:19–20).

It's a statement. It's imperative that the church planter write out the church's mission in the form of a mission statement. If he can't write it on paper, chances are good that he doesn't have a mission; that is, he is directionless.

It's a statement of what the church is supposed to be doing. In a business sense, a mission articulates what business we're in. That raises another question: What are you supposed to be doing? The answer is the Great Commission.

Having said that your mission is the Great Commission isn't enough, however. (The Great Commission is found in Matthew. 28:19–20; Mark 16:15; Luke 24:46–48; and Acts 1:8). People may not understand what that means. If I were to state it so that it fit on a T-shirt, I would say that Christ's mission for the church is to proactively make and mature believers at home and abroad.

Developing a Mission Statement

The following is a four-step process for developing a written mission statement that's tailor-made for your planted church. Remember that your mission will not have the authority of a leadership statement until it's clear enough to be committed to paper. Work your way through each step by answering the questions.

Step 1:   What are you supposed to be doing according to the Bible? If
          you're a church, Christ has already predetermined your mis-
          sion (the Great Commission). It must be at the core of your
          mission statement.

Step 2:   Can you articulate your mission in a written statement? Here
          are some mini-questions:
             What specific words best communicate with your
          people? (This will help you personalize it for your unique
          congregation.)
             Do your people understand what you've written? For
          example, if you use the terms *disciple, glorify God,* or
          holiness, will they know precisely what you mean or
          will you need to clarify? For example, Willow Creek
          Community Church in Barrington, Illinois, clarified what
          they meant by the term *disciples* with the words "fully
          devoted followers of Christ."
             Does your format convey well your mission? Here are
          several mission formats that will help you shape your
          statement. Which works best for you? Simply fill in the blanks.

          The mission of (ministry's name) is to _____.
          Our mission is to _____.
          (Ministry's name) seeks to _____.

Step 3:   Is your mission statement broad but clear? Is the statement
          broad and all-encompassing? Is the statement clear and
          understandable?

Step 4:   Is the mission brief and simple? You say more by saying less.
          Here are the mini-questions:
             Does your mission pass the T-shirt test (brevity)?
             Have you expressed it in one clear sentence? Is it memorable?

I once pastored Northwood Community Church in Dallas. The following was Northwood's mission statement:

The mission of Northwood Community Church is to develop people into
fully functioning followers of Christ.

This statement calls for several observations. First, since we were a church, our mission was the Great Commission; however, rather than simply quoting one of the Bible passages, we personalized it to fit who we were.

Second, we hoped to reach people—lost and saved—in the Dallas metroplex. We left the term *Dallas* out in favor of brevity.

Third, we served people by developing them into fully functioning followers of Christ. The latter was our definition of a disciple. Disciples at Northwood were characterized by the three Cs: conversion, commitment, and contribution.

Fourth, we placed this statement on the bulletin cover underneath the logo. I commented on it often from the pulpit, and we covered it every time we held a newcomer's class. We also placed it on church business cards and distributed them to our congregation so that our people would know it well.

Finally, it obviously passed the T-shirt test, and most of our people memorized it.

The following are several other mission statements that I've collected:

"Our mission is to know him and make him known" (The Navigators).

"Our mission is to present Christ as Savior and pursue Christ as Lord" (a church plant in San Antonio, Texas).

"Our mission is to turn irreligious people into fully devoted followers of Christ" (Willow Creek Community Church).

"Our mission is to equip you in grace to influence our community with grace" (church plant in Kingsport, Tennessee).

Communicating Your Mission

Once you've drafted a dynamic mission statement, you must communicate it to your people. Steven Covey has said something to the effect that the main thing is to keep the main thing the main thing. That's your job as a leader. The main thing is your mission statement, and communicating your mission statement serves this purpose. There are several ways to accomplish this:

Preach on it periodically (at least once a year) and refer to it often in your sermons. You could cover it in a "state of the church" message given at the same time that our president gives his state of the union address.

Put it on your bulletin masthead.

Print it on business cards and pass them out to your people. Ask them to keep a card in their wallets or purses.

Develop a logo for the church. The logo will help you communicate the church's mission and vision.

Frame the printed mission and mount it on the wall in the foyer.

Put it on your website.

Make it part of the appraisal of your staff and even of the congregational appraisal. (The idea is that what gets appraised gets done.)

Conducting an Environmental Scan

The third step in the conception stage is to conduct an environmental scan.

The Purpose of the Environmental Scan

The environmental scan helps the church planter and the team avoid the peril of the ostrich. It poses the question: What's going on out there? Unlike the proverbial ostrich, who buries its head in the sand, the church needs to remain alert as to what is taking place in the world surrounding it—like the men of Issachar, understanding its times (1 Chron. 12:32). The danger for too many church ministries is that over time they become inward-focused and lose all perspective as to what is taking place in their culture and their national and international environment. The result is cultural irrelevance—they cease to communicate the gospel clearly to new and different generations. From this point on you will need to conduct regular scans so as not to lose touch.

The Contents of the Environmental Scan

The environmental scan involves two particular environments—the general environment and the church environment.

The General Environment

The general environmental scan enables the church to address the trends and practices of the world in which its people live and work. This includes the international, national, and local scenes. The scan covers trends in at least five areas:

Social trends. You will need to keep abreast of the trends and practices in the areas of gender, family, health, crime, race, aging, athletics, the generations (Builders, Boomers, Busters, Bridgers, and new generations), psychographics, demographics, as well as others.

Technological trends. This covers the information revolution, computers, communication, the environment, medicine, genetics, energy, warfare, robotics, transportation, entertainment, education, and other technological innovations.

Economic trends. This includes the national debt, the federal deficit, the trade deficit, inflation, taxes, Social Security, the effects of downsizing, and so on.

Political/legal trends. Developments in the legislative and judicial processes, Supreme Court decisions, elections, church-state issues, the White House, zoning issues, and other such trends are included here.

Philosophical/religious trends. You will want to keep abreast of secularization, privatization, pluralism, relativism, modernism (philosophical naturalism), postmodernism, and so forth.

The Application. Select what you believe are the most important trends in each of the five areas above that will affect your church. Turn to the general environment table—under Environmental Scan in the Conception Stage Worksheet of the Church Planter's Workbook—and place each trend in the Trends column and your response in the Response column. For example, under "Social trends" you might note the trend that people are so busy they tend to value their time more than their money. In the response column you might put: The church will attempt to schedule its primary disciple-making ministries so that its people have to make as few trips as possible to the church facility to attend these ministries. You may address these trends in your sermons. They will also affect your strategy.

The Church Environment

The church environmental scan keeps the church planter abreast of the trends, practices, and programs of international, national, and local churches. It's a way of keeping track of what God is and isn't doing in our world. The purpose of the scan is not to mimic the entire program of another church but to learn from those practices and programs that God is blessing.

The Application. Turn to the church environment table in the Conception Stage Worksheet of the Church Planter's Workbook. Identify a particular church in the left column and the trend in the right column. One example is Yoido Full Gospel Church in Korea. It's the largest church in the world. From this church we learn how to minister to people individually in a large church context. This church's answer is small or cell groups. You write the name of the church in the column on the left and write "cell groups" in the column on the right.

Developing a Vision

The fourth step of the conception stage is the development of a vision.[6]

Why Is a Vision Important?

A vital element of the church planter's ministry is his vision.[7] Both the mission and the vision address the ministry's direction. The vision, however, is different from the mission and is important for several reasons.

First, the vision communicates where the church is going. It's the function of the mission statement to help plan where the church is going. The vision is a communication tool that functions to help you communicate where the church is going.

Second, the vision provides a snapshot of the church's direction. Whereas the mission articulates the ministry's direction, the vision provides a picture or snapshot of that direction. People need to see it in their head as well as see it on paper or it won't happen.

Third, the effect of the vision on the church is to challenge your people to accomplish the ministry whereas the job of the mission statement is to clarify what that ministry is.

Fourth, the purpose of the vision statement is to inspire people to greater efforts for God. It motivates or energizes activity. The mission statement is usually written and informs the people of the efforts for God they can make. The vision may or may not be written but is preached. It creates a picture of the efforts the people can make.

Fifth, the vision touches the emotions. Its source is the heart. The mission is a "head thing." It affects the intellect.

Finally, the vision is unique to every church. It spells out all the particulars—you see people, facilities, and land. On the other hand, the mission is broad and general. Most churches share essentially the same mission—the Great Commission.

What Is a Vision?

An organizational vision is a clear, challenging picture of the future of your ministry as it can and must be.[8] This definition has six essential ingredients.

A *vision is clear.* People can't act on information they don't understand. The goal is that everyone in the church understand the vision so that they can clearly articulate it.

A *vision challenges.* Once a vision is conceived and born, it may die a quick, untimely death. If the vision doesn't challenge the people, there is no vision, just a collection of lifeless words on a sterile sheet of paper.

A *vision consists of a mental picture.* Vision is a "seeing" word. A good vision probes people's imaginations and conjures up positive pictures, images, and memories in their minds.

A *vision relates to the future.* A vision is what is seen in the future regarding the ministry of the church. It concerns the exciting possibilities that the future holds, a picture of what we want the church to become.

A *vision can be.* A significant vision has great potential. A vision "can be" in the sense that it's possible. It's not some wild-eyed dream but is based squarely on the bedrock of reality.

A *vision must be.* A critical sense of urgency exists about a vision. It taps into our passion to the point that it has the potential to keep people awake at night!

Developing Your Vision

Once church planters realize the importance of a vision and have arrived at a clear, working definition, they need to give birth to a vision for the ministry. In birthing a vision, we must ask two important questions: Who develops the vision? How do you develop a vision statement?

Who Develops the Vision?

The first question is a personnel question. It attempts to determine the participants in the envisioning process. The answer is twofold.

Initially, the pastor of the new church is the point person who is responsible to see that the vision is birthed. In a cold start, where no core or launch group exists, he will develop the entire vision himself and cast that vision as he gathers such a group. However, in a hot start, where the leader-starter is working with an already existing launch group, he will facilitate the development of the vision along with that group, depending on its size. If it's a small group of people, say thirty or fewer, he will work directly with them. If a larger group, he'll need to limit the size to thirty who are leaders and work with them through the process. The critical factor is that he works with them in such a way that they get their fingerprints all over the process. It's imperative that they have ownership—it must be their vision as well as his.

How Do You Develop a Vision Statement?

The second question deals with process. Now that we know *who* is primarily responsible for birthing the vision, we need to understand *how* that process works. There is a period of preparation prior to the process.

The preparation. This preparation involves six events, which take place in cycles and not necessarily in this order.

1. Envisioning prayer is prayer that specifically focuses on the development of a vision. An example would be Nehemiah's prayer in Nehemiah 1:4–11. Church planters must devote time to this kind of prayer.
2. Small visions don't motivate. Church planters must not think small. Paul indirectly exhorts us in Ephesians 3:20 both to ask and think big: "Now to him who is able to do immeasurably more than all we ask or imagine."
3. In the process of developing a vision, you will generate lots of ideas. Write them down! This is a brainstorming process. Put on paper what God is putting on your heart. Write down everything that comes to mind. Later you can determine what is and isn't important.
4. Peruse what you have written and attempt to organize it. This serves as a skeleton for ideas that can be fleshed out later. Some of the "bones" or contents could include the following: a statement of the purpose for the church, some of the values, the strategy, the target group, the place of ministry, as well as other features.[9]
5. The visionary and others might probe the ideas with numerous questions. Is the vision clear? Is it challenging in the sense that it

inspires people to action? Does it create mental pictures? Is it future-oriented? Is it both realistic and stretching?

6. The developmental process, like good soup, must be given lots of time to sit on the back burner and cook. Give the process adequate time. It could take place quickly, but most often it comes together over a period of time.

The process. How do you develop a vision statement? There are at least three ways. One is to expand your mission statement. Let's assume that your mission statement is to make and mature believers at home and abroad. To expand this statement, you would ask: What will this look like two, five, ten years from now when it begins to happen? Then you describe what you see.

Another way is to build your vision on each of your core values. You take each value, state it, and then describe what the church will look like when that value is realized in the lives of your people.

A third way is to take someone else's vision statement that touches you and your people deeply and tweak it to fit your congregation. There is an example below of how we at Northwood Community Church tweaked Rick Warren's vision for Saddleback to fit our particular unique situation.

Northwood Community Vision

Vision is not about reality or what is. Vision is all about our dreams and aspirations or what could be.

At Northwood Community Church, we envision our sharing the good news of Christ's death and resurrection with thousands of unchurched friends and people in the metroplex, many of whom will accept Him as Savior.

We envision developing all our people—new believers as well as established believers—into fully functioning followers of Christ through people-friendly worship services, Sunday school, special events, and, most important, small groups.

We envision becoming a church of small groups where our people model biblical community: a safe place where we accept one another and are accepted, love and are loved, shepherd and are shepherded, encourage and are encouraged, forgive and are forgiven, and serve and are served.

We envision helping all our people—youth as well as adults—to discover their divine designs so that they are equipped to serve Christ effectively in some ministry either within or outside our church. Our goal is that every member be a minister.

We envision welcoming numerous members into our body who are excited about Christ, experience healing in their family relationships and marriages, and grow together in love.

We envision our recruiting, training, and sending out many of our members as missionaries, church planters, and church workers all over the world. We also see a number of our people pursuing short-term missions service in various countries. We envision planting a church in America or abroad every two years.

We envision a larger facility that will accommodate our growth and be accessible to all the metroplex. This facility will provide ample room for Sunday school, small groups, Bible study, prayer, and other meetings. While we do not believe that "bigger is better," numerical growth is a by-product of effective evangelism. Thus we desire to grow as God prospers us and uses us to reach a lost and dying world.

This is our dream—our vision about what could be!

What Does a Good Vision Statement Look Like?

Good vision statements can take numerous forms. One of the best examples is Dr. Martin Luther King Jr.'s "I Have a Dream" speech. You can find it and other samples in my book *Developing a Vision for Ministry in the Twenty-first Century*.

If you haven't completed them already, turn now to the Church Planter's Workbook at the end of the book and complete the parts of the Conception Stage Worksheet on values, mission, the environmental scan, and vision.

8

We're Going to Have a Baby!

The Conception Stage, Part 2

Once a church planter has discovered and articulated the church's core values, developed a mission statement, conducted an environmental scan, and developed a compelling, significant vision, three steps remain. One is designing a strategy that accomplishes the church's direction (make disciples), the second is implementing that strategy, and the final step is evaluating the ministry's performance.

Designing a Strategy

Designing a strategy for your church is important for a number of reasons. Here are four:

It's the strategy that accomplishes the church's God-given direction (mission and vision). Without a strategy the mission and vision will not happen.

A clear strategy facilitates understanding. When people grasp your strategy, they'll understand how all the ministries of your church work together, tie back into, and contribute to the mission-vision. For example, a Sunday school class will not only know that it is the church's mission to make disciples but also what part the Sunday school ministry plays in this.

It supplies a sense of spiritual momentum. People feel and see that they're growing spiritually. For example, Rick Warren's baseball diamond analogy helps his people discover where they are spiritually. People who are at second base can rejoice that they are no longer at first base but, at the same time, they are challenged to move toward third base.

Strategy signals what God is blessing. Though God uses many forms or ways of ministry, some work better than others. A strategy manifests this and shows what God is currently using to reach a generation of people.

However, here's a warning: A church's strategy has the potential to cause divisions. Discovering a church's core values and developing its mission and vision create little controversy. This isn't the case with the strategy, because the development of a strategy forces you to select a style of worship. And anyone who is familiar with the church at the end of the twentieth and the beginning of the twenty-first century knows that this has proved to be a major battleground in established churches, much to the chagrin of the Savior.

I define a strategy in the church context as the process that determines how you will accomplish the vision and more specifically the mission of your new church. First, a strategy is a process for moving people from wherever they are spiritually (prebirth-lost or new birth-saved) to where Christ wants them to be—mature (Col. 1:28–29; Gal. 4:19; Phil. 3:12–15). I refer to it as the journey from prebirth to maturity. Second, the strategy addresses how you'll accomplish the church's direction (mission and vision). You can have the best mission and vision statements, but if you don't have a good strategy, you'll never accomplish your mission. Finally, the purpose of the strategy is to help the church accomplish its mission in particular. Every church will have a strategy of sorts. It may be a good or bad one and is represented in the church's programs. Not every church has a mission, however. This makes no sense because the purpose for a strategy is to accomplish the mission. This is the proverbial cart *without* a horse.

Each of the prior steps in chapter 7 will exert some influence on the strategy. The values will dictate what does and doesn't go into the strategy. The mission will give direction to the strategy while the vision will picture and energize it. The environmental scan will update the planter on current cultural trends and provide sample strategies from other churches as examples.

A mistake that many aspiring church planters make is trying to model their new ministry after some highly successful contemporary church. This is the product approach. While this may work, the failures far exceed the successes. Rather than attempt to duplicate a successful church product, it's wise to pursue the process of strategy development. Following a process will result in a unique product or ministry model that is tailor-made for your unique ministry situation. It's imperative that in a post-Christian America or Western Europe (or anywhere for that matter) planter-leaders and any other lead pastors be strategic thinkers, or their ministries won't survive. This chapter explains how to think and act strategically.

This process includes five ingredients that answer five core questions:

Who are you trying to reach? The answer involves discovering your focus group.

How will you reach your focus group? The answer is to design a disciple-making process to reach them.

Who will take part in reaching this group? The best answer is a gifted ministry team.

Where will the church meet; where is the best place to reach your focus group? The answer is your facilities.

How much will it cost to reach the group? The answer involves finances. You must raise and manage well your financial resources.

Discovering the Focus Group

The first ingredient in the strategy process is to decide on whom you'll focus your ministry. There's a certain amount of naïveté in this area. For example, many seminarians think that they'll go out into the world and reach everybody! The desire to reach everyone in general, while very noble, could result in reaching no one in particular. This isn't only naïve; it's unrealistic! While we must be willing to minister to anybody, the truth of the matter is that no church can or will minister to everybody (that's why I use the term *focus*)! Once a group of people opts for a particular style of worship and preaching, it has already limited itself culturally in terms of its potential congregation. (You would benefit greatly by reading appendix B that deals with culture, especially if you have any questions or desire to explore this further.)

Discovering your focus group involves three stages: determining the group, locating it, and connecting with it.

Determining the Focus Group

Church planters must, like Paul and Peter, determine who their focus group will be (Paul focused on Gentiles, while Peter focused on Jews—Gal. 2:7–8). This involves four areas.

1. Identify the Focus Group

Identify your particular group by answering in order each of the following questions.

Will you purposely pursue lost people? Church planters must answer this question honestly. Most evangelical churches would answer in the affirmative. After all, who would vote against evangelism? But in reality, according to an article in *Christianity Today*, 80 percent of the churches in America that are growing are experiencing transfer growth, not conversion growth.[1] They're merely "reshuffling the Christian deck."

Christ's Great Commission mandate begins with reaching lost people. Christ came for the specific purpose of reaching lost people (Luke 5:27–32; 15:1–10; 19:1–10). Any church planter who starts a church today must catch a strong vision for reaching lost people. If not, then he should forget about starting a church and become a part of one that's reaching the unsaved.

Will you focus on unchurched lost people? Lost people can be divided into two groups: those who are churched and the majority who are unchurched. There are still a number of lost people in parts of America, such as the South and the Bible Belt, who attend a local church, though their numbers are dwindling. While the new church will want to reach these people, it is not wise to focus on them alone. Consequently, when the church planting team comes into a new area, they can assure any pastors who might feel threatened by their presence that they have no intentions of "stealing sheep." Whom will they reach? The obvious answer is the unchurched lost in the community.

Will you focus on people like or unlike yourself? No church can reach everybody, because there is no church that can conduct all the ministries necessary to meet everyone's diverse needs. About the time you feel that you're addressing the needs of a particular group, you discover that you've tuned out a number of other groups with totally different needs.

People who are attracted to the new church initially and for several years after are usually close to the church planter/pastor in terms of age (ten years older or younger), marital and family status, and other socioeconomic factors. Since people, both lost and saved, respond best to others who are most like themselves, it would seem wise to reach out to them *initially* because they're the ones who will be most responsive. As you grow, you'll find that you will attract some who aren't like you, and you'll become more diverse, which is even better.

On the other hand, God may call you to focus on people who are different from you, perhaps of a different ethnicity or generation. One way to determine if you're called to reach a different ethnicity is to assess if

God has given you a gift for cross-cultural ministry, as he did Paul (Eph. 3:7–8). Most church plants in the growing inner cities of the world will need to focus on reaching a diverse people.

Will you reach receptive people? The principle of receptivity (covered in appendix D on evangelism) tells us that some people will be more receptive to the new church than others. People who are naturally like us will be attracted to us. Because of their affinity to us, they will be more likely to listen to our message. Also there will be people in the community whom the Holy Spirit has been convicting and who are therefore interested in spiritual matters (see John 16:7–11). They will be receptive to a conversation about spiritual things or an invitation to church.

Will you focus on needy people? The key to unlocking the closed mind and touching the calloused heart is to address people's felt needs (see 2 Cor. 8:14; 9:12; Eph. 4:29; Phil. 4:19). Then you should use them, in turn, to address their spiritual needs. For example, as the Savior demonstrated, hungry lost people listen better to the gospel when their physical need for food has been met.

The church planter must realize that the way to penetrate and gain the attention of a community is to become involved in that community and address positively its felt needs. Barna writes:

> If we expect the Christian Church to attract more people, we will have to become more sensitive to their felt needs. The competition of the local church is not other churches down the street. It is television, sleeping in on Sunday, the weekend special at Bloomingdale's, games and picnics in the park and so forth. As people's lives become more tense, their time more valuable, and their skepticism about the influence and benefits of the church more confirmed, attracting people will be more difficult.[2]

The question is what are the community's needs? Generally speaking, every community has certain broad basic needs and specific needs. The first consists of those needs that the community shares with all other communities across America, as reflected in Maslow's hierarchy of needs. The second consists of certain needs that are unique to a community. For example, an inner-city community may struggle with various addictions, AIDS, unemployment, crime, destitute single parents, and so on.

Another question asks how can we discover these needs? One way is to survey the focus group. Simply stated, this involves asking them what their needs are. In addition, a good source is the media, such as radio and television news. Another way is to observe the group. This may involve moving into the community and spending some time there. A fourth answer is to use demographic and psychographic studies.

Other factors to consider. There are other factors that the church planter-leader should consider in identifying the focus group. A major consideration early in the twenty-first century should be the different generations. At this point in time most generations will fit into the modern or postmodern context. While there are always exceptions, the moderns consist largely of the Builder and Boomer generations, while the post-moderns consist of Generations X, Y, and possibly Z (newer, younger people). Other terms that are used for postmoderns are Bridgers, Busters, and Millennials.

Churches like Willow Creek Community Church near Chicago and Saddleback Community Church in southern California have focused primarily on moderns, such as the Boomers, though they are now attempting to reach out to postmoderns as well. We need churches to focus on a rapidly growing postmodern generation that now outnumbers the modern generation. The simple reason is that it takes all kinds of churches to reach all kinds of people, and postmoderns think very differently from modern generations. See appendix G to learn more about postmoderns.

2. Gather Information on the Focus Group

Once you've identified your focus group, you'll need to gather as much information as possible about them. In particular, determine who they are (demographics) and what they want out of life (psychographics).

Who are the people in your group? Demographic information provides details on the people who make up the focus group. A demographic study will give the following information about people in the community: age, sex, race, population, number and types of households, median income, level of education, occupation, and purchasing power.

What do the people in your group want out of life? Psychographic information presents what people are searching for in life. A psycho-graphic study seeks to discover the focus group's basic attitudes, wants, needs, and values that affect their lifestyles.

Church planters can obtain this information in several ways.

1. Ask people for the information. This would involve conducting some kind of personal survey.
2. Move into the area and begin to observe the people.
3. Read local periodicals and newspapers, since they give this kind of information.

4. Read material on psychographics. An excellent periodical is *American Demographics* magazine. Though dated, two good books are Arnold Mitchell's *The Nine American Lifestyles*[3] and Tex Sample's *U.S. Lifestyles and Mainline Churches.*[4]

5. Obtain professional help. An organization that provides this service is Percept. It's a Christian organization that's aware of church planting and the kinds of help church planters need. It also supplies both demographic and psychographic information.[5]

This material relating to psychographics and demographics will prove vital to targeting and reaching the lost people in a community. It will affect almost every aspect of the new church—from marketing the church (positioning the new church in the community) to the kinds of sermons that are preached on Sunday.

How do you minister to moderns and postmoderns? You will also need to gather information on the modern and postmodern generations. While there is much available on moderns, there is not as much on postmoderns. Again, I have provided some information in appendix G that will help you understand who they are and how to reach them.

3. Construct a Profile Person

Third, you'll use the important information you gather from your demographic and psychographic studies to construct a profile of a target individual. This is optional and has appealed more to moderns than postmoderns. This person or persons could be a man and/or a woman and could be given a name. Several churches have done this. For example, Willow Creek Community Church has created profile persons they call "Nonchurched Harry and Mary." Saddleback Community Church has created "Saddleback Sam." One of my former churches targeted "Community Charley and Cathy."

You could actually draw a picture of this person, dressed in clothing that's typical of the community and even have something in his or her hand, such as a tennis racquet or a golf club.

The profile will serve to facilitate communication among the leaders, the team, and people in the church and aid in focusing the church's efforts. The profile person's name and/or picture reminds everybody that the church is focusing on a certain group.

4. Determine the Kind of Church That Will Reach Your Focus Group

To determine the kind of church that is needed to reach your focus group, you should ask the following questions.

What kind of pastor should lead your church? In light of the particular group, what kind of person would be able to minister most effectively? Take into account such factors as age, education, family, and so on.

What kind of team will minister most effectively to this group? If you're attempting to reach a mixed ethnicity, you would be wise to have those people represented on your team. For example, if you're focusing on blacks and whites, then have them on your team.

What kind of people should be in your core group? These people should be committed, caring, evangelistic, friendly, and warm but not "smotherers."

What kind of meetings should you have? The meetings should be the kind that people in the focus group will attend. Also consider such factors as the meeting's purpose, time, structure, frequency, and size.

What kind of sermons should you preach? Consider appropriate topics and length, along with the interests, needs, hopes, dreams, and aspirations of the focus group.

What kind of worship should you implement? In terms of the focus group, a certain style of worship will be most effective. This will involve decisions about contemporary versus traditional versus ancient worship, including musical instruments, worship teams, communion, the liturgy, and other worship-related matters.

What kind of ministries should you sponsor? There are certain basic ministries that are common to all churches, such as an evangelism ministry. However, specific ministries should take into account the particular needs of the focus audience. For example, if the group consists of young families, ministries need to be designed accordingly. My view is that these ministries will expand considerably into areas that few have even imagined, especially those that seek to reach out evangelistically. This is where godly creativity comes in. I know of one church in Western Europe that meets in a pub, shows video clips of perceptions of God from the film industry, and uses them as a launching pad for discussions about who God is.

Locating the Focus Group

Once the church planter has identified the focus group, the second stage is to discover where that group is located in the community.

The idea is to target urban, suburban, and rural areas for new churches. A key aspect of a geographical strategy for church planting is to target specific areas for new church starts. Today the majority of people in the world live in cities, so, to begin with, the urban areas of the country should be our target.

Approximately 60 percent of the people who live in the state of Colorado live in the Denver metropolitan area. Peter Wagner indicates that 74 percent of Americans lived in urban areas as early as 1976.[6] Greenway and Monsma write that by 2050 approximately 79 percent of the world's population will live in urban centers.[7] Thus the world's cities have increasingly become fertile ground for the gospel. In fact, in his book *Apostles to the City*, Roger Greenway writes: "He who wins the city, wins the world."[8] This shouldn't surprise us because Paul targeted strategic urban centers (a total of twenty-three cities!) on his first three missionary, church planting journeys.

We must also target the suburbs, because people continue to move to them. Churches tend to grow fastest in high-population areas that are experiencing rapid rates of growth.

What about the rural areas of America? What typically happens is that information flows from urban areas to rural areas. In other words, to reach urban areas is to reach rural worlds as well. For example, Paul targeted the city of Ephesus (Acts 19:1), which was known as the "gateway to Asia." The result was that after two years of intense church planting, the gospel had spread throughout Asia (Acts 19:10). However, we must intentionally plant churches in rural areas as well. If we desire to reach America with the gospel, we must start with our cities but must not neglect rural America.

The method for targeting urban areas is demographics. In the book *The E-Myth*, Michael Gerber writes, "Demographics is the science of marketplace reality. It tells you *who* your customer is."[9] The importance of knowing the target group can't be overemphasized. A church can't reach people it knows nothing about.

William Frey is one of the more widely respected demographers in America. He has written an article in the *American Planning Association Journal* in which he argues that our nation can no longer be understood in terms of urban, suburban, and rural population centers.[10] He writes that these centers may only be useful in describing locales within a region. Instead, he suggests that the 2000 census shows we can better understand America from a regional perspective. He places all of America into three regions: the "New Sunbelt," the "Melting Pot," and the "Heartland."

What Frey calls the New Sunbelt ("the American Suburbs") has thirteen states (Arizona, Colorado, Delaware, Georgia, Idaho, North Carolina, Nevada, Oregon, South Carolina, Tennessee, Utah, Virginia, and Washington) and contains 20 percent of the population. It includes the fastest-growing states, due to domestic migration. Those who largely make up the New Sunbelt are young adults and retired persons. The fastest-growing areas within this region are the suburbs, exurbia, and the smaller metro areas. Obviously, this region is ripe for church planters who would focus on reaching both modern-minded Builders and postmodern-thinking young people. It's likely that methods that reached those in the suburbs would work as well in this "American Suburb."

Nine states make up what Frey calls the Melting Pot region (Alaska, California, Florida, Hawaii, Illinois, New Jersey, New York, New Mexico, and Texas). They contain 41 percent of the American population, including 74 percent of America's Asians and Hispanics. This is fertile ground for those who would plant ethnically diverse churches. (I'm convinced that we've done a poor job of reaching Hispanic and Asian people.) Some churches would be multiracial, blending into churches of other ethnicities. The majority prefer to be reached as a distinct Hispanic or Asian ethnic group.

The remaining twenty-eight states, including the District of Columbia, make up our nation's Heartland. They consist primarily of Anglos and African Americans, making up 39 percent of the population. Most living in this region are native Americans (born in America), who are modern-minded Baby Boomers. The principles that worked in reaching them in the 1980s and 1990s will likely reach them in 2000 and 2010. However, as they age, they'll be looking for churches that address issues of mid-life and aging.

Church planters can do much of their own demographic work by following five steps.

1. Determine where in the world you want to plant a church. (Let's assume for the sake of an example that it's somewhere in the United States.)
2. Determine where in the United States you desire to plant a church. This would include the region (the New Sunbelt, the Melting Pot, or the Heartland) and where within this region (state, city, suburb, exurb, and so on). *American Demographics* magazine is most helpful for those who are open to going anywhere in the United States because periodically it publishes a list of the top fifty fastest-growing metropolitan areas in the country. Church planters could pray about this list and see if God directs them to start a church in one of these areas.
3. Determine where in the city, suburb, or other area you want to plant a church. This is the step where the focus community is identified. Bob Roberts (the pastor of Northwood Church near Fort Worth, Texas) has developed the *glocal* concept. He encourages the

church plants that he sponsors to plant a church globally at the same time they plant locally, hence the term *glocal*.

4. Do a feasibility study of the focus community. My website (www .malphursgroup.com/Church Planting) contains an excellent feasibility study done by Carol Childress for a potential church in Kingwood, Texas. Though somewhat dated, it illustrates the contents of a good feasibility study: a statement of the purpose for the study, such as planting a church; a community profile presenting the population, housing, education, occupation, and income of those who live in the target community; a lifestyles and values profile based on a psychographic study; a list of area churches; a list of potential meeting sites; a pastoral leadership profile that predicts what kind of pastor would be best for the community in terms of education, skills and abilities, experience, age, and marital and family status; a list of possible core group members and families; and an assessment of the future growth potential of the area.

Obviously, the usefulness of demographics depends on their accuracy. Good information results in good decisions, while bad information results in bad decisions. Primary demographics are the most reliable, because they are gathered by church planters at the actual site of potential location and ministry. Secondary demographics are less reliable, because they're gathered by others, such as a professional company that might be located on the other side of the country. Most likely, they get much of their information from the census, which is taken every ten years. The longer the time since the last census, the less accurate will be the information. Consequently, any secondary demographic studies must be confirmed by actually visiting the potential target area and doing some work yourself.

Connecting with the Focus Group

Once you have identified and located your focus group, you'll need to make contact with them to minister to them. The following are some approaches that have proved highly effective in making such contacts.

Connecting with the relational community. This particular approach is covered in appendix D on evangelism. It attempts to involve those in the church in reaching out to others who are a part of their relational community, such as neighbors, workmates, and family members. It should also extend beyond them to those in the broader area where you live. I'll say more about this below under community service. Some other approaches may be used along with it, such as direct mail. However, other methods may cease to be used at a point in the life of the church, whereas targeting the relational community will always be practiced.

This is at the very heart of what Willow Creek Community Church has done over the years. In fact their program depends on people inviting their lost, unchurched friends who are a part of their relational community to a weekend "seeker's service."

Direct mail. This program involves sending some kind of mailer to the homes of people who are in the new church's community. The purpose is to attract a lost, nonchurched person to a service or a small-group meeting. This is a good method for smaller core groups because it doesn't require a lot of people to accomplish it. However, an effective program could prove costly. The new group may want to send a mailer from two to four times a year. Good times are early in September, early December, before Easter, and in early summer.[11]

Early in its ministry, Saddleback Valley Community Church used direct mail very effectively to attract a number of unchurched lost people to its services. Some of my former students have also used this method successfully to draw unchurched people to a new church. They make sure the mailer is attractive and accurately targets their community. They're convinced that this is the best way to bring in lost people despite the cost involved.[12]

Telemarketing. Some church plants have used a telemarketing program. Perhaps the best known and the one used most for church planting has been "The Phones for You!" program developed by Norm Whan in California. People in the core group call every household in the target community to invite them to church. The telephone call is followed up by several letters and one final call to encourage those who have responded to follow through.

Community service. This approach seeks to provide programs that meet the various needs of the community according to Galatians 6:10: "Therefore, as we have opportunity, let us do good to all people." It could involve the new church in offering classes in sewing, crime prevention, aerobics, self-defense for women, computers, and simple auto repair. The church might also offer certain events like a fitness fair, a 10K run, a weight-lifting contest, a "red apple" day for teachers, honoring the police and fire departments, Christian camping for inner-city kids, mentoring kids in the public schools, a sports program including soccer and other similar sports, and a rocket club for children. Finally, the church might sponsor a MOPS (Mothers of Preschoolers) or DADS program. Unchurched people respond to these activities because they target their felt needs.

Special attendance Sundays. Some churches select two to four Sundays or more each year and sponsor a special event on them. The people in the group are encouraged to invite those in their relational communities. The event could feature a testimony by a popular Christian personality or sports star. Often they feature a musical program performed by a professional musician. They could feature a band.

A prayer ministry. A program that has proved effective is one that solicits prayer needs from people who live in the target community. This can be done either through the mail or by canvassing the neighborhoods. These requests are given to people in the new church who will pray every day for a given period of time. Then they'll make a contact with the person who submitted the request for an update and any new requests. Eventually, through these contacts, a relationship develops and there are opportunities to present the gospel.

A welcome wagon. In this program, the church obtains a list of all the new people moving into the focus community. Next, they'll either write a letter or send a team of people to welcome the newcomers to the community and invite them to the church. Often, with the latter approach, the visiting team brings a gift, such as an apple pie, a liter of Coke, or—in Texas—salsa and chips. This approach attempts to reach people at a time in their lives when they may be open to spiritual matters and would consider coming to a church. Ezra Jones notes that most people moving into a new area will either find a new church or become confirmed nonchurchgoers within the first three years.[13]

"Farming." This is a regular visitation program developed by Mark Platt, who works with Conservative Baptists in the area of church planting. He got the idea from a young real estate salesman in Simi Valley, California. Basically, the church planting pastor visits the people in his focus area several times. Platt discovered that, after repeated visits, the pastor wins the right to be heard and people respond. The secret to "farming" is consistency. It takes at least six visits before people even begin to recognize the pastor. This calls for at least one visit a month.

But where does a busy church planter find time to make all these calls? Platt spent only two hours a day in visitation and was able to cover five hundred homes per month. He reports that in one six-month period he had more than fifty families visit the church as the result of "farming."

Media. An approach that has been used for many years to communicate the message of the church has been the media—newspapers, radio, and television. There are several problems with the typical approach to the use of the media. The first is the cost, especially those associated with television. The second is the fact that the media has typically reached more

Christians than lost people. For example, most churches advertise on the church page of the newspaper. The only problem is that unbelievers and especially the lost don't read the church page, and some even avoid it. Most churches place advertisements on Christian radio stations. But who listens to Christian radio stations?

The media is still a good place to advertise and can be used to reach unchurched lost people. However, the church might place its advertisements in some part of the newspaper other than the church page. The church could use an ad with a cartoon character that highlights an upcoming sermon that addresses the felt needs of lost people in the focus area. Have the newspaper run the ad in the sports section if you desire to reach out to men. Broadcast radio advertisements on the most popular non-Christian station in town. The church might also inquire if there is any free public service time available.

Another possibility is to volunteer to host or conduct a religious talk show on a popular, local non-Christian radio station. Begin the program by addressing a particular problem or felt need in the community and then show what Scripture says about the issue. Provide time for listeners to call in with questions.

The key to discovering and designing these approaches is creativity. Allow the team some time to be innovative and think creatively about programming. Brainstorm together. Discern the methods that God is blessing in the country and in your area, especially in churches that are reaching lost people. Attend conferences and stay on the leading edge.

At this point you may want to turn to the Church Planter's Workbook and complete the section of the Conception Stage Worksheet on the focus group, under Strategy. It will summarize this material for you and ask you to respond to it.

Developing a Disciple-Making Process

As we have seen, the first core ingredient in designing a strategy is to discover your focus group. The second is to design a disciple-making process. This answers the all-important question, How will we move the focus group from prebirth to spiritual maturity? Following is an abbreviated five-step process that answers this question.

Step 1: Articulate Christ's Mission for Your Church

We've already discovered that Christ's mission for your church is the Great Commission—make disciples. Earlier I encouraged you to develop a mission statement that is short and memorable, with the Great Commission at its core. In this first step, you'll need to return to your mission statement, which has as its ultimate goal spiritual maturity (Col. 1:28–29). Remember, God is using you to move people along a spiritual continuum or journey from prebirth to the new birth and then to maturity. This continuum is well represented by Engel's Scale below.[14]

Engel's Scale

God's Role	Communicator's Role			Man's Response
	General Revelation		−8	Awareness of Supreme Being but no effective knowledge of the gospel
Conviction	Proclamation		−7	Initial awareness of the gospel
			−6	Awareness of the fundamentals of the gospel
		Rejection	−5	Grasp the implications of the gospel
			−4	Positive attitude toward the gospel
			−3	Personal problem recognition
			−2	Decision to act
	Persuasion		−1	Repentance and faith in Christ
Regeneration				New Creature
			+1	Postdecision evaluation
	Follow-up		+2	Incorporation into body
Sanctification			+3	Conceptual and behavioral growth
	Cultivation		+4	Communion with God
			+5	Stewardship
			•	Reproduction
			•	Internally (gifts, etc.)
			•	Externally (witness, social action, etc.)

Eternity

Step 2: Identify the Characteristics of a Mature Disciple

Since your ultimate goal is to encourage spiritual maturity, you'll need to identify the characteristics of a spiritually mature person. Here you answer the question, Since my mission is to bring believers to spiritual maturity, how would I know a mature believer if I saw one? In this step you'll need to answer two questions that establish these characteristics.

1. What are the characteristics of a mature disciple? A brief biblical study will help you identify these (Matt. 5:48; Gal. 4:19; Eph. 4:13, 15;

Col. 1:18; Heb. 6:1). Some examples are that mature disciples are saved; they worship, pray, know and apply the Word, serve, give, and care about others. You should decide on at least two but no more than five characteristics, otherwise your list becomes unwieldy, and your people won't remember them.

2. *How will I communicate these characteristics to my core or launch group and later to my church and potential members so that they understand and remember them?* You may want to use alliteration, an acrostic, a person, pictures, and other approaches. For example, a church that I pastored used the three Cs: conversion, commitment, and contribution. (Later we added a fourth C for community.) We took the biblical characteristics for a mature disciple and put them under the Cs. One church developed an acrostic using the acronym grace (G for glorifying God through meaningful worship, R for relating together in community, A for applying God's truth, C for cultivating a lifestyle of service, E for expanding God's kingdom through evangelism). Another church used the figure of a person and four Ws that related to a particular part of that person's body (the Word went with the head; worship went with the heart; work with the hands; and witness with the feet—Rom. 10:15).

Step 3: Determine the Primary Ministries That Best Accomplish the Characteristics

How will your people appropriate these characteristics of maturity? How will they get them into their lives? This is the purpose of your church's ministries. They are the ministry means that help accomplish the maturity ends (the characteristics). There are two kinds of ministries. One is the primary ministries. These are the two, three, or more ministries that help your people incorporate the characteristics of maturity into their lives. You communicate to your congregation that to become mature Christians, they must commit to involvement in these core, primary ministries. A typical example would be a large-group meeting, such as a worship and preaching service on Saturday night or Sunday morning, a Sunday school class on Sunday morning, and a small-group meeting during the week. (Note also that not only do the primary ministries aid the congregation in embracing the characteristics of a disciple, but they also aid in assimilating people into the church.) The secondary ministries are those that are not essential to disciple making but will supplement and support the process in some way. These would include a men's ministry that meets once or twice a month, or vacation Bible school.

Next you will need to create a sanctification matrix. Across the top of the matrix place a horizontal axis or line and write your characteristics of a mature disciple above it. Down the left side of the matrix, place a vertical axis or line along which you write your primary ministries in assimilation order (this is the natural order in which people will most likely get involved in your church—first a large-group meeting, next a small-group meeting, and so on). This will help you make sure that you have a primary ministry to implement each discipleship characteristic. You can discover this by moving horizontally across from the primary ministry to the characteristic it implements and placing an X there. If any ministry isn't incorporating a characteristic, then you will need to justify its existence. If a characteristic is without a primary ministry, you will need to design such a ministry.

Sanctification Matrix

	Conversion	Commitment	Contribution
Worship Service	X		
Sunday School		X	
Small Group		X	X

What primary ministries should you offer to encourage the development of each characteristic? I suggest that you examine the people that you're attempting to reach (your focus group) along with your launch group and consider their needs and what they'll respond to. It's important that you brainstorm. Also, use an environmental scan to determine what others are doing who are planting in similar situations to yours. You may get some excellent ideas from them.

Decide how and when these ministries will meet. For example, how many times should you expect people to meet per week? What is reasonable to develop spiritual maturity? In the churched culture of the 1950s and 1960s, the answer was three times per week (Sunday morning and evening plus a Wednesday evening prayer meeting). Today people will probably want to meet fewer times. You must also determine the days and times of the day when groups will meet. Some will meet on Sundays, some on Saturdays, and others during the week. I've observed that often Gen Xers prefer to meet in the evening.

Finally, determine how you will communicate the process to your people so they'll understand and remember it. A visual is a good way to communicate the process. In my last church, we communicated it by using

A Fully Functioning Follower of Christ

a three-legged stool. You could use a baseball diamond or the layers of an apple. Northpointe Community Church in Atlanta communicates this process by using the rooms of a house—foyer, living room, and kitchen. Other ways to communicate this information is through a sermon, a new member's or attender's class, church brochures, or the church's website.

Step 4: Decide How You'll Measure Spiritual Progress

There are two questions in step 4: Why measure progress? How will you and your people accomplish this? The answer to the first question is twofold. Your people need to evaluate their personal progress toward Christ's goal of spiritual maturity. And you as a leader need to be able to evaluate the church's progress so that you can determine how the church is progressing corporately and make ministry corrections in process.

There are a number of ways to measure this progress. One is to assign performance indicators for each characteristic so that you'll know how people are developing spiritually. Scripture contains a number of performance indicators, such as baptism (Acts 2:41; 8:12; 9:18; and more), attendance (4:4; 5:14; and more), sharing possessions (2:45; 4:32), and others. Thus, if you used the three Cs, the indicator for conversion would be baptism, commitment would be the number of people attending Sunday school, and so forth. Another way to measure progress is to have small-group leaders evaluate people individually. This works if you have an active small-group program. A third way is to measure on a broader scale. For example, Watermark Community Church in Dallas, Texas, offers its people a congregation-wide assessment on its website and also offers it during a corporate service.

An Example of a Specific Working Strategy

Below is a condensed example of a disciple-making process that may serve as a model. Every strategy implements a mission, so this strategy begins with a restatement of the mission.

Mission
Our mission is to be used of God in developing people into fully functioning followers of Christ.

Goals
The strategic goals (to realize our mission):
Fully functioning followers have three characteristics (the three Cs). They are converted, committed, and contributing members of the church body.

1. Conversion to Christ (they know Christ as Savior). The goal is to see people converted to Christ (interest in *becoming* a disciple).
2. Commitment to Christ (they are committed to growing in Christ). The goal is to bring people to the deepest of commitments to Christ (to become a deeply *committed* disciple).
3. Contribution to Christ (they serve the body, share their finances, and seek the lost). The goal is to equip people to make a contribution to Christ (to become a *contributing* disciple).

Steps
The specific action steps to accomplish our goals. The following three action steps are vital to our plan to move people from prebirth to maturity. The steps are represented by using the visual of a three-legged stool. Each leg represents a level of commitment. The range is from level 1 (the least commitment) up to level 3 (the maximum commitment).

1st Leg: Conversion to Christ
Goal: To lead people to faith in Christ and active involvement in the church (interest in becoming a disciple)—Luke 15:1–10; 19:1–10; 1 Cor. 14:22–25; Col. 4:2–6.

Action step 1: A "people-friendly" large-group meeting at 10:45 AM on Sunday to interest unchurched lost and saved adults and young people in becoming Christ's disciples. It will include the sermon, drama, celebrative worship, and a regular presentation of the gospel.

Action step 2: Other events to minister to lost and saved people and assimilate them into the church, such as vacation Bible school, men's and women's ministries, aerobics, Pioneer Boys and Girls Clubs, Awana, sports events, and community events.

2nd Leg: Commitment to Christ
Goal: To bring people to a commitment to Christ (to become a committed disciple)— Eph. 4:12–13; Col. 1:28; 1 Tim. 4:7–8; Heb. 6:1–3. (What does a committed disciple look like? The answer is found in Acts 2:41–47.)

Action step 1: Discipleship Small Groups (fully functioning communities).
Lay leaders will oversee small-group communities who help one another
become more like Christ. Meeting twice a month, these communities could
include the following: shepherding, studying the Bible, exercising spiritual
gifts, biblical community, accountability, prayer, and evangelism.

Action step 2: Christian Education.
Christian education consists of children and adult Sunday school classes, a
nursery, and children's church. The adult Sunday school consists primarily
of classes that will cover more in-depth than the sermon topics that are vital
to commitment and spiritual growth.

3rd Leg: Contribution to Christ
Goal: To equip people to make a contribution to Christ (to become a contributing disciple). This involves three things: serving the body, sharing our
finances, and seeking the lost.

Action step 1: Serving the body (Eph. 4:12).
A staff or lay Minister of Involvement will use our Sunday classes to assess
our people and provide the necessary information for them to discover their
divine designs (required of new members). The staff or lay minister will
match the people with the church's ministry for which they are best suited
according to their design.

Action step 2: Sharing our finances (Acts 2:44–45; 4:32; 2 Cor. 8:1–24;
*   9:1–15).*
We will use the Sunday service, the Sunday school, and the small groups
to teach our people the biblical principles that will help them handle their
finances in a Christ-honoring way.

Action step 3: Seeking the lost (Luke 15; 19:1–10).
We will provide classes in evangelism so that our people will understand the
importance of evangelism and discover their style of evangelism and how to
share their faith with the lost. We will involve our people in missions abroad
as well as at home. We will plant churches as we grow.

At this point you may wish to complete the Developing a Disciple-
Making Strategy, part of the Conception Stage Worksheet in the Church
Planter's Workbook.

Building a Gifted Leadership Team

After you've developed your disciple-making process, the third
ingredient of your strategy is to recruit and build a gifted leadership

team. These are the people who will help you plant the church and implement the total strategy. This step answers the question, Who will be involved in reaching the focus group? Far too many church planters attempt to start their churches by themselves or with the aid of a small core group. A much better option is to recruit a dynamic, gifted church-planting leadership team who will own and have a major role in implementing and realizing the dream. While the process may already be under way, this is the point in the strategic planning process when you must address the issue of personnel. But even if it begins here, it does not end here. It is a never-ending process; you will always be recruiting personnel. In addition, you must understand that your church will only be as good as the people who make up the leadership team. Thus I can't emphasize enough the importance of this ingredient.

Why Recruit a Team?

There are two strong reasons for recruiting a church planting team. The first concerns the importance of a team ministry and the second is the advantages of that ministry.

The Importance of a Team Ministry

A team approach to ministry is important for several reasons.

Christ ministered through a team. Christ chose to accomplish his ministry on earth using a team approach. This is important to note because he is God, the all-powerful Creator of the universe. Therefore, he doesn't need mortal men to do his work. Yet, instead of doing it alone, he chose to work through a band of fallible, inept disciples (Mark 6:7).

Paul ministered through a team. Paul did not attempt to carry out the Great Commission vision alone but ministered through a team. It consisted of people such as Barnabas (Acts 11:22–30), John Mark (Acts 13:2–5), Silas (Acts 15:40), Timothy (Acts 16:1–3), Luke (Acts 16), and others (Acts 18). Also Acts 19 and 20 mention Erastus, Gaius, Aristarchus, Sopater, Secundus, and Tychicus.

New Testament ministry was team ministry. Though not a biblical imperative, the ministries of Jesus and Paul demonstrate that New Testament ministry was team ministry. Lyle Schaller indicates that the key to reaching a new generation is starting churches, but to be effective it requires teamwork. "Starting a new church is one of the loneliest jobs in the world. I wouldn't do it unless I were part of a team."[15]

The Advantages of a Team Ministry

There are several advantages to ministering in a team context, especially if you recruit those who can lead the ministry to the next level of excellence.

Multiple ministry. First, a team brings together several individuals with multiple gifts, talents, and abilities. This results in a more diverse ministry menu. When we look at all the gifts described as belonging to the body of Christ (Romans 12; 1 Corinthians 12; Ephesians 4), we wonder why anyone would want to attempt a ministry all alone!

More ministry. Second, a simple but often overlooked fact is that a team can accomplish more than an individual. Ecclesiastes 4:9–10 says, "Two are better than one, because they have a good return for their work: If one falls down, his friend can help him up. But pity the man who falls and has no one to help him up!"

Self-ministry. Third, a team can minister to each other. This also seems to be the point in the passage above from Ecclesiastes: "If one falls down, his friend can help him up."

How Do You Recruit a Team?

The second question concerns the team recruitment process. It requires us to ask what we should look for in potential team members. The following three qualifications are musts: character, competence, and chemistry.

Character. The number one qualification for any person on a team is godly character. Such passages as 1 Timothy 3:1–13; Titus 1:6–9; and Acts 6:3 set the standard. These passages teach that there are various character qualifications for leaders in a team context in the church.

Competence. Competence refers to the team members' special abilities to function well at what each does. There are two kinds of abilities—God-given and developed. God-given abilities are one's natural and spiritual gifts, passion, and temperament. Developed abilities are character, knowledge, and skills.

Chemistry. Chemistry refers to how the team members relate to one another. A team member can have good character and exceptional competence but not be able to get along with others, which jeopardizes the team's survival. The chemistry of the team affects its ministry, doctrinal, and emotional alignment. Ministry alignment means agreement on the future church's core values, mission, vision, and strategy, including worship style. Doctrinal alignment is agreement on doctrinal essentials (deity of Christ, inspiration of Scripture, and others) and also on nonessentials (speaking in tongues, divorce, women's role in ministry, and so forth).

Emotional alignment is compatibility of temperament, passion, and emotions. It determines the emotional climate of the ministry. I'll say more about alignment of temperament under What Kind of Teams? below.

Where Would You Recruit a Team?

The school campus. A number of schools train men and women for various roles and positions in vocational Christian ministry. These range from unaccredited short-term schools to accredited graduate seminaries.

The local church. Another excellent source for recruiting teams is the local church. A major obstacle, however, for the contemporary church in America is that not enough churches are involved in starting new works. While a church doesn't have to be involved in the church planting effort, it helps if it is, because often church members are open to the church planting idea, and team members can be found there.

Planted churches will also provide fertile soil for recruiting church planting teams. As the church adds professional staff and implements an intern program, and as gifted laypeople surface, all could be recruited and trained within the church to extend its ministry through establishing new churches. In this role, the new church would serve as an incubator for future church leadership teams.

Other potential sources for church planting team members are a denomination and a mission agency that support church planting and would network naturally with potential team members.

What Kind of Teams?

The temperament of individual team members is an important factor in recruiting a team. Here we need to ask the configuration question: What are the best temperament combinations for recruiting and developing gifted, significant church planting teams? The best way to answer this question is to examine briefly the information on temperament from the *Personal Profile* and the *Myers-Briggs Temperament Inventory* (MBTI) (see chapter 5). It must always be kept in mind that these inventories are merely tools. They are to be used as helpers not final determinants of who functions where on a team.

The Personal Profile. In chapter 5, we looked at the DiSC model that relates to developing effective teams for church planting. The question is, how do the various combinations relate to one another in terms of effectiveness in the work environment? The Performax Company, which publishes the *Personal Profile*, has developed a compatibility chart that shows the various degrees of compatibility of the DiSC temperaments with one another in the areas of social interaction and work tasks.[16]

This chart indicates that the two best temperament combinations for accomplishing a work-related task is the person with a high *D* or one with a high *I* teamed with a second person with a high *S*. The next best combination is a person with a high *S* working with another who is a high *C*.

It's important to observe two things. First, as indicated earlier, the high *D*s and *I*s benefit a team the most by functioning or leading in the point position. Second, the high *S* temperament serves in all three team combinations (rated as excellent) as the best possible backup person on the team. In other words, the high *S* temperament makes for excellent team compatibility in accomplishing a work-related task.

This doesn't mean that other temperament combinations can't get the job done. What it does mean is that, all things being equal, these temperaments function best in these positions and relationships in a task-oriented team environment.

The *Myers-Briggs Temperament Indicator.* There are four effective team combinations in terms of temperament according to the MBTI. The first is extroversion or introversion (*EI*), the second is sensing or intuitive perception (*SN*), the third is thinking or feeling judgment (*TF*), and the last is judgment or perception (*JP*). (If these preferences seem a little vague at this point, turn back to chapter 5 and read the brief description of them.)

How do these preferences and their combinations affect recruiting teams for church planting? From her work in the field of temperament combinations, Myers concludes that the stronger teams consist of people who scored differently on the *MBTI,* showing a preference for either sensing (*S*) or intuition (*N*), or for thinking (*T*) or feeling (*F*) but not both. They should be alike on at least one other preference. In other words, they should both show a preference for either extroversion (*E*) or introversion (*I*) or for judgment (*J*) or perception (*P*).

In working with the MBTI, Roy M. Oswald and Otto Kroeger wisely add the following caution.

> One caution: the more the staff members differ in type, the better able they will be to minister to a diverse congregation; but it will be more difficult for them to communicate and get along with each other. This is a trade-off. Be aware that when differences in type abound on a parish staff, more time and energy must be applied to maintaining support and communication.[17]

In addition to considering temperament when we recruit and develop a team for church planting, we must also think of the optimal number of team members, their roles or functions on the team, and their giftedness.

The two-person staff team. On the basic two-person team, an effective combination would be a leader and a manager. The leader would be the one with the spiritual and natural gifts of leadership (Rom. 12:8) and possibly the spiritual gift of faith (1 Cor. 12:9), which involves vision. The manager would be the person with the spiritual and natural gifts of administration (1 Cor. 12:28). This team, most likely, would function better than two leaders or two managers teamed together.

Ed Stetzer's research indicates that attendance was demonstrably higher in planting situations when there were at least but not more than two staff on the team. He postulates that one would be the lead planter and the other would have evangelism and worship competence.[18]

The three-person staff team. Lyle Schaller believes that all church planting teams should include at least three people—a pastor, an evangelist, and a music specialist. He also suggests a five-person team that would include, in addition to the three just mentioned, someone to minister to families with children and a person responsible for developing church life.[19]

The three- to five-person staff team. Willow Creek Community Church is encouraging three- to five-person teams with certain spiritual gifts. For example, they strongly encourage that teams be led by someone with the gift of leadership. The other two members should be a teacher and a programmer. Ideally, there would be two additional members—a youth worker and an administrator.[20] The teacher in the Willow Creek strategy would teach the believers at the New Community services during the week. The programmer would be responsible for what takes place in the various congregational services, such as the drama and worship.

Perhaps the best way to determine the right combination for the team is to consider the church's ministry strategy. For example, if the team desires to plant churches that reach lost people, then they'll need an evangelist. If they want good worship, they'll need someone gifted in music. If they desire a church with an emphasis on small groups, they'll need someone with gifts and experience in small-group ministry. If they are trying to help their people develop certain characteristics in their lives that lead to maturity, such as the three Cs, they need a lead person who champions each characteristic.

Lay teams. Reality is that most church planting teams will not have more than two people. Again, Stetzer indicates that this is good because his research demonstrates that a team of more than two people isn't as effective as a team with more members. However, you would be wise to fill other positions with qualified, talented laypeople. Stetzer, citing Bob Logan, advises that you have at least the following laypeople on your team: a volunteer preschool children's minister, an assimilation coordinator, an evangelism networker, a spiritual gifts mobilizer, a welcome coordinator, and a financial organizer.[21] Perhaps another person who would be immensely valuable to the team would be a fundraiser. This person's sole responsibility would be to raise funds for the ministry in general and any full-time team persons in particular.

Mini-bios. Once you've recruited your team, ask each to develop what I refer to as a "mini-bio." It is a brief statement that identifies who the person is and gives information about his or her family, ministry training, areas of expertise, and other pertinent information. Place this in a well-done, attractive church-starting brochure and on your website. A photo of each person adds a nice touch. The purpose of the bio is to introduce the team to anyone interested in some way in the church plant.

The team should meet together and develop a board of reference, consisting of people who have worked with the team and/or with individuals on the team and can recommend them on the basis of their character and past performance.

In the context of the typical church, the days of the specialist pastor who attempts to minister without a team are numbered. If such church plants survive, most will remain small and drain the leader's energy and the sponsor's finances. Organizations and denominations would be wise to send out one church planting team, consisting of four or five people, and invest in it rather than in four or five separate individuals to plant four or five separate churches.

Turn to Building a Gifted Leadership Team, part of the Conception Stage Worksheet in the Church Planter's Workbook, and work through the questions.

Locating the Ministry's Facilities

The fourth ingredient in strategizing is to locate a place for the church to meet. You must ask, What facilities are necessary and best for reaching our focus group?

Here the age-old maxim "form follows function" applies. The facilities must align with the working strategy. If your strategy dictates a Sunday school program, then the facilities must have adequate rooms for classes. If you target people with infants, you must have a nursery. If you have a worship service, you'll need a place to hold that service.

I deal more in-depth with facilities in the development stage (chapter 9). There we'll look at the characteristics of a facility, such as location, appearance, visibility, accessibility, size, cleanliness, and many others. I'll also probe the prospects that buildings such as a school, public center, storefront, or movie theater hold for serving as good facilities.

You should consider the possibility of remodeling. You may find the right facility in a good location but have to remodel it to suit your needs.

Some church planters have the option of purchasing land and a facility or purchasing land and building a facility. If you plan to build, be sure to ask lots of questions and be on the lookout for hidden costs and problems. I knew of one five-acre piece of land that was for sale in a new, growing suburb. It looked like a fantastic deal. However, the city wanted at least one acre of the land for a second road, which the buyer would have to pay for. Also, a Mormon Stake (church) had bought the adjoining property. The agent handling the property didn't volunteer this information; the church discovered it on its own.

Raising the Ministry's Finances

The fifth ingredient in developing your strategy is finances. You must ask, How much will it cost to reach our focus group? The answer is two-fold. This involves raising and managing your financial resources.

Raising the financial resources. For you to raise adequate financial resources for yourself and the ministry, you need to determine your precise financial needs. The way to accomplish this is with a budget that reflects most accurately the costs of your ministry community. As I discussed in chapter 3, your budget will consist of such items as salaries; housing (rent or mortgage plus utilities); insurance (liability and health); automobile; rent or lease of meeting facilities and an office; facility improvements; office supplies, furniture and equipment; Sunday school curriculum; and equipment, such as sound, musical instruments, lighting, and chairs. (You may wish to review the worksheet on budgeting in the Church Planter's Workbook.)

The next step is to raise those funds. I have covered the topic of fundraising in chapter 3. It's important here to note that many denominations have discovered the need for church planting and are providing help for those who desire to plant churches through them. Some will match the funds that the church planter raises, and others will even match every dollar raised with two dollars. In addition, a few churches have caught the vision to plant and fund new churches. Consequently, at this point—if you haven't already—you need to decide if you want to affiliate with a particular denomination. You would also be wise to seek out a sponsor church.

Managing the financial resources. Once you've raised the necessary funds for your church planting ministry, you need to properly manage those funds. This involves such practices as receipting gifts, using several people of known high integrity to collect and count any offerings, living by the budget, and at least a yearly audit of funds. The public is all too aware of the televangelists in the 1980s and 1990s who misappropriated the funds given to their ministries by well-intentioned people. They're looking for integrity in this area, and we must not disappoint them. I'll say more about this in the developmental stage (chapter 9).

Implementing the Strategy

After you have developed your overall strategy, the next step in the conception stage is to implement the strategy. The greatest problem in developing an overall ministry strategy is implementation. Church planters can catalyze and articulate a fresh, innovative, powerful strategy, but somehow never get around to implementing it. They fail to follow through. Thus it dies a quick death for lack of implementation.

It's imperative that we take action if we want to translate the vision into the very fabric of the organization. We must make it happen. To fail at this point in the conception stage is as demoralizing as getting to the goal line and not scoring, or getting to the marriage altar only to change your mind. The implementation step consists of six key components.

Determine specific actions. The first key component is determining the specific actions you need to take to accomplish the strategy. You can't implement the entire strategy all at once. Thus you must ask, What are the specific actions we must take at the beginning to afford the greatest impact? They will be several. At the last church I pastored, Northwood Community Church, our focus group was primarily Baby Boomers with children. Consequently, it was imperative that we bring our Sunday school program "on line" as soon as possible. These people wanted something good for their kids.

Formulate specific priorities. Once specific actions are identified, you must prioritize them. This serves to focus your resources, energy, finances, people, and creativity. Again, at Northwood, our number one priority was our Christian education program.

Decide on specific deadlines. The third component of the implementation process is deciding when each action should be accomplished. Assign a specific month and year to each one.

Assign responsibility. Next you must assign responsibility to someone for the implementation of the specific action. You ask, Who is the best person to carry out this assignment?

Communicate the specific priorities. The fifth key component is communication. Here you ask, Who needs to know about these specific actions? People need to know what you're implementing if they are to buy in and be involved in any way in the program.

Schedule a monthly implementation review. The final component is a monthly implementation review (MIR). This allows the church planting team to review the monthly operational performance of the ministry and to assure accountability.

Evaluating the Ministry's Performance

The final step in the conception stage is evaluation. Few churches formally appraise what they are doing. That doesn't mean, however, that evaluation doesn't take place. People are constantly judging whether or not they like their Sunday school class, their small-group leader, last Sunday's sermon, and so forth.

For churches to grow and improve, they need to conduct regular evaluations. (Note that evaluation also leads to constant change or transformation of the ministry, so that it becomes increasingly better.) This practice makes sure that the ministry recognizes people's strengths and contributions to the church as well as their weaknesses and failures. While most don't like evaluation, it allows the church to confront problem people and problematic performances that would otherwise be ignored. Rather than hurt ministry morale, our system has encouraged it. It reminds us to reward people and forces us to deal with our problems.

The rule is: What gets appraised gets done. To accomplish good appraisal, you must answer the following questions: Who evaluates? Whom and what do they evaluate? How often do they evaluate?

Appraisal is based on and works from each person's job or ministry description. First, each individual needs to have a ministry description that spells out clearly his or her responsibilities.

I suggest that you use a 360-degree evaluation process. Each one on the team evaluates the team as a whole, each member on the team (including the lead pastor), and any other staff. All also evaluate themselves with a self-appraisal. Do this at least once a year.

This appraisal process allows everyone to know his or her assessed strengths and weaknesses. Be sure to applaud the former. Look at the weaknesses, discuss them, and ask the person to work at improvement. This lets the worker know where he or she stands. Should the individual not improve, you may have to dismiss him or her after a time. Should this be necessary, the person is well aware of the problem and reason for dismissal. Often these people resign before the church releases them.

Now, turn to the Church Planter's Workbook and complete the Conception Stage Worksheet on implementation and evaluation.

This chapter has covered the basic steps that church planters must take to put the new church in place.[22] However, this is only part of the battle. I believe that technical skills and job knowledge are only a small part of why you get an advance in a job. It's your people knowledge and skills that make a difference. I'm convinced that this is doubly true of ministry. You can accomplish all that's in this chapter and more and still fail, due to a lack of people skills. What's the message? Work hard at relating well to people. Let the Spirit help you (see Gal. 5:22–23).

9

Childbirth Classes

The Development Stage

While in seminary, Bill Smith worked his way through much of the conception stage. He has developed his core values, a mission, and a strong, significant vision statement that involves pursuing and reaching unchurched lost people. He has also recruited one other man at seminary as part of a gifted, aggressive church planting team. While both men possess different gifts and abilities, they're strongly committed to each other and to the accomplishment of the same vision to reach the unchurched. They've also outlined a ministry strategy to accomplish their dream. They've focused on a group of people, located that group in a particular community, and developed a disciple making strategy to reach them. One final important event has also transpired. Both have just completed their seminary training and received their degrees. Where do they go from here? What's the next step in the process of church planting?

The second stage in the process of starting a church is the development stage. The primary purpose of this prenatal stage, as with a newly conceived child in the womb of its mother, is to prepare this new life for its birth (the third stage). The new church faces two potential problems at this point. On the one hand, it could start too soon—the birth would be premature. On the other, it could wait too long and be delivered past term. How long then should the development take? What time is necessary to prepare for birth? In most cases, this ranges from three months to a year, depending on whether there's a preexisting group of interested, committed Christians in the focus area. For the new church to be ready for its birth in the focus community, the planting team must gather, cultivate, and grow the launch group.

Gathering a Core Group

A church can't exist without people! People are the church. The development stage assumes that there will be people to develop, so the development stage begins with the gathering of an initial core or launch group[1] of people who are interested in starting a new church. This will involve either a "cold start" or a "hot start." In a sense you never leave this stage in that you'll be gathering people for the rest of the church's existence. Should this cease, you'll plateau and begin to die.

A Nonexistent Core Group

What Is a Cold Start?

A cold start involves gathering believers together who are not already part of a group. There are Christians already living in the target area, but they may not know one another and are not meeting together for the purpose of planting a church.

Bill Smith and his team have targeted a particular community in an urban setting where they don't have any contacts. Most likely, they've been praying over a list of the fastest-growing metropolitan areas in America as listed in the *American Demographics* magazine, and God has directed their hearts to this one. They've completed a feasibility study on the area and have determined their focus community. The next step is to move into the area and begin to locate and raise up a core group of committed, relatively mature Christians.

It's also possible to move into the area and focus primarily on lost people. However, this would require that time be set aside to develop them because of their initial immaturity. The planting of the church would have to be delayed until these new believers were ready.

What Are the Advantages and Disadvantages?

There are both advantages and disadvantages to gathering a core group that does not already exist.

An advantage. One of the definite advantages of this approach is that the people who become involved "join you." The result is that they grant you the authority and the necessary power to lead them. They're committed to your leadership and DNA from the very beginning of the work. In contrast, when pastors take established churches, they "join them." At the beginning, they aren't given the authority and power to lead the people. The power likely rests with a church patriarch or matriarch. The new pastor has to earn the authority, which takes time and providence.

The disadvantages. There are at least two disadvantages to this approach. The first is that you can't get started before you move into the area. You have to be in the area to make contacts with the people. The second disadvantage is a result of the first. This approach takes a lot of time and patience. Discouragement is likely to set in unless a lot of good contacts are established early.

What Are Some Methods?

There are several ways to make contact with potential core group members in a target area.

Prayer. The first and most important is to get on your knees before the sovereign God of the universe and ask him to help you raise up the right people for the new church. Ask him to put you in the right places with the right people at the right times.

The constituency of a school. Second, if the church planters are seminary or Bible college graduates, they could ask the school to write a letter to its constituency in the target area informing them of the new church and encouraging them to contact the team. If the school will release the names, the planters could make the contacts themselves and assess any interest in the new work.

Parachurch. Another approach is to make contact with any parachurch organizations in the area. Some examples would be Christian Businessmen International, Campus Crusade for Christ, or Young Life. Explain the church's vision and strategy and see if there's any interest. Often parachurch groups will share the same vision and will be delighted to help a church that desires to reach out to lost, unchurched people. These organizations can provide the names of contact people in the community as well as encourage their own people to come your way.

"Leading-edge" churches. A fourth approach is to contact a biblically based, spiritually healthy, leading-edge church and articulate your vision. Once you feel you've gained their confidence, ask if they have any contacts in the focus community. They might be willing to send some of their own people your way. Often there will be people who write them from around the country desiring to find a similar church in their community. These contacts can be valuable.

Advertising. Place an ad in the church page of the community newspaper explaining the vision and plans to start a church. Since Christian people read the church page, you will stir up some interest. I used this method effectively in planting my first church. You could also send out a letter of explanation to the community. While this may create a lot of interest, one drawback could be a negative response from other pastors in the area.

Networking. As you circulate in the community, you will come in contact with Christians, and you'll want to pay particular attention to unchurched Christians. (For a biblical example of networking, see John 1:39–45.) You'll come across them at the mall, grocery store, soccer practice, and elsewhere. Ask them if they know people who aren't going to church anywhere. You could recruit people by conducting a neighborhood survey. Regardless of where you find Christians, invite them to join the core group.

Gathering an Existing Core Group

What Is a Hot Start?

A hot start involves gathering and working with a group that has already come together in some locale before the church planting team arrives on the scene. There are several potential hot start situations. The first is a group of people from a sponsor church who desire to begin a church. They might be Christians who live in the same community, which is located a substantial distance from their church. Rather than drive all that distance, they would like to begin a church nearer to them. In a similar fashion, a mother church might desire to plant a daughter church in a particular community and recruit some of its people who live in that community to form the core of the new church.

Another situation involves gathering a group of people without a mother church who are located in an area of the country where there aren't many evangelical churches. They may have contacted the placement office of the seminary, which put them in contact with the church planting team. One of my students who planted a church in Memphis, Tennessee, used these gatherings (he referred to them as a "prequel") to prepare his people spiritually and intellectually for what was to come.

What Are the Advantages and Disadvantages?

The advantages. The most obvious advantage in this situation is that not as much time is required to locate and recruit people to make up the initial core group, because they are usually already in place. Also, if there are enough people in the initial core group, they may be able to come up with a strong financial package.

The disadvantages. There are several disadvantages. The group may have a different vision and different DNA from that of the church planting team. For example, they may be more interested in having someone come and teach them the Bible than in reaching their lost friends and neighbors for Christ. The critical issue here is whether the group is willing to own the new vision and share the same DNA. There is no way to know for sure, so you're taking a chance if you continue with people who initially don't share your vision. Personally, I would give them my blessing and move on.

Another disadvantage, as I mentioned earlier, is that the church planters are joining the group, and it may take a while to gain their allegiance especially if the group has been in existence for a period of time. If a leader in the role of a patriarch or matriarch has emerged, this could be another disadvantage, especially if he or she is unwilling to let you lead the plant. For the church plant to work, the former leader must let go both intellectually and emotionally and let the church planting team lead.

Whether you are involved in a hot or a cold start, look for people who are what I refer to as "magnet" or "attractor people." These are individuals or couples who have strong people skills (often high *I*s on the *Personal Profile*) and have developed large or multiple webs of relationships in the community. Their presence contributes to quick growth and strong outreach into the community.

My experience with hot starts, along with that of other church planters, is that within a year or two the initial core group will often leave the church. This is because some don't understand the sacrifice that it takes to plant a church. Others had something else in mind or believed that they could change the vision and direction of the ministry. And some are simply looking for a Bible study. The greater problem is that many will not share the same DNA. Consequently, in time, they will be replaced by those who do. Therefore, it's most important that church planters take great pains to explain repeatedly to their initial core groups the church's DNA (values, mission, vision, strategy) as well as other vital concepts.

What Are Some Methods?

What does the church planter or the planting team do when they first meet with an existing core group? What's their agenda? What are the kinds of things they should discuss? The purpose of the first meeting is for the leader to get to know the core group and to assess if they're the right match for the team. The following considerations should determine the tenor of the first meeting.

Allow for a large block of time. It's important that there be plenty of time for discussion and interaction between the team and the core group. One possibility is to get away together for a weekend in a place where there will not be a lot of interruptions. Children should be left with a sitter.

Get to know one another. There should be sufficient time to get to know one another, or as one of my planters words it—to hang. This will help in bonding and developing a sense of community. Both the team and the core group could give information about themselves. Participants should make a point of visiting with one another during breaks and the evenings and mornings when people are relaxed and together. Playing a game of volleyball or some other team sport is a good mixer that will help accomplish this goal.

Ask lots of questions. The more questions you ask, the better you'll be able to assess the situation and the existing core group.

1. Find out about the origin of the group, their backgrounds, and their beliefs.
2. Determine the group's purpose, vision, and felt needs. Most important is their DNA. What is their vision, and do they all have the same vision? What are their values and are they shared? Do you share their values? Before this meeting, you might ask each person in the group to listen to a tape, view a video, or read some literature that communicates your vision. Determine if they're open to it or not.
3. Ask if there is a need for the new church. The answer is always yes, but it's important for them to verbalize it.
4. How serious are these people about starting a new church? Try to determine their level of commitment.[2]

Gathering a Committed Core Group

Secure a commitment. The commitment of the existing, potential core group is critical if a church is to be planted. The truth is that you'll lose some people along the way, and that may be good or bad. It's good if certain people don't align with the church in its essence or have a different agenda. It's bad, however, if you've not done a good job in casting the church's vision and clarifying its DNA. (Losing people can also be emotionally painful.) However, you can "cut your losses" by asking for a commitment. To secure a commitment, three things must be done.

1. *Discuss the nature of the commitment.* The core group must realize the need for a commitment. It's vital to the ultimate realization of the vision. The level of commitment is important as well. The group must make the strongest of commitments to the new work, different from that which they would make to an optional Bible study. Commitment involves the whole family, with both a husband and wife committed to the new church. Commitment will involve their time, talents, and treasure. How much are they willing to give to the new work?

2. *Discuss the areas for commitment.* There must be alignment in several areas. One is ministry alignment. Spend a significant amount of time discussing the DNA (core values, mission, and the vision and the strategy) to accomplish the dream. This should lead to a discussion of what kind of church will be planted. Will it be a seeker-type church, or will it be primarily focused on Christians? If so, what does that mean and what is involved? Consider other topics for discussion such as a commitment to excellence and the structure of leadership. Other areas of alignment are spiritual and doctrinal. Discuss the importance of a commitment to personal, spiritual growth, the doctrinal stance of the church, and the team's position on such issues as the role of women, the place of the sign gifts, divorce and remarriage, and involvement in political issues. There also needs to be emotional alignment. Can you all get along together? And what happens when you disagree? How will you handle disagreements and other problems?

3. *Call for a commitment.* Eventually, both the team and the core group will need to make a decision whether or not to proceed with starting a church together. Both groups may need time to discuss this among themselves. Try to allow some time for this while all are still together. This will provide time in which to answer any questions that may surface. It's possible that both groups will decide to commit to the new work before the weekend is over. Otherwise, more time may be needed to discuss the matter. Take no longer than a week.

If the decision on commitment is affirmative, several things must be done. First, ask who has decided to be part of the core group. Next, ask these people to make a financial commitment and to write on a piece of paper how much. (Finances have a way of surfacing the extent of one's commitment. It's amazing how many people lose interest when finances enter the picture.) Finally, have them complete a commitment card with their names, addresses, financial commitments, and a personal signature.

Before moving on to the next phase, you may want to complete this portion of the Development Stage Worksheet in the Church Planter's Workbook.

Cultivating a Core Group

The potential core group is now an official, committed core group, and the church planting team is ready to move on. What happens next? The second phase of the development stage is to cultivate the new core group in preparation for the birth of the church. This cultivation takes place in three primary areas: *spiritual formation* that's vital to the spiritual development and life of the new church, *ministry implementation* that involves implementing many of the decisions you made during the conception stage, and *ministry administration* that involves the daily operations and functioning of the new ministry. Be aware that the cultivation stage has much in common with pouring cement. Initially you're able to dictate the shape the ministry takes, but it hardens quickly. And once it hardens, it's hard to change.

Forming Spiritually

Spiritual Formation Supports the Birthing Process

Church planting will not happen well without spiritual formation. It will undergird the entire planting process. It's imperative that people develop spiritually from the day that the church begins until it closes its doors. *Initially*, the leadership team must call the core group to spiritual revival and renewal. This sets the tone for the church's future. It encourages all to examine carefully their spiritual walk and to make necessary corrections.

Spiritual Formation's Results in Transformation

The goal of spiritual formation or sanctification is the transformation of each person's life, resulting in the transformation of the entire congregation. (In theological language, we call this personal sanctification. In this case, it's congregational sanctification.) All other change is subordinate to and subsequent to this.

Over the years the church will experience much change as it seeks to better accomplish spiritual growth or formation. Thus we change what we do (ministry forms or methods) not to aggravate or get rid of people, as some suppose, but to enhance the Christ-likeness of our people. In our change strategy, we must communicate and never forget this.

Spiritual Formation Is a Lifelong Process

The following process may prove helpful initially in the spiritual formation of your group. Be sure to modify it to your particular planting situation. Meet together with your people early in the cultivation phase and instruct them in the following (likely you can accomplish this in one meeting of three to four hours). Remember, this is only the beginning of your spiritual development process. It doesn't cease once you've covered point 11. As you work through each point, be sure to read the Scriptures together.

1. Ponder and acknowledge your individual, personal sinfulness (1 John 1:8–10; Rom. 7:14–25).
2. Confess your sins to God (Psalm 51).
3. Forgive those who have sinned against you in some way (Matt. 18:21–22; Eph. 4:31–32; Col. 3:8).
4. Spend time in intense, positive prayer for the church (Matt. 7:7–12; James 5:16).
5. Put off the "negative stuff"—complaining, finding fault, and so forth (Eph. 4:22, 25, 29–32).
6. Pursue reconciliation with an estranged brother or sister (Matt. 5:23–24; 18:15–19).
7. Become a better listener (James 1:19–21).
8. Speak the truth in love—avoid all gossip (Eph. 4:15).
9. Pursue personal, spiritual holiness (Rom. 6:1–15; 12:1–2).
10. Adopt a servant mentality (Phil. 2:3–18).
11. Commit the church to Christ (Matt. 16:18).

Implementing Ministry

After you initiate the spiritual formation process, what's next? You must begin to implement the strategy and its ministries that you developed in the conception stage. You want to focus on the disciple-making portion that consisted of choosing the characteristics of a mature disciple. You've already selected those characteristics; now you begin to implement the ministries under each that the Holy Spirit will use to create those characteristics in the lives of your people.

Mobilizing the Core Group

Assess your people. In addition to spiritual formation, one of the very first things the team must do is assess the people who have committed to being part of the core group in preparation for mobilizing them for ministry. This is an exciting process that answers the question, Whom has God sovereignly brought together? The assessment should be the responsibility of a particular, trained person on the staff team. This person trains another person or several people, who, in turn, serve on a mobilization team.

The team should assess all who make up the core group. This is an assessment of their natural and spiritual gifts, passion, temperament, potential leadership abilities, and any other abilities. My book *Maximizing Your Effectiveness* (Baker Books, 1995) will help you with this assessment. Most likely, assessment will be new to all the people in the group, but it will help all involved become delighted and excited about what God has done in their lives. They will also be anxious and motivated to implement their gifts in a ministry in the new work.

Determine their ministries. Once you know their divine designs, determine your people's potential ministries in the emerging church. Because God is working sovereignly behind this process, you will discover the ministries that you need (whether or not you know it) and those that he wants you to emphasize. As you implement your strategy, you'll determine what those ministries are and move people into them. Scripture is clear that the congregation is to be involved in the church's ministry (Eph. 4:11–12). Thus the mobilization process will continue for the life of the church.

At this point, I encourage you to turn to appendix A. I've developed it to help you with your mobilization ministry.

Implementing the Strategy

Once you've assessed the core group, the team will be ready to implement some of the ministries that will help to develop the characteristics of maturity. Use the strategy implementation process covered in the last chapter (determine actions, formulate priorities, set deadlines, assign responsibility, and conduct MIR meetings).

Design ministries. As you worked on your DNA, you designed a disciple-making process as a vital part of your ministry strategy. The process likely consisted of your determining the characteristics of a mature disciple, such as the three Cs, the four Ws, or some other method you decided works best for you. Now it's time to review and determine the specific ministries that will fit under and implement each characteristic. Again, you should determine these ministries in light of the people God has sovereignly provided. Don't attempt to institute any ministries unless God has provided the people who are gifted to lead and implement them (don't succumb to the idea that something is better than nothing). It is often difficult to find people who are gifted in junior and senior high ministry. If this is the case, you may not be able to have such ministries.

Determine the critical ministries. Several ministries are crucial early in the development stage. One is your small-groups ministry. I suggest you or someone else on the planting team have the expertise to develop and lead this program until you can train a lay group member to take it over. Small-group ministry is so vital to the life of the forming church that you can't wait for someone to come along to lead it. Small groups are vital because they promote the necessary assimilation and growth and they encourage biblical community. There is information on how to develop your small-group ministry in appendix E.

Ministry to children is also critical. Most church planters tend to be married with young children and they attract similar people who are looking for a church that ministers to the whole family. While ministry may not be possible at the junior or senior high level, it should be available at the younger levels.

You may not be able to implement the entire strategy and its ministries up front. That's okay. This may have to wait until the birth stage or later. Do what you can with the people God gives you. Determine which ministries will help the group reach the lost people in their relational community. For example, you might begin a "seeker friendly" Bible study.

Ministry to the core group is essential for its maturing. It will be necessary for the group to meet together for worship and Bible study. There should be a regular weekly meeting of the entire core group that's led by the point person on the planting team. This meeting will eventually become the church's worship service. If the church has a large, well-endowed core group of people, the church's strategy may include a "seeker's service" for the lost and a believer's service for Christians. In this case, the meeting of the core group will become the believer's service. If the strategy is to have only a seeker-friendly service, the core meeting will become that service.

Initially, the corporate meeting will serve to orient the group to the church's DNA, using the Scriptures. It will also include time for worship. It's important that the team's DNA be or become the core group's DNA.

In this meeting, the pastor, as the primary vision caster, will teach on such concepts as the Great Commission vision; a strong servant-leadership; a well-mobilized lay army; a culturally relevant ministry; a holistic, authentic worship; a biblical, culturally relevant evangelism; and a robust network of small groups. I cover all these concepts in-depth in the appendices at the end of this book.

Selecting and Training Lay Leaders

Not enough can be said about the importance of lay leadership to the new church. As your leaders go, so goes the church. The church planting team simply can't lead by themselves. Whether the new church survives and accomplishes its vision will depend on its ability to recruit and equip quality lay leaders.

Recruiting lay leaders. The church planting team should begin to recruit lay leaders as soon as possible. Actually, this process begins at the initial meeting with the potential core group. The team should discern which individuals have already gravitated toward leadership in the group.

The basic requirements for leadership in addition to natural and/or spiritual leadership gifts will be character, vision, and influence, undergirded by the same DNA. Determine which individuals in the group walk with Christ on a consistent basis. Everyone attempts to look good at the first few meetings, but how do they respond when problems and differences of opinion surface? Also, determine who has caught the vision and shares the values. If people do not yet own the vision and values, they're not ready for leadership. Godly leaders who have a vision attract followers.

Training lay leaders. There are several methods for training lay leaders. A good method is to train leaders both corporately and individually. One member of the church planting team, probably the point person, could assume the responsibility for training the leaders as a group. They could meet once or twice a month, emphasizing development in such areas as character (heart work), knowledge (headwork), and skills (handwork). Those on the staff team and leaders in a sponsoring church could disciple the lay leaders, meeting individually once a week. Will Mancini and I have written the book *Building Leaders* (Baker Books, 2004) specifically to help people just like you know how to develop leaders at every level of your church.

The ultimate purpose for recruiting and training these leaders is for service and ministry to the church body (Eph. 4:11–12). It isn't intended to make them members of a powerful governing board (lay elder or deacon board) that makes decisions affecting the direction of the ministry. The church planting team will serve in that capacity and take care of these matters. The lay leaders will be training to lead small groups or various other ministry groups in the church, not to sit on a board or committee. It's most important that this be clarified in the early meetings with the core group before a final commitment is made to start the church.

Initially, you may have an advisory board consisting of people from both inside and outside the church (those with the sponsor church, a denominational representative, a coach, and so on) with the primary role of providing accountability for the staff team. You would be wise to wait until the maturity stage to establish a governing board comprised of spiritually qualified laypeople. When that time comes, select those who have proved themselves by leading well over a significant period of time—one to two years (1 Tim. 5:22).

The emphasis at this point is the training of lay leaders in the growing core group. Also, the birthing team in general and the lead planter in particular need to continue to develop as leaders. Key to the lead planter's development will be a ministry coach with whom he'll meet on a regular basis for spiritual encouragement and ministry knowledge and wisdom.

Designing a Membership Process

As the group grows, you would be wise to set up a membership process. Membership is all about commitment. When new people want to become part of the emerging church, you will need to inform them of what is involved and ask them to make a strong commitment to it. This process is similar to that described earlier in this chapter for gathering the committed core group.

To what will you ask them to commit? They should align with your DNA (values, mission, vision, and strategy) and agree with your doctrines—especially those essential to the faith. You will need to decide where to draw the line on the nonessentials (your position on divorce, women's role in ministry, charismatic gifts, and others). This means that you as the staff leadership team have arrived at a consensus position on these issues prior to or in the conception stage. You should ask them to pray for and reach out to their lost friends and to go through the mobilization process with the intent of committing to a ministry in the church.

Designing a Marketing Strategy

During the development stage, the new church begins to think through its marketing strategy. I want to be careful how I use this term, as it's greatly misunderstood in the Christian community. Church marketing is positioning the church in its community. It has to do with what it wants to be known for—the church's reputation and how that affects God's reputation. Every church has a reputation in its community; it's a matter of knowing what it is and whether it honors God. Theologically, marketing gets at the purpose of the church, which is to glorify God (1 Cor. 10:31; Eph. 1:12, 14; 3:21). You want your church to be a lighthouse for God in the community, representing and presenting him to a lost and dying generation. Marketing helps you work intentionally to accomplish this end.

Effective marketing usually involves understanding the church's DNA, capturing it in a catch phrase and a logo, and communicating it to the church's focus community through various well-designed, attractive pieces of literature and through other means.

You need to decide if you should seek professional help or attempt the marketing on your own. If the team knows very little about marketing, which is often the case, they'll need professional counsel. Some sponsor churches have become creative and innovative in this area and are often willing to help.

Good marketing costs money. There are some techniques that don't cost a lot of money, such as hand delivering a brochure or inviting a friend to attend a service. However, there are a lot of advantages to implementing marketing such as a direct mail program, and this will involve some expense. Consequently, the team and the church will need to decide how committed they are to establishing a good, God-honoring reputation and the degree to which they'll use it as a means to attract unchurched people to the new church. (My view is that it's vital.)

Conducting Preview Services

Some planting churches have found it most helpful to conduct preview services in preparation for the birth stage. A preview service is a worship service or large-group meeting that most (the churched and the unchurched) prefer to attend when first exposed to a church. It is similar to a regular worship service and usually consists of a worship time (singing songs, prayer, communion, liturgy) and a sermon, but it doesn't meet regularly. Preview services take place toward the end of the development stage.

There are multiple purposes for the preview service: building critical mass, weeding out and addressing potential problems, encouraging churched people who are pushing to start the birth stage prematurely, giving people a taste of what's to come, encouraging the launch group to develop relations with lost people, and building momentum and anticipation for going public.

Administering the Church's Affairs

Not only is spiritual formation and leadership important to the new church, but the management and administration of its affairs are also necessary.

Managing the finances. The new church will need to establish a credible, efficient financial control program. This includes such things as establishing the church's financial policies; raising, collecting, recording, banking, monitoring, and disbursing its funds; a budget; and a yearly audit. It's essential that the financial program be squeaky clean. The church must avoid doing anything that might cast doubt on its financial integrity.

Evaluating the team, leaders, and ministries. Evaluation is critical to the growth and improvement of the ministry as we learned in the last chapter. A regular program of evaluation should be implemented by the development stage. The evaluation process should involve those on the church planting team, the lay leadership, and the various ministries of the church. The key is to develop agreed-on job or ministry descriptions and base the evaluations on them.

Monitoring attendance, growth, and finances. According to Luke, numerical growth is a performance indicator of whether the church is making progress toward the accomplishment of its vision (Acts 1:15; 2:41, 47; 4:4; 5:14; and others). The leadership team will need to monitor its attendance, growth, and finances. Records should be kept of who is involved in the ministry and the weekly attendance and any giving at the various ministries. The team should begin to look for patterns in attendance and giving. For example, does attendance and giving go down in the summer but increase in the fall? If so, what can be done to address this pattern?

Naming the church. More than likely, the group will be ready to select a name for the church early in the development stage, if the selection hasn't taken place already. Most people in the core group will want to identify themselves with a name. This will also be necessary if the church decides to incorporate. Names are very important to people, especially to the unchurched. I'll say more about how to select a church name in the next chapter.

Drafting a constitution and bylaws. The constitution presents what the church believes (articles of faith), its DNA, and how it will organize to function as a church. It should also contain a policy on church discipline. Often bylaws address how the church will accomplish its constitution. A planted church would be wise to look to a sponsor church or another newly planted church for examples and samples that will assist it to draft good statements that are in line with local and state regulations.

Incorporating the church and filing for IRS tax exemption. If planting a church in America, the team will need to consider incorporating the church, because it gives the organization the legal right to solicit financial contributions. It's relatively easy—you need to file articles of incorporation with the proper state office (most often the secretary of state). The requirements for incorporation should be available online. Often an attorney or a certified public accountant can provide information and assistance. If finances are limited, ask for help from the mother church or a recently incorporated church in the area. In many states, incorporation protects individuals in the church from any lawsuits that might be brought against the church. You can sue an incorporated church for its assets but not its people for their individual assets.

Also, incorporation or its equivalent is necessary for IRS tax exemption so that contributors can receive tax deductions. You'll find IRS publication *557 Tax-Exempt Status for Your Organization* is most helpful. It describes the forms needed for obtaining tax-exempt status and is available from any IRS office or online at http://irs.ustres.gov.

Locating a place to meet. The group should constantly assess its needs. This involves monitoring attendance and growth to determine if the present facilities are adequate. Project when the church might need to relocate and where, and begin to look for future relocation sites in the focus area.

Preparation of the facilities. Most churches aren't in a position to begin with their own facilities. They'll have to rent the facilities of a school, a business, strip mall, daycare, or some other organization. In most cases, before each meeting, they'll need to arrive early and prepare the facilities for worship, child care, and nurture programs. This requires the efforts of a team of unsung heroes who are willing to come early and stay late to accomplish this task.

Anticipating contingencies. Good and bad things happen to churches. You would be wise somewhere in the development if not in the conception stage to address how you'll deal with these contingencies. Brainstorm what good things could happen to the church (a large gift of money, a celebrity attends the church, sudden growth) and what bad things could affect it (a heart attack during a service, a church split, a false accusation, a serious accident, and others). Decide how you would handle each situation. For example, in case someone had a heart attack during a worship time, you might train the ushers to handle the situation. I've placed some material on my website, www.malphursgroup.com/ChurchPlanting, to aid you with this.

Designing a website. I'm surprised at the number of churches that have a website, because churches are often slow to use technology—either being suspicious of it or thinking they can't afford it. A website is a must if you want to reach postmoderns, because they spend so much of their lives online. Whereas the Boomer seekers would visit a church to see if it was for them, Gen X and Gen Y people will first visit it via its website. And international people will also have access to your site, which creates the potential of reaching them for Christ. Use a website for ministry as well as for information about the church. It can be an effective way to do evangelism, teaching, preaching, fellowship, and a host of other ministries. If you're interested, see a book that Michael Malphurs and I have written on E-ministry: *Church Next* (Kregel, 2003). Should you be interested in website design, contact us through my website.

Planning for the future. The church that doesn't plan for the future may not have a future. Since the development stage prepares the church for the birth stage and beyond, the team must always be thinking and planning ahead. There are numerous factors that must be worked through to birth the new church. At this point, you would be wise to complete the portion of the Development Stage Worksheet in the Church Planter's Workbook that addresses cultivating the core group.

Growing the Core Group

The team has gathered the core group and is cultivating it. The third phase of the development stage is to grow the core group. The term *grow* is used here in the sense of numerical growth—both conversion and transfer growth. The object of the church is to reach people, and this must begin in the development stage. In fact the church will not be ready for the birth stage until it reaches a numerical size that's sufficient to sustain its birth. Church growth researchers refer to this as critical mass. I'll say more about it in the next chapter. Growing the core group involves evangelizing unbelievers and recruiting believers.

Evangelizing Unbelievers

The church's vision and a critical core value should be to reach lost people and unchurched lost in particular. This vision has been used as a means to recruit many of the people who make up the new core group. They're present because they've made a conscious decision to own the new church and what it represents. In their minds, they see their relational community coming to faith in Christ, and they're excited and motivated to get on with it.

Thus the church planting team must strike while the proverbial iron is still hot. Not to act will result in losing valuable momentum toward weaving the direction (mission and vision) into the very fabric of the church. The strategy should accomplish this.

Implement a Strategy for Individual Evangelism

Two things are necessary for individual evangelism. The core group must assume personal responsibility and they must develop an evangelism strategy.

Assume personal responsibility. People in the core group will need to assume personal responsibility for pursuing the lost people who make up their relational community. Preparation for this should begin in the initial meetings following the formation of the core group. Core group members should understand that their relational community consists of their family, workmates, and neighbors. They need to think about the people who make up these communities and make a list of those who may be receptive to spiritual truth. Often it's helpful to draw a family tree, an organizational work chart, or a map of the neighborhood immediately surrounding their houses.

Develop a strategy. Next, they should develop a strategy to reach these people. Here is one:

1. Put responsive people on a "focus or target list."
2. Pray daily for them.
3. Cultivate relationships with these people.
4. Look for times of receptivity to spiritual truth and reach out accordingly.

Initial training will help people discover their individual styles of evangelism. Most laypeople view evangelism as confrontation. Consequently, since many aren't good at confrontation, they don't share their faith. They must become aware that there are other styles and then discover their own natural style if they're to be effective in sharing the gospel.

Implement a Strategy for Corporate Evangelism

Not only will people need to be involved individually in evangelism, but the church or core group needs to be involved corporately. Basically what this means is that the core group will need to have a corporate strategy for evangelism. Most likely, this will involve ways in which the entire core group can assist individuals in their evangelistic endeavors. For example, the church could implement a "seeker-friendly" Bible study as a vital part of its ministry. The pastor or someone on the team could lead this study. This would provide a meeting to which people could invite their lost friends to hear a positive presentation of true Christianity. Later this might develop into a Sunday morning or Saturday night "seeker's service."[3] I've provided you with information in appendix D that will help you design and implement your strategy for evangelism.

Recruiting Believers

The vision of the new church is not to steal sheep from other churches (transfer growth) but to win sheep from the community (conversion growth). At the initial planting, however, the new church will need a group of mature believers as an important part of its foundation. It will also attract some Christians who are unchurched for some reason. So there may be some transfer growth initially. There are basically two sources of mature believers for the new core group.

The Sponsor Church

The first and best source of mature, committed believers is the sponsor church. In fact the best way to plant a church is through the efforts of a sponsor church. The advantages are numerous, one of which is the provision of a core group of people.

Some sponsor churches are so committed to church planting that anyone in their church is subject to being recruited for service in the new church, even the staff. Other parent churches will either train as staff the church planting team or provide staff members to assist the new group with certain vital ministries such as music and youth.

Christian Friends and Acquaintances

Christian friends and acquaintances of the people who make up the core group may also be a source of mature believers. As those who are a part of the group catch the vision for planting the church, they should be encouraged to share the vision with their Christian friends. The result is that others will catch the vision and be attracted to the new church as well.

The problem, most likely, is that these individuals will be part of another church in the community. That church may not be open to the idea of losing its people to a new church, especially if it's plateaued or in decline and hurting financially. Therefore, the new group may be criticized and accused of "sheep stealing." Perhaps one way to defuse this response is to encourage the potential core group members to meet with their pastors and explain what's taking place and why they're getting involved in a different ministry.

I must tack a warning on to all of this. You should be aware that people will attempt to join your launch for the wrong reasons as well as the right ones. Some are disgruntled people who are looking for a pastor and church that they can control so they can "have it their way." Though not many churches enforce discipline, some people may be under discipline at a church for a sin issue, or they should be. This is why you need to be careful about who joins the group. I suggest that you consider some kind of background check. Ask them the last couple of churches they attended. Then call those churches for references. See if the pastor knows and endorses them.

Be sure to complete the last few questions on the Development Stage Worksheet in the Church Planter's Workbook before leaving this stage.

The development stage involves gathering, cultivating, and growing the new core group. Its purpose is to prepare that group for the birth of the church, which is the next stage in the process of church planting. This stage is the subject of the next chapter.

10

It's a Baby!

The Birth Stage

Bill Smith and his team are excited. Things have progressed unusually well. While they've implemented a cold start, Christians in their community have responded enthusiastically to their dream of planting a church to reach the unchurched in the northeastern part of the United States. They quickly gathered a sizable core group of fifty adults and are currently in the stage of cultivating and growing this core group. What thrills Bill most is the fact that these people are inviting their lost friends to a seeker-driven Bible study, where fifteen people have accepted Christ over a five-month period. This would bring the total to sixty-five adults. In addition, the core group has made a strong financial commitment to the new church, which has provided a decent financial package for the team.

Now it's time to ask the questions, Where does the church go from here? What's the next stage of church planting? The answer to these questions is the birth stage. This is the stage where the new church goes "public" with its first meeting. It's at this point that the church is ready to pursue its geographical community (those in the focus area) in addition to its relational community (the friends and acquaintances of its people). The primary purpose of this stage is to provide an opportunity to pursue and reach the geographical community for the Savior. From the perspective of the community, this is where the church is born. Up until this time the community has probably not been aware that there's a new church in the area. Now all that will change. The birth stage consists of the steps that are necessary to prepare for the first public meeting or the "birth event" of the church.

Knowing When to Birth

The growing core group must determine when to birth the church. While much of the development stage is general preparation for the birth stage, the question is, when does the development stage end and the focused preparation for the birth event begin? Most church planting teams will start too soon. People tend not to feel that they're a church unless they're involved in a large-group worship service. Resist this pressure. At least three ingredients make up the answer to the important question of when.

The Elapsed Time

The first ingredient involves the amount of time that has elapsed from the initial gathering of the core group to the birth event. Much depends on whether the church was initiated with a hot or cold start.

The Hot Start

Since the hot start involves gathering a core of committed believers from a group of people who have already come together in some locale for the general purpose of starting a church, the development stage may be relatively short, probably three to six months. This will depend on the amount of time and preparation the planting team puts into the new work during the conception stage and any problems that might surface during the development stage.

In his book *Church Planting for a Greater Harvest*, Peter Wagner essentially agrees with this estimate:

> It takes nine months for a human baby to develop. Experience has shown that this might be a little too long for the nucleus building phase of a new church. If the proper planning is done and a competent feasibility study produced, it is well to plan for a nucleus building phase of four to six months. A longer period might have been called for in the past when we did not have today's know-how. But any church planter who is up-to-date on the field should have the techniques to make it happen in four to six months.[1]

The Cold Start

As we have seen, the cold start involves gathering a core of committed believers in a community where the planting team doesn't have any prior contacts. The team has to raise up an interested group of Christians by making a number of initial contacts in the focus community. This situation can be more difficult and may add several months to the length of the development stage, so it could take three months to a year to get to the birth event. It will take even longer for the "lone wolf" church planter who goes into a focus area and attempts to build a core group with lost people whom he wins to Christ. The "lone wolf" approach is not the best, because New Testament ministry is team ministry and core groups need to be formed with solid, mature believers.

The Number of People

Not only is the amount of time that has elapsed during the development stage an ingredient affecting the birth event, but the number of people who are in the core group is an important consideration as well. Veteran church planters differ as to the ideal number of people.

Ten to Twelve Seed Families

Donald MacNair is a church planter and has written the book *The Birth, Care, and Feeding of a Local Church.*[2] He believes that at least ten to twelve families are needed before a church can proceed with what he calls phase 2, which lasts from nine to twelve months.[3]

This was excellent advice for those who were planting churches in the 1950s through the early 1970s when MacNair wrote his book. At that time, America was a churched culture and it was easier to gather an interested core group of people. Today the culture is predominantly unchurched and post-Christian and people are slower to respond. Consequently, if the core group desires the church to grow and reach a lot of people for Christ, it should wait until it is large enough to attempt the birth event. Most likely, more than ten to twelve seed families will be needed to staff the various positions to make the first public meeting possible.

Fifty to One Hundred Adults

In *Church Planting for a Greater Harvest*, church growth expert Peter Wagner suggests that the church needs to decide at the outset how large it wants to grow. If it desires to grow larger than two hundred people, it should have from fifty to one hundred adults in the core group before it goes public. He writes, "If the long-range plan for the church is to be under two hundred, the critical mass can be as small as twenty-five or thirty adults. However, if the plan is for the church to grow to over two hundred that is too small. The critical mass should be between fifty and one hundred adults."[4]

You must keep in mind that some variables could make a difference in this figure. One is the geographical location of the new church. An urban church plant would require a larger core group, whereas a rural plant might allow for fewer people. Churches that focus on Muslims in North Africa might also allow for fewer people. Wagner indicates that another variable is the group's "collar color." He writes, "There may well be many variables that determine ideal nucleus size, but I am so far aware of only one study. It suggests that for a blue-collar, working-class church you can start near the lower end of the range, but for a professional, white-collar church you do better toward the top part of the range."[5]

More Than Fifty People

Wagner cites some research from the Southern Baptists that indicates that the size of the core group at birth may affect the new church's ultimate survival. He writes, "Research by the Southern Baptist Home Mission Board has shown that Southern Baptist churches going public with under fifty have three times the rate of failure as those that start with over fifty. It wouldn't surprise me if this applied to most other denominations as well."[6]

Jim Dethmer, a former pastor at Willow Creek Community Church near Chicago, says that if you desire to plant a seeker-driven church as Willow Creek has done, you need more than fifty people. He advises that seeker-driven churches need at least one hundred people in the core group, a sizeable church-planting team in place, and from $100,000 to $150,000 in the bank.

The Conclusion

The conclusion from all this information and research is this general rule: *the bigger the better.* Critical mass is essential. If you want to break through the two hundred barrier and other growth barriers (which is the position of this book), you need a minimum of fifty adults before you go public. And the more people you have in the core group beyond fifty adults, the better your chances are of reaching a significant number of lost people for the Savior.

The Right Sunday

A final ingredient that can help in determining when the core group is ready to have its first public meeting is the particular Sunday on which the event will be scheduled. Over the years, it's become evident that certain Sundays on the calendar are better than others for attracting unchurched people from the focus community.

Easter Sunday

Unchurched people are more likely to go to church at certain times of the year. While this may vary from community to community, good times are Christmas, Mother's Day, possibly Father's Day, and Easter. Of these four, one of the best has proved to be Easter Sunday. Many church planters have concluded that if a lost, unchurched person is going to go to church at all, he or she will probably go on Easter. This may be because Easter is observed internationally as well as nationally, and people are given time off from work or school. At this time, the thoughts of many turn naturally to spiritual matters.

Since this is the case in so many communities across America, a good time to have the first public "birth meeting" of the new church is on Easter Sunday. The church planting team should develop a timeline that would determine when they would need to gather the initial core group and the length of time for the development stage if they are to birth the church on Easter. The church could mark Easter Sunday on its calendar and then go back three to six months if it's a hot start or longer if it's a cold start to see when they need to begin.

Perhaps an even better choice for birthing the church is the Sunday before Easter—Palm Sunday. (See my comments later in this chapter under Publicizing the Meeting where I discuss the problem of getting people to return the following week.)

A Special Sunday

If Easter Sunday isn't feasible, another approach is to create a special Sunday and have the birth event on that Sunday. This could take place on practically any Sunday on the calendar, except those covered in the next category. We implemented this strategy at one of the churches I pastored. To give our people an opportunity to invite their lost, unchurched friends to our church, we held two events: a Fall Harvest and a Spring Celebration. We advertised these two events and planned for lots of food, fun, and fellowship. The result was an excitement in the air and many new faces in the pews.

There are numerous other possibilities. For example, some churches feature a Celebration of Friendship Sunday to which everyone brings a person who's a friend and part of their relational community. Other churches might invite a special speaker, such as a radio, television, or sports personality. Some will feature a contemporary Christian music group. Other options would be to honor the local policemen, firemen, military personnel, teachers, and others on a particular Sunday. In fact the only limit on what you can program is your imagination.

Holiday Sundays

While Easter Sunday may be the best time for the first public meeting of the new church, several other Sundays have proved to be the worst times for this meeting. Some of these Sundays fall on holiday weekends. When a holiday falls on a Monday or Friday, the three-day weekend becomes an ideal time to take a trip. Consequently, people often plan to leave town or relax at home. The worst Sundays for the birth event tend to be those that fall near Memorial Day, Veteran's Day, Thanksgiving, and July 4, as well as Super Bowl Sunday.

The Sundays each year that are affected by daylight saving time, when we either set our clocks forward or back, are also difficult Sundays to encourage new people to come to church. Most churches have found these to be low-attendance Sundays.

Choosing a Name

Another step in preparing for the first public meeting is the naming of the church. Many new church starts will do this as early as the conception or development stages. The point here is that if the church hasn't yet selected a name, now is the time to do so.

Some will delay this decision because they don't believe that choosing a name for the church is important. Using one of his characters, Shakespeare once asked, "What's in a name?" The answer in church planting is everything! Enough research has been done to indicate that people, even unchurched people, pay attention to church names. A number of factors should be considered.

The Focus Group

One factor to consider in choosing a name for a church is the focus group or the people whom the church has singled out for evangelism. The setting in which the group and the church are located will influence this.

An Urban Setting

Today denominational labels, such as Baptist, Methodist, Presbyterian, and Episcopal, do not attract people in an urban setting. Whereas denominational loyalty was strong in the 1940s and 1950s, that loyalty had greatly diminished by the 1990s. Some believe that the early twenty-first century is a post-denominational age. People, especially Baby Boomers and Busters, are more interested in what churches have to offer them than in denominational affiliation.

In fact, in some unchurched areas of the country, such as the Northeast, the Northwest, and the West Coast, denominational affiliation can work against a new church. Saddleback Valley Community Church near Los Angeles is a Southern Baptist church. However, many of the people who attend don't know this. One of my students planted a Southern Baptist Church in Washington State. He used "Baptist" in the name but removed it a year later because of the negative effect it had in the unchurched community.

A Rural Setting

What we have just observed about church names in an urban community may be reversed in many rural communities, especially in the South. One of my students wrote a master's thesis on planting churches in rural east Texas. He discovered that people there viewed churches without denominational affiliation as either charismatic or a cult.

The Community

Another factor to consider in choosing a name for the church is the particular community in which it's located. The church may want to use the same name in combination with the term *community*. For example, the Southern Baptist church mentioned above, Saddleback Valley Community Church, is located in the Saddleback Valley area around Mission Viejo, California. Another example is Willow Creek Community Church. The church I pastored was Northwood Community Church.

Using the term *community* was very popular in the 1980s and 1990s across denominational lines. It communicates warmth, is inoffensive in unchurched areas of the country, and imparts a sense of identity with the actual community. However, it's becoming most important that churches with *community* in their name be involved in their community. Today communities are asking churches: What are you contributing to the community?

The Generation

The generation of the focus group can affect the church's name. Builders of the modern generation have identified with denominations. They look for churches named First Methodist Church or First Baptist Church, while Boomers tend not to. They look for names with *community* in them. Some postmoderns have pursued a different track using unique names that include such terms as Mosaic, Sojourn, Journey, Jacob's Well, and Solomon's Porch.

Some Suggestions

If your desire is to reach lost people and unchurched lost in particular, you may want to consult with them regarding a church name. Try putting yourself in their shoes and create names that would attract not distance them. Once you and your people have decided on several names, ask some unchurched lost people which names they would choose and why. This should prove most illuminating.

Keep the name as short as possible. It should be easy to spell and pronounce. An exception might be a name that's commonly known in the area, such as the name of a community or a major road or highway.

Be careful to avoid names that could unnecessarily alienate people. Some names are pejorative.

While there's no reason to be ashamed of what you believe, it's wise not to put your doctrinal statement in your name. For example, avoid names such as Faith Independent Closed Communion Predestinarian Bible Baptist Church, Pentecostal Fire-Baptized Holiness Church, or the First Two-Seed-in-the-Spirit Predestinarian Baptist Church. Most unchurched people don't care what you believe. They care more about who you are and whether you incarnate what you say you believe!

An exception might be some rural areas where pride and tradition are important parts of the people's religious heritage. An example would be the hills and mountains of southern Tennessee where people have historically been Southern Baptists and Freewill Baptists.

Don't use names that may be misunderstood. People who have been Christians for a long time might recognize them, but an unbeliever wouldn't. One example would be the use of the term *Catholic* in the name of a Protestant church, such as Zion Catholic Church or Redeemer Catholic Church. Another example is the use of the term *reform*. Some older people hear this term and the first thing that comes to mind is a reform school—a prison for youthful offenders in the middle of the twentieth century.

Other names that can be misunderstood are Mennonite, Moravian, and, even in some cases, Evangelical Free Church. Not that there's anything wrong with these names! In many cases each has a rich heritage that's traceable back to Europe and a group of Christians who held to the faith in spite of intense religious persecution. Again, the important consideration is how an unbeliever responds to these names. Would some people not come to our church because of the name? In an area of Christian liberty such as the name of a church, we as mature believers must be willing to defer to the lost people we're attempting to reach. If a name would unnecessarily offend or bring a negative response, we must choose something else. There are too many good names not to do so.

One caution about the term *metropolitan*. This term is often used in urban areas in an attempt to include a large number of people. But those naming a church should be aware that there's a group of homosexual churches (Universal Fellowship of Metropolitan Churches—MCC) that commonly uses the name Metropolitan Community Church.

There are some names that have the potential to communicate negative impressions. One example is the term *memorial*, which may be used of a church that's named in memory of a person. The problem here is that it reminds unchurched people of death or even a memorial service for someone who's just died.

Another example is the name of a church that I spotted one day on a drive through rural east Texas. Apparently a Baptist pastor, Paul Powell, who's from that part of Texas, also spotted the same sign. I'll let Paul tell you the story.

> But many of our churches mirror the despair of the age rather than proclaim the hope. I was driving down the highway the other day and saw a sign with an arrow pointed down a country road that said, "Little Hope Baptist Church—3 miles." I thought to myself, My soul, I'm glad I'm not the pastor of that church. If I were, my first action would be to start a movement to change its name. I would have them call it: "Big Hope Baptist Church" or "New Hope Baptist Church," or "Living Hope Baptist Church," or "Coming Hope Baptist Church" or "Everlasting Hope Baptist Church," or "Glorious Hope Baptist Church," or "Flaming Hope Baptist Church"—anything but "Little Hope Baptist Church."[7]

Now to be completely fair to this little church, someone told me that it's located in a small rural community called Little Hope. In this situation, the name doesn't sound so bad except to those who live outside the community of Little Hope. However, in terms of reaching the lost in general, Powell makes the point as he continues the story.

> The only name worse than "Little Hope Baptist Church" would be "No Hope Baptist Church." That's exactly what many of our churches are presenting

to the world today: little or no hope. . . . If we hold up hope, our despairing world can be reached.[8]

Locating a Place to Meet

Along with knowing when to start and choosing a name, the new work will need to locate a place suitable to hold its first public meeting and its subsequent meetings. It could be the same location as that used for the development stage, but it will probably be different to allow for growth.

The Characteristics of a Location

In church planting and church renewal, there are a number of characteristics that should be thought through in terms of site selection. It would be a shame if people avoided a church because of a lack of one of these characteristics. Use them as a checklist to be reviewed quarterly if not monthly.

Appearance

A critical characteristic of a good facility is its appearance. It affects two groups of people.

The core group. A facility's appearance affects congregational self-esteem. Most people view their church and its facilities as a reflection on themselves, and in many ways it is. People intuitively want what they identify with to look good, whether it's their car, house, or church facilities. When they don't, it may indicate that the people themselves are struggling in their present situation. They may have lost their sense of pride and don't care anymore.

Some people in a church with declining facilities get used to leaks in the roof and peeling paint on the walls. They learn to tolerate these conditions. However, others in the church don't. Consequently, when there's a big push to invite their friends to the services, they politely say, "No thanks." They'd be too embarrassed, especially the young people. They don't want their lost friends to see where they go to church. While they may understand, their lost friends wouldn't.

Lost people. The other group who is affected is lost people. Keep in mind that many of today's unchurched lost have high expectations due to the pursuit of excellence in the marketplace and the media. If the facilities are in poor condition, they'll assume people don't care and they won't come, or they'll come only once and reject the message because they reject the facilities.

A good approach in selecting the facility is to see it through "lost eyes." We must ask ourselves: *What would lost people in our focus group expect when they arrive at our church on Sunday morning or Saturday night? If they were responding to a direct mail campaign, would they take one look at our facility and drive back home, or would they stop and come in?*

Visibility

The visibility of the building is a second characteristic that affects location. Can the building be seen? When people drive by, can they see the facility? Sometimes the storefront church simply blends in with all the other storefronts.

What can a church do to gain greater visibility? It should attempt to locate in a place where it's not simply one of many buildings. A location along an expressway is ideal because the building can be seen by all who use that expressway every day. Often a sign will help. It catches people's attention and directs it in a positive way toward the building.

Accessibility

Whereas the second characteristic concerns seeing the building, the third concerns finding the building. How easy is it for people to locate and access the facility? The ideal location would be near a major artery, such as an expressway or a busy road. Then church is both easy to see and easy to locate. While this may appear to be a major obstacle for the new church in terms of cost, keep in mind that at this stage you're renting, not purchasing facilities. Consequently, there's a good chance that you can rent a building, such as a public school or a place in a shopping center, that's quite accessible to the community.

Size

The facility and grounds should be the right size for the vision of the core group. The building must be large enough to hold a significant number of people (one to four or five hundred) who might respond to a mailer. At the same time, if it's too large, people will feel overwhelmed by the facility. They will develop a feeling of insignificance.

Ezra Earl Jones recommends that a church consider locating on three to five acres depending on its growth goals. He believes that three acres are adequate for a church of eight hundred to one thousand members. If it expects to grow larger, then he recommends five acres.[9] Some would argue that this isn't enough acreage. The need to provide adequate parking affects much of this. Consequently, with the ability of telemarketing to attract lots of people and today's transportation-oriented culture where many families have at least two cars, it is preferable to rent a building on approximately three to five acres. Some postmoderns would shun large facilities on a large lot, arguing for more of an emphasis on simplicity and community. They prefer to put their money into people than bricks and mortar.

Why so big when the group is small? The church may stay in rented facilities for three to five years. It is best that it not have to move too many times during this period. The church needs to have enough room for future expansion.

Cleanliness

Cleanliness isn't next to godliness; cleanliness is godliness! Dirty facilities reflect negatively on a congregation. One well-known pastor believes this is so important that not only are the facilities regularly cleaned each week, but nicks and scratches are repaired and painted as well.

There are two areas of the building that need particular attention. They are the nursery and the women's bathrooms. As new parents, one of the first things that my wife and I checked in a church was its nursery. And the number one thing we looked for was its cleanliness. I've heard horror stories of rat droppings on the floors and roaches crawling across soiled linen in the cribs! No parents would want to leave their baby in such a place, and it would be foolish to expect sophisticated unchurched people to do so. Also the women's bathrooms, like the nursery, must be immaculate.

Location

An obvious but often overlooked characteristic of a temporary facility is its location in the community. Someone in the business world once said that the three most important elements for a successful business are location, location, and location! The simple rule in church planting is that you must locate in a building that's in your target community.

The church also needs to take into consideration the location of the people in the core group. While they should be willing to be flexible and perhaps drive a little farther, they shouldn't be inconvenienced. In fact some of the lost people who will come to the new church will be from the core community's neighborhoods—especially if it's a new area.

The church should also be alert to any nuisances in the vicinity. There could be an airport nearby that often diverts its traffic over an area that would make it difficult to hear on Sunday mornings. Also, there could be a pharmaceutical plant or a paper mill nearby that emits noxious odors. The way to find out about these possible problems is to ask people who live or work in the area near the building under consideration.

Potential Ministries

When considering a facility, you must ask how conducive it would be to the planned ministries of the church. A building should be evaluated in terms of its possibilities for a nursery, classrooms, and worship. Every church must have a nursery for infants and small children. Is there a room that could function well as a nursery? Does it look and smell clean, and would it be easy to keep clean? Churches must also provide some rooms for Christian education. People are most concerned about what kind of education their children are getting in church. They often decide for or against a church on this basis. Finally, is there adequate space for congregational worship? Will people be able to see and hear well? Are the lighting and acoustics adequate?

Cost

Sometimes churches fail to take into account all the expenses involved in renting and using a building for their meetings. They may look at the rental costs alone and fail to anticipate other costs. For example, what will the utilities cost? What is an adequate amount of insurance? What renovations will be necessary to prepare the building for church services? Is the sound system adequate? Will cribs, tables, chairs, and other items have to be purchased? All of these factors—and more—must be taken into consideration.

Storage

Another characteristic that church planters may overlook is adequate storage space. Often churches are started in buildings such as schools, where folding chairs, cribs, portable signs, and tables must be put away after the services are over. If adequate on-site storage is not available, what does the church do? Usually facilities have some room for storage; however, it's best to discuss this with the landlord and reach an agreement before moving into the facility. Some landlords have a way of dragging their feet after a contract has been signed.

Should there be no on-site storage space, there are some other alternatives. One is to obtain permission to place a small portable building on the site. Another would involve the purchase of a vehicle such as a mid-size truck, which could be used for storage and to transport the contents to the building each Sunday. Of course, either alternative would involve additional cost to the new church.

Signage

Not only is it important to advertise the church, but it must have some way of identifying itself visually in the community, if not during the week, then at least on Sunday mornings. One of the ways most churches do this is with a sign.

Build a sign. For your temporary facility, build a collapsible wooden sign. In my first church plant, we put together two four-by-eight-feet sheets of plywood with hinges at the top and legs at the bottom. A sign painter volunteered his time, and we had a sign. On Sunday mornings, we simply lifted it out of storage and placed it in front of the building where we met. After the service, it was stored until the next Sunday.

Purchase a sign. You could also purchase a vinyl or canvas sign. Most sign shops have the capability to produce these at a reasonable price. There are several advantages. The first is storage; all you have to do is carefully roll it up. You could even keep it in the trunk of someone's car. Another is placement. You can place signs anywhere. Some churches mount the canvas on two poles and put the sign out by the road so everyone who passes by sees it. Others will hang it over the existing sign on the building in which they're meeting. For example, if it's a school, on Sunday morning, place the vinyl sign over the school sign so that, in effect, their sign becomes your sign for the morning or evening.

Parking

Another factor to consider is parking. The size of the entire facility and grounds should be big enough to include adequate parking. Sometimes those in the target group may drive two or even three cars to church on Sunday morning: his, hers, and the kids! If people can't find a place to park their cars, they'll not attend the church. Most will drive through the lot, and if no parking spaces are available, they'll return home. Some people are nervous and are looking for reasons to talk themselves out of coming to church. Let's not make it easy for them by failing to provide adequate parking!

Sometimes the best facility doesn't provide adequate parking. Several alternatives exist for facilities with small parking lots. Ask the core group to park in the remote areas and leave those spaces close to the building for guests. Or ask core group families to come in one car and park it in a lot adjacent to or near the facility. Finally, the core group could park some distance from the building, and a van could shuttle people back and forth.

Reputation

Another important characteristic of a good location is the facility's reputation in the community. You may question this one, so I must tell you a story. When I first accepted Christ in college, I attended a new, small church that was located in a rented facility that obviously had been built originally for a church. This new church didn't grow, and hardly anyone in the neighborhood came to any of the services. Later we learned that every bizarre religious group that had come to town had rented and used this facility. The neighborhood was suspicious of us for good reasons.

Before renting a facility, especially a former church building or a public community center that's located in a neighborhood, ask the people living near the building about its past history and occupants. Some locations are haunted by the "ghosts of Christmas past," to borrow a line from Charles Dickens.

The Prospects for a Location

One of the questions that all church planters need to ask is, What are some potential places where our church could meet until we find a permanent facility? There are several possibilities, all of which are affected by the church's vision, strategy, and focus group.

A School Building

In *44 Questions for Church Planters*, Lyle Schaller indicates that public schools are one of the three most commonly used temporary places for new mission churches in spite of resistance from some school boards.[10] The church plant could use a public or private elementary, junior high, or high school. It might also consider a community college or university facility.

The reason for this is obvious. Most schools are set up to provide the various facilities that a church needs. There's usually an auditorium for large-group congregational worship and lots of classroom space for a Christian education program. However, there are some disadvantages to using a school building. One is that some school districts will allow the church to use their facilities only for a limited period of time, often one year. Another is that the church will not be able to use the building during the week. This results in having to set up and take down certain things each week, such as chairs, cribs, or a sound system. Also it could mean renting other facilities for office space during the week at extra cost to the church.

A Church Building

Another possibility is using or renting a church building.[11] A number of ethnic church plants meet on Sunday afternoons in an existing church's facilities. If the existing church is the mother church, then there may be no cost involved for the daughter church.

Another possibility is to rent the facilities of a church such as the Seventh Day Adventists who meet on Saturdays. There are several advantages to this approach. One is the available facilities, such as the nursery, auditorium, and classrooms. Others would be the advantages of parking and a sound system. Some disadvantages could be a possible bad reputation in the neighborhood on the part of the church that owns the building, a location that's not close enough to that of the focus group, the design of the building itself, and a poorly maintained facility.

A Public Center

Public centers include recreation centers, community centers, or day care centers. These centers usually are very open to renting their buildings or rooms to churches, especially those that are privately owned. Also most people in the community are aware of their locations.

There are some disadvantages. Often public facilities are difficult to clean and maintain. Each group that rents the facility may be responsible to clean up after themselves; consequently, the facility may be poorly cleaned if at all. Also, these centers are not always set up conveniently for the church in terms of a place for a nursery and a large-group meeting. In addition, there may be inadequate parking space, and the church might have to purchase its own sound system.

A Storefront

Often a good choice for the location of the new church is a storefront, especially one that's located in an inner-city area or a shopping mall in the center of the focus community. These malls are usually frequented by young and old alike. They provide the church with lots of visibility in the area because of the location and because the church has use of the facility during the week as well as on weekends. The church could minister to the community by offering special programs during the week, such as counseling services or a neighborhood crime watch. The only disadvantage might be the cost.

A Movie Theater

Another good option is a movie theater, which would provide an auditorium with a stage, screen, and sound system already in place. Also, theaters are often located in shopping malls where there's high visibility and lots of parking. Schaller notes that some theaters contain several rooms of different sizes that can be used as the church grows larger.[12] The disadvantages are the lack of space for a nursery and a Christian education program. Also, the new church would not have the use of the facility during the week, and its time of use would be limited to Sunday mornings prior to the start of the first show.

Several churches have used theaters in the past. One example is Willow Creek Community Church. One of its early meeting places was in a theater in Palatine, near Chicago.

One of my friends has begun a church in an older, well-known fine arts theater located near a university in the downtown area of Denton, Texas. They call the new church Sunday Morning on the Square. They've cleverly used this location in all their advertising to attract the unchurched in the community. For instance, one of their mailers looks like a piece of film and contains the following: "If life has you feeling like a rebel without a cause, check out the new feature at the Fine Arts Theater." Another says, "If your life's dreams seem to be gone with the wind, check out the new feature at the Fine Arts Center."

Other Possibilities

New churches have sometimes used parachurch facilities, hotels, motels, bank buildings, coffee shops, restaurants, pubs, YMCAs and YWCAs, and funeral homes. Each of these has both advantages and disadvantages. Perhaps the most questionable facility is the funeral home. On the one hand, they have some excellent facilities for congregational worship because so many have chapels. On the other, the idea of meeting in a funeral home could discourage a significant number of unchurched people who are looking for an excuse not to attend. However, a clever marketing ministry in the church might be able to use a location in a funeral home to the church's advantage, much as the Denton church plant used the fine arts theater.

Some postmodern churches that celebrate the arts have met in art studios, theaters, restaurants, and other similar establishments in the arts district of their city.

Publicizing the Meeting

If the new church is going to have an impact for the Savior in its focus community, it will have to make its presence known to that community. A fourth step in preparing for the birth event is publicizing the meeting. Far too many established churches fail to make their presence in the community known to the unchurched. They assume people know they're there. Of course, for a church plant, which doesn't as yet own a permanent facility for people to drive by, it's particularly important that they let people know they are there.

This is where marketing and advertising come in. The primary purpose of marketing during the birth stage is to encourage and help a church with an "invasion mentality" to reach to its community. There are two primary ways to accomplish this.

Reaching the Geographical Community

The first and primary way is to publicize the church in its geographical community. To accomplish this, the church will need to have a strategy and a method.

The Strategy

The church planting team is already aware of the importance of publicizing the new plant in the target community and has made a decision to do so in the conception stage. Early in the development stage, the team will need to develop a strategy as to how the new work will publicize itself in the community.

The problem. One of the problems experienced by churches that have adopted the birth event approach is a sizable drop-off factor. They spend a lot of money advertising the opening day event, and a considerable number of unchurched people in the community show up. The problem is that a significant number, as many as one-third to one-half and even more, don't come back the following Sunday![13] Stetzer notes that the typical church plant averages 50 percent of the launch attendance one month later.[14]

The people who fail to return haven't been offended by the gospel or the sermon. Rather, they simply aren't in the habit of going to church! That's one of the reasons why they're unchurched! Those with a herd mentality who do return the following Sunday wonder what happened to all the people, and they may not come back the third Sunday.

Some solutions. The team must develop a strategy that encourages people to return. One strategy that doesn't work is to attempt each Sunday to top what took place the previous Sunday. For example, "We had a great day last Sunday, but wait until you hear who'll be here next Sunday!" This appeals to the wrong motives, and it's just a matter of time before the entire strategy crashes.

Rather than pour all of its efforts into one meeting on the first Sunday, the church should focus attention on the first three or four Sundays. An example of one church that did this is Kensington Community Church near Detroit. On the first Sunday, the church attracted people in the community through newspaper ads and a direct mail campaign. But it didn't stop there. Early in the following week, it passed out numerous brochures in the target community located around the church's facility publicizing the next Sunday. Finally, the church asked their core group to invite the people in their relational communities to come on the third Sunday. To some degree this helped minimize the drop-off problem.

Another technique is to encourage people who visit to return on the following Sunday. There are several ways to accomplish this. One is to invite them verbally to return next Sunday. At the end of the service, you could say, "If you enjoyed the service today, and God used the message to touch your life, then why don't you come back next Sunday?" You might add the following: "If you think you might need a reminder, then leave us your phone number on the card in your bulletin, and we'll give you a quick call on Friday or Saturday."

Another method is to preach a short series of sermons on a highly relevant, need-oriented biblical topic. The first Sunday you begin the series and invite everyone to come back for the second part in the series. Perhaps you could leave something hanging at the end of the sermon that will be resolved the next Sunday. You could work in a story that raises a conflict that will be resolved the next week. This might also be accomplished with drama.

An additional technique is to celebrate the birth event on Palm Sunday, one week before Easter. The very fact that the following Sunday is Easter may encourage the unchurched to return. You could remind them that next Sunday is Easter and encourage them to come back for the second part of the series of sermons you've just begun.

The Method

Once the team has developed a strategy, it will need to decide on the methods it will use to implement the strategy. Some methods to accomplish the strategy of bringing people back on successive Sundays are newspaper ads, a direct mailing, and a hand-delivered brochure.

The two methods that seem to have reached the greatest number of people in the past are direct mail and telemarketing.

Direct mail. Some favor using direct mail because it doesn't require a large core group and it can be screened demographically. The church could send a letter to the community or pass out a brochure about the church or a birth announcement similar to the type parents send out to announce a new baby. One great disadvantage is the cost of direct mail. Another is the possibility that the post office may not deliver the mail at the right time.

Telemarketing. The team might prefer to use telemarketing instead of direct mail. Norm Whan's The Phone's for You! has been out there the longest. Another is Tellstart, which is an automated calling system and mailings that some have used successfully. George Thomasson has a most helpful section in *The Church Blueprint* on how to conduct a telemarketing campaign.[15] Key factors in deciding to use telemarketing are the cost, the community, and the core group.

If the new church isn't able to reduce the costs of a telemarketing program by the use of a phone bank or a significant discount from a printer, then the program may not be cost-effective.

Some communities have been over-telemarketed. Thus people in these areas don't respond well to a phone call, especially if it comes during the evening meal. They view it as an invasion of their privacy.

The core group may not be large enough to make all the calls necessary if they attempt it on their own. The average response to a telemarketing campaign is one person per one hundred or more calls. Consequently, if the church's goal is to have two hundred people at the first service, it will have to make twenty thousand–plus phone calls. If a group of volunteers could make one thousand calls in an evening, it would take twenty evenings to make all the necessary calls. A small group of people would quickly burn out in attempting to accomplish this.

Another concern is recent technology that allows a growing number of people to use caller ID, which allows them to identify and block incoming calls. The general dislike for telemarketing on the part of the public has resulted in legal restrictions on the telemarketing industry as a whole. The Federal Trade Commission is involved, and the public can now register on a do-not-call list. There are some loopholes for political organizations, pollsters, and charities, but all isn't clear at this point. These drawbacks along with the public's growing antagonism toward telemarketers have limited its effectiveness.

Advertising in the newspaper is another favorite method for publicizing the church in the focus community. The ad would need to be placed in the part of the paper that the focus group reads. Cost would also be a factor. However, it's possible that the local paper would feature a story on the church and run it the week prior to the birth event. This would be free publicity. The article should appear in some place other than the religion section of the paper if you're targeting lost and/or unchurched people—they tend not to read the "church page."

Reaching the Relational Community

While the primary emphasis is usually placed on reaching the geographical community, the church may use the birth event to reach its relational community as well. In this case they will also need a strategy and a methodology. Now is a good time for core group people to invite those in their relational communities (family, coworkers, and neighbors) to visit the church.

The Strategy

An important part of the church's strategy for reaching unchurched lost people is to encourage its core group to pursue their lost friends. The church can't reach its focus community simply by using a direct mail or telemarketing approach alone. The people who make up the church must develop significant relationships with those in their relational communities. Some churches use this approach as the primary means for contacting and reaching lost people. In fact it's the best approach for long-term results. Most churches use a mailer or telemarketing approach at the beginning, but eventually use these strategies less as they grow. The one approach that can be used throughout the life of the church is individual members reaching their relational communities.

Early in the development stage, the church planting team will need to impart the vision and promote a passion for reaching nonchurched lost people. Next, they'll need to help the core group develop a strategy that focuses on those who make up their relational communities. These are the most natural prospects for evangelism and the easiest to reach. A good approach is to examine the relational community, develop a "target or focus list," pray for those on the list, cultivate a relationship with them, discover their needs, and look for times of receptivity. All of this could culminate with an invitation to the "birth event." Appendix D will help you think through and develop this strategy.

The Method

The launch group can use various methods in developing significant relationships with the lost people in their communities. It's important that lost people see what we believe by our lives as well as hear about it from our mouths.

Mutual participation. One way to develop relationships is doing things together. Our tendency is not to spend any time with lost people because their lifestyles are so different from our own. We simply don't feel comfortable around them, so we avoid them as much as possible. The core group will need to get over this and pursue and spend time with these people. They should do things together, like jogging, aerobics, cooking, sewing, traveling, and dining.

Open homes. Another method is to invite these people into our homes for coffee or to share a meal together. This could be preliminary to doing other things together. They would be able to use this time to discover what they have in common and might enjoy doing together. The conversation might go like this: "Bill, you enjoy playing golf? Well, so do I. Let's get out and hit some balls together. What are you doing this Saturday?"

Other methods. Some other methods involve helping people in the community during times of personal need, involvement in mutual events such as neighborhood cleanup, or inviting them to an informal Bible study or MOPS event at your house. Pastor Steve Sjogren describes more than three hundred such events in his book *Conspiracy of Kindness.*[16] Actually, the only limit to these methods is the creativity of the core group.

An approach that I've found to be most effective with postmoderns is prayer evangelism. When I'm around them and others as well, I listen for things that I can pray about for them—good or bad. I ask their permission to pray for a specific situation and then do so daily until I connect with them again. I ask how the situation is progressing and mention that I've prayed for them daily. This surprises them. They often respond by telling me about their spiritual journey and by asking me questions about mine. I use this as an opportunity to share the gospel. One reason it's effective with postmoderns is that they can't accuse me of pushing my faith on them (a common response)—they're the ones pursuing the discussion of spiritual matters.

Planning the Meeting

The first meeting and the ensuing meetings are so important that you should plan them carefully. While this may not be the last step, it must be one of the steps in the birth stage. This is because first impressions are lasting impressions. Your planning should focus on at least four areas: the service, facility, nursery, and children's ministries.

Focus on the Service

The team and the core group should put extra effort into planning the service, because the Sunday morning worship service is what most people in the community will attend. It will serve as the litmus test as to whether they'll come back to the next meeting.

The sermon. The sermon must be a word from God that addresses the audience in terms of its felt needs. It must also be relevant and interesting. It could be the first of a three- or four-part series. An example would be the three-part series "Dealing with the Three Deadly Emotions: Stress, Anger, and Depression." The first sermon would be entitled "The Solution to Stress." The second would be "How to Defuse Your Fuse," and the last one "How to Defeat Depression." Such sermons should be based squarely on the Scriptures and can serve as hooks to bring people back next Sunday as well as address their spiritual needs.

The worship. The worship must be done well. Good musicians and vocalists from the core group or a parent church should be included in the service. Because of the importance of this first meeting, a professional musician could be invited to perform. The degree to which this event is targeting lost, nonchurched people (seeker-driven) will determine audience participation. Most unchurched people aren't used to singing and come more to "check things out" than to worship. (Note, however, that David viewed worship as an opportunity to reach others—Ps. 40:3; 57:9—and Paul did as well—1 Cor. 14:22–25.) Consequently, most of the singing could take place up front and be performed by accomplished vocalists. Be sure to consult appendix C as you plan and implement your worship service.

The drama. Like the music, if you choose to use drama, it should be performed well. The use of a good four- to six-minute mini-drama to introduce the sermon will surprise and delight most unchurched people. The worship team should rehearse several times with everyone present, including the sound person.

Don't try to do too much in the service. The more you attempt, the greater the likelihood that something will go wrong. A few events done well are better than many events done poorly.

The greeters. Locate greeters in at least two places. Some could stand in the parking area and direct people to the front entrance of the building. Keep in mind that they are the first people associated with the church whom the guests will see. They must smile and be friendly. If the crowd is large enough, they may need to direct traffic. Other greeters should stand at the entryway to the building where they smile, shake hands, greet people, hand out bulletins, and give directions. It would be most helpful if several people are available to take parents with infants and young children to the nursery.

Focus on the Facility

Everyone should make a special effort to arrive early. Make sure the facility is spotless. If you anticipate a problem, bring some cleaning equipment. Check out the auditorium, the bathrooms, and the nursery. Also, determine how well the sound equipment is functioning. The service depends to a great degree on everything operating well. A lot of failures during the worship service are due to faulty audio and video equipment.

Determine if you can use the facility in some way to enhance the birth event. For instance, if the facility has a foyer, it's a nice touch to serve coffee and possibly a snack there. Station some people where coffee is being served, so they can meet guests and answer their questions about the church and its programs. Having an information booth or table in the foyer is also helpful.

Finally, be prepared for any facility emergencies. Chances are good that something will go wrong!

Focus on the Nursery

You want to reach young couples because they're the future of Christianity as well as the church, and most of them will have small children. Therefore, you have no choice but to provide a nursery for their kids. You began planning for this in the development stage, but it's just as important in all the following stages in general and the birth event in particular. Remember that parents will be paying close attention to the condition of the nursery. They'll be asking themselves questions such as, *Is the nursery clean? Is the nursery safe? Do they have enough workers to watch all the kids? Are the workers friendly and do they love children? Do I feel good about leaving my infant or child here while I'm in the service?* If you have a registered nurse in the church, ask that she or he be available or even serve in the nursery. Also, advertise her or his presence so that couples are aware of it. It will make a significant difference in their attitude about leaving their child in the care of the nursery.

Focus on Children's Ministries

I can't emphasize enough the importance of children's ministries in church starting. If the church has a Christian education program that will be advertised and attended by the children of unchurched couples, plan to do more than just babysit them. It's important that children have classes specifically designed for them. The church will look ridiculous if it advertises programs for all the family but can't provide for children. Whether or not the family returns the following week may depend on how well their children liked the classes. Often parents ask their children three questions: "Did you like it?" "Did you learn anything?" "Do you want to go back?"

Make sure that your children's ministry is served by warm, caring people. Today it's imperative that you perform a criminal background check on those who work with children. Child abusers often prey on unsuspecting churches. We worry about someone objecting to such a check; however, those who have nothing to fear will understand the wisdom of it. If a person objects to such a check, I would not use him or her in the children's ministry (as Shakespeare said in one of his plays: "The lady doth protest too much, methinks"!).

Some church planters conclude that once they've completed the birth stage they're no longer in the planting stage. Yet there is a fourth stage in church planting—the growth stage. It's essential that churches that want to influence a significant number of unchurched lost people in their target community focus on growth following the birth stage.

Before you move to the growth stage, turn to and complete the Birth Stage Worksheet in the Church Planter's Workbook.

11

Feed Them and They Grow!

The Growth Stage

"Three hundred people actually showed up at our first meeting!" exclaimed Robert Andrews, one of the new church's promising lay leaders. "I expected a decent crowd, but not that many people."

It wasn't that anyone doubted that God could do it. The question was would he do it for them? But it happened. The new church sent out thirty thousand mailers and three hundred people from the focus community responded—approximately 1 percent. Nobody could believe it! Nobody, that is, but Bill Smith and the church planting team. The team and a number of lay leaders had gathered together at a restaurant after the birth service for a late lunch to celebrate what God had done. There was a lot of backslapping and handshaking. Everyone was smiling. A sense of divine destiny hung in the air, a feeling that God was going to do something spiritually significant in the community through these people in this church.

The core group had grown from sixty-five to ninety people. Some were Christians who came because they liked the vision. They had lots of lost friends whom they wanted to see come to Christ. Some were lost people who accepted Christ through the ministry of the seeker's Bible study.

These ninety people launched the first public meeting of the church and were simply delighted at the response. They were aware that not everyone would be back the following Sunday; yet they anticipated another good crowd because it would be Easter Sunday, and many of their unchurched friends indicated they would come for Easter. But what would happen after Easter? The church was off to a good start in the community, but what would sustain its spiritual and numerical growth? What would keep it from plateauing at around two hundred people?

The next stage in the church planting process is the growth stage. When I use the term *growth*, I'm talking about both spiritual and numerical growth. While numerically growing churches may not necessarily be spiritually healthy, with few exceptions most spiritually healthy churches are growing numerically. Numerical growth isn't the goal or mission of a Great Commission church. However, it's the by-product of most spiritually healthy, biblically functioning Great Commission churches according to Acts.

You must understand from the very outset that leaders in general and church planters in particular can't make a church grow. That is God's work. The biblical principle is that some will plant and others will water, but God makes churches grow (Matt. 16:18; Mark 4:26–29; 1 Cor. 3:5–7).

The growth stage is a critical time in the church's life that will determine its ultimate size in terms of numbers. The church will either reach a certain level—the two hundred barrier—and plateau, or it will push through this barrier and continue to grow. There are certain growth factors that church planters and their teams should be aware of that will help their churches continue healthy growth and minimize growth inhibitors. This chapter covers six of these church growth factors. Based on my awareness of the various growth plateaus, I have intentionally implemented these growth factors in the earlier stages to anticipate such plateaus. This chapter isn't meant to be an exhaustive treatise on church growth. The goal is to cover four of the more important church growth principles and two that may be overlooked. All six are important to planted churches.[1]

Leadership for Growth

Leadership is a critical factor for growing churches, whether newly planted or established. Leadership includes not only the senior pastor but the church planting team and the church's lay leadership as well. Leadership begins with the senior pastor or point person on the team. If this individual isn't in favor of growth, it simply will not happen. What kind of point people will encourage growth?

Gifts

Several spiritual and natural gifts facilitate growth, and they're found in most pastors of growing churches.

Leadership. The first is the gift of leadership (Rom. 12:8). Peter Wagner writes, "I have observed that pastors who tend toward being leaders, whether or not they also are administrators, will most likely be church growth pastors."[2] Leaders have vision that provides a sense of direction and the motivation to move in that direction.

Not only do these pastors have the gift of leadership, but they are also strong servant-leaders. They do not work under a lay elder or deacon board but lead these boards as a leader of leaders. That's why they are point persons. Lyle Schaller has made the same observation: "The pastor must be willing to accept and fill a strong leadership role and serve as the number-one leader in the congregation."[3]

Faith. Another spiritual gift is faith (1 Cor. 12:9). This gift is not exactly the same as vision but it enhances the visionary capacity of Christian leadership. Wagner believes that faith is so important to church growth that he devotes an entire chapter to it in *Your Church Can Grow.*[4] Faith helps pastors want the church to grow and believe that it will. Faith overcomes the fear of failure and helps pastors take risks for Christ's kingdom.

Evangelism. A third gift is evangelism (Eph. 4:11). Obviously a person who strongly desires to see lost people come to the Savior and works to this end will grow churches. Not only will such leaders reach lost people, but in church planting situations they will exert a strong influence and encourage others to do the same. Their example is infectious!

Communication. My experience is that most pastors of growing churches have a communication gift, whether preaching or teaching (1 Tim. 1:11). They're good communicators, and people respond to their ability to communicate Scripture well.

Strategy. I have also noted that church growth pastors tend to be strategic thinkers. This is more a natural than a spiritual gift. They have the ability to think ahead and not only anticipate needs but come up with fresh, creative ways to address those needs. For example, they're not only aware that their churches are growing but have thought ahead about how to address future growth problems.

Passion

I commented on passion earlier in this book. Your passion is what you care deeply and feel strongly about. Church leaders will have a passion for something. Usually it's preaching and teaching Scripture. Lyle Schaller and others of us who are consultants have noted that church growth pastors seem to have a passion for the Great Commission as well. They care deeply about seeing lost people come to faith and saved people grow in their faith.

Temperament

As with spiritual gifts, there are certain temperament types that are found in many of the pastors of growing churches. Peter Wagner observes in *Leading Your Church to Growth*:

> The fifth and final limitation on how strong a given pastor's leadership role can be is highly personal. It depends on the temperament of the pastor himself or herself. Some pastors are take-charge people, and some could never bring themselves to take charge. . . . I myself feel that each of us needs to regard ourselves as a product of God the Creator. He has not created every pastor for pastoring a large, growing church.[5]

Church growth pastors tend to display similar patterns on both the *Personal Profile* and the *Myers-Briggs Temperament Inventory*.

The *Personal Profile*. Leaders who go out and plant churches or help established churches grow significantly are usually high *D*s in combination with a secondary *I*, or they are a high *I* in combination with a secondary *D*.[6]

D type persons like to get immediate results, love a challenge, and are catalytic. They tend to be quick decision makers who question the status quo, usually take authority, and are good at managing trouble and solving problems. They are risk takers who are task oriented and are upfront, out front kinds of people.

Individuals who are *I* types like to be around people, and are articulate and motivational. They tend to generate lots of enthusiasm, enjoy participating in a group, and genuinely desire to help other people. They are very people oriented, and, like the *D* profile, they are risk takers who don't like the status quo and are upfront, out front people.[7]

There are some other potential combinations that characterize growth pastors. These would be either a high *D* or a high *I* in combination with either a secondary *S* or *C*. While these aren't as strong as the *D-I* combination, they show an inclination toward growth. Those who are high *S* or *C* tend not to function as well at leading churches to growth but work better on a team led by a high *D* or *I*.

The *Myers-Briggs Temperament Inventory*. Those who are strong church growth pastors usually show either an *NT* or an *NF* on the MBTI profile.[8] The *N* indicates a preference for intuition. These people are visionary and tend to focus on the future and the exciting possibilities that the future holds. The *T*s show a preference for making decisions based on logic and objective analysis, whereas the *F*s prefer to make decisions based primarily on values and people-centered concerns. Extroverts (*E*) also have an edge on introverts (*I*). What all this means is that leaders with the *NT* or *NF* pattern should be in the point position on the ministry team if the team wants the church to grow and reach people.

This type of person should not be an afterthought. He or she must become the team leader at the very beginning of the process—in the conception stage. The field of church growth has been very helpful in discovering what kinds of pastors grow churches. The problem is that this information comes too late for many churches. They already have a person in place who doesn't have the temperament for growing a church, and it's already plateaued. Church planting allows us the luxury of starting with these kinds of people.

Now that we understand what kinds of leaders God has "wired" for growing churches in terms of their gifts, passion, and temperament, we need to examine what they do. Such leaders function as ranchers more than shepherds.

The Shepherd

Our culture has deeply affected how pastors function in the church. Over the years, a particular model has emerged that has influenced the typical role of the North American pastor. This role is that of a pastoral caregiver in a small flock of people. Consequently, most traditional churches expect their pastor to visit church members in the home and the hospital, marry couples, bury those who die, and preach sermons on Sunday morning.

As ironic as it may seem, this is actually an unbiblical model that encourages churches not to grow. After you get over the shock of what you just read, consider the following. First, where do you find this model in the Bible? Second, the pastor or shepherd of a flock of sheep (on which the biblical term is based) was first a leader who functioned in a number of ways (to feed, protect, discipline, and so on), only one of which was that of pastoral caregiver. Actually, the term *shepherd* is equivalent to that of *leader*.[9] The reason that it limits growth is that pastors who are wired as pastoral caregivers prefer to minister to most of their people in person than delegate this to others. As the church grows, they're limited in the number of people that they can care for, so they tend either to discourage new growth or burn out.

While there's nothing wrong with providing pastoral care (as long as that's not all a pastor does), how does a pastor in a church of two thousand accomplish it? The simple answer is that it's impossible! The reality is that churches with this kind of pastor rarely break through the two-hundred-member barrier and most have fewer than one hundred people, because one person cannot give care effectively to more than one hundred people. There simply aren't enough hours in the day!

The Rancher

Those who pastor larger, growing churches serve as leaders. They function primarily as ranchers in relation to the rest of congregation. In *Leading Your Church to Growth*, Wagner summarizes this role: "in a church led by a rancher the sheep are still shepherded, but the rancher does not do it. The rancher sees that it is done by others."[10] (Note that here Wagner falls into the habit of using the term *shepherd* for the pastoral caregiver.)

Several characteristics distinguish ranchers from pastoral care-providers in growing churches:

1. Ranchers primarily minister *through* people and train them to do the work of the ministry. Pastoral caregivers minister *to* people, and they attempt to do the work of the ministry.
2. The rancher has a broad view of ministry, and sees it as involving leadership and other functions as well as pastoral care. The pastoral caregiver limits ministry primarily to pastoral care along with preaching and teaching.
3. Ranchers believe that God wants people to minister in the body of Christ because they're capable of doing so. Caregivers believe that they are the most qualified to minister in the church. Most people aren't capable of serving others in the church because they haven't attended seminary.
4. Ranchers believe that they are dispensable in the sense that if they become incapacitated, they have trained others to carry on the work of the ministry (Eph. 4:11–12; 2 Tim. 2:2). Care-providers make themselves indispensable. If they become incapacitated, the church struggles without them.
5. Ranchers realize that they can't control all that takes place in the church; thus their leadership is characterized by a decentralized power. Caregivers feel they must have a say in all that takes place in the church; consequently, their leadership is characterized by a centralized power.
6. Ranchers prefer to be on the visionary leading edge of what's taking place in ministry, whereas care-providers prefer the status quo.

Vision for Growth

If a new church is to grow, then the people who make up the church, and its lay leaders in particular, must have a strong vision for spiritual and numerical growth. If they don't want the church to grow, then it doesn't matter who the pastor is or what the pastor does. It simply will not happen.

Negative Growth Factors

There are a number of negative growth factors associated with people in established churches that have prevented these churches from experiencing any substantial numerical growth. Three of these factors are fairly common. They are presented in the context of church planting so that the church planting team will be aware of them and prevent them from surfacing in the new church. Should they surface, then the team will recognize them quickly and deal with them before they cause any damage.

A Family Atmosphere

The first common negative factor is the desire to maintain a family atmosphere in the church. At first, this may sound strange. Why wouldn't we want our church to be one big family? Lyle Schaller answers this question in *The Small Church Is Different*:

> First, the strong commitment of the members to one another, to kinfolk ties, to the meeting place, to the concept that the congregation should function as one big family and the modest emphasis on program tend to reinforce the single-cell character of the small church. When combined with the intergenerational nature of the typical long-established small church, these forces tend to enhance the caring nature of the fellowship, but at the cost of potential numerical growth.[11]

A large number of the smaller American churches are basically family clan churches. They're a small group of people who commit to take care of one another. They may also be related to one another. While there's nothing wrong with people caring about one another, they really aren't a church in the biblical sense. These people have missed the Great Commission mandate. They're not pursuing, evangelizing, and edifying lost people. These small clans exist exclusively for themselves. It's all in-reach with no outreach.

A Comfortable Community

A second negative factor is the desire on the part of people to maintain a certain level of personal comfort in their lives. One of the problems in many of our American churches is the pursuit of a "comfortable Christianity." In America it's the American way: the pursuit of life, liberty, and personal happiness. In response to an invitation to involvement, far too many would respond, "Church is great as long as all I have to do is show up every week and put something in the offering plate. When I've done this, I've done my part! Please don't ask me to do anything else; that's not my job, and I really don't have the time to help."

We must face the fact that today's typical churched people place a high priority on personal comfort. They've developed their own comfort zones and strongly resist any attempts to be moved out of them. They don't share their faith because that could lead to confrontation, which makes them uncomfortable. They don't reach out to new people who might reject them, because that would make them very uncomfortable. In short, any change is threatening.

In the field of church planting, many people who catch the vision will move out of their comfort zones and work hard initially to grow the church. But once the church is established and growing and purchases or builds a facility, some tend to relax their involvement. Their ultimate goal is to return to their comfort zones.

A Powerful Person

A third negative factor is one layperson or a group of laypeople in the church who desire to control much of what takes place. In an established church, this could be an affluent person, a board member, the spouse of a board member, or even the board itself. Most often their motives are noble. They want to control things so that liberalism doesn't creep into the church or to protect the people in the church from young, zealous pastors who want to change things.

If the church begins to grow, the chances of maintaining control are slim indeed. These people argue: "New people don't understand these things. They don't understand how we work around here. They don't realize how we've always done things. Furthermore, they tend to side with the pastor." They realize that they can control only a small, loyal group of people. When new people come into the church, they'll be loyal to the pastor who's probably had an influence on their lives. Consequently, these powerful people strongly resist any efforts toward church growth.

Positive Growth Factors

Church planters can do several things both to facilitate a positive attitude among their people toward growth and to prevent some of the negative factors from occurring. The first positive growth factor is broad and general and the other three are specific and designed to counter the three more common negative factors covered above.

A Single, Clear Vision

Consistently casting a clear, significant vision is critical to facilitating a positive attitude toward church growth. Vision is important to any church, whether planted or already established, because it provides direction and motivation as well as other important elements.

Small Groups

The church that implements a robust network of small groups at the very beginning avoids the problems encountered in the family clan church. It allows its people to have the best of two worlds. On the one hand, the small group provides the kind of loving, caring community that the family clan seeks to protect. On the other hand, it provides this community in the context of a Great Commission mandate. The new church isn't only reaching in through its groups, but it's reaching out through a Great Commission strategy.

A Lay Army

Another specific factor that encourages church growth is a well-mobilized lay army. The church planting team takes the core group through an assessment process early in the development stage. This brings about a change in attitude concerning the pursuit of personal comfort. The discovery of one's divine design and place of ministry motivates Christians to step outside their comfort zones and get involved in ministry. They're excited about the fact that God has uniquely designed them with spiritual and natural gifts, passion, and temperament. This is all new to most of them, and they have a burning desire to serve and discover what God can accomplish through them.

Lay Leaders as Ministers

A third factor that enhances church growth is training lay leaders to minister in the new church. The new church should be planted with the understanding that the pastoral team will handle the church's administrative affairs. The purpose for this is to free lay leaders from such affairs so that they can lead and minister to the church body. Some will lead specific ministries such as a worship or outreach ministry. Others will lead and serve a small group. Regardless of what they do, they'll minister within the context of their giftedness (see 1 Corinthians 12–14).

This system also prevents one person or group of people from taking control of the church. First, they never get into these control positions to begin with. Second, it gives lay leaders power and authority, but this is exercised effectively within their individual ministries, not over the ministries of others or the entire church! The final result is that lay leaders are busy serving Christ, and the church experiences the necessary freedom to expand and grow.

Other Growth Factors

In Christian Schwarz's book *Natural Church Development*, he argues from his research of churches around the world that healthy, growing churches have eight essential quality characteristics. They are the following: an empowering leadership, a gift-oriented ministry, a passionate spirituality, functional structures, an inspiring worship service, holistic small groups, need-oriented evangelism, and loving relationships.[12] I believe that Schwarz's research is well done, and you'll find all these essential quality characteristics at some place in the process that is presented in this book.

Staffing for Growth

A third critical factor for growing churches involves the staff that will lead the church to spiritual and numerical growth. Two questions directly affect church growth: How many people should be on the team? Who are they?

How Many?

If you were to ask the pastor of any church with more than one hundred attenders whether they had enough people on staff, undoubtedly the answer would be a resounding no! This is because so many churches across America are understaffed. In terms of church growth, Lyle Schaller writes, "If measured in simply quantitative terms, the majority of the large congregations are staffed to remain on a plateau or decline in size. They are not staffed to grow!"[13] So how do you staff for growth?

The ratio. In dealing with the topic of staffing for growth, Schaller begins by talking about staffing for a plateau. He indicates that a church that plans to remain on a plateau should have one staff person for two hundred people attending an average worship service, two staff for three hundred people, three staff for four hundred people, and so forth up to eight hundred. Then he suggests that a church averaging four hundred at worship have the equivalent of four full-time staff members if it desires significant growth.[14] Others seem to indicate as well that staffing for significant growth involves having a minimum of one staff person for every one hundred people attending the average worship service.

The problem. The problem for most established churches that desire to grow is that they're staffed for a plateau at best and for a decline at worst. When they discover the above information, they have to scramble to try to come up with the right staff person and enough money to hire that person.

Using teams to plant churches helps circumvent this problem. A team ministry is biblical and provides gifted people for mutual ministry and encouragement. It also enables a church to staff for growth. The church planting team could begin with two or as many as four or five people on staff. By recruiting a team of two or more people, the new church will be staffed to grow far beyond its initial size and will probably grow at a faster rate as well.

The question. Church planters must ask some important questions: What is our vision for growth? In terms of this community, how big could this church become? If the vision is to plant a church that will reach a significant number of people, the leadership should consider recruiting a team of four or more staff people at the inception of the church. While only a few churches have been started with a sizable team, these have achieved significant growth in a short period of time.

Who?

Not only is the ratio of staff to congregation important to church growth, but the individuals who make up the staff team are critical as well.

The Source for Staff

One question in staffing a church is, Where do you find the right people to join the team? Initially, for church planters the team may be recruited on a college or seminary campus. The potential point person begins to share a vision and others are attracted to that vision. Another source is the staff or congregation of a mother church. However, once the church is born and has been in existence for a while, where does it find its staff?

Inside the congregation. Team members can be recruited from the congregation. The advantages are that you know these people and whether or not they'll be a good fit. Many will have been with you from the beginning of the church. They've caught the vision and have been around long enough to prove their character and display their gifts. The disadvantage is that they've come up in the present paradigm or way of doing things and may not be as innovative as someone from outside the church.

There are several excellent examples of this approach to staffing. One is Hoffmantown Baptist Church, located on the outskirts of Albuquerque, New Mexico. Norman Boschoff, a Dallas Seminary graduate, is the pastor. In his system, any person in the church can attain a staff position. They begin by working with a neighborhood group. As they're successful they move up until they qualify for a full-time position on the staff. Another example is Willow Creek Community Church, which also recruits from within the ranks. In fact many growing churches tend to follow this method.

. *Outside the congregation.* Another approach is to recruit staff from outside the congregation. The advantage is that these people bring fresh, new ideas to the team that can bring positive change and benefit the ministry as a whole. In *Discovering the Future,* Joel Arthur Barker writes the following:

> How often has an important innovation in technology, or business, or education, or any field where there are rules and regulations, come from the established practitioners? Rarely. . . . So, where is the logical place for innovation to come from? The edges, the fringes, where there are outsiders who do not know that "it can't be done."[15]

Both are valid methods for recruiting staff for the church. Churches should use the method that best fits their particular circumstances.

The Criteria for Staff

You should consider the following important criteria when going through the process of staff selection.

Personal character. The first and most important is character. Does this person walk with God? A person's character forms the foundation on which ministry is built. As character goes, so goes the ministry!

Ministry DNA. A second criterion concerns the ministry's DNA (core values, mission, vision, and strategy). Can this person own and align with the church's DNA? When people on a team have the same DNA, they appreciate those with different gifts, talents, and abilities (divine design) and recognize the contribution they make to the ministry as a whole.

Different design. A third criterion involves a different design. It's important that you staff to your limitations. God didn't gift and design us to do everything. We must view those areas outside our designs as limitations not weaknesses. Leaders should minister in areas where they're strong and recruit others to minister in their areas of limitation. Therefore, you should look for people whose gifts, talents, and abilities are different from but complement your own.

Loyalty to the pastor. Peter Wagner adds a fourth criterion for staff selection—devotion to the senior pastor.[16] If, for some reason, a staff person can't be loyal, then that individual should move on. Loyalty doesn't mean being a clone of the pastor; it means respecting the pastor. It's impossible to work well with leaders you don't respect.

Mobilization for Growth

A fourth growth factor concerns the mobilization of the people in the church. Peter Wagner refers to this as "lay liberation" and calls it one of the vital signs of the church.[17] He writes, "Pastors of growing churches, whether they be large or small, know how to motivate their lay people, how to create structures which permit them to be active and productive, and how to guide them into meaningful avenues of Christian service."[18]

Who Mobilizes the Laity?

The Point Person

The ultimate responsibility for lay mobilization in the church falls on the point person of the team. While this could be the responsibility of another team person, team leaders should be able to take people through the assessment process. This is because the process, not the idea, is a relatively new concept to the church. Initially, they may not be able to find anyone else who understands the process. Most likely, they'll conduct the ministry until they've trained another leader to take their place. Thus it's important that they have training in the mobilization process or have someone on the team who is trained accordingly.

A Staff Person

In the cutting-edge churches of the twenty-first century, there will be staff specialists who will function primarily in the capacity of lay mobilization. It's possible that this specialist could be a part of the initial church planting team. However, there should be someone on that team who can serve in a variety of roles, one of which would be as a mobilizer of the laity. The goal of this staff person is to train laypeople to take over the church's lay mobilization program.

A Layperson

Of course, another good option is to train a gifted, capable layperson to serve in this capacity. We must not forget that God has equipped laypeople in such a way that many of them can accomplish ministry-related tasks far better than those who are paid to do so. In fact, in this particular ministry, you're mobilizing laypeople to mobilize laypeople!

How to Mobilize the Laity

The Problem and the Solution

In the 1960s there was a revival or an awakening to the importance of the ministry of laypeople and the exercise of their spiritual gifts. Pastors like Ray Stedman of Peninsula Bible Church in Palo Alto, California, began to teach and write about the importance of laypeople and their gifts to the local body of Christ. They not only taught on the spiritual gifts but also conducted body life services where people in the congregation could publicly exercise their gifts.

The problem is that now we've developed a good theology of the gifts but not a practice of the gifts. There's been lots of good exposition from the pulpit concerning the biblical teaching on the topic, and there may be some time set aside in the services for the exercise of the gifts. However, there's been little, if any, help given to people in terms of discovering their gifts and then implementing them in the ministry of the church as a whole.

In the 1980s, this began to change. Churches such as Willow Creek Community Church began to develop methods to mobilize the laity. In particular, Pastor Bruce Bugbee developed the *Networking* program, which proved highly effective in mobilizing numerous laypeople in the Willow Creek congregation.[19] In fact it has served as the prototype for many of the lay mobilization programs in the churches of the twenty-first century. Bruce now leads Network Ministries International, and you can learn more about this excellent ministry from his website (www.brucebugbee.com).

The Program

A good assessment program consists of three phases. The first is the discovery phase, where laypeople receive biblical and practical instruction on spiritual gifts, passion, temperament, and so forth. The purpose of this phase is to help them discover their unique divine design.

Next is the consultation phase. Here laypeople meet with either some-one from the staff team or a trained lay leader who helps them analyze and synthesize the results. The purpose of this stage is to make sure people have correctly analyzed themselves, answer any questions, and discuss some possible ministries in the church.

The last phase is the mobilization phase. In this stage, the consultant helps believers discover where they can minister either within or outside the church body. Then laypeople are assigned to a specific ministry that will train them for that particular service.

It's important in church planting that you institute this mobilization program early in the process. As stated earlier, you should implement it in the development stage with the initial core group. Then you can take everyone who identifies with the group from that point on through the process. This should be a requirement for membership in the church because it sends a loud, early message that the people who are a part of this local body are here to "stand and serve," not just "sit and soak." If you haven't yet read appendix A, now is the time to turn there for more information on the ministry of mobilization.

Assimilation for Growth

An important factor that is often overlooked in terms of church growth is assimilation. Most newly planted churches will attract a lot of new people through the front door. The problem is that many will eventually exit through the church's back door. Assimilation focuses on discipleship and ways to involve people in the church so that there will be fewer people who leave (see chapter 8 to review the disciple-making process).

The Characteristics of Assimilation

Church growth researcher Win Arn lists eight characteristics of what he calls an "incorporated member."[20] These are also characteristics of an assimilated person and are very helpful in developing some processes for assimilation.

1. New members should be able to list at least seven new friends they have made in the church. (These friendships could be and often are with other new members.)
2. New members should be able to identify their spiritual gifts.
3. New members should be involved in at least one (preferably several) roles/tasks/ministries in the church, appropriate to their spiritual gifts.
4. New members should be actively involved in a small fellowship (face-to-face) group. Many churches keep their new member groups together indefinitely.
5. New members should demonstrate a regular financial commitment to the church.
6. New members should personally understand and identify with the goals of the church.
7. New members should attend worship services regularly.
8. New members should identify unchurched friends and relatives and take specific steps to help them toward responsible church membership.

Some Methods for Assimilation

A Culture of Acceptance

One primary method for assimilating new people is to make them feel accepted.

The research. In *The Pastor's Manual for Effective Ministry*, Win Arn writes the following:

> New research underscores *why people select one church over another.* "A good church location" was only tenth on a list of sixteen. "My spouse was a member" was fifteenth.
>
> The *number one reason* people select a church today is: "I felt accepted."
>
> Dr. David Jones, a researcher in Jackson, Mississippi, says, "persons are looking for a group of individuals who will first and foremost make them feel accepted" (*RD Digest*, 1/85). This #1 reason is in contrast to the predominant reason researchers found people attended church in the 1950s and early 1960s. A generation ago Americans attended church most often "for the benefit of our children." But in Jones' study, this reason was listed only eighth.[21]

The responsibility. Creating a culture of acceptance by making people feel accepted is the responsibility of the entire core group or church. Though one leader may take responsibility for the oversight of this ministry, no one person can accomplish this single-handedly. In the planted church, this must be ingrained in the core group's thinking early in the planting process. It should be fully discussed and implemented in the development stage.

A Small Group

One of the more effective ways to assimilate people is the implementation of a small-groups ministry. In *Natural Church Development* Christian Schwarz writes, "Continuous multiplication of small groups is a universal church growth principle."[22] He proceeds to describe the kinds of groups in particular: "They must be *holistic* groups which go beyond just discussing Bible passages to applying its message to daily life. In these groups, members are able to bring up those issues and questions that are immediate personal concerns."[23] Finally, he concludes: "If we were to identify any *one* principle as the 'most important'—even though our research shows that the interplay of all basic elements is important—then without a doubt it would be the multiplication of small groups."[24]

A Newcomer's Class

A newcomer's class helps not only in communicating vision but also in assimilating new people. Most often the class is directed at returnees or regular attenders who are interested in the church.

The purpose of this class isn't the same as in most churches. It shouldn't focus on the church's doctrine, such as the meaning of baptism and the sacraments or any denominational distinctives. Neither should it be a Bible study or an opportunity for spiritual growth. That's not to say that these things aren't important. In fact they'll be covered later. The problem is that some of the people attending might not yet be Christians.

The purpose for the newcomer's class is to tell people what the church is all about and what it expects from those who want to be a part of it and to answer any questions. The content of each class would include most of Arn's characteristics of an "incorporated member." The desired result of the newcomer's class should lead to the next ministry, a new member's class.

A New Member's Class

A number of the people in the newcomer's class will desire to become a part of the church. Invite them to attend a new member's class or small group.

In the 1980s a number of churches moved away from having a church membership. Some argued against it because membership isn't found in the Bible. (This was a weak argument because much of what they were doing isn't found in the Bible.) Others may have done it because some denominations place undue emphasis on membership. Yet membership can be used to the church's advantage in terms of assimilation. This advantage is found in the requirements for membership.

Those requirements are found in Arn's characteristics. Since most people who are considering joining a church are at a reasonably high point of commitment in their lives, they need something to commit to. These characteristics form the object of their commitment.

Commit to the vision and goals. First, they need to commit to the vision and goals of the church (characteristic 6), which is the Great Commission mandate. You could ask everyone to develop a "focus list" consisting of those people who make up their relational communities (characteristic 8). Their job is to begin to pray for and gently pursue these people.

Join a small group. Second, each person should agree to be part of a small group (characteristic 4). This group would be one source of the seven new friends Arn mentions (characteristic 1). If the affinity is good among those in the new member's class, they might form their own small group, depending on the church's purpose for small groups. This small group would also provide a means for monitoring the members' worship attendance (characteristic 7), as well as their spiritual condition.

Experience the assessment process. Third, each will enthusiastically go through the assessment process. It might be accomplished with or apart from their small group. This would not only help them determine their spiritual gifts (characteristic 2) but their entire divine design. Usually the result of this process is a natural desire to become involved in a ministry of the church (characteristic 3).

Support the ministry. Finally, it's at the time of membership that the church explains its financial expectations (characteristic 5). Some churches make the mistake of addressing their financial needs repeatedly in the worship service. This could be a real turnoff to unchurched people. Rather than attempting this when people are merely checking out the church, it should be done when they've decided they like the church and genuinely desire to be a part of it.

Organization for Growth

One other factor affecting church growth that is often missed is the general organization of the church.

The Role of the Staff

The Problem

Currently, in most churches across America, the staff (which consists primarily of one pastor, since the majority of churches are small) and the committed lay leaders of the church join together as a governing board once or twice a month to take care of what are mostly the administrative matters of the church. These may range in importance from the church's future ministry direction to the color of the carpet in the closet. Most spend the bulk of their time micromanaging matters relating to the latter!

Since many lay leaders have grown accustomed to churches that are organized in this manner, they assume that these board meetings are what ministry is all about. They tend to see their ministries in the church primarily in terms of functioning on the board. However, even if they didn't view ministry this way—and some don't—these meetings are often so time-consuming that there's little time left in their busy schedules for anything else.

The Solution

Since the ministry of laypeople is so valuable, and because they have such little time available for it, one solution is to let the staff take care of these matters. There are several advantages to this approach. Usually the church employs pastors and their staffs, depending on the size of the church, on a full-time basis, which allows them to spend more time in the areas of administration. They may have been trained in church administration and generally know what to do.[25] If they haven't been trained or when they don't know what to do, they know where to go to get answers.

In addition, I suggest that the church not even have a governing board until well into the maturity stage. If the planter-leader desires some accountability, which a governing board might normally afford, he could set up an advisory board that might eventually become a governing board. However, he should take great pains to make sure that all understand that it's an advisory board and not a governing board.

The Role of the Laity

The Problem

Those who have grown up in churches that have adopted a more rural, cultural model from the twentieth century for ministry that ignores Ephesians 4:11–13 are convinced that they aren't capable of ministering to anyone. They believe that to minister to people, church leaders must first go to college and then to seminary. Therefore, when they're in need of ministry, they expect the pastor or at least a staff professional to call on them. A layperson might visit and minister more effectively than the staff person, but in their minds this doesn't count! It was nice but not the real thing. If the pastor doesn't visit me, I've not been visited!

The Solution

In a world that's quickly moving toward urbanization, we must abandon the rural ministry model for a more practical, relevant model that focuses more on biblical principles. Probably the best model is one that puts most of the administration in the hands of the staff and places the ministry in the hands of the laypeople.

The principle. Scripture indicates that the entire body of the church is to be involved in the ministry of the church. First Corinthians 12–14 clearly teaches that all believers in the body of Christ have spiritual gifts and are necessary to the life and vitality of the church. A healthy, growing body is one that places a balanced emphasis on all the gifts and the involvement of all the people in the ministry of the church.

The practice. The following are several ways to facilitate lay ministries in the planted church. There should be a philosophy of ministry that values lay ministry. The lay ministries are constantly lauded and given high visibility in the church. The key slogan could be "Every member a minister." An ongoing program of assessment should be in place so that laypeople can discover their "tools" and places for ministry (their ministry niche). Also the church must not start ministries until God raises up qualified laypeople to lead and staff them. These lay leaders should have the authority to lead their ministries with only minimal rules and outside interference. They, and not some board, own their ministry.

The information on church growth in this chapter isn't meant to be exhaustive. The purpose is to stress some of the more important factors and some that are often overlooked in terms of church planting. This is because this book isn't simply about planting churches but about planting spiritually and numerically *growing* churches. The two go hand in hand. Church planters must not only be familiar with church planting but must also study and know the principles and practices of biblical and sociological church growth.

Now turn to and complete the Growth Stage Worksheet in the Church Planter's Workbook.

12

I'm No Longer a Kid!

The Maturity Stage

Bill Smith gives credit to God every time he's asked about it. The church has been in existence for twenty months and it already has three hundred people attending the morning worship service! It barreled right on through the so-called two hundred barrier as if it didn't even exist. Each week the church picks up more and more people. Some are still coming as the result of the mailers that were sent to the focus community before Easter. Most are coming because of word of mouth; the new church has gained a growing, positive reputation in the community. Most of these are unchurched, lost people who are curious.

Those in the initial core group and others who joined them have invited a number of their unchurched friends, and about half of those who have responded have accepted Christ as Savior. This has resulted in some changed lives and the rescue of a number of failing marriages. While some in the original group were a little tentative at the beginning, now they're sold on the vision and committed to the future of this church. In fact many have begun to ask when the church is going to purchase some land and build a facility.

Currently this church is in the growth stage; however, it's advancing toward the maturity stage. Actually one stage does not abruptly end and then the next stage begin. Instead, over time the growth stage blends into the maturity stage. How can you know when you're in the maturity stage? There are several clues. One is that the church no longer thinks of itself as nor communicates that it's a new church. Second, some of the founders, who could be still relatively young, begin to tell stories about the beginning of the church. Third, the body may have purchased permanent facilities or is thinking about it. Fourth, its ministries are expanding, and the church is in the process of developing additional ministries to implement the strategy more effectively. Fifth, some of the people are spiritually mature in the sense that all of the characteristics (three Cs, five Gs, and so forth) of a mature disciple are evidenced in their lives. This is why I call this the maturity stage—believers have had time to mature spiritually.

This chapter on the maturity stage covers three aspects: some prescriptions for maintaining vital, spiritual maturity; the changing leadership of a maturing ministry; and the church's land and facilities. The last section will give some direction to those in Bill's church and others in similar situations as to when a church should seek permanent facilities and the various decisions they'll have to make in doing so.

The Prescription for a Maturing Church

Biblically based, spiritually healthy churches move naturally toward spiritual maturity. However, there are some diseases that can invade and infect the body along the way and cause it to focus inward, rather than outward to a lost world. Whenever an inward focus exceeds the church's outward focus, the numerical and spiritual growth and thus the maturity of the church plateaus, followed not long after by a decline that leads to the death of the organization. Church growth research and practical ministry experience have helped us identify the common diseases that attack the church. Thus we can practice preventative medicine by writing vital prescriptions that keep our churches from becoming spiritually sick.

Regularly Cast the Church's Vision

The direction of the church is determined by its mission and vision—the Great Commission (Matt. 28:19–20). Normally you communicate the mission in writing and the vision orally, such as when you preach. Thus this prescription for health looks primarily at regularly communicating the church's vision, which forces it to look to the future not to the past. When I say regularly, I'm urging you to ask, How can we communicate our vision in some way every week? It doesn't have to be through the sermon (see chapter 7 that addressed vision along with the other DNA of the church). When you stop casting the vision, you stop looking to the future and begin to die.

The problem in the maturity stage is that we can be too focused on the church and not its vision. The church itself is only a means to the end. The vision depicts that end.

Another similar issue that affects the church primarily in the maturity stage is living in the past. The church must focus on and live in the future not the past. It should periodically celebrate its past, but it must never live in its past. If it does, it is a sign of impending death.

Focus on Ministry instead of Money

When churches move into the maturity stage, there's a natural inclination to focus on money instead of ministry. The reason is that ministry costs money. Most churches find that their two biggest costs are staff and facilities. By the maturity stage, the church has likely experienced some change in staff. Whereas it began with a team who practically volunteered their time or worked other jobs, that's no longer the situation. In addition, the church's leadership understands that if it wants to hire good personnel, it will have to pay them. Volunteer staff in more established ministries are rare. Also it's likely that the ministry has a permanent facility or is close to purchasing one (I'll address that shortly), which adds up to a mortgage payment.

The church must resist the subtle temptation to focus on money and, instead, put its attention on its ministries that move people from prebirth to maturity. This is what the church is all about. When you cease to concentrate on ministry, you cease to function as a biblically based church. Rather than trust God to meet your needs as in the early days, you begin to worry about the finances. This shows up in various fundraisers and too many sermons throughout the year on giving or stewardship.

Evaluate and Make Strategic Changes

Few churches have established a regular system of evaluation where they assess what they're doing and those who do it. However, I encouraged you to implement such a ministry back in the conception stage. This serves to make needed, strategic changes in your ministries and the personnel that serve in them.

The advantage of regularly making changes along the way is that you're constantly fine-tuning the ministry engine as opposed to taking it occasionally through deep change. Deep change is needed when churches have not experienced any significant change over the years. Unfortunately, few churches survive to tell about it.

One of the difficulties in making any change is the fear of angering and losing people. I have two responses. First, no matter what you do—change or no change—you're going to lose people. People die, become disillusioned, change jobs and move, ad infinitum. Second, my experience is that some who leave are likely the ones who needed to leave or would have left anyway. Ultimately, this can be good for the church and promote its health.

Focus on Evangelism over Edification

While no ministry is easy, I have found that most people find it easier to involve themselves in ministries of edification than evangelism. I believe that Matthew 28:19–20 presents the two in balance. Again, the natural inclination is for churches in the maturity stage to turn inward and lose that balance, as the Jerusalem church had done by Acts 8. I believe that's why the various passages in the Gospels on the Great Commission that we examined earlier in this book appear to emphasize evangelism more than edification. By focusing on evangelism over edification, you're more likely to reach a biblical balance between the two.

Feed Your Believers Meat Not Milk

It may appear that this book emphasizes evangelizing lost people over edifying or building up saved people. Again, my focus has been on evangelism because I have realized that the average believer is inclined toward discipleship. However, I'm convinced that far too many of the more contemporary churches can so emphasize evangelism that they don't take their people deep enough in their knowledge and application of the Scriptures. The writer of Hebrews warns us that you can't become mature on milk alone. Mature people must have meat or "solid food" (Heb. 5:12–6:2). Thus, if we are moving our congregation from prebirth to maturity, deep biblical teaching in the maturity stage must be somewhere on the menu.

I suspect that, contrary to what most Bible churches believe they are doing, they do not necessarily communicate meat in a Sunday sermon, unless it's in a service specifically focused on believers. Perhaps we need to revisit the Sunday school and deepen its teaching of the Word of God. An alternative is to offer various classes for in-depth Bible study.

Preach to Unchurched Lost and Believers

When the lead pastor and others who preach address their sermons to unchurched lost, it serves as a constant reminder of the need to pursue evangelism in the context of cultural relevance. Again, the tendency of most of us is to preach to believers in general and our members in particular, especially in the maturity stage of the church, when we expect people to be mature spiritually. That's not wrong and should take place. However, too often believers are our focus to the extent that we don't address the lost.

While some can address both groups effectively, such as my pastor (Steve Stroope of Lake Pointe Church in Rockwall, Texas), I'm not sure that most of us can. One answer is to create at least two services, one of which addresses lost people. Our congregations know that they can invite their unsaved friends to such a service and that they'll understand the message because it will be culturally relevant.

Emphasize the Disciple-Making Process

In the maturity stage, your church can become program or ministry oriented rather than process oriented. I introduced you to the disciple-making process in the conception stage in chapter 8. At that time, you identified the characteristics of a mature disciple such as the three Cs. Then I showed you how to identify your ministries that would help your people to realize these characteristics in their lives. The ministries align with the characteristics. Over time the characteristics don't change, but the ministries must. That's because every ministry is a means to a characteristic that is its end. Thus ministries, not characteristics, have a shelf life.

A church that becomes program oriented focuses on the ministries and misses the characteristics that lead its people to maturity. These ministries become sacrosanct, rigid, an end in themselves. Yet we continue to fund and operate them because we've always done it that way.

Mobilize Your Members for Ministry

A problem facing the church in the maturity stage is the formation of a ministry caste system that separates people into the staff and the laity. The understanding is that the church hires a competent, gifted professional staff to do the ministry. When the church was just starting, most everyone got involved in some way, using their gifts to accomplish the ministry. However, now that the church has a little age under its belt, the mind-set becomes, "Let the professionals step in and take control and we'll stay out of their way. The rest of us can retire and sit back and watch the pros do their thing for God."

The obvious problem with this view is that it's unbiblical. It violates such clear passages as Ephesians 4:11–13. Instead of turning over the ministry to a professional staff, the church must mobilize its people to minister along with them and at their direction. Again the biblical prescription and goal for the laity is "Every member a minister" or 100 percent lay involvement. This must not change. What's a good ratio of ministries to people? How can we know when we're doing a good job? Church growth expert Win Arn advises: "There should be at least sixty roles and tasks available for every one hundred members in your church. A role or task refers to a specific position, function, or responsibility in the church (choir, committee member, teacher, officer, etc.). Any fewer than sixty roles/tasks/ministries per one hundred members creates an environment which produces inactive members."[1]

Train Your Leaders to Lead

Probably the biggest neglect that I've observed in churches in the twentieth and now the early twenty-first century is the failure to train leaders for leadership in the church. (A few churches are addressing the problem but most only develop the leaders at the higher levels of their churches.) While this may not be as apparent in the earlier stages of church planting, it becomes obvious in the maturity stage. Leaders are the lifeblood of the church. Without them much goes undone and, in time, the ministry begins to unravel.

The obvious prescription is that the ministry must enter the maturity stage with a strong leadership-development ministry in place that trains leaders at every level of the church. This is accomplished by addressing each leader's character, knowledge, and skills. If you need help in how to accomplish this, and most do, see the book that I coauthored with Will Mancini—*Building Leaders* (Baker Books, 2004).

The Leadership of a Maturing Church

In the first section of this chapter, we discovered some sources of spiritual disease that often infect and in time destroy established churches. Now we know how to practice preventative medicine that addresses these problems before they invade the ministry organism. Thus we can keep our church out of the hospital. Next we need to revisit the spiritually maturing church's leadership at the pastoral and governing board levels.

The Pastoral Leadership

In chapter 6 on pastoral leadership, I argued that the planting pastor must be a strong leader. My research and ministry experience have shown that he must step up to the leadership plate and be the leader of leaders, the proactive point person on the planting team, the one with whom the proverbial buck stops.

This doesn't mean that he's the only leader. He will want to raise up other leaders in addition to those already on the planting team. These will be lay leaders or what I refer to as E. F. Hutton people. This is a reference to an ad that the E. F. Hutton Company, a securities brokerage firm, used in the 1990s. Perhaps you'll recall that whenever someone mentioned their name, everyone in the room stopped to listen, implying that they were a leader in their field. E. F. Hutton leaders are those with circles of influence in the church. They're lay leaders to whom others listen. You want these people on your team.

The lead pastor is neither a tyrant nor a despot. However, those that want to control or influence him or accomplish their own agendas may make such accusations. While they'll move on to other churches, he must lead the church to spiritual maturity and growth, using a blend of integrity and strength.

This pastor works closely with the staff, whom he values highly. They truly consider themselves a team. This doesn't mean that they don't have disagreements. The key is that they've learned to work through them.

Amazingly, the lead pastor also finds time for unchurched people. He has the gift of evangelism and, like a magnet, has a way of attracting lost people. When he is not spending time with his family, he may be playing racquetball with a lost neighbor or someone he has met at the health club.

The Board's Leadership

You have noted in earlier chapters that I discourage planter-leaders from establishing governing boards early in the start-up process, because most governing boards have power and may, through ignorance or misdirection, use it to block or stymie his leadership. Scripture also warns us about placing people in positions of leadership too soon (1 Tim. 5:22). The planter may want to put in place an advisory board that would consist of people outside the church who advise him on the planting of the church and ask him the hard questions about his spiritual walk with the Savior.

These could be people in the sponsoring church(es), a ministry coach, a denominational agency, and others.

The Governing Board

At the maturity stage in its spiritual and numerical growth, the church needs and should be ready for a single, central governing board. You may want to call it a trustee, deacon, or elder board—the name may not matter. (However, the term *elder* carries certain biblical, spiritual connotations.) It's also possible that your denomination may give it a different name.

The governing board should consist of the senior pastor and five to six of the spiritually mature men of the church (an odd number would eliminate the possibility for ties when the board votes). The biblical qualifications for these board members are found in 1 Timothy 3:1–7 and Titus 1:5–9, especially if they are an elder board. I suggest that they be men (1 Tim. 2:11–13; 1 Cor. 11:2–16; 14:26–34). Anyone in the church could nominate a board member; however, the pastor (and later other board members) would have veto power over any nominees (he/they might know of reasons why some aren't spiritually qualified). The congregation would elect them by majority vote if the church is congregationally ruled (the constitution and by-laws adopted in the development stage would dictate this).

The governing board would operate based on a policy governance system in accord with Scripture. This system would spell out the policies that direct the senior pastor, the board, the senior pastor–board relationship, and the overall direction of the church. I am currently writing *Leading the Leaders: A New Paradigm for Board Members*, which will help you develop these policies with examples of what they could look like. Another book that would be helpful, though written from a secular perspective, is John Carver's *Boards That Make a Difference*.[2]

Any church committees will function only in an advisory capacity. They exist to help or advise the board (board committees) or the staff (staff committees) with such areas as finances, strategic planning, a building program, or stewardship campaign. They must have absolutely no power. I've worked with churches where a committee had a stranglehold on the governing board. In one case, a committee had the power to determine who was nominated for membership on the governing board. This must not be.

Guidelines for the Use of Power

The following guidelines address the issue of power in the church, seeking proper checks and balances, in this case in a congregational context.

Another option, however, is an elder-rule system. Various leaders and theologians mount arguments for both systems. My view is that Scripture isn't clear and gives the church freedom to select the system that best enables it to accomplish its purpose and mission in its ministry context. You should note that this is an important time in the pastor's leadership of the church because until now he's held most of the power. At this juncture he will begin to share power with a group of lay leaders.

The congregation has power only when acting corporately as the congregation (for example, voting on issues). When acting as a congregation, the people have power over the governing board and the senior pastor. However, no individual congregant or church member has power over anyone else.

No individual board member has power over anyone in the church. The board has power only when acting corporately as a board in behalf of the congregation. However, the board is responsible for the senior pastor, who answers to it. In an elder-rule situation, the board would be acting for the benefit of the congregation but wouldn't be responsible to the congregation.

As the designated leader of the church, the pastor has power over all the people (Heb. 13:17) as individuals (spiritual direction, discipline, and so on). He doesn't have power over the board when it acts corporately nor does he have power over the congregation when it acts as a congregation. He must have power over the staff (hiring, firing, and so on) and is responsible to the board and the congregation for the staff's performance.

The various members of the leadership staff have power over those who are serving under them, regardless of whether they're board members, church members, or any others. This includes hiring and firing staff who work under them.

Each member of the board should serve for either four or five consecutive years for maximum ministry continuity and then must rotate off for a minimum of one year.

Other Boards in the Church

You may wish to have a deacon board or some other board. For each board, you must decide what function(s) it will perform. For example, a deacon board could serve as a precursor to the elder board. Thus the governing board could place on it those who might be future governing board members, and they could serve the church in some way. However, they must not have any power that would affect the governing board, the pastor, or the staff.

The Facilities of a Maturing Church

So far, the church has met in temporary facilities. This has been by design. The staff team desires to reach many in the community for Christ. Yet they realize that if they attempt to purchase land and build a facility too soon this will limit the ultimate size of the church. As Pastor Rick Warren at Saddleback Community Church near Los Angeles says, "It's a case of the shoe telling the foot how big it can get!"

However, it's in the maturity stage that the church will need to make a decision regarding permanent facilities. By this time the leadership (likely a governing board) should have some idea as to the church's ultimate growth potential. The church's growth will have either slowed down or still be increasing rapidly. Again, this is a major decision in the life of the church because facilities affect the ultimate size of the church. Actually, this decision consists of at least three tensions: permanent versus temporary facilities, new versus used facilities, and where to locate geographically.

Permanent versus Temporary Facilities

The Advantages of a Permanent Facility

There are several advantages to purchasing or building a permanent facility. First, it communicates permanence and stability to those in the focus community. This affects the church's longevity in the community. Also, a permanent facility allows the church, not a landlord, to be in control. As long as another person or organization actually owns the building(s) and the property, the church doesn't have the final say regarding what can be done with those facilities. Some buildings, such as a storefront, can be physically altered to fit the church's needs, while others, such as a movie theater or a school, can't.

Another advantage is that a permanent facility ends the set-up and takedown process that must occur every week in a temporary facility. This process has a long-term demoralizing effect on the people who serve in certain ministries of the church, such as the nursery and the Christian education areas. They never have their own "nesting space" where they can leave their stuff and find it again the following week. Finally, if the church outgrows a facility it owns, the church could possibly sell it at a profit (depending on the market) and use the funds in purchasing a larger facility.

The Disadvantages of a Permanent Facility

The first disadvantage of a permanent facility is the cost. Over the past three decades, the church has witnessed rising costs in terms of land and facilities. The cost of land in most new, growing areas of urban and suburban America today can be high. Then there is the "people factor." Not only do the purchase of property and the construction of buildings on that property cost a lot of money, but the process puts the money into brick and mortar not people. The point is that if the money were invested in a staff team, part-time personnel, and other people-related areas, the church would benefit more from a ministry perspective.

The disadvantage of a permanent facility that I've already mentioned is that once a facility is built, its size limits the church's future growth. Zoning laws in every community declare that a church can build only to a certain extent on their existing property. In most areas, there are also strict guidelines for allowing maximum space for parking cars.

New versus Used Facilities

If the church decides to reside in temporary facilities, it doesn't have to make any further decisions about land and buildings outside of those affecting the rented facilities. However, if the church decides to purchase a permanent facility, it will have to make a second decision. This involves whether the permanent facility will be new or used.

The Advantages of a New Facility

A new facility carries with it a natural attraction. The latest styles in construction and design signal that the church has a strong, vital future. It invites people to come and experience the latest and the best. A new facility also enhances the congregation's esteem. People tend to identify with the facilities in which they work and worship. The feeling is that not only do these facilities represent the place where I serve or go to church, but to a certain extent they represent me, because I've chosen to identify with this place. Consequently, the facilities say a lot about me and who I am.

Another advantage is that the church can design a new facility to meet its unique needs. Every church is different in some way from every other church. This isn't necessarily bad because the same is true of people, and churches consist of people. If they were all alike, things would become very boring! Also, it takes all kinds of churches to reach all kinds of people. These differences mean that each church has its own unique needs. Often the design of its buildings reflects these needs. If the church emphasizes a Sunday school program with large classes, it will need large rooms to accommodate those classes. If it opts for a small-group approach, the rooms can be smaller but more numerous. If, in the worship service, the church projects the words of its songs on a screen, as opposed to using hymnals, it will need to allow for front or rear projection in its design.

The Disadvantages of a New Facility

Of course, a new facility is the most expensive way to go. The problem here is that some churches risk going into heavy debt to cover these costs. If the church should fail to grow, or if the pastor should suddenly leave, the people may be left in a vulnerable position financially. Once you've finished the facility, you can expand and add onto it only so many times. When the number of services reaches a point of saturation, the church can't grow any larger numerically.

Another disadvantage of a new facility is the effect of urban sprawl. Not too far from Dallas Seminary where I teach, there's a beautiful, large church facility. The auditorium has room for several thousand people. The baptistery is ornate and lined with large slabs of expensive marble. The only problem is that only about two hundred people gather there every Sunday, and baptisms are rare. What happened? After the church was built, the neighborhood changed from suburban-urban to an inner-city complexion. A large but poor ethnic community developed in the immediate area around the site, and the people who lived in the area and attended and supported the church moved to suburbia.

The Advantage of a Used Facility

The advantage of a used facility essentially is the cost factor. Even though purchasing used facilities is sure to be relatively expensive in today's economy, it isn't nearly as expensive as putting up a brand-new building. This is why the only option for a number of less affluent churches is the purchase of some type of used facility, whether it's a church facility or some other.

It's interesting to note that churches in some areas are exercising all kinds of creativity in terms of purchasing used facilities, especially when their area experiences a real estate recession. Some buy vacant shopping centers. Others buy failed restaurants or smaller office buildings.

The Disadvantages of a Used Facility

While it's much cheaper to purchase used facilities, several disadvantages come with this option. Of course, there are some initial costs involved in occupying a used facility. The general rule is that the cheaper the purchase price for the facility, the greater will be the costs for occupying that facility. For example, the older the building, the more it will be in need of repairs before occupancy. A second disadvantage is the possibility of a poor reputation in the community. Some buildings may have been occupied by a cult or questionable organization so that people in the area will avoid the church because of the facility's reputation.

A Conclusion

Having examined the factors mentioned above, the question is, what should a new, growing, spiritually mature church do? Should they remain in a temporary facility or move to a permanent one? If they move, should they erect a new building or purchase a used one?

The evidence indicates that the advantages of a permanent facility outweigh those of a temporary one. In *Growing Plans* Lyle Schaller writes, "Most of the congregations that chose to avoid owning and operating their own meeting place eventually concluded that the disadvantages outweighed the apparent advantages."[3]

Not only is a permanent facility advantageous, but a *new*, permanent facility is even more advantageous. If the new church can come up with the funding, then the advantages of a new facility outweigh those of a used facility.

A key factor is that the church must take enough time to get an idea of how big it will become. Not only does this give the leadership a feel for the ultimate growth of the church, but it allows the church to expand to a size necessary to raise sufficient funds to purchase the land and new facilities that will allow for present and future expansion.

Locating Geographically

In the process of purchasing a new, permanent facility, the church will need to decide where to locate in the focus community. You need to keep several factors in mind when making this choice.

The Church's Core Community

One factor is where the people who make up the church's core community are located geographically. They are the majority of people who regularly attend the church. You should locate ideally in the midst of the core community or reasonably near them and definitely in the focus community. First, if the core community lives too far away, it will be difficult for them to invite unchurched, lost neighbors, and community friends to the church. These people might come once or twice, but the fact that they are unchurched means that they're not in the habit of going to church. Consequently, if they have to travel very far from home, they'll probably not make the effort.

Second, if the core community lives too far away, they will find it difficult to drive a long distance to church. Over a period of time, they'll discover that the drive becomes longer and harder. Win Arn presents some research on the driving time of people to church that affects both groups. His work indicates that the maximum drive time for most people is fifteen to twenty-five minutes.[4]

Third, if the core community doesn't locate in the focus community, the latter may view them as outsiders, especially in small towns and rural areas. They will not see them as a viable part of their community and may reject them and the church.

Other Area Churches

Another factor in locating the church is the other churches in the vicinity. In some areas of the country, such as the Northwest, this isn't a problem because there aren't many churches. In the South it can be a major factor.

As much as possible, the church should be located far away from other churches for two reasons. First, it eliminates any spirit of competitiveness and accusations of sheep stealing. Second, it increases the chances of reaching those in the immediate community of the church. However, if the focus area is heavily churched but unreached by those churches, then the church may locate not far from other churches, especially if they are not evangelical churches.

Urban Sprawl

A third factor in locating the new church is the direction of urban sprawl. Wise leadership will attempt to determine if the proposed area will change rapidly in the next few years. If the answer is yes, they will need to decide if this will affect the church's focus group. They've chosen this site for the purpose of reaching a distinct focus group. Will this change in the next twenty to thirty years? If so, what will happen to the church and the possibility of reaching its focus group in the process of that change?

Now turn to and work through the Maturity Stage Worksheet in the Church Planter's Workbook.

13

Let's Have a Baby

The Reproduction Stage

The words "Don't forget your roots" had somehow lodged themselves in the recesses of Bill Smith's mind. His church-planting professor had said them often in seminary, and now the time has come to realize them in his ministry. The church is almost four years old and is averaging four hundred people in attendance for the past month. The growth has slowed only a little, finances are good, and the church is investigating the purchase of a large piece of land near their present facility.

Bill is having problems sleeping at night. The last time this happened was back when he was in seminary, contemplating the planting of this church. What's keeping him awake? It's his dream about reaching the entire city. In fact, when he moved to the suburb of this large city in the Northeast, his vision was to take the entire city for the Savior. Having planted the church, he believes that now is the time to start another church. His desire is literally to circle the city with biblically based, spiritually healthy churches and to use them to finance and plant other churches in the inner city, certain rural areas, and in other parts of the world. Consequently, in his prayers, he isn't asking God if they should plant another church. That's already been settled long ago. His prayers focus on exactly when and where they should locate the next church.

At this point, Bill's church is growing and is spiritually mature enough to begin the process of planting daughter churches at strategic locations around the city—an integral part of any church's ultimate vision. Therefore, a vital aspect of the church's future ministry isn't only to carry out the Great Commission mandate but also to plant church planting churches

(churches that will also carry out the Great Commission mandate both at home and abroad).

This is the reproduction stage. It's not meant to be a separate, distinct stage from the growth and maturity stages but could be concurrent with the first and should begin at least by the latter. It involves planting churches not only all over the large metropolitan areas of America but in other countries as well. This stage focuses on three areas: the reasons for, the timing of, and the process of reproduction. It's designed to help established, maturing churches know why, when, and how to parent new churches.

Three Reasons for Reproduction

For a growing, maturing planted church or an established church to start a daughter church, it must think carefully about its reasons for desiring to reproduce itself. People will want to know why the church wants to start another church. Some will ask, "Why should we start another church?" Others will point out, "This church is taking all of our time and attention; how could we possibly consider birthing another church? Aren't there already enough churches around here?" There are three important reasons for starting a daughter church: the need, the examples, and the advantages.

The Need

Few Churches Have the Vision

Few churches have a vision for reproducing themselves through starting other churches. They are plateaued or in decline. For those that are plateaued, the emphasis is maintenance, and for those who are dying it's survival.

Not many churches in America have taken the initiative to birth churches. Many simply aren't interested. They would perhaps like to start a church but feel that their church isn't ready yet. They respond, "Maybe, some day." But "some day" never becomes "today." Others have helped start daughter churches, but at the initiative of the group of people who desire to form the daughter church. After the church is planted, it's "business as usual."

Because I have seen the need for churches to reproduce, I have written *Vision America* (Baker Books, 1994) as a tool to help these churches and their pastors catch a vision for church planting in North America and abroad.

Few Churches Are Reaching the Cities

All over the world in general and America in particular, people are moving from rural to urban areas. In *Your Church Can Grow*, published in 1976, Peter Wagner indicated that 74 percent of Americans live in urban areas.[1] This figure has not diminished any over the years.

If the church of Jesus Christ envisions reaching North America and the world, it will have to reach its cities. The problem is that few churches are reaching the cities and even fewer are thinking about it. There are some exceptions. For example, one pastor planted a church in Rockwall County located east of Dallas, which grew to a large size rather quickly. However, it has not remained only in Rockwall County; it has circled the Dallas metroplex. First, it planted a church in north Dallas County, which is also growing quickly. Second, it planted one in south Dallas County, and then others in surrounding rural areas. Next, hopefully, it will plant churches abroad. As these churches grow and plant other churches, they'll have a strong impact on the entire metroplex and ultimately the world. This kind of vision is the hope for Christianity in America.

Most Churches Resist Change

A third need for established churches to plant other churches is the fact that it's so difficult for established churches to change. Some indicate that of the 350,000 churches that existed in America in the decade of the 1990s, 100,000 closed their doors. Probably even more will close in the twenty-first century.

The problem is that most of these churches were started prior to the 1960s and developed their ministries in the context of a churched, so-called Christian culture. With the shift from a churched to a nonchurched, post-Christian culture, not all that different from the first century, these churches are no longer reaching their communities. The problem is compounded by the fact that some aren't aware of what has happened, and those who are, in general, aren't willing or able to make the changes necessary to influence their communities. This is because none of us likes change; it makes us uncomfortable. It's so much easier to remain cloistered in our comfort zones. Therefore, rather than change what we're doing, we argue that what we've done in the past will also work in the future, and the ministry begins to die.

A number of the people who leave changing churches aren't necessarily opposed to implementing new ideas and ways of doing things. They're opposed to doing them in their own church but would be open to seeing them implemented elsewhere. Consequently, pastors who take established churches and see themselves as change agents need to do two things. First, they must become experts on change. This means reading everything available on the topic. They must be patient and realize that it's difficult to sew a patch of new, unshrunk cloth on an old garment without badly tearing the garment (Matt. 9:16). And they should consider implementing their new ideas and methods in new daughter churches, where they can pour new wine into new wineskins (v. 17).[2]

Examples of Reproducing Churches

Even though not enough churches are reproducing themselves through sponsored churches, there are some good examples of churches that have done this in the past, and there are some notable examples that have a vision for accomplishing it today.

The Church at Antioch

Perhaps the best example of a church that reproduced itself through starting churches was the church located in the city of Antioch in Syria. The missionary journeys described in the book of Acts were vital to the spread of Christianity. However, these were largely church planting ventures that came out of the church at Antioch.

What's important to observe here is how the early churches, such as the one at Antioch, understood the Great Commission mandate. Jesus said, "Make disciples!" The Antioch church accomplished this through sending out two missionary church planters who began a number of daughter churches in Asia Minor, Macedonia, and Achaia. What better way to spread the gospel than to plant a number of significant churches in the areas targeted for evangelism. Is there any reason why established churches or growing mature planted churches shouldn't follow suit?

Modern-day Examples

Not all of the churches in America have missed the opportunity of reproducing themselves. One notable example is Saddleback Valley Community Church. Pastor Rick Warren began this church in 1980 as a home Bible study with seven people. Today the church is one of North America's largest, and a majority of its people have accepted Christ as the result of its ministry.

But Warren hasn't "forgotten his roots." In an article in 1988 on the church, Sherri Brown wrote, "Church growth extends beyond the immediate church, Warren believes. When the church began in 1980, he proposed they start a church a year. To date they've started nine churches—eight of which have continued and grown to be self-supporting. They plan to start ten more churches the next year."[3] Warren's vision is to spread Great Commission churches across much of Southern California. The results for Christ will be phenomenal.

There are many other churches that are reproducing. Calvary Chapel of Costa Mesa, California, spawned more than 250 daughter churches across Southern California and the continent in the latter part of the twentieth century. The average size of most of them is between 200 and 300; however, 13 average more than 1,000 worshipers on a Sunday.

Under the leadership of Bob Roberts, Northwood Community Church in Keller, Texas, has trained church starters and sponsored numerous church starts at home and abroad. Bob's strategic thinking is displayed in his global concept that encourages the planting of an international church for each local church planted in America. This concept balances a local versus an international approach to reaching this planet for the Savior.

Ten Benefits for Daughter Churches

There are numerous benefits of reproducing daughter churches for both the sponsor church and sponsored churches. This section will focus on some of the benefits for the daughter churches.

Finances

One of the major problems in planting a church is financing the venture. The costs can be high for a core group, especially if it pursues its community through a mailer or a technigrowth program that uses some kind of telephone system. Some planted churches have the momentum to implement the vision but are slowed in the process because of a lack of funding.

This is where a sponsoring church can be an extremely valuable asset. It can give strong financial assistance at the very start and then cut back each year until the new church becomes financially self-supporting. A church's commitment to reaching its community and others can be measured by its financial commitment to church planting.

Core Group

Another benefit is that the mother church may supply some or all of the people who make up the initial launch group, including some key lay leaders as well as followers. This could take place in several different contexts. If the new church is not too distant geographically from the sponsoring church, the launch group could come from it. In fact the new church might locate in a community where a number of members live who have been driving a significant distance to attend the sponsoring church.

Even if the new church would be geographically distant from the mother church, a launch team could come from the sponsoring church. For example, Willow Creek Community Church, before they discontinued directly planting churches, allowed their interns to recruit laypeople in the church for their church planting teams. Keri Kent writes:

> However, interns are not making public appeals within the church to recruit their teams. "It's based on natural relationships," Bugbee says. "We've given them the freedom to share their vision with those they are ministering to. A year from now, I wouldn't be surprised if they (each) took 25 or 30 people. Eventually, it would be great if they (a team) took 100 people with them."[4]

The result of this aggressive approach was that laypeople got involved in a team and, if necessary, moved to some other large metropolitan area and planted a church there. Kent writes, "Some have given up jobs and homes in the Chicago suburbs to move to another part of the country to be part of a new church."[5]

Along the same lines, Leith Anderson implemented a "Hunting License" approach at his church in Minnesota. They allowed church planters to recruit practically anyone in the church to be a part of their ministry. Others have taken a similar approach, asking only that the leader-planter communicate who they were targeting so that he didn't recruit people who might harm the new church in some way. Regardless, this demonstrates the strongest of commitments to church starting.

Accountability

A third benefit is that the sponsoring church can provide necessary accountability for the new work. This will affect several areas. One is corporate finances. Are they using financial gifts from individuals and the sponsoring church as intended? Another is the matter of moral integrity, especially in the area of sexual promiscuity. Is anyone on the staff of the new church struggling in this area? A fall here will destroy the new church. The staff can also be held accountable for their family life. Are they balancing their time in planting the church and their time with their families? Some planters have allowed the new church to be their mistress or replace their family!

Encouragement

A fourth benefit surfaces during times of ministry discouragement. Those who serve the Savior will face times of discouragement. Unfortunately, it comes with the job. Even Paul, who was a church planter par excellence, faced times of intense discouragement (2 Timothy 4).

Here is where the sponsor church can be extremely helpful. It's most difficult to face discouragement alone. The senior pastor or the person assigned to the new church can serve as a comforter and source of encouragement during the leader-planter's times of discouragement.

Prayer

Those who plant churches without a sponsoring church must recruit intercessory prayer warriors. This is because the battle isn't simply that of determining where to find the necessary physical resources to get the job done. The battle is being fought in the spiritual realm (Eph. 6:10–20). Often when seminary students go into ministry and experience a lot of success initially, something always goes wrong! This is the result of spiritual warfare. We need to remember that one of the primary weapons against Satan and his forces is prayer (Eph. 6:18–20).

Credibility

Credibility is another benefit for the daughter church. How do people who might get involved in the new church know that the work is legitimate? How might people distinguish this work from some "fly by night" operation? These are the questions that people will be asking, and they're good questions that demand answers.

Proving credibility could be difficult for the church planting team without a mother church. Church starts in this situation should form a board of reference, consisting of people who can recommend them to those who don't know them. Also a degree from a known theological institution grants limited credibility. However, some church planters have neither. The best solution is the sponsoring church. When a known, established church births another church, it conveys its credibility to that work.

Counsel

A seventh benefit is the availability of counsel from those on the staff of the parent church. One of the problems in ministry in general and church planting in particular is the knowledge problem. Often leaders find themselves in positions of having to make important decisions but not knowing what to do. The problem is compounded in church planting because so often the church planter and the team are recently out of school and don't have a lot of pastoral experience to fall back on. This is where the counsel of a seasoned senior pastor and church staff can be of much benefit to the daughter church.

Talent

An eighth benefit is that the new church may have access to talented individuals in the parent church. A problem for new churches, especially at the time of inception and later at the birth event, is coming up with enough good talent to put together a quality worship time. Too often the church attempts to use people who by their own admission are mediocre vocalists or instrumentalists. Usually this has dire consequences.

The sponsoring church can alleviate this problem by making its talented people available to the new work. A church that is rich in talent isn't able to use all their talent all the time. Therefore, people could take turns performing in the new church on Sunday. This might include the help of the staff worship leader as well.

Personnel

A ninth benefit is in the area of staff and ministry personnel. Most new churches tend to be understaffed or their staff may be inexperienced. The sponsoring church can make their personnel available to help with the new work. Some send in what they refer to as "swat teams" to give the new ministry a jump start. The worship leader could advise the worship team and offer limited services. The youth leader could help set up a youth ministry and be available for advice and training. A few churches hire trained people in these capacities and then loan them to the new churches until they're up and running. This assumes that the planted churches are similar in makeup to the parent churches and reflects a strong commitment on the part of those churches to the Great Commission mandate.

Shared Events

A tenth benefit of having a mother church is shared events. A complaint often heard from people involved in the new church is that they or their children miss some of the programs and events they experienced in the parent church.

One solution to this problem is for the daughter church to participate in some of the programs or events. For example, every year a number of the churches in Dallas sponsor a family camp or a ski trip to the mountains in Colorado. Some of the families in these churches have made this a family tradition to be observed every year. The new church could join the parent church for this event. In time, the new church will grow large enough to sponsor their own trip, but until then, they can share this time with the other church. Other events could also be shared, especially those affecting adolescents in the new work.

The Preferred Time of Reproduction

Now that we've looked at some of the reasons for parenting a daughter church, the next question concerns when this should take place. What is the best time to plant a church? Several considerations should prove helpful to the parent church in answering this question.

The Size of the Parent Church

One consideration is the numerical size of the sponsor church. How big should the parent church be to plant a new church? Is there an ideal size?

A Perception

The perception among most if not all churches considering church planting is that they're not big enough to start a new church at their present size, no matter what it is. The ideal size is always larger than they presently are.

This same perception can affect the church not only in terms of its size but in other areas as well. For example, the same argument could be mounted in terms of finances. The church may feel that it does not have quite enough finances to start a new church now, so it decides to wait until next year or the year after. However, the ideal amount will always be larger than what the church presently has! And, at this rate, the church will never become involved in birthing new churches.

A Survey

In the summer of 1984, *Leadership* conducted a survey of its readers, asking them to share what they had learned about parenting new churches.[6] Here are some comments about size that still apply even in the twenty-first century.

One church with only eighteen people planted a new church. The pastor explained: "I begin with Bible studies and wait until we have forty in regular attendance before launching the new church. We started with eighteen and now have about seventy to eighty" (Foursquare; California).[7]

Another church planted a daughter church when they had twenty people. They commented, "Start with a larger core group (we had twenty). This was very tiring when trying to fill even the basic needs" (independent; Illinois).[8]

A church, which didn't disclose its size when it parented its first church, suggested, "You need at least seventy-five people to function as a complete body" (nondenominational; Illinois).[9]

One church planted when they had 150 people. They believed this wasn't large enough. Their comment was, "Wait until we have a larger congregation. We had 150 at the time" (independent; California).[10]

It would appear from this brief sampling that there's no ideal size at which to begin a new church. Each church in the survey states that, in retrospect, it should have been larger when it birthed a daughter church—whether it consisted of 18 people or 150 people. This would seem to indicate that churches that have parented a church as well as those that are considering this endeavor are still under the perception that the ideal size at which to start a church is always larger than their present size—regardless of what that size may be.

A Conclusion

There doesn't seem to be any ideal size at which a mother church should be before it plants. In general, all agree that the larger the size of the church, the easier it is to plant another church. Yet if these churches had not started when they did, they would never have thought they were large enough and would not have started churches.

I suggest that, based on the information above and birth stage research, a church can launch a new work when it has a minimum of fifty adults. You'll recall from the chapter on the birth stage that research indicates that a planted church needs a core group of at least fifty people or more before going public if it desires to grow larger than two hundred people.[11] This figure is helpful to a church that has a vision to plant other churches. If it keeps planting churches before it reaches fifty, it could be delayed in reaching the birth stage, and this will hinder its ministry long term.

The idea that we can't plant a church yet because we're not big enough is questionable. The church must remember that this perception will always be there regardless of its current size. If it has more than fifty people, then it needs to take a step of faith and parent a new church.

The Growth of the Parent Church

Another consideration in terms of the best time to plant a church is the growth of the parent church. At issue here is whether the parent church is growing, plateaued, or in decline.

The Growing Church

Certainly an ideal time at which to plant a church is when the parent is experiencing numerical and spiritual growth. Many examples exist from the first, the twentieth, and the twenty-first centuries. The research indicates that planting new works while a church is growing doesn't inhibit that growth. Instead, unchurched people who couldn't find a parking space at the parent church are able to locate one after a group launches out to start another church.

The Plateaued Church

It's not too difficult to understand that growing churches should plant other churches. But what about the 80–85 percent of churches in America that are either plateaued or in decline? Should they consider starting new churches?

Most of these churches tend to be focused inward not outward. They're concerned with getting themselves off their plateau or turning their situation around. However, what most don't realize is that one means of accomplishing this is parenting a church. Gary Carter, the pastor of Eastwood Fellowship Baptist Church in Saint Thomas, Ontario, believes that churches, like gardeners, must prune themselves for growth if they desire to continue to grow.[12] If they don't, then one of two things may happen: stagnation or accidental pruning. The latter refers to people in the church who take the initiative and split off on their own.

But how can a church know when to prune itself, and what effect this will have? Carter writes the following:

> Thus, when a church has not seen recent growth, it may be a signal that it is time to prune—by planting a daughter church. Such a move is likely to stimulate the church to new heights by breaking in on established relationships and patterns in a positive way. Growth will be spurred again by the recent memories of how the sanctuary used to be full. Everyone will know that these pews are now empty because the church selflessly gave people to

the daughter church. A holy dissatisfaction will engender enthusiasm to fill those places once again. The new-found momentum may take the mother church to the next plateau that previously seemed out of reach.[13]

The Declining Church

Churches stay plateaued for only a short time. If they continue "to conduct business as usual," they'll begin to decline, which is a nice way of describing the death process. Much of what Gary Carter wrote above applies to the declining church—especially those in early decline. In the latter stages of decline, a church is facing the death of the ministry. These churches find it difficult to close the church because of memories and resulting emotional attachments, thus they tend to hang on until forced to shut the doors.

Rather than hang on until the inevitable, these churches and any denominational advisors would be wise to consider closing the church and releasing the people to minister or attend elsewhere. They could sell the facility and its property and invest the money in new church starts.

Another option is to close the church for a period of time, such as six months. During this period a church planting team or a sponsor church could refurbish the facility. Then they could plant a new work on that same site that would be more endemic to the neighborhood and able to reach out to it. Even dying churches can be involved in starting new works.

The Conclusion

It would appear that church planting should characterize a church regardless of whether it's growing, plateaued, or in decline. The evidence seems to indicate that parenting a church is natural for growing churches and is important to plateaued and declining churches that desire a new direction. Consequently, a church can know that it's time to become a parent by the very fact that it's a church, regardless of whether it's growing, stagnant, or dying.

The Age of the Parent Church

My experience as a pastor, church planter, and ministry consultant is that if a church hasn't birthed another church within the first three years of its existence, it probably won't happen. Most healthy, spiritually growing churches should be in the spiritual maturity stage by then, which is an ideal time to begin a new work in a focus community.

The Process of Reproduction

A parent church may know all the reasons for starting another church and when to do so but not how to go about it. This can result in a birthing process that is full of unnecessary pain and that may not even produce a daughter church. Either result has the potential of giving church planting a bad reputation in the eyes of the congregation, discouraging any future attempts at reproducing another daughter church. There are at least six steps that must be taken if the birthing process is to be successful.

Step 1: Praying for Daughter Churches

Precede the birthing of any church with much prayer. Prayer must permeate the entire process, because the prayer of faith is most effective and powerful (James 5:13–18). This prayer begins with the leadership team but includes the entire church.

A church will never rise above its leadership. If the leadership of the church isn't committed to church planting, the membership will not be committed. If the leadership doesn't pray for daughter churches, the membership will not pray for daughter churches. The leadership must set the example for the congregation.

You should cast the vision for church planting in such a way that it will motivate people to pray for the project. It's not realistic to expect everyone to share the same burden and to pray to the same extent, but the goal is to have some people praying all the time.

One way to involve the congregation in praying for daughter churches is to encourage them to become involved in these churches. Those who plant these churches, whether interns or others, could spend a certain amount of time in the church recruiting both a core group and prayer support for the venture. Leith Anderson has encouraged this approach, which he calls the "head-hunter" approach, in his church in Eden Prairie, Minnesota.

Another way is to recruit special daughter-church prayer teams. These would consist of people who have expressed an interest in church planting and missions. The primary purpose of these groups is to pray for specific daughter churches long before they're conceived and long after they've been weaned.

Step 2: Casting the Vision for Planting Churches

Another step in starting a daughter church is casting the vision for the same. If the vision isn't cast, chances are good that it will not happen. The two issues here are the time and methods for accomplishing this.

The church needs to cast the vision for another church all the time. Church planting is the primary if not the only vehicle for the evangelization of America. Therefore, any church plant should have as a part of its ultimate vision the planting of other churches. It must not forget its "roots."

A mother church should begin to cast the vision for daughter churches long before it's in a position to start them. (The best time is at its own inception.) The result is that people will not be surprised when the time comes and the church begins to move in that direction. In fact, if the vision is cast properly, the people will grow impatient with the church, and their constant complaint will be that it's taking too long to become a parent.

The methods for vision casting are much the same as those enumerated in chapter 7. They include such things as the pastor's example, the sermon, visual images, brochures, and audio- and videotapes.

Step 3: Identifying a Focus Group

A vital step in parenting churches is the identification of a focus group. This involves a specific group of people in a specific community, whether they're close to or a long distance from the church. The general procedures for accomplishing this are found in the strategy section of chapter 8. They consist of the following:

1. Identify a unique focus group. (Determine if it will be similar to or dissimilar from the sponsor church.)
2. Gather information on the focus group.
3. Construct a profile person.
4. Determine the kind of church necessary to reach this focus group.

When the sponsoring church is in the same city as the focus group and shares its demographics, it will be relatively easy to gather the necessary demographic and psychographic material firsthand. The church can probably also supply the people who'll make up the initial core group. This could be a sizable number of people who live beyond the normal driving distance to the church and desire a church with the same vision in their area of the city. However, it could consist of any cluster of people from the church who desire to target a particular area of the city where they live. Again, all this assumes that the planted church shares the same demographics as the sponsoring church(es), which may not and should not always be the case.

Step 4: Selecting and Equipping a Leadership Team

Everything rises or falls on leadership. *Who* is as important as *how*! The right person in the right position with God's blessing usually gets the right results. The right person in the wrong position gets the wrong results. The parent church that understands this can play an important role in the success or failure of the future church. An aspect of this role is the selection and equipping of a church planting leadership team.

Chapter 5 describes how God has designed each person in a unique way for leadership and ministry. Chapter 8 has a section on team ministry that includes some instruction on how to select the individuals who make up the team. This selection process involves a consideration of each person's character and competence (God-given and developed), and the chemistry of the proposed team (ministry, doctrinal, and emotional alignment).

Once they've selected the team, the parent church can serve that team by equipping it for the ministry that's ahead. There are at least two ways to accomplish this task, depending on the size of the church. One approach is to set up an internship program. This could be coordinated with a Christian college or seminary. This would be a good approach for a smaller church that has only limited funds available. The advantage for students is that they receive a small stipend and room and board from the church plus they meet the graduation requirements of the school.

Another approach is to place church planters in staff positions in the sponsoring church. They would serve the church in a full-time capacity, including preparation for church planting. They would be paid full-time and could recruit a team from among the congregation. Once they leave, other church planters could take their places. This is a good option for medium and larger churches.

Step 5: Recruiting a Committed Core Group

Another step in parenting a new church is the recruitment of a committed core or launch group of people who will form the nucleus of the new church. If the mother church can accomplish this, it will save the church planting leadership team the time of having to build a core group in the context of a cold start. But who will make up the group, and how will they be recruited?

The primary source for the nucleus could be people in the congregation, assuming that the church is attempting to reach people who are similar demographically. The congregation is a good source for several reasons: They'll already have the vision. Also there will be clusters of people who live beyond the average driving distance to the church (fifteen to twenty-five minutes). These people are already aware of how long it takes to get to church and will probably be interested in something closer to home. The church should chart where its people are located geographically and look for its clusters. Another reason is that these potential core group people are accessible. The church will discover who they are and will have the ability to communicate regularly with them.

The church should follow two steps in recruiting these people:

Cast the vision. The first is to prepare the soil by planting the vision. The vision of the mother church from its very inception should include the planting of daughter churches. Thus the vision should already be well established. Indeed, the church will have cast the vision so well that people in the congregation are looking forward to becoming involved in a church plant to reach unchurched lost people.

Ask for volunteers. The next step is to ask for volunteers to be a part of the new work. This has proved to be a simple but highly effective method. A survey of parent churches conducted by *Leadership* in 1985 indicated that three-fourths of them followed this approach.[14] According to Dean Merrill, "The vast majority of these turned out to be permanent transfers, not temporary aids. In the case of Oak Grove Church, Milwaukie, Oregon, for example, '75 members came for a one-year commitment; 72 remained.'"[15] This continues to be a good approach in the twenty-first century.

Step 6: Financing the Future Church

An important step in nurturing new churches is for the parent church to help in the area of finances. It should work through at least four areas: the amount of money, the source of that money, what the funds are to be used for, and how long the support should last.

The Amount of Money

You must ask, How much money do we need to provide to plant a daughter church? There is, however, no set figure. Each situation is different because leaders plant churches in different places under different circumstances.

In *Leadership* Dean Merrill provides encouragement: "Mothering a new church is not as costly as we had expected." He continues, "Few investments totaled more than $25,000 (excluding real estate purchases). Many daughter congregations were started with as little as $5,000. *Some start-ups required no money at all* from the mother church treasury."[16]

However, the pattern seems to be that the more money the church is willing to invest coupled with good leadership, the greater the return on that investment. An example is Hope Chapel in Hermosa Beach, California, which has started thirty daughters in the past twelve years. Merrill quotes the pastor, Ralph Moore:

> "We spent $3,000 in our first attempt back in 1973. And we were only 125 people at the time. Lately we've been spending in the high twenties with a proven leader, and the daughter church ends up with usually 100+ people in six months." In mid-1983 Moore ventured out himself, with 40 others from the 2,700-member mother church, to plant a new Hope Chapel in Kaneohe, Hawaii. A year later, attendance was running above 400.[17]

Of course, these figures don't include costs for the acquisition of land and facilities. The church will need to determine if it desires to become involved in this aspect of financing.

The Sources of Money

Several different ways exist for a parent church to financially support new church starts. It can create a special fund for church planting that is outside the church's regular budget. It would depend on the gifts of people in the congregation who are interested in seeing a network of daughter churches in the area.

A parent church can allocate part of its missions budget for planting churches, which is definitely an aspect of any church's missions program. These funds would be designated specifically for new churches.

Funds for planting churches can also be a line item in the regular budget. This would serve to give it special treatment and would communicate the church's commitment to it. The parent church could also designate and use funds in its budget for the salaries of the church planting team.

The Use of the Money

You may use the money for a variety of necessities. At the top of the list would be salaries. In Merrill's *Leadership* survey, the most common provision was for salaries.[18] Another common use would be for renting appropriate facilities. After facilities and salaries, other possibilities include such expenses as publicity, mailers and brochures, sound equipment, lighting, curriculum, Bibles, and so forth.

The Length of Time

How long should the parent church help or support the daughter ministry? The objective of the new work is to become self-sufficient as soon as possible, so the answer to the question is as long as necessary but not for very long.

A suggestion. The parent church should probably make a three-year commitment with hopes that it will not take this long. If it should take longer than three years, something is probably wrong. The exception to this might be some ethnic works, new churches in the inner city, and some plants that target special groups, such as the cults, Muslims, and other religions.

A survey. In the *Leadership* survey, Merrill asked the question, "How long was the road to self-supporting status, and thus an independent existence?" The answer was the following:

> Two-thirds of the daughter churches in our survey had reached that milestone in an average of twenty months. The median time, however, was only twelve months, and almost a fifth of the sample reported being on their own financially from Day 1. By contrast, a few cases reported receiving outside aid as long as ten years.
>
> The other third of the respondents were still working toward self-sufficiency and had been doing so for an average of thirty months. The clear preference, of course, was to end this phase as soon as possible, because "as long as the parent is helping to pay the bills," says John W. Fogel, an Alliance pastor in Fulton, New York, "the new church is not totally independent."[19]

The average. The average time for a church to become self-supporting appears to be somewhere between twenty to thirty months. The median time would be closer to twenty months. This should give encouragement to both new churches that desire independence and parent churches that desire to see them become independent and self-supporting as soon as possible.

Now turn to and complete the Reproduction Stage Worksheet in the Church Planter's Workbook.

It's most fitting that this book end with this chapter emphasizing the need for planted churches to reproduce other spiritually healthy, biblically based churches—in short, to plant church planting churches. This ties in with the vision in the book of Acts. It's to encourage and equip individual Christians and churches to seed American soil with relevant, significant Great Commission works that will assault and crash through the gates of Hades (Matt. 16:18). This is to take place at home and abroad. Not only are we to sow new works to reach the various people groups here on the North American mission field, but these, in turn, can sow churches on the mission fields of other countries. The vision is for the world! This has been the means through which God has accomplished revival in the past and will be for the future as well. Will you become a part of this vision?

Church Planter's Workbook

This workbook is designed to help you implement the material in this book and plant a church planting church. Over the next few days, weeks, or months, work your way through the following worksheets as you complete the various chapters in the book. If you're planting with a team, be sure to include them in the process.

Financial Worksheet

Fund-Raising

1. Have you met the requirements of Matthew 6:33? Do you believe that God will take care of your needs? How might you demonstrate this belief? What would you be willing to give up in order to start a church?

2. Check any of the following from chapter 3 that are potential financial sources that might be of help to you. Do you have any other sources of funding that aren't listed among these six? Write them down.

   ___Sponsor church(es)
   ___Core group
   ___Interested friends and acquaintances
   ___Denomination or organization
   ___Personal employment
   ___Prayer team
   ___Other:

3. Of the two problems in fund-raising, which would characterize you?

___Pride
___Fear
___Both
___Neither

4. Make a list of any Christians you know or come in contact with who might be in a position to help financially, whether you think they will or not. Include their addresses and phone numbers. Keep this list in an easily accessible place, and add names as they come to mind. This will be an important source for raising funds.

Budgeting

Work through the following personal and ministry needs in light of the costs where you plan to locate the church (some areas are more expensive than others). Attempt to give actual expenses where possible. The idea is to come away from this exercise with a personal needs and ministry budget in hand.

Personal Needs

1. Salary
2. Housing allowance
   Mortgage/rent
   Utilities
     Electricity
     Gas
     Water
     Sewage
     Telephone
   Repairs and maintenance
3. Medical/life insurance

4. Giving/tithing
5. Automobile
   Payment(s)
   Expenses
      Gas
      Maintenance
      Repairs
6. Clothing
7. Food
8. Continuing education
   Subscriptions
   Books
   Conferences/seminars
   Classes
9. Retirement
10. Contingency fund

Ministry Needs

1. Salaries
   Pastors/staff
   Secretarial
   Maintenance/custodial
2. Office space
   Rent/lease
   Utilities
   Office equipment
      Phones
      Fax
      Computer
      Printer
      Internet
      Copier
      Tape reproduction
   Office furniture
      Desk
      Chairs
      Lamps
   Office supplies
      Bulletins
      Stationery
      Tapes

3. Meeting facilities
   Rent/lease
   Utilities
   Insurance
   Storage
4. Audiovisual equipment
   Microphones
   Projectors
   Sound board
   Sound system
   CD and DVD players
5. Worship
   Music
   Instruments
   Communion
   Pulpit supplies
6. Children and youth ministries
7. Babysitting
8. Missions/outreach
9. Denominational/organizational support
10. Travel and moving expenses
11. Telemarketing
    Advertising
    Stationery
    Logo
    Postage
    Printing
12. Contingency fund

Assumptions Worksheet

1. What are some of the key assumptions that you bring to the ministry of church planting?

2. Which of the six assumptions in chapter 4 do you agree with? Place a check by them. Which do you disagree with? Why?

___Evangelism must be taken seriously.
___Numerical growth is important.
___Functions are more important than forms.
___We must pursue excellence in ministry.
___God wants people of strong faith.
___God uses courageous Christians.

Ministry Design Worksheet

1. Based on the information in chapter 5, what are your spiritual gifts? List them below. Is one a primary gift about which the others cluster? If so, then list it first. Also, identify any natural gifts.

   Spiritual Gifts:

   Natural Gifts:

2. What is your passion? (What do you care deeply and feel strongly about?)

3. What is your temperament? Circle the appropriate answer. If the information in chapter 5 doesn't help, take the *Personal Profile* (DiSC), the *Myers-Briggs Type Indicator* (MBTI), or Temperament Indicators 1 and 2 in my book *Maximizing Your Effectiveness* (pages 209–15).

DIRT	Primary:	DIRT
	Secondary:	DIRT
PPS	Primary:	DiSC
	Secondary:	DiSC
MBTI	E	
	S	N
	T	F
	J	P

4. How do your spouse and family feel about being involved in a church planting situation? Do they meet the qualifications for the family in chapter 5? Is your spouse excited about or at least open to church planting?

5. Based on your personal divine design and your family situation, what is your answer to the question, "Am I a lead or point church planter?" If your answer is no, or you're not sure, how might you fit into a church planting team?

Leadership Worksheet

1. In light of chapter 6, what is your definition of leadership? What is your definition of Christian leadership? Does it agree with the one in this book or does it differ? Why?

2. What are your motives for wanting to plant a church? Are they the same as those found in 1 Thessalonians 2:2–6?

3. How would you describe your character? Does it match up to that of Paul in 1 Thessalonians 2:2–8?

4. What are you currently doing to develop your character?

5. Do people naturally follow you? If they do, why are they following you? Conversely, if they don't, why don't they follow you? If you're not sure about any of these questions, ask someone you can trust to tell you the truth.

Conception Stage Worksheet

You'll need to recruit an intercessory prayer team. Write down the names of your team.

Core Values

1. According to the information in chapter 7 and the values audit in appendix F, list below your ministry core values. Mark in some way those that are aspirational.

2. If you're a lone church starter, these will likely be the ministry's core values. However, if you're working with a team, you'll probably need to consider their values in the process and come to an agreement on the team's final core values (it all depends on how you recruit the team). If the latter is your situation, what is your team's final values statement?

3. Develop a values statement or credo and write it below, using the information in chapter 7. Have you distinguished your aspirational from any actual core values?

4. How do you plan to communicate your values to later staff, the core group, and others who express an interest in being a part of the ministry?

Mission

1. Based on the information in chapter 7, what is your mission statement? Write it below. Is it broad enough to include your entire ministry? Is it brief—short enough to fit on a T-shirt? Is it biblical? Is it what you're supposed to be doing—Christ's Great Commission?

2. How will you communicate your mission statement to your launch group and others?

Environmental Scan

1. Based on the information in chapter 7, fill in the general environment table below. You will want to return to this scan and add to it later.

Trend	Response
Social trends	
Technological trends	
Economic trends	
Political/legal trends	
Philosophical/religious trends	
Other	

2. Fill in the church environment diagram below. Identify the particular church in the left column and the trend in the right column. (Adjust the categories accordingly if you're planting in an international environment.)

Churches	Trends
Local churches	
State churches	
National churches	
International churches	
Other	

Vision

1. What is your vision for the new church (what do you see when you picture this church and what it will be like in your mind)? Write it in the space below or on a separate sheet of paper. If you're working with a team or this is a hot start, did you include the others in the vision development process?

2. Does the vision statement comply with the definition in chapter 7? (Is it clear, challenging, and so forth?) Where might it fall short?

3. How do you plan to cast the vision to those who would be interested?

Strategy

Discovering Your Focus Group

1. Determining your focus group
   Identify your focus group. Place a check by those that apply.

___Lost	___Saved
___Unchurched	___Churched
___Like you	___Unlike you
___Receptive	___Resistant
___Modern	___Postmodern
___Needy (if so, list their particular needs)	

   Gathering information on your focus group
   Who are your focus group (demographics)?

   What do they want out of life (psychographics)?

   If they're moderns, how will you minister to them? If they're postmoderns, how will you minister to them (see appendix G)?

Construct a profile person. Would a profile person help you and your team to remember the identity of your focus group? If so, then create such a person.

Determine the kind of church that would reach this person.
  What kind of pastor?

  What kind of people?

  What kinds of meetings (large, medium, small)?

  What kinds of sermons (see appendix C)?

  What kind of worship (see appendix C)?

  What kinds of ministries?

2. Locating your focus group
  Where in the world is God leading you to start a church?

  Where within that country (state, province, etc.)?

  Will it be in an urban, suburban, or rural context?

3. Connecting with your focus group
Check below the methods that you plan to use to connect with your focus group.

___Building personal relationships
___Direct mail
___Telemarketing
___Community service
___Special Sundays
___Prayer ministry
___Welcome wagon
___Farming
___Media
___Others:

Developing a Disciple-Making Strategy

Step 1: What is your church's mission statement? Write it below:

Step 2: Identify the characteristics of a mature disciple. What will be your characteristics of a mature disciple (at least two but no more than five)?

How will you communicate them to your people? Write them in the appropriate place below:

___alliteration (for example, the three Cs)

___acrostic

___person

___picture

___other:

Step 3: Determine and write down the primary ministries that best accomplish the characteristics (include a sanctification matrix).

How will you communicate your developmental path?

___Visual (identify it)
___Sermons
___New member or attenders classes
___Brochure
___Website
___Other:

Step 4: How will you measure spiritual progress?

___Performance indicators (write down the performance indicators for each characteristic)
___Small-group leaders
___Congregation-wide survey
___Other:

Building a Gifted Leadership Team

What kind of character, competence, and chemistry are necessary for your team members?

Where will you recruit your team?

___School campus
___Local church
___Denomination/organization
___Mission agency
___Other:

What kind of team will you recruit? What temperament combinations are you looking for? If you already have a team, what are the temperament combinations? According to chapter 8, how well will you work together?

How many people do you want on your team?

___Two-person team
___Three-person team
___Three- to five-person team
___Other:

Have you developed mini-bios for each team person? Try writing yours out in the space below.

Who are some people that you've ministered with or who know you well who would serve on a board of reference?

Implementing the Strategy

Write below the initial specific actions that you need to take to begin to implement your strategy.

Prioritize these specific actions in the order of importance.

Determine a date (month and year) when each action should be completed.

Who will take responsibility for seeing that the specific action will be accomplished by the due date?

Who needs to know about these actions (leadership team, core group, membership, others)?

When will you have your MIR (monthly implementation review) meetings?

Note: You may want to put this information on a chart such as the following example that we used in my last church for the Christian education program.

Priority One: Christian Education Program

Develop a Sunday school program, nursery, and children's church that provide Christian education for all the people in our church.

Actions	Deadlines	Responsible Person
1. Recruit pastor of Christian Education	November 2005	Tom Smith
2. Recruit teachers, helpers, and director	December 2005	Greg Jones
3. Train teachers, helpers, and the director	January 2006	Greg Jones
4. Remodel rooms where necessary	January 2006	Greg Jones
5. Implement Christian Education program	February 2006	Greg Jones

Evaluating the Ministry's Performance

Design job/ministry descriptions for the professional and nonprofessional people who will serve in the church.

Who might lead the evaluation process?

Who will be conducting evaluations?

Who and what will they evaluate?

How often will evaluation take place?

Development Stage Worksheet

Gathering the Core Group

If your church is a cold start, according to chapter 9, how will you connect with a potential core group?
___Prayer
___Constituency of a school
___Parachurch
___Area leading-edge churches
___Advertising
___Networking
___Other:

If your church is a hot start, how will you get to know the people in the core group? How will you know if they'll make a good core group? How would you secure a commitment from them?

Cultivating the Core Group

Forming Spiritually

What process will you follow to implement your spiritual formation process?

Implementing Ministry

What is your plan for mobilizing your core group for ministry? Do you have the training or do you have someone on your team who is trained to mobilize your people?

What ministries did you select to accomplish your characteristics in the conception stage? Will you have a small-groups ministry? What will you do to minister to kids?

What is your plan for selecting and training leaders?

Will you have a membership? If so, what is your new member process?

Will you have a marketing ministry? If so, what's your plan for marketing the church?

Will you have preview services? When will they start?

Administering the Church's Affairs

What is your system for credibly managing the church's finances?

How will you evaluate the team, your leaders, and your ministries?

What is your plan to monitor the church's attendance, growth, and finances?

Have you selected a name for the church? If so, what is it?

Have you drafted a constitution and bylaws?

Have you incorporated the church and filed for IRS tax exemption?

Have you located a place for the church to meet? If so, where?

Have you found adequate facilities for the church to meet? If so, what are the advantages and disadvantages of this facility? How will you offset the latter?

What are some contingencies that the church might face, and how will you deal with them?

Do you have a website? If not, when will you have one?

Are you making a practice of planning ahead?

Growing the Core Group

What is your plan for implementing personal and corporate evangelism with your people?

How will you recruit believers?

Birth Stage Worksheet

Knowing When to Start

Is your church a cold or hot start? Using chapter 10 as a guideline, when might you have your birth event?

How many adults do you plan to have when you birth the church?

___10 to 12 families
___50–100 adults
___100-plus adults

On what particular day will you birth the church?

___Easter Sunday
___Palm Sunday
___Special Sunday
___Another day:

Based on the birth date, create a timeline back to when you will begin the church (development stage). When will that be? Is it a good time?

Choosing a Name

If you've not yet chosen a name, you'll need to do so by the church's birth day. What is the name of the church?

Locating a Place to Meet

If the place where you'll hold the birth service is different from where you've been meeting, you'll need to select a place for the birth event. Use the following as a location checklist:

___Appearance   ___Cost
___Visibility   ___Storage
___Accessibility   ___Signage
___Size   ___Parking
___Cleanliness   ___Reputation
___Location   ___Other:
___Potential ministries

Which of the following locations would be best for the church?
___School building
___Church building
___Public center
___Storefront
___Theater
___Other:

Publicizing the Meeting

What is your plan for publicizing the church in your geographical community?

What is your plan for publicizing the church in your people's relational communities?

Planning the Meeting

What will be your sermon topic for the birth event?

What is the plan for the worship service?

What will you need to do to the facility (if anything) to prepare it for the meeting?

What are your plans for the nursery?

What are your plans for children's ministries?

Growth Stage Worksheet

Leadership for Growth

Do you have the spiritual and natural gifts that help to grow a church? Mark the following gifts that are a part of your gifts mix.

___Leadership
___Faith
___Evangelism
___Communication (preaching, teaching)
___Strategy
___Other:

What is your passion (what do you care deeply and feel strongly about)? How will your passion affect the church's growth?

Identify your temperament. How will it affect church growth according to chapter 11?

Would you classify yourself as a pastoral caregiver or a rancher?

Vision for Growth

Which of the following characteristics are or will be true of your ministry?
___Family atmosphere
___Comfortable community
___Presence of a powerful person
___Single, clear vision
___Robust small-groups ministry
___Mobilized lay army
___Trained lay leaders who minister

Staffing for Growth

What is or will be your staff to worship attendance ratio?
___1 to 100
___1 to 150
___1 to 200
___1 to 250
___Other:

Where will you find leadership staff people?
___Within the ministry
___Outside the ministry
___Combination
___Other

What is or will be your criteria for your leadership staff?
___Character
___Ministry DNA (alignment on values, mission, and so forth)
___Different design
___Loyalty to the lead pastor

Mobilization for Growth

Who will be responsible for mobilizing the church's people?

Who will actually be involved in leading and conducting this ministry?
___Lead pastor
___Staff person
___Layperson
___Combination
___Other:

What will your mobilization ministry look like? How many phases? What will they be? What will you do in each?

When in the life of the church do you plan to implement your mobilization ministry?
___Development stage
___Birth stage
___Growth stage
___Maturity stage

Note: Be sure to read appendix A: A Well-Mobilized Lay Army.

Assimilation for Growth

Which of the following characteristics are or will be true of your church?
___Atmosphere of acceptance
___Robust small-groups ministry
___Newcomer's class
___New member's class
___Other:

Organization for Growth

What is or will be the role of the board?
___Micromanage the church
___Micromanage the pastor
___Micromanage the staff
___There will be no board
___Other:

What is or will be the role of the staff?
___Administer the church's affairs
___Conduct the church's ministry
___Train people to do ministry
___Other:

What is or will be the role of the people?
___Be ministered to
___Do ministry
___Other

Maturity Stage Worksheet

The Prescription for a Maturing Church

Which of the following does or will characterize your ministry?

___Regularly casts the church's vision
___Focuses on ministry not money
___Regularly evaluates and makes strategic changes
___Focuses on evangelism over edification
___Provides solid, biblical teaching (meat not milk)
___Messages for unchurched lost as well as believers
___Emphasis on making disciples (making mature believers)
___People are mobilized and doing ministry
___Leaders are trained to lead at every level of the church

The Leadership of a Maturing Church

Which of the following will characterize the lead pastor in the maturity stage?

___Strong leader
___Proactive point person
___The only leader
___Raises up other leaders
___Works closely with staff

Does or will the church have a governing board? If so, when? What is or will be its role? What is or will be the church's polity (congregation rule, elder rule, other)? How will power be distributed among the congregation, the board, and the lead pastor?

The Facilities of a Maturing Church

What kind of facilities does or will the church have long term?

___Temporary
___Permanent

If permanent, will they be used or new facilities?

___Used
___New

Where will the facilities be located?

___In the church's core community
___Away from other churches
___In a stable community
___In a changing community
___Other:

Reproduction Stage Worksheet

Reasons for Reproducing Churches

If someone asked you why the church should start other churches, what would you tell them?

Do you have a vision for planting church planting churches?

Benefits for Daughter Churches

Check below what you believe are some benefits for daughter churches, according to chapter 13.

___Finances   ___Counsel
___Core group   ___Talent
___Accountability   ___Personnel
___Encouragement   ___Shared events
___Prayer   ___Other:
___Credibility

Preferred Time for Reproducing

Your size is a factor in determining the best time for your church to start another church. What is your size and what do you believe is the best size?

___Doesn't matter
___20 people
___50 people
___100 people

Your growth is another factor that determines when you might plant a church. What is your growth situation and what do you believe is the best growth situation?

___Growing
___Plateaued
___Declining
___Dying
___All of the above
___Other

What will be your process for starting new churches? Does it agree with the process in chapter 13? If not, where does it differ?

Appendix A

A Well-Mobilized Lay Army

In his book *Honest to God?* Bill Hybels describes the following scene:

It's August. Throughout the country, the late summer ritual begins. And it's not a pretty sight.

Pastor Bob has just received his annual flood of resignation notes. Sunday school teachers, ushers, Bible study leaders, youth leaders, and assorted other "servers" have called it quits. He's not surprised. It happens every year. Some people offer lengthy explanations. Others say simply, "I've done my part."

Now Pastor Bob knows that the ministries of the church can't continue unless someone fills all these empty positions. So, with unprecedented determination, he begins psyching up for the annual "August Recruitment Campaign."

Pastor Bob isn't the first to fight this battle. His predecessor fought it, too. In fact, it's become somewhat of a tradition—one that even his most tradition-bound congregants would like to do without. So while Pastor Bob is psyching himself up, his two hundred members are doing the same. They know they'll have to be tough to resist this year's recruitment campaign. It's going to be war!

A man named Jim says to himself, "He's not going to get me this year. So help me, I don't care what he preaches on, or how often he threatens God's judgment. I'm not going to cave in—even if he starts to cry! Three years ago he cried and I ended up as a center aisle usher—and I don't even like people. This year I'll resist to the end."

Pastor Bob does know how much resistance has surfaced in his congregation. So this year he's bringing out the heavy artillery. He's planning a four-sided series called "Serve or Burn." Every week he'll use a dramatic illustration from *Foxe's Book of Martyrs*. There's nothing like true-to-life stories of people who gave up their lives for serving Christ.

He's already decided to wear a lapel microphone. Then he can walk the length of the stage, raise his voice, perspire a little bit, and wave his Bible in the air.

On the fourth week, he'll bring out his secret weapon. Seven-year-old Suzi Miller. He'll cradle the little darling on his lap and ask her what it will be like to spend a whole year in second grade Sunday school with no teacher. He hopes against hope that she'll cry. If she does, he'll win the war hands down. Sure as shootin' he'll win the war.

So the stage is set. It's going to be an interesting August.[1]

Unfortunately, all too often the above scenario describes the typical solution to a problem that every church across America faces—the unemployment problem. Not that people in the church are looking for things to do. In fact there's lots to be done, but no one's particularly excited about doing it—even those who are presently involved. Consequently, the church has no alternative but to hang a "Help Wanted" sign out front.

A vital principle for church planting is lay mobilization. Peter Drucker writes, "People determine the performance capacity of an organization. No organization can do better than the people it has."[2] Lay mobilization is the solution to the unemployment problem and involves the process of recruiting and equipping a well-mobilized lay army to accomplish the various ministries of the church. The object in church planting is not to pursue a corrective approach in order to take down the "Help Wanted" signs, but to pursue a preventative one to see that no signs go up in the first place.

In 1 Corinthians 12 Paul compares the church to a vibrant, healthy human body. Just as it is critical that all the parts of the human body be present and functioning in their proper places, so it is in the life of the church. This is the task of lay mobilization. This principle is placing the right people in the right places for the right reasons with the result that every member becomes a minister.

The Plan for Lay Mobilization

An important part of the Father's plan for blessing is our involvement in fruitful service for him in the church. This is evident from his divine accomplishments in our lives. First, he's created each of us with a unique design (Job 10:8–9; Ps. 139:15–16; Jer. 1:5; Luke 1:14–15; Gal. 1:15). As we've already seen, this includes our temperament, natural skills, talents, and abilities.

All of us who are Christians have the Holy Spirit within us. At the point of conversion, God, the Holy Spirit, indwells each of us. He, in turn, supplies us with all the power we need to accomplish his ministry in this world (Eph. 3:16, 20). Consequently, it's the Holy Spirit, not us, who provides the divine power and accomplishes Christ's work through us.

The Savior has placed us in his body, the church, and given us spiritual gifts, special God-given abilities for service that are listed in 1 Corinthians 12–14, Romans 12, and Ephesians 4:7–11. All Christians have at least one gift and probably more.

All Christians are believer-priests (1 Peter 2:5–9; Rev. 1:6). This priesthood involves such services as sacrifice, worship, and prayer. Sacrificial service includes the commitment of ourselves to God along with our praise and giving. Worship concerns the acts of adoration, confession, and thanksgiving. Finally, prayer involves intercession for God's people as they attempt to carry out his work.

The Father has placed us in various difficult circumstances in life for more effective service. This is the point of 2 Corinthians 1:3–7. No one Christian, including a pastor, can or ever will experience all the difficulties of life. However, God allows different individuals to experience various trials and tragedies so that they can minister effectively as others go through similar trying circumstances.

God has accomplished all of this for us and much more. Does he desire that his people merely show up on Sunday morning and occupy space? Is there more to Christianity and local church involvement than "sitting and soaking" in some pew?

God's divine accomplishments are for the purpose of enabling us to be instruments of his grace in the lives of both believers and unbelievers alike in this world. The New Testament shows little patience for noninvolvement in the body of Christ.

The Problem of Lay Mobilization

The great tragedy is that far too many Christians are either not involved or not properly involved in any service for Christ or his church. The Lay Renewal Movement of the 1950s and 1960s was a great idea and did result in more lay involvement in church ministries. However, this movement didn't survive well in the 1980s and 1990s.

The evidence for this lack of lay involvement is the 20-80 principle. Essentially, this is the time-tested Pareto principle that 20 percent of the people in the church are doing 80 percent of the work of the church. These are the serving contributors. This means that 80 percent of the people in the majority of our churches are soaking consumers who aren't using their gifts and talents for the Savior. As far as the church is concerned, they're unemployed! Their names are on both the membership rolls and the unemployment rolls of the church at the same time. Consequently, there's a small, faithful but exhausted group in every church who are doing much of the work of the church.

According to a survey by George Gallup, the Pareto principle is too optimistic. Gallup indicates that only 10 percent of the people in the church are doing 90 percent of the ministry of the church. Thus 90 percent of the people are typically unemployed "sitters and soakers." Of the 90 percent, approximately 50 percent say they'll not become involved for whatever reason. The remaining 40 percent say they'd like to become involved, but they've not been asked or trained.

The church in America doesn't simply have an unemployment problem; it has a massive unemployment problem!

In his book *Say It with Love*, Howard Hendricks laments the unemployment problem. He refers to an analogy between it and the game of football:

> Make no mistake: the greatest curse on the Church today is that we are expecting a small corps of professionals to get God's work done. No way!
>
> Bud Wilkinson, former football coach at the University of Oklahoma, was in Dallas for a series of lectures on physical fitness. A TV reporter interviewed him about the President's physical fitness program and asked: "Mr. Wilkinson, what would you say is the contribution of modern football to physical fitness?" The reporter expected a lengthy speech.
>
> As if he had been waiting 30 years for this question, he said, "Absolutely nothing."
>
> The young reporter stared and squirmed and finally stuttered, "Would you care to elaborate on that?"
>
> Wilkinson said, "Certainly. I define football as 22 men on the field who desperately need rest and 50,000 people in the stands who desperately need exercise."
>
> I thought to myself: What a definition of a church! A few compulsively active people run around the field while the mass of the people rest in the stands. But not according to the Word of God![3]

Frank Tillapaugh reported that "Larry Richards and his colleagues asked 5,000 pastors what the greatest needs are for strengthening the church. On a scale of five from a twenty-five-item list, nearly 100 percent gave a first or second priority to 'Getting my lay people involved as ministering men and women.'"[4]

The state of lay involvement in the church today raises the obvious question: Why is it that so many people are so uninvolved in the ministries of their churches? There are several reasons.

1. *A faulty recruitment process*—one that is based on emotion and coercion. A good example is Pastor Bob, who began his August recruitment campaign using such coercive techniques as *Foxe's Book of Martyrs* and his four-sided series of sermons called "Serve or Burn." If that tactic didn't work, he would abandon it for an emotional technique! His plan was to bring out his secret weapon, little seven-year-old Suzi Miller. If Pastor Bob prays hard enough or accidentally pinches the precious little girl, maybe she'll cry. And if she does, he's won the day. Even the most calloused, task-oriented person would have difficulty resisting the tears of Suzi Miller. Many laugh at all this on the outside, but cringe on the inside.

People in the church grow weary of hearing tired and disgruntled church people telling all sorts of "tear-filled" or "arm-twisting" recruitment stories. For example, "When the pastor began to cry, I broke down and gave in. I can't stand to see grown men cry!" "The pastor kept bugging me. He called me at home and at work, regardless of the hour. It was either give in or get out, and we weren't ready to look for another church." And finally, "He thinks so highly of me! He'd be so disappointed if I said no."

2. *A lack of knowledge and expertise on the part of those who would attempt to mobilize laypeople.* Seminaries, Bible colleges, and various Christian schools offer little or nothing on lay mobilization training.

In churches, evangelical pastors teach their people about spiritual gifts. But that's all they know to do. They expect people to respond based on information alone. Most pastors don't know how to devise a system to help the "unemployed" discover their gifts and implement them in ministry. Pastors have a good biblical theology of the gifts but lack a practical theology.

3. *Laypeople are waiting for a personal invitation.* Many people will not respond to a public invitation to service but will respond to a personal, private invitation. They want to serve in some capacity, but they want to be asked personally. Perhaps the public invitation is too informal, or they feel special if someone approaches them individually. Regardless, the church will have to take a more aggressive, personal approach to lay recruitment in the future.

4. *A failure on the part of some pastors to appreciate and value the layperson's abilities to minister in the church.* In some cases, pastors assume that ministry is their responsibility. They're the ones who've been specifically trained for ministry. A significant number have attended seminary

or some equivalent. Why involve inexperienced laypeople who wouldn't know what to do and wouldn't have the time even if they did?

In other cases, this attitude may be due to problems of codependency on the part of the pastor. A church consultant once asked a non-Christian psychiatrist his opinion of church pastors in general. The surprising response was that a number of them are codependent. They derive a sense of significance from feeling needed. When someone requests help, they respond partly because if feels so good to be needed.

5. *Laypeople are convinced that ministry is the pastor's job.* They sincerely believe that pastors are the ones who are supposed to do the work of the ministry. After all, they're ordained and have been trained for ministry. They know what to do. In fact that's what we pay them for.

Many feel that laypeople aren't qualified or as able to minister to other people. Their job is to be faithful and to be there on Sunday mornings and to support the church financially. They sincerely appreciate it when other laypeople in the church visit with them whether at home or in the hospital, but that isn't the same as when the pastor visits. This is a common view held by many who are of the generation of Americans preceding the Baby Boom. We call them Builders, Pre-Boomers, or the Harry Truman Generation. Often, their roots are in rural America, and they've grown up with a traditional, more rural view of the pastor's role.

The Need for Significance

One very basic need of every person is a sense of significance. In his book *The Search for Significance*, Robert McGee emphasizes the importance of this need: "Whether labeled 'self-esteem' or 'self-worth,' the feeling of significance is crucial to man's emotional, spiritual, and social stability, and is the driving element within the human spirit. Understanding this single need opens the door to understanding our actions and attitudes."[5]

There's a subtle difference between self-worth and significance. Self-worth affects who we *are*, that is, our sense of value or personal worth. Good self-worth means we feel good about ourselves. Significance relates to what we *do*, a sense that what we accomplish has value. Good significance means we feel good about what we do. In essence, we want to believe that our lives make a difference, that they really count for something. We do not want to think that we're just taking up space here on planet Earth. Regardless of any difference between significance and self-esteem, both are critical to our emotional and spiritual health.

Significance and Ministry

Those who aren't mobilized and involved in the ministry of the church find their significance in other pursuits. Most commonly, they find it in their work or in leisure time pursuits, such as sports or a hobby. They believe that their lives make a difference because of their expertise in their vocation or hobby. As long as this is the case, they may never become involved in the ministry of their church. Their private response is, "Who needs it?"

Those who are involved but are in the wrong place, the round pegs in square holes, eventually realize that they lack a sense of significance in their ministry. They begin to wonder if what they're doing will make a difference. Then they question if their ministry and possibly their church count for anything. The eventual result is burnout and potential disillusionment with the church and possibly Christianity. Often they join not only the "unemployed" in the church but the ranks of the unchurched as well.

The Task of Lay Mobilization

The primary task of lay mobilization is to equip and mobilize laity for ministry. This is the thrust of Ephesians 4:11–12: "It was he who gave some to be apostles, some to be prophets, some to be evangelists, and some to be pastors and teachers, to prepare God's people for works of service, so that the body of Christ may be built up." The local church must be a place where people are pursued, won, enfolded, discipled, and mobilized for ministry. The goal is "Every member a minister!" Our people need to be equipped and mobilized for several important reasons.

First, all Christians in the church, whether professional or laypeople, are happiest and healthiest when they're both equipped and mobilized for ministry. There needs to be a balance as shown in the two columns below:

Equipped	Mobilized
Consuming	Contributing
Soaking	Serving
Taking in	Giving out

It's good for people to "sit and soak" because that's a legitimate part of the equipping process. In fact, in the two columns above, many of the items in the column on the left are sometimes used in a negative way although they're all essential to the process. Actually, there's a time for God's people to consume, to "sit and soak," to absorb or take in.

A second reason is that *problems occur when a person is not involved in either process or is involved in one but not the other.* Some aren't "soaking" at all, whereas others are "soaking" and that's all that's happening. Here the task of the church is to correct both problems. In the first situation, our job is to bring people from a state of noninvolvement to one of involvement. In the second, it's to correct an imbalance. Both professional and laypeople typically experience a lack of balance. Laypeople tend to gravitate to the column on the left, and the pastoral staff to the column on the right.

On the one hand, potential lay ministers are equipped but in desperate need of mobilization. They've heard numerous messages on the spiritual gifts and may have discovered their unique gifts, but they aren't using them. They could be compared to a basketball team that's always practicing but never plays any games. After a while, they'll grow weary, lose interest, and either look for another team or retire early.

On the other hand, the pastor and possibly the staff are mobilized to the maximum but are in need of additional equipping or retooling. Typically, they begin ministry with some training but become so overwhelmed with ministry that they don't have or take time for more equipping. As time passes, they need exposure to new ministry ideas. They need to become aware of what others are doing who are effectively ministering to our generation. They're like a basketball team that plays so many games that they don't have time to learn any new plays or develop the different aspects of their game. The result is that they lose a lot of games and grow tired of playing the same old game. The crucial need in both situations is for a healthy balance.

A final reason why all need to be involved is because *everyone is a 10 somewhere.*[6] God doesn't make mistakes when he creates people, brings them into this world, and then into his kingdom. His design is intentional and with an ultimate purpose in mind, which includes some form of service in relation to the local church. Everyone fits somewhere and the closer they come to that fit, the greater will be their ministry satisfaction and personal feelings of significance. Again, it becomes the task of lay mobilization to help them come as close as possible to their proper fit.

The Solution to Lay Mobilization

The equipping and mobilizing process begins with personal assessment. Assessment is vital in helping believers discover how God has designed them and how to minister accordingly. The principles covered in chapters

5 and 6 and in my book *Maximizing Your Effectiveness* not only apply to church planters but also to those who in a lay capacity minister in the local church.

The Preparation for Lay Mobilization

A good lay mobilization program must be planned before it is implemented in the church. This planning process involves several important decisions.

The Philosophy of the Program

The first is philosophical and involves both an issue and an answer. The issue is twofold. Do you create a structure and attempt to place the people you have into that structure, or do you start with the people you have and design the structure around them? The rationale behind beginning with a structure is that every church requires certain basic core ministries that are necessary for it to function. While these may vary from church to church and tradition to tradition, most consist of such areas as evangelism, worship, preaching, and Christian education. If a new church doesn't have some of these bases covered, then potential members will look elsewhere. For example, families, which make up the backbone of any ministry, will be attracted to a church that has something for the children.

The other option involves starting with the people that God has attracted to the core group and designing the church's ministries around them. The rationale is that God is in control and has sovereignly brought together those who make up the core group. Rather than attempt to force them into a predesigned structure, why not design the structure around them in light of their gifts, temperaments, talents, and so on? Then each will serve in ministries for which they have the right gifts and passion.

For church planters the answer lies somewhere in between. It would be wise to start with a general structure that consists of the ministries that will be necessary to reach a particular target group. People should not be forced into ministries that violate their divine design, however. While people may have to serve in areas for which they are not designed, this service shouldn't exceed 40–50 percent of their ministry time. From a practical standpoint, it's not always possible to place people in their precise ministry niche. Life simply doesn't work that way! However, the church can move too far in the other direction and violate divine design, which will eventually cause ministry burnout.

God sovereignly attracts people with the right designs to staff the necessary programs. In fact it is fascinating to take the core group through an assessment program and observe the various designs God has brought into the church. If, however, the people needed for a certain ministry are not in the group, the church planter should delay starting that program—and possibly the church—until the right people are available. There are some options. Either take a passive approach and wait for God to bring them along as new people join the core group, or go out and attempt to recruit the right individuals for the ministry. An example would be quality musicians for a band. Pursue these individuals by talking to other worship leaders and band members. Often God provides through persistent pursuit.

The Design of the Program

A second decision involves the design of the assessment program. If there's someone on the church planting team who's trained in assessment, it will be that person's responsibility to make these determinations.

There are several design decisions that have to be made. One concerns the length of the program. The discovery phase, which will be explained below, should last no longer than a few evenings or one or two Saturday mornings at the most, unless the interest of the group dictates otherwise.

Another design decision involves the areas to be assessed. These should include spiritual gifts, passion, temperament, and any natural gifts or talents. In addition, assessment tools, if any are to be used, must be chosen. The information in chapter 5 should be most helpful in determining this.[7]

The Recipients of the Program

A third decision concerns those who will be assessed. Probably everyone should be assessed. This sends a clear message to all that the church desires that every member be a minister. There are people who have never been very active in a church ministry who will be motivated to service as the result of a good assessment program.

Most people become excited about the process and require little motivation to become involved. It's a good idea to explain at the beginning that this approach is more developmental than psychological to relieve any anxiety on the part of those who have undergone assessment for counseling purposes.

The Length of the Program

A fourth decision is how long the program should last. Should the program be used initially as the church is planted and dropped later, or should it become a permanent ministry of the church? Here there's little debate. A divine design assessment program is a must for any church that desires to mobilize its laity. It's also an essential ingredient of the assimilation process. It encourages new people to stay and get involved. Consequently, this program should be established for the life of the church. The initial core group should go through it and so should everyone who joins thereafter. It's wise regularly to evaluate and expand the ministry as the church grows in size.

The Process of Lay Mobilization

A good assessment program will accomplish lay mobilization by taking people through a minimum of three phases.[8]

The Discovery Phase

First is the discovery phase, which attempts to help laypeople discover their basic divine design. It consists primarily of two parts: instruction and assessment.

The instruction portion is necessary to introduce the core group and any new believers to the various areas of assessment. This involves teaching them about such topics as spiritual gifts, passion, temperament, and other design elements. The aim is to provide them with a general, biblical understanding of these areas. For example, they should know what the Scriptures teach about spiritual gifts in general and the definition and uses of each gift in particular. This may take place over a few evenings or a Saturday morning. Should this process last too long, however, people will begin to lose interest.

At the same time, evaluation also takes place. Each person listens with an "evaluative ear." They're absorbing all the information while, at the same time, evaluating and determining what is true of them. This can best be accomplished both by explaining the various areas and by using selected assessment tools, such as a spiritual gifts inventory or one of the personality profiles. The aim is to help people come up with at least an initial feel for their divine design that they can put down on paper. I have written *Maximizing Your Effectiveness* to help accomplish the Discovery Phase. It instructs believers in the divine design concept and then provides a number of assessments (spiritual gifts inventory, temperament tools, and so forth) in the appendixes.

Of the few churches that attempt some kind of program of assessment, most prematurely conclude with the first phase. This serves only to excite people and then kill their initial enthusiasm. There are two more critical phases as well.

The Consultation Phase

The second critical phase involves consultation. Here people meet with a designated staff or layperson who provides personal consultation one-on-one or in a small-group context.

The consultant could be an individual who is a member of the initial church planting team and specializes in personal assessment. However, this is such a new field that there simply aren't many people who are trained and available to do it. Because there's such a need for this kind of ministry, we'll be seeing more assessment people in ministry in the future. We could call them ministers of discipleship or involvement.[9]

Most likely the consultant will be someone on the planting team who enjoys and serves the team in this as well as several other capacities. This person should select and train key laypeople in the church who show a gift or inclination for assessment. They should be allowed to take over this vital ministry. Chances are good that God will provide a gifted layperson who is stronger in this area than the original pastoral staff person. Then as the ministry grows, this person can recruit others as lay consultants.

The consultant will accomplish several objectives. The first is to provide individuals with personal help in determining and confirming their designs. This may involve spending time helping them through the process and answering their questions or simply confirming the results of the Discovery Phase.

Once this is accomplished to the satisfaction of both the consultant and the individual, the second objective is to aid them in discovering their personal ministry niche in the church. The consultant will help them decide what ministries they're best suited for in light of their individual design. This objective will be the most difficult and will require some time and expertise.

The Mobilization Phase

The final phase is mobilization. In this phase the consultant helps believers discover where they can minister either within or outside the walls of the church. This is the stage at which people discover their ministry niche. It's twofold.

The first concerns the church's ministry positions. The consultant will need to be aware of the various ministry needs within the church body. This information may come from a variety of sources, depending on the size of the ministry. If the church has just been planted, then the source will be the team. If the church is already established, then the information will come from the various ministries within it. Regardless of the source, the team or ministries need to develop job or ministry descriptions for each position in their ministries to guide placement. These would include the necessary spiritual gifts, passion, and temperament, the supervisor, and any other pertinent information. All of this data could be loaded in a computer database so it can be accessed in the placement process.

The second part of an individual's discovering his or her ministry niche concerns the church's ministry leaders. The consultant will send the person to the leader in charge of the ministry that seems to be a match for the individual. Then it becomes the responsibility of the ministry to orient and equip the person for service. Should things not work out, the person returns to the consultant, who may reassess the individual, make some adjustments in the ministry vision, and suggest another ministry.

Should people have ministry missions that don't presently coincide with any of the ministries of the church, one of two things can happen. The team will need to make a decision as to whether they're ready to start a new ministry. Perhaps they could become involved in a target ministry of the church, such as outreach to international students at the local college or street people in the inner city area.[10] Another possibility is to encourage their involvement in some ministry beyond that of the church. It could be a parachurch ministry or possibly a ministry in another church in the area.

Lay Mobilization Exercise

1. Are you familiar with the method of lay mobilization described by Bill Hybels at the beginning of this chapter? Can you add anything to it from your own personal experiences? Are you satisfied with this approach?

2. Do you agree with the explanation of why so many laypeople aren't involved in our churches? What reasons would you add, if any, to the list in this chapter?

3. In preparation for developing a lay mobilization plan, will you create a structure and attempt to fit people into it, or will you develop the structure around your people? Will you attempt both?

4. Do you like the lay mobilization process that's presented in this chapter? Why or why not? What would you change or add to it?

Appendix B

A Culturally Relevant Ministry

With a smile on her face, a friend gave my wife a sheet of plain, typed paper. She read it, laughed, and passed it on to me. I've read it and chuckled, and now I pass it on to you just as it came to me.

FOR ALL THOSE BORN PRIOR TO 1945
We are survivors!!!!! Consider the changes we have witnessed:
We were before television, before penicillin, before polio vaccines, frozen foods, Xerox, contact lenses, Frisbees, and the Pill.
We were before radar, credit cards, split atoms, laser beams, and ball-point pens; before pantyhose, dishwashers, clothes dryers, electric blankets, air conditioners, drip-dry clothes—and before man walked on the moon.
We got married first and *then* lived together. How quaint can you be?
In our time, closets were for clothes, not for "coming out of." Bunnies were small rabbits and rabbits were not Volkswagens. Designer jeans were scheming girls named Jean or Jeanne, and having a meaningful relationship meant getting along well with our cousins.
We thought fast food was what you ate during Lent, and outer space was the back of the Riviera Theatre.
We were before house-husbands, gay rights, computer dating, dual careers, and commuter marriages. We were before day-care centers, group therapy, and nursing homes. We never heard of FM radio, tape decks, electric typewriters, artificial hearts, word processors, yogurt, and guys wearing earrings. For us time-sharing meant togetherness—not computers or condominiums; a "chip" meant a piece of wood; hardware meant hardware; and software wasn't even a word!
In 1940, "made in Japan" meant junk and the term "making out" referred to how you did on an exam. Pizzas, McDonalds, and instant coffee were unheard of.

We hit the scene when there were 5 and 10 cent stores where you bought things for five and ten cents. Sanders and Wilsons sold ice cream cones for a nickel or a dime. For one nickel you could ride a streetcar, make a phone call, buy a Pepsi or enough stamps to mail one letter *and* two postcards. You could buy a new Chevy Coupe for $600 but who could afford one? A pity, too, because gas was only eleven cents a gallon!

In our day, cigarette smoking was fashionable, grass was mowed, Coke was a cold drink, and pot was something you cooked in. Rock music was a Grandma's lullaby and AIDS were helpers in the principal's office.

We were certainly not before the difference between the sexes was discovered but we were surely before the sex change; we made do with what we had. And we were the last generation that was so dumb as to think you needed a husband to have a baby!

No wonder we are so confused and there is such a generation gap today!

BUT WE SURVIVED!! What better reason to celebrate?[1]

Most people who read this little essay laugh, but for different reasons. Some people laugh because it's nostalgic. It reminds them of the "good old days" when life seemed so much simpler and easier. These Builders make up the generation that preceded the Baby Boom Generation. They are the Harry Truman Generation. Other people laugh because they take much of what is said for granted. They tend to assume that life has always been like it is today. This group consists of the Baby Boom Generation and Generation X.

What all of this depicts is change. Times have changed drastically! And there's more—much more—to come. In terms of information alone, George Barna noted in the 1990s: "We now have only 3 percent of the information that will be available to us by 2010."[2] Someone has said that, currently, the amount of information doubles every five years! Obviously, all this massive change has deeply influenced our culture. Life during the 1940s and 1950s is completely foreign to life as it is in the twenty-first century.

As our world changes, the evangelical church must change as it attempts to communicate the message of Jesus Christ. The cultural leap from the unchurched community to most American churches is too vast. Consequently, our planted churches must be culturally relevant if they're to reach this and future unchurched generations for the Savior. They must be relevant when they begin, and they must remain relevant. When I use the term *culturally relevant,* what do I mean? *Being culturally relevant means communicating the Christian message in general and the gospel in particular in ways that each new generation not only hears it but also understands it.* Churches become culturally irrelevant when they allow their time-honored practices and traditions to confuse and cloud the message and the gospel. This must not be if churches hope to reach younger and future generations.

It's also imperative that church planters develop a biblical theology of culture. They must understand that culture in itself is neutral. For example, Adam and Eve lived within a culture before the fall, and cultural diversity will be with us in heaven (Rev. 7:9–10). However, culture was devastated by the fall and now may be used for good or bad (a good example is the use of language—James 3:9–10).

There are at least six principles that will help church planters realize and maintain cultural relevance.

The Principle of Cultural Recognition

In terms of what it values and practices, every church must distinguish between its unique culture and biblical truth.

The Explanation

While every church exists within a culture—the world out there—every church also has its own unique culture—the world in here. A church's culture consists of its beliefs in general, its values (the core beliefs that guide and direct what it does), and how these values manifest themselves in the congregation (the church's rituals, ceremonies, heroes, ministries, clothing, and so on). In short, the church's culture is "the way we do things around here." This culture is affected by the general culture of the community in which the church is located—the world out there. Whether we like it or not, every church is affected to some degree by the culture of its community. The world out there is reflected in various ways in the world in here. Though some Christians resist this truth, it's simply part of living in a community.

The Christian often views the general culture of the community in a totally negative light. It's important to recognize, however, that not everything in the world out there is necessarily bad. There are a number of areas that are morally neutral, such as participation in the arts or the pursuit of a particular talent, like singing or playing a musical instrument. Ultimately, the question isn't whether we reflect the culture of our community. That's a given! The question is which culture we reflect—that of the twentieth or that of the twenty-first century.

Evangelical churches attempt to follow the teachings of the Scriptures and to apply them to what they do in the church as well as at home and in the marketplace. Thus the world in here is a mixture of the application of the Bible to the life of the church and the influence—whether great or small—of the world out there. Again, the latter can be good or bad (Rom. 14:14–15). The point is that the church's values and beliefs consist of a mixture of scriptural truth and the world in here.

The problem is that over time the church begins to confuse the two and values the style and practices of the world in here on an equal basis with eternal biblical truth. This affects choices of clothing, hair styles, music (both instruments and songs), times for the church service, versions of the Bible, the order of worship, the number of services per week, the name of the church, prayers, and pews.

For example, the church may have used an organ for years as the primary instrument in facilitating worship. Many in the congregation have become so accustomed to singing with the accompaniment of an organ that they think there's something sacred about this particular instrument. Yet it's only a matter of time before the culture changes, and the organ declines in popularity as a musical instrument in the world out there. How do churches respond? Most churches continue to use the organ because they now believe that it's a sacred instrument. After all, they've been using it for all these years, so there must be something special about it.

The Application

The principle of cultural recognition seeks to help the church distinguish between that which is truly biblical and eternal (functions) and that which is temporal and subject to change (forms). Knowing and understanding this principle is beneficial because it makes us aware of the two categories and allows us to consider change in the second category. Far too many people aren't even aware of the fact that they have placed a church tradition on the same plane as biblical truth. This results in little or no change at all.

Church planters must be aware of this danger from the very beginning. In fact they must be sensitive to both the culture of the community and the culture of the church. They should not be afraid to make changes in the church that don't violate Scripture. For example, many churches are using guitars and drums in their worship services. While these are morally neutral instruments, they are more in vogue with the world out there than organs.

In some areas of the country, when unchurched people walk into a church that still uses an organ, they're turned off by it and aren't willing to consider spiritual truth. While they have no problems with the organ as a musical instrument, it just seems so outdated to them. Sometimes this means the sermon is prejudged as outdated as well. It would be a shame for an unchurched person to walk away from a service where Christ is proclaimed because a group of people have insisted on using a musical instrument that is merely a part of their tradition.

The Principle of Cultural Adaptation

The mature church must be willing to be flexible in areas that relate to its unique culture (the world in here) but not in areas that relate to biblical truth.

The Explanation

There are two areas in which a church can adjust in response to changes in the world out there. It can change its functions or its forms.

The functions have to do with the foundational principles of belief and doctrine. We looked at these in chapter 4. They consist of principles of evangelism, worship, fellowship, leadership, community, and other similar principles. The evangelical church for the most part holds to the Scriptures as its authority and the basis for what it believes. Since biblical truth is eternal truth, the church cannot and must not compromise its biblical functions.

There are some churches, however, that have chosen to respond to the massive changes in our culture by making changes in the areas of faith and functions. In response to pressure from gays and lesbians, many denominational churches have begun to take steps to ordain them as priests. Others are considering softening their stance on homosexual relationships and sexual relationships outside of marriage.

The other area has to do with the church's forms that carry out its functions. We also looked at these in chapter 4. Forms are reflected in a church's strategies, programs, and lifestyles. Most of these are morally neutral areas where the church has freedom to change and adjust to what is taking place in the world out there. This is God's way of keeping his church relevant to its culture so that the church can get a fair hearing from those who are not or have never been a part of it. The evangelical church must not change or violate the clear functions of the Scriptures, but it must change and adjust what it does in terms of its programs and strategies (its forms) if it is to remain relevant. I'll say more about this under The Principles of a Biblical Hermeneutic.

It is sad that many evangelical churches have refused to adjust their forms and stay relevant. They think they're maintaining biblical integrity, but in reality they're preserving the forms and culture of a bygone era. If you want to know what life was like in America in the 1940s and 1950s, then attend one of these churches, because things haven't changed much. Unfortunately, unchurched people walk into these churches and experience culture shock. They're repelled—not by the message of Christ but by the lack of relevance. They know a dinosaur when they see one!

The Application

The planted church must be willing to be flexible in areas of Christian liberty and the world in here, especially when it comes to reaching unchurched people. In 1 Corinthians 9:19–23 Paul indicates that while he has various rights within the realm of Christian liberty, he is willing to set them aside to reach lost people. This involves moving in their direction. In verse 20 Paul says that he became like those who were under the law in order to reach them with the gospel. This is a reference to the religious Jews of the first century, who would be somewhat parallel to churched lost people today. In verse 21 Paul states that he became like those who weren't under law to reach them as well. This is a reference to the nonreligious Gentiles, who would be very similar to today's unchurched generation.

In this passage and in 10:23–33, Paul isn't talking about compromising the faith. He's talking about a willingness on the part of the church to be open to change and to adapt its traditions and practices (the world in here) to reach the unchurched. But many are unwilling to be flexible.

Inward focus. One problem is that a significant number of evangelical churches focus inwardly, not outwardly. They plan their programs around themselves, around their wants and desires. For example, they find it most convenient to meet on Sunday mornings at 11:00 AM. This is a matter of Christian liberty, and there's nothing wrong with it.

But what if they conducted a survey of unchurched people in their community and discovered that, if invited, these people would come to church but only for the 11:00 service? Would they be willing to give up the convenience of this time slot to reach the lost? Would they be willing to get up an hour earlier, worship at 9:00 AM, then bring their lost friends to an 11:00 AM meeting that is designed to reach them with the gospel of

Christ? Would they be willing to give up their favorite place in their pew so a lost person could sit there?

Unrealistic expectations. Another problem is that far too many of our churches expect lost people to behave like saved people—before they've become saved people. We're asking them to adjust to us and the way we do things at church rather than our adapting to them and where they are in life.

Many of these people are "traveling incognito" when they visit our services. They don't want to sign, sing, or say anything. They're simply "checking things out." They don't want to be singled out or embarrassed. Yet many of our churches conduct their evangelistic services as if these people were Christians. We speak Christianeze and expect them to understand our language. We use such terms as reconciliation, redemption, and propitiation in our sermons (terms that lost people in the first century understood because they were used commonly in everyday life). We sing older, traditional hymns of the faith that employ such King James verbs as "wert" and "art" and expect them to understand our music. We ask them to sign a visitor's card and stand and introduce themselves so we can know who they are. This is done in spite of the fact that speaking in public is the number one fear of most Americans. Then we wonder why none of our lost visitors ever come back for a second look.

If we truly desire to reach the lost in general and the unchurched lost in particular, we must be willing to be flexible and adapt what we do to them and where they are in life. We need not abandon any biblical principles. We should not schedule a "happy hour" to get to know these people. Nor should we fill our music with popular contemporary themes such as sexual immorality and suicide.

But we can begin to move in their direction in an attempt to reach them with the saving message of Christ. For example, we can demonstrate that we're not a cloistered community by addressing current issues in our sermons. We can present what Scripture has to say about healthy families in contrast to dysfunctional families. We can address the benefits of sexual intimacy within marriage as opposed to outside the marital bond. We can hold out the hope and help found in Romans 6 for those who find themselves in bondage to some addiction.

We can also adapt and move in their direction in terms of our music. Scripture doesn't consecrate a particular musical instrument. The fact that a number of churches today still use an organ or a piano in worship doesn't mean that these are sacred instruments. The church needs to be open to the use of other instruments such as guitars and drums. The fact that secular institutions use these instruments doesn't mean the church can't. Lost people will quickly see that how we use these instruments is different from how the world of secular entertainment uses them.

The same is true of music with a beat. The fact that secular music may have a beat to it doesn't mean Christian music shouldn't. (I would argue that the distinguishing characteristic of Christian music is the lyrics, not the beat or instrumentation.) The key is what the church does with the music that has a beat. Certainly, wisdom and moderation are necessary. Far too many churches, however, have not thought this through and often overreact (have overreacted) in the opposite direction.

It's interesting to note that many of these churches are flexible when it comes to reaching young people. They recognize the value of what Paul is saying in 1 Corinthians 9 and 10. They realize that if youth ministries aren't relevant, they die a quick death. Yet they draw a line and refuse to apply this principle to the other programs of the church in which they're involved.

It's also interesting that a number of today's pastors who are reaching unchurched lost people in great numbers were formerly in youth ministry. What they've done is to plant innovative churches using the principles they learned in working with and ministering to young people.

The Principle of Cultural Evaluation

The church should regularly evaluate the cultural aspects of its ministry and make whatever adjustments are necessary to stay in touch with the people to whom it seeks to minister.

The Explanation

The purpose of this principle is to keep the planted church on the "ministry edge." A large number of evangelical churches remain anywhere from ten to as many as forty or even fifty years behind the times. It's important that the church of Jesus Christ not become a memorial to a generation that has passed from the scene long ago, unless it's specifically targeting people who were a part of that generation. There's nothing wrong with remembering and valuing some aspects of life as it was forty or fifty years ago, but this should not be done in the church.

Pastors who apply the principle of cultural evaluation will involve their churches in regular evaluation. This involvement means change, which will upset people. For some reason most of us don't like change. We like to stick with that which is familiar, the tried and true.

Yet change is the key ingredient in both salvation and sanctification. To be saved, people must repent or change their thinking about working their way to heaven and accept God's way through Christ. But change doesn't end at the cross. The whole of sanctification involves the process of change. In 2 Corinthians 3:18, Paul writes, "And we, who with unveiled faces all reflect the Lord's glory, are being transformed into his likeness with ever-increasing glory, which comes from the Lord, who is the Spirit." If change is critical to salvation and sanctification, we must be open to the idea that change could benefit us in terms of what we do in the church.

The merit of regular evaluation and updating of the church's programs and ministries is that the church will grow and expand in its outreach. Without regular evaluation, churches get involved in too many programs and activities. A particular ministry such as a Sunday school class will go on and on, even though it may no longer serve the purpose for which it was intended and attracts only a few people. Other programs are begun and eventually the church has far more than it can possibly manage.

The result is that the church adopts a maintenance mentality and shifts into a maintenance mode. Should it have to hire a new pastor, it finds a maintenance person whose ministry is primarily to keep everything running smoothly. This will plateau the church and eventually send it into decline.

The Application

Churches should regularly evaluate their forms or practices but not their functions. A function is permanent and eternal and isn't subject to change because it's based on an eternal, unchanging God. The same isn't true concerning our practices and how we implement that faith in our churches. But what are we to evaluate, who does it, and how often is "regularly"?

The church should evaluate everything it does. Nothing should be exempt. There should be no sacred cows that are beyond the scrutiny of good evaluation. This is healthy for the church and prevents various ministry forms from becoming institutionalized and perpetuated eternally. This doesn't mean that everything gets changed all the time, for this would lead to chaos. What it does mean is that some change is constantly taking place so that the various ministries improve in their effectiveness.

The best people to carry out the evaluation process are those involved in particular ministries. The church should give them the freedom to evaluate and innovate within the purview of their unique ministries. If they've been properly placed, they should know best what their ministries are to accomplish and whether or not they're succeeding. Occasionally, someone could come in from the outside to bring in fresh ideas. These individuals should be under another person who is responsible to make sure that good evaluation takes place. But evaluation is best left to those who are involved in the ministry—who know the ministry well.

The time when evaluation takes place depends on the particular ministry being assessed. For example, the Sunday morning service should be evaluated weekly. All facets of what takes place should be looked at, asking, How did we do? and What can we do better the next time? This includes not only the sermon, the choice of songs, and how well they were performed, but other things, such as the pace of the service.

Programs in Christian education, evangelism, and outreach can be evaluated over a longer period of time. This evaluation should be done at least quarterly and at a minimum annually. It's helpful to implement "shelf-life" ministries. The various perishable items found on the shelves of grocery stores have a shelf life. A date is stamped somewhere on the item giving the time after which it should no longer be used or consumed. The various ministries in the church could also be assigned a shelf life of one year. After that time is up, the ministry would have to justify its existence if it is to continue. The basis for this justification would be the quarterly evaluations. The shelf life of most church ministries ranges from eighteen to twenty-four months, unless they're regularly evaluated and updated. After that they need to be either dropped or overhauled.

The Principle of Cultural Exegesis

The church must be a student of the world out there as well as of the world in here. If our churches are to remain relevant to our culture, they must spend time exegeting that culture as well as the Scriptures.

The Explanation

What does the term *exegete* mean and how does it apply to the Bible and to the culture?

Exegesis involves the skillful application of basic Bible study methods to Scripture to understand and present its meaning. It takes time and is critical to the teaching and preaching ministries of the church.

The real importance of exegesis is that it helps us both discover and communicate divine truth. In times when truth is viewed by so many in our culture as relative, the church must articulate and apply the absolute truths of Scripture to the needs and problems of the contemporary world. The postmodern concept of relative truth leads only to a loss of hope and despair; the concept of absolute, divine truth brings hope and leads to salvation.

Not only must we know how to exegete the Bible, we must be able to exegete the culture in which we live. A vital aspect of communicating divine truth is the application of that truth to life. This can't take place, however, unless we understand what's happening in people's lives, both lost and saved. It might seem strange to include here Christians as well as the lost. Yet in the twenty-first century many of our churches are microcosms of the larger macrocosm of the world in general. To study what's taking place in the world out there and to address it in terms of God's truth will help add authenticity to sermons and ministries—whether they're directed to lost or saved people or both.

First Chronicles 12:32 is a key passage in illuminating this principle. The writer presents the numbers of those who had decided to join David in his battle with Saul. When he gets to the men of Issachar, he describes them as those "who understood the times and knew what Israel should do." Understanding one's times involves cultural exegesis. Apparently the men of Issachar were exegetes of the culture that resulted in their being in touch with what was going on around them.

The Application

How can planted churches exegete their culture and thus understand their times? There are at least five ways to accomplish this.

Build Friendships with Lost People

The first way to exegete the culture involves a practice followed by a problem.

The practice. The practice is to pursue contacts with lost people in an attempt to develop relationships that result in friendships. This means that Christians will have to spend some time with the unsaved and get to know them well enough to understand their needs, hurts, dreams, and aspirations. Every Christian should be doing this with at least one lost person or couple regularly.

The problem. The problem is that far too many Christians have few if any lost friends. They have lots of lost acquaintances, but not many lost friends. In some cases this may be due to a false view of separation. Some teach that Christians should associate with lost people as little as possible; otherwise, they'll become "worldly." Christians may have to work with unbelievers, but they should avoid spending time with them away from the workplace.

Actually, the Savior taught that we're to be *in* the world but not *of* the world (John 17:14–19). If this means that we shouldn't associate with lost people, then we would need to revive the ancient practice of monasticism. Jesus, by example, demonstrated that it's important that we spend time with lost people, that we get to know them and address their needs (Luke 5:27–32; 15:1–2; 19:5–7). At the same time, however, we're not to live like them. The problem that many churches are facing is that their people aren't in the world (they don't know many lost people), yet they're of the world (their behavior is little different from that of their lost neighbors and workmates).[3]

Another reason Christians don't associate with lost people is because they don't appreciate some of their bad habits. For example, most believers prefer not to be around people who use profanity or tell obscene jokes, especially in front of the family. Yet this need not be a barrier to befriending these people. There are ways to deal with their habits and not lose the relationship. If you take these people aside and explain that you value them and their friendship but ask that they respect your feelings in these areas, most will understand and appreciate your candor. You will come across as authentic.

Listen to the Culture

In his book *Thriving on Chaos,* Tom Peters suggests that executives develop what he calls "naive listening." He writes, "Listening to customers must become everyone's business. Listening means: (1) hanging out (on their turf), (2) listening naively and with intensity, and (3) providing fast feedback and taking action."[4]

Few of us listen very well to begin with, much less to lost people. This has to stop if we have any desire to reach them. But as Peters indicates, this will take some effort on our part. Not only will we have to listen to them, but we'll have to do so intensely and on their turf. "Their turf" includes, among other things, their areas of interest. The temptation is to pay attention only to things that interest us. Yet we must begin to take an interest in things that matter to them. Often we have things in common with them. We simply may not be aware of it, unless we ask and listen.

READ, READ, READ!

Read what people are reading. Read the newspaper and know what's going on in the community. Consider subscribing to *USA Today* and know what's going on in the world. Be conversant on matters that affect the community and our world. Read magazines such as *Time, Newsweek,* and *People.*

Discover what topics are hot and what topics are not. Ask if the sermons on Sundays are addressing any of these issues. Is the church in general dealing with these issues in terms of its programs and ministries? For example, hardly a day goes by that the typical newspaper doesn't have a story or article about various addictions, such as drugs and alcohol. Is the church confronting these problems?

Attempt to read a good novel at least once a year. Select one that has been at the top of the best-seller list. What issues does the novel deal with? Is the author sending a message, and, if so, what is it?

Collect and Interpret Demographic and Psychographic Data

The term *demographics* refers to general information about people, such as where they live, their income, their education, their marital status, and so on. The term *psychographics* refers to what these people value and how it has influenced their lifestyles. This kind of information will reveal much about the culture.

You will be able to find a lot of excellent information in the local newspaper. Other sources are public utilities offices, local colleges and universities, realtors, land developers, chambers of commerce, and city planning departments. There are also some professional organizations that provide this information for a price.

Develop and Implement a Community Survey

A good way to exegete a community is to survey it. If you want to know what people are like, why not ask them? The idea here is to go straight to the source. The only problem is that people aren't always truthful. Nevertheless, the contact with them is invaluable.

A sample survey. The following community survey has been used effectively in starting up new churches among unchurched lost people:

1. Are you currently attending a local church?
2. What do you think is the greatest need in this community?
3. Why do you think some people don't attend church?
4. If you were looking for a church in the area, what would you want?
5. What advice would you give to a new pastor?
6. Would you be interested in more information?[5]

Let me comment on this survey. The first question is an attempt to discover if the individual is churched or unchurched. It's important to ask if people are presently attending a church—*not* if they're *members* of a church. There are still a significant number of people in America, especially in the South, who are members of churches but don't attend them.

The second question is designed to identify felt needs from the community's perspective. While these needs may vary, if enough people are surveyed, there should be some consistency.

The third question will underscore what turns people off to spiritual things. Use their responses in advertising. For example, a number of people will list money as an objection. They claim that all the church is interested in is their money not them. Another objection is dull, boring sermons. A well-done, attractive mailer could tell them to leave their wallets at home. Relevant sermon titles might catalyze some interest in spite of their disappointment with sermons in the past, especially if these messages probe felt needs. For example, in the 1990s, when the O. J. Simpson not-guilty verdict came in, I preached a sermon on God's justice: "What God Would Say to O. J."

The Principle of Cultural Homogeneity

The church will not reach everybody but will initially attract those who are culturally similar to the people who make up the core group.

The Explanation

What does this principle mean and what problems has it encountered in its application to ministry?

The Definition

The homogeneous principle was developed by Donald A. McGavran, who is undoubtedly one of the twentieth century's premier missiologists and the founder of the Church Growth Movement. The principle states: "Men like to become Christians without crossing racial, linguistic, or class barriers."[6] Lost people are most comfortable with those with whom they feel an affinity.

The Controversy

The homogeneous principle has become one of the most controversial principles of the Church Growth Movement. Its critics have attacked it as racist and classist. Yet their reaction is "knee jerk" and due to a failure to understand what McGavran is saying. He is talking about the way lost people think and respond. He's describing the thinking of the unregenerate mind. He's not saying this is the way things ought to be. It's not his contention that this is the way *God* thinks and acts, but it's the way *lost people* think and act. McGavran approaches this principle from the perspective of the lost mind-set and the way things are in this world, not from the perspective of the divine viewpoint or what should be.

The Reality

No church can be culturally neutral. This is because what churches do (preaching, worship, the offering, and other practices) are all culturally conditioned. As I said at the beginning of this chapter, this isn't necessarily wrong because culture itself is neutral (Rom. 14:14–15).

It's also important to note that Paul, who wrote Ephesians 2:11–22 also wrote Galatians 2:6–10, and targeted Gentiles while Peter targeted Jews.

In reality, the church has practiced the homogeneous principle for years as reflected in several areas of its ministry.

Missions. Here I want to address two areas. First, missionaries have to focus on a single group of people when they plant churches internationally, because they have to learn a people's or tribe's culture (language, customs, and so forth). They can't reach people if they don't know their language or culture. My wife works with a mission organization that focuses on Spanish speaking peoples around the world. And most missions practice the same. Is this wrong? It's no different in North America. We now live in what is officially a mission field. And even though we all speak English, that doesn't mean that we speak the same language or share the same culture or even begin to understand one another.

Second, it's a common practice, and a good one, in missions to turn works that have been started by foreign missionaries over to nationals after a period of time. Why? Because we all recognize that nationals have a greater opportunity to minister to other Christian nationals and the lost of their country. They understand the culture and the needs, hopes, and aspirations of their people. They have affinity with their people.

Christian education. Most if not all Christian education programs in churches of any size provide classes for males and females, singles, couples, adults, young marrieds, youth, children, and newcomers. Why do they do this? Simply because they realize that there's a sense of affinity among some groups. Singles tend to prefer to meet with other singles for a variety of reasons, such as commonality of needs. The same is true of couples. Why don't we mix older adults with our high school-age young people? They don't share the same language or interests. Is this wrong? Most think not.

Other. When you select a worship style, you've focused on a particular segment of the culture. This includes traditional or contemporary as well as Latino, African American, and even Asian styles of worship. When you choose to speak in a particular language, such as English, you've limited the people that you'll reach to those who speak the language. Some would be quick to criticize those who focus on the rich. However, they laud those who focus on the poor and marginalized. The same is true of those who focus on Caucasians and those who focus on other ethnicities. Let's face it—this not only *seems* inconsistent, it *is* inconsistent.

Church planting. Ethnic peoples are attracted to churches started by the same ethnic people. For instance, Koreans are attracted to new churches that have been started by Koreans. African Americans prefer to attend churches started by African Americans. The same is true for Hispanics, Latinos, other Asians, and whites. And this is particularly true of lost Asians, Hispanics, African Americans, and whites. This practice violates Scripture only when these churches choose to purposely exclude people of another culture. A painful example would be the treatment of some African Americans by white churches in a segregated America.

An Illustration

Mark Platt, a church planter on the West Coast, illustrates the homogeneous principle with a story about a young African American preacher named Larry.

It was Larry's desire to start a church for *all* people. Mark was interested in how he planned to accomplish this goal, so he asked Larry several questions. The first concerned how he planned to preach to this multiethnic congregation. Larry's answer was that he would "whoop," which is a style common to preaching in many African American churches. Next, Mark asked how he would take the offering. Larry said that they would have an "offering walk," which is a common way to take the offering in African American churches. This involves placing the offering plate at the front of the church and asking people to walk by and place their money in it while the preacher watches.

The question we must ask about Larry's church is whom will it attract? The answer is obvious. We can't escape our roots.

I once had a most interesting conversation with a fellow faculty member's wife. She is a highly educated woman who considers herself to be very open-minded. She was upset that her church didn't have other ethnic people in attendance, especially African Americans and Hispanics. She'd also heard of the homogeneous principle and was adamantly opposed to it. I agreed with her on the first issue regarding the ethnic makeup of her church but not the second concerning the homogeneous principle. So I decided to ask her some questions.

The first was, "So, you want your church to reach out to and attract more people of different races? That's excellent, I agree with you and so does the Bible!" Then I asked, "And what are you willing to give up to attract these people to your church? Would you be willing to listen to a different preaching style on Sunday morning? For example, would it be permissible for your pastor to whoop rather than teach with his normal heavy Bible content? Also, would you be willing to involve yourself in an offering walk, rather than sitting in a pew and passing the plate? If you want to reach people of other cultures through the worship service of your church, especially lost people, what changes are you willing to make?" She responded with silence. She wasn't ready to give up the way they "did church."

The Application

Planted churches should recognize that, whether right or wrong, the homogeneous principle is true and is practiced by most lost people. Therefore, churches will attract and win those who are of the same culture and nationality unless God has gifted (Eph. 3:7–9) and thus called them to reach a different ethnicity, much as missionaries have been doing in other cultures for centuries.

The Initial Focus Group

Churches will be wise *initially* to focus their efforts on lost people in their communities who are culturally similar. This doesn't mean that they shouldn't minister to people of other cultures should the opportunity present itself. It does mean that it would be a mistake for a white Anglo church to focus on a Hispanic community if that church isn't willing to make some huge cultural adjustments in its approach to ministry. For starters, its people could learn Spanish.

Yet it would be far wiser for this church *initially* to target a white Anglo community consisting of people much like themselves. There would be an affinity present that wouldn't be true of the other community. Those who minister, such as the pastor, could then preach in a style that's more natural to them.

The Ultimate Focus Group

As the church grows, it will attract people from other ethnic groups and become more heterogeneous. Some people are willing to give up their particular style of worship for other values. For instance, some value good Bible teaching to the extent that they'll attend a church of another culture to get it. Some churches have excellent ministries for the hearing- or seeing-impaired that encourage the crossing of stylistic boundaries.

Once the church becomes more heterogeneous, it will be able to pursue more aggressively a ministry to people of other ethnic groups. As it attracts some Asian people, it should consider targeting Asian people in the community. Again, when they begin to reach these people, it would be wise to provide either classes or services for them in their own language and style so that they'll attract and reach other lost Asians.

The Principles of a Biblical Hermeneutic

How can church planters know when they may have crossed the cultural divide? How can they know when, in their attempts to be relevant to the culture, they may have conformed to the culture and bought into the spirit of the age? The answer is found in applying six key hermeneutical principles to the church.[7]

Form versus Function

In chapter 4, we studied the principle of form and function as an assumption that undergirds this book. There we learned that the Scriptures fix the functions of the church, such as evangelism, worship, and giving. Functions are as true in the twenty-first century as they were in the first century. Scripture, however, doesn't dictate the forms the various functions may take. This allows churches the freedom to remain relevant to their culture.

Church planters must be careful to determine whether they are dealing with a function or a form in conducting ministry. For example, must churches have small groups? The answer depends on if they are a form or function. Small groups are a form. The function they serve may be biblical community, evangelism, or worship.

Tradition versus Scripture

A church tradition is a nonbiblical custom or practice (form) that church people attempt to observe, often preserve, and pass on to the next generation. The Bible teaches that traditions can be good or bad. In Mark 7:1–23, Jesus condemns the Pharisees' practice of setting aside funds that could help their parents by declaring them *corban* (a gift devoted to God). They placed their tradition ahead of scriptural truth. In Acts 17:2–3 Paul observes the custom of entering the synagogue and interacting with the Jews in attendance. This tradition didn't violate Scripture.

How might church planters observe this principle? First, they must distinguish between what is tradition and what is Scripture. Many parishioners confuse Scripture with tradition and cling to the latter as if it was the former. An example is the old-timer who quipped, "If the organ was good enough for Paul, it's good enough for us!" The other is not to place traditions as equal to or above Scripture. This was the error of the Pharisees in the first century and the Roman Catholic Church in later centuries.

The Negative versus the Positive Hermeneutic

The negative hermeneutic teaches that if a custom or practice (form) is not found in the Bible then it's wrong and unbiblical. It may be expressed with such clichés as "Where the Bible speaks, we speak; where the Bible is silent, we're silent." Those who hold to this view condemn the use in church of such things as drama, drums, guitars, and, in some cases, any instrumental music.

The problem with this view is that it's neither biblical nor logical. The same churches have Sunday schools, nurseries, hymnals, pulpits, pianos, even indoor plumbing. Where do they find these practices in the Bible?

I prefer the positive hermeneutic. It teaches that though you can't find a practice in the Bible, it's permissible as long as it doesn't contradict or disagree with the Bible.

Patterns versus Principles

"Patternism" teaches that the church must not only follow the biblical principles of the early church but its practices or patterns as well. If one of the early church's patterns was to meet on the first day of the week (Acts 20:7), then twenty-first-century churches must follow suit.

This position is incorrect for five reasons. First, it assumes that all the churches of the first century followed the same patterns. No evidence exists for this. So then we must ask, Which church's patterns do you follow? The Corinthian church exercised various gifts in the public worship service (1 Cor. 14:26–39). We don't know that others followed the same pattern. Another reason the position is incorrect is that there doesn't appear to be enough information to know what the early churches practiced—just bits of information here and there. The position is incorrect because patternism locks the church into a first-century culture, as the Amish have locked themselves into an eighteenth-century culture. Finally, we must ask, Can we apply a biblical principle? The biblical principle regarding when a church meets for worship is that we are free to make up our own minds (Rom. 14:5–12).

Descriptive versus Prescriptive Passages

Descriptive passages are those in the Bible that describe what took place in the early churches. For example, the church at Troas may have met on the first day of the week (Acts 20:7). Consequently, some argue from this that the church in all the other centuries must follow suit.

The fallacy with this view is that just because a practice is described in the New Testament doesn't mean that it was mandated by the New Testament. We must not allow nonabsolutes of the early church to become binding absolutes for the twenty-first-century church.

Prescriptive passages are those in the Bible that prescribe what ought to take place in the church. Various biblical imperatives, prohibitions, and other indicators help us to identify them. Some examples are the Great Commission, the Lord's Supper, baptism, and church discipline.

The Secular versus the Sacred

Since the Middle Ages, many in the Christian church interpret that which takes place outside the church as secular and, therefore, bad. For example, to look to the business community and those who write in this context for insight in conducting church business is sacrilege.

This isn't biblical. Scripture draws no such line that divides sacred from secular or the church world from the business world. The question is, does what you're doing fall under the lordship of Christ—whether inside or outside the church? Because all truth is ultimately God's truth (either revealed in or outside the Bible—special or general revelation), church planters may learn from the business community, much as Moses learned from his father-in-law, Jethro, who likely was an unbeliever (Exodus 18). However, they must be careful to use their biblical training (their theological grid) to evaluate all that they read from these other sources to discern what is, in fact, truth.

An Exercise in Cultural Relevancy

1. When you read "For All Those Born Prior to 1945" at the beginning of this chapter, what did you think? Were you attracted to it, or did it simply amuse you? What does it tell you about the impact of the culture on people regardless of whether or not they're Christians?

2. In the churches you've attended, what are some practices or traditions that you believe have been commonly confused with biblical truth? How has this confusion affected the church?

3. Are you willing to be flexible in areas that involve the practices of the church? Where might this be a problem for you (music, clothing, length of hair)?

4. How do you feel about being evaluated? Have you ever been in a church that regularly evaluated itself? If you have, what were some of the benefits of evaluation? What were some of the problems that developed? How might the latter be avoided?

5. Do you believe you understand the culture in which you live? Do you have any lost friends, people with whom you spend time away from work? If the answer is no, what do you plan to do about it?

6. Do you believe that you understand Donald McGavran's homogeneous grouping principle? How do you respond to this principle? Does it have a place in church planting? What is it?

7. Are any of the hermeneutical principles for the church new to you? Have you violated any of these in the past when interpreting matters that relate to the church?

Appendix C

A Holistic, Authentic Worship

When I was a child, one of the games we played involved word association. Someone would say a word, and we'd all blurt out the first thing that came to our minds. For a moment, I'd like to play the game with you. What first comes into your mind when you hear the words *worship service*? Obviously the answer will depend on your experience of worship in the various churches you've attended over the years. Perhaps you think, *That's what we do at our church on Sunday morning at 11:00 AM.* Then again, you may think of the great hymns of the faith, announcements, and a pastoral prayer.

Now I'd like to change the game a little and ask you a second question: What do you *feel* when you hear the words *worship service*? Please note that I didn't ask what you *think* but what you *feel* about these two words. The difference is that the former is a cognitive exercise while the latter is emotive. Do you have warm feelings and pleasant memories, or do you feel bored and a little empty on the inside?

It would be interesting to play this game with Christian laypersons. Their responses to the questions would probably be real eye-openers for those of us who are in the professional ministry and in positions of leadership in the church. What we think and feel varies considerably from person to person, colored by our expectations and disappointments. (I would also challenge you to consider playing this game with formerly churched Christians—church dropouts—and unchurched lost people.)

Finally, it would be most informative to ask a few other questions: Do you value the worship services at your church? Do you look forward to worship on Sunday morning? Is your worship service a regular encounter with God? The expectations of those who worship and what's actually taking place in many of our churches are far apart.

There is a solution to this problem that involves planting churches that implement a holistic, authentic worship. In explaining what this means and how it works, we need to look first at the problem of inauthentic worship and then at the philosophy and practice of authentic, holistic worship.

The Problem of Inauthentic Worship

The Problem

The problem in far too many evangelical churches at the beginning of the twenty-first century is that they fail to realize how crucial authentic worship is when it comes to reaching their people and younger generations.

The Typical Service

Ronald Allen and Gordon Borror describe a worship service that is typical of what takes place on Sunday morning at 11:00 in many evangelical churches across America.

> An organ prelude was played, but no one paid much attention. The service began with a reading of a psalm of praise, followed by an urgent plea for Sunday school teachers, presented by a well-intentioned lay leader who needed help. He asked for two or three volunteers to rescue a class of junior boys from running around the parking lot. This presentation was followed by a greeting from a recently returned missionary, who was doing great work in the field but took too long to tell about it. The opening hymn (twenty minutes into the service) had nothing to do with the sermon. After the hymn, the Scripture reading was dropped because there was no time.[1]

This account reminds me of how worship was conducted at a church that I pastored. The service was normally accompanied by a piano and an organ. For a time we were without a pianist, so we had to depend on the organ. The organist was an elderly lady who was on some medication that made her drowsy. She regularly fell asleep during my pastoral prayer. This wouldn't have been a problem except that one of her hands would fall and hit the keyboard. I would be waxing eloquent in a great prayer and all of a sudden there would be a loud bonk! We eventually grew somewhat accustomed to it. In fact, if it didn't happen, I'd always wonder if she were all right. As I think back over it, this wasn't the problem. The problem was that was the most exciting thing that happened during our worship time! Unfortunately, there are many who listen to these examples and say, "That describes what's happening at our church on a *good* morning!"

In light of all the struggles of a small church, we got by. The problem is that from God's perspective, we were offering up "blemished lambs" in response to the perfect Lamb he offered up for us. From a ministry perspective, such a service is totally inadequate when it comes to transforming lives, which is what worship is all about.

The Typical Attitude

The typical attitude in a significant number of evangelical churches, especially on the part of pastors, is that worship is merely the preliminary before the main event—the sermon. It's viewed as comparable to the appetizer before the meal or the warm-up before the game. In their book *Worship*, Allen and Borror have sensed this same attitude:

> As pastors, we evangelicals have not been much concerned with worship either. In many of our circles the Sunday morning event is considered a "preaching service" in spite of the fact that the official title in the bulletin reads "Morning Worship." Viewing the preacher's singular act of proclamation as significantly more important than the entire congregation's acts of adoration, praise, confession, thanksgiving, and dedication, is espousing an expensive heresy that may well be robbing many churches of their spiritual assets.[2]

The Result

The result of all this is that worship is poorly done, predictable, boring, and irrelevant. Consequently, rather than attracting people *to* Christ our churches are distracting them *from* Christ. The unchurched visit to "check us out" and don't return. Our young people leave as soon as they finish high school to join the ranks of the unchurched, vowing never to be bored again. One of my students told me that he had invited a lost, unchurched neighbor to go with him to his church. He said that about halfway through the service, his neighbor elbowed him and said, "If I'd had to pay to get in here, I'd be wanting my money back about now!"

But what can pastors and church planters, especially those of us who have had little or no training in the areas of worship and music, do about this? We need to rethink our philosophy of worship before starting a new church. Most likely, we have inherited our present philosophy, and if it's not adequate, it's imperative that we construct a new one. The solution to the problem of inauthentic worship lies in developing an authentic, holistic philosophy of worship.

A Philosophy of Authentic, Holistic Worship

What's involved in a worship service that's authentic and holistic? What do these terms mean? The answer is found in five key areas of worship.

The Importance of Worship

Churches and pastors must recapture the importance of worship in the life of the church. There are three reasons why.

Worship is emphasized in the Bible. Worship is important because the Bible says it's important. In fact worship is emphasized in Scripture from beginning to end. (It's mentioned more than preaching!) In his book *People in the Presence of God*, Barry Liesch presents five worship models that he finds revealed in Scripture. These five basic models are: "pre-Sinai (family worship modeled by the patriarchs), tabernacle-temple, synagogue, Pauline, and worship in the book of Revelation."[3] (Note, however, that, as important as worship is, in Matthew 5:23–24 the reconciliation of a relationship takes priority over worship—the offering of a gift at the altar.)

Worship edifies people. Worship is important because, when it's done well, it has the potential to influence people spiritually as much or more than the sermon. The goal is for people to be spiritually refreshed, nurtured, and transformed through worship. When this takes place, Christians are willing to give themselves away in sacrificial service. It's essential that believers' souls be satisfied in worship if they're to function as believer-priests. If something happened to the pastor so that he wasn't able to preach one morning, people should still leave the service with their souls nourished and spiritually satisfied as the result of having attended the worship service.

Worship is integral to the church. Worship is important not only because it matters to God and should matter to us, but because it's an integral part of what takes place in the service that occurs in most churches on Sunday morning. The people in our churches, their guests, and visitors judge the church on the basis of what happens in the public worship service. This service attracts the largest number of people in most cases and is viewed as the church at its best. Much of the week's preparation time is focused on this one main event. Consequently, it serves as a litmus test for the church as a whole. Most people determine whether or not they want to be a part of the church based on the worship service—even before considering the church's programs and events. If worship is not done well, then, in most minds, this is a reflection on the other programs of the church, and they don't come back for a second look. However, this is not to say that worship is the purpose of the church or that it takes precedence over everything else, such as fellowship, evangelism, and the reconciliation of a relationship.

The Definition of Authentic Worship

Authentic worship is an active response to God in which we acknowledge his great worth. This definition has three important elements.

A response to God. God is proactive in the sense that he has pursued us as lost people rather than the reverse. "There is no one righteous, not even one; there is no one who understands, no one who seeks God" (Rom. 3:10–11). God's pursuit of us is clearly seen in such great divine events as the incarnation, death, and resurrection of Christ. Once we come to faith in Christ, it's in worship that we respond to him and what he's done for us. Therefore, worship is responsive.

An active response. Worship is an event that requires some effort on our part. We don't simply sit in a pew or kneel and wait for something to happen. According to Scripture, there should be an active response on the part of God's people. For example, in Revelation 5, which is one of the great worship chapters in the book of Revelation, the saints (the twenty-four elders) sing (v. 9) to God.

Worship may also include an active physical response. For example, in Revelation 5:8, the saints as well as others in heaven fall down before Christ, who is worshiped as the Lamb. I've noted that in my own worship experience, I pray best when I'm on my knees as opposed to sitting or standing.

It acknowledges his worth. In discussing the English word *worship*, Allen and Borror indicate that "this term comes from the Anglo-Saxon *weorthscipe*, which then was modified to *worthship*, and finally to *worship*. Worship means 'to attribute worth' to something or someone."[4]

Whatever we worship—whether an object or a person—we attribute various degrees of worth to that object or person. Of course, the point in Christian worship is that we're attributing supreme or ultimate worth to God. We're acknowledging that of all that we value in life, we value him the most. We're attempting to elevate above all else his great value and worth in light of who he is and all that he's done.

The Elements of Worship

Adoration. Adoration involves acknowledging publicly and privately the attributes of our God and his great works. This honors God in a most wonderful way. It also involves praising him for all he's done for us personally. One of the great books of the Bible that is full of examples of adoration is the Psalms (see especially Pss. 33, 36, 105, 111, 113, 117, 135).

Confession. Confession, like adoration, can be both public and private. Here we acknowledge our "dark side" or what the Bible refers to as the "flesh." After celebrating the goodness of God, it's only natural that we gain a deeper sense of our own sinfulness and guilt. Confession is God's provision for dealing with our dark side. First John 1:9 points out that while it can be personally painful and even embarrassing for us, our God is pleased when we confess our sins to him. Not only does it serve to "flush out" our spiritual system, but it sensitizes us to the sin in our lives and makes us more dependent on him (see Psalm 51).

Thanksgiving. As with adoration, the Psalms offer many examples of worship through giving thanks to God for all his many benefits. For example, there are individual thanksgiving psalms (Pss. 30, 32, 34, 92, 107, 116, 118, 121, 138). There are also communal thanksgiving psalms (Pss. 65, 67, 124).

Thanksgiving is another way of honoring God. After a sincere time of confession, the natural response is to spend some time expressing our thanks to him for his forgiveness and blessings. These include such things as answered prayer, spiritual blessings, and material blessings.

Commitment. The natural outcome of adoration, confession, and thanksgiving is the commitment of ourselves to Christ and his service, whatever that may be. This commitment involves sanctification. When we begin to understand God's great love and forgiveness in light of our sinfulness, our natural response is to present our bodies as instruments for his service (Isa. 6:8–9; Rom. 6:12–14).

Supplication. Prayer is a time when we talk to God and make requests for ourselves and others within and outside the body of Christ. This is done publicly by one or two people and privately by all who are present in the service. These requests may involve such areas as marriages, ministries, jobs, friends, health, finances, and decisions. Various books of the Bible record the prayers of God's great people. Some New Testament prayers can be found in Matthew 6:9–13; John 17; Ephesians 1:15–23; 3:16–21; Philippians 1:9–11; and Colossians 1:10–12. There are some who have studied these prayers and wisely patterned their own after them.

Proclamation. Proclamation is the preaching of the Word of God. Certainly, preaching involves worship in that it too is a response to God that acknowledges publicly his great worth. Proclamation could occur at the beginning or middle of a public time of worship, but most often occurs at the end. It's a means for communicating a word from God that heals and edifies his people and saves the lost.

The Result of Worship

A Commitment of Our Lives to Christ

A major effect that worship can have on God's church is to bring its people to a fresh commitment of their lives to Christ. This is the message of Romans 12:1: "Therefore, I urge you, brothers, in view of God's mercy, to offer your bodies as living sacrifices, holy and pleasing to God—this is your spiritual act of worship." In other words, the commitment of ourselves to the service of Christ *is* worship. Wouldn't it be honoring to Christ if our worship services so glorified him and satisfied people's souls spiritually that they committed their lives afresh to him each week! This is the goal of our worship.

The Importance of Holistic Worship to Authentic Worship

But how does this process happen? Authentic worship is holistic and culminates in a Romans 12:1 experience.

The cognitive aspect. As worship occurs, it first touches the intellect or the cognitive aspect of our being. If, for example, we're singing, then we think about the words and their spiritual meaning and significance. This enables us to understand the songs and prevents us from singing heresy.

The affective aspect. Next, worship touches our emotions or the affective aspect of our being. If we're singing, then the songs influence us emotionally as well as intellectually. Not only do we understand what we're singing to and about God, but we're feeling it as well. Certainly, we sense David's intense emotions as he worships in the Psalms. Even more so, we sense those of the Savior as he prayed so intensely in the garden before his crucifixion.

The balance. The fact that worship touches both these aspects of our being is important because the result is balance in these two areas of our lives. The temptation is to tilt one way or the other. Some people are very cognitive and approach worship intellectually. The message never gets past their mind. This happens to a lot of seminarians in an academic environment. Others are very emotional and approach worship looking only for a deep emotional experience. They may be singing heresy to God and aren't even aware of it. What's important to them is that they feel something. Holistic worship serves to avoid both extremes by involving both aspects in worship.

The result. When both the intellect and the emotions are involved, the result is a changed life. Again, this accomplishes a Romans 12:1 type of commitment. We begin to love God with all our heart, soul, and mind (Matt. 22:37). Our heads and our hearts are touched, and through an act of the will we surrender our bodies as living sacrifices to Christ.

The Requirements of Worship

What kinds of things encourage authentic, holistic worship?

Leaders Must Be Worshipers

It takes a worshiper to lead worshipers. Therefore, the leaders in the church of Jesus Christ must be authentic worshipers of Christ. In the past most pastors involved themselves in public worship through proclamation of the Bible and pastoral prayer. The trend today is toward more pastoral involvement in other areas of worship as well—not so much in leading singing but in leading the congregation in a time of corporate adoration, confession, thanksgiving, commitment, and prayer.

Such leadership requires an intensive, regular time of private, personal worship on the part of pastoral leaders and all who lead God's people in worship. The leader's private worship becomes public on Sunday morning.

Worship Should Be Culturally Relevant

All that was said in appendix B about cultural relevance applies to worship. One of the reasons the youth in so many churches drop out and join the unchurched is because some of our churches are still worshiping much as they did in the 1950s and 1960s, using hymns in the King James English— which young people don't understand—and instruments preferred by an older Builder generation.

Young people and unchurched Christians enjoy worship when the form is relevant to them—that is when they experience authenticity and depth. For example, moderns, such as Boomers, prefer fresh, fast-paced contemporary Christian music that is based on Scripture, such as the Psalms, to the older hymns of the faith. The music seems more upbeat and uses words they can understand. They also prefer instruments that are more popular today such as guitars, other stringed instruments, and drums. However, a characteristic of some postmoderns is a "return to their roots," emerging as a fresh fascination with ancient church rituals, stained glass windows, candles, the liturgy, the Eucharist, creeds, and other ancient forms of worship. (Note that some interpret this as a return to the 1950s and 1960s vintage worship. This is hardly the case as it's a yearning for something much older—a return to the first few centuries.)

What is interesting is that each new generation seems to react to the former generation in terms of its preference for worship. Boomers move away from the traditional preferences of the Builder generation toward a more contemporary style. Then Generation X and possibly Y respond to the Boomers by returning to a more traditional first-few-centuries style. Do we discern a pattern here? If there is such a pattern, then we should expect more of the same out of future generations. The next generation will react with a desire for a more contemporary approach (whatever that may be) and on and on it goes. I don't think that this is bad or wrong as long as it honors God and is true to Scripture. What it means is that church planters will need to be aware of where each new generation is in their worship preferences and be sensitive to them. In addition, it's important that you explain your worship preference. The reason that liturgy fell by the wayside is not because it was bad worship but because churches failed to explain its meaning to its younger generations, and so it became meaningless. People were going through the motions without it affecting their souls. Early in the twenty-first century, as we return to the liturgy, creeds, and stained glass, we must make clear their meaning and intent in worship.

Worship Must Be Done Well

It's important that the church pursue a "reasonable" excellence in all that it does. This especially includes worship. There must not be any "flying by the seat of the pants." People who sing off-key during special music or who play untuned instruments detract more than they facilitate good worship. Being unprepared conveys inauthenticity.

It would be better that churches not attempt certain aspects of worship rather than do them poorly. For example, if there's no experienced, reasonably accomplished pianist available, sing a cappella. If the hymnals are in bad shape or contain songs that are mostly in King James English, don't use them. If a slide projector works one Sunday but not the next, repair it or stop using it.

Worship Needs a Proper Environment

One of the difficulties in church planting is locating and keeping an adequate facility in which to meet. It's not advisable to buy land and build too quickly, so church planters may meet in temporary facilities for as long as three to ten years.

It is important to locate the better facility in the focus area in terms of cost and other requirements, including seating, lighting, sound, cleanliness, and accessibility. Sometimes church planters overlook these things to their detriment. They must realize that if they should focus on lost seekers, many of them are used to decent facilities and will not tolerate a substandard environment. It's difficult for visitors to worship when they are distracted by frayed carpeting, water stains on the ceiling, and pews or seating in need of cleaning.

Worship Must Be Creative, Authentic God-Encounters

A turnoff for many is worship that's boring or entertainment focused. Instead, younger adults prefer encountering God in fresh, authentic ways. They want substance; biblical, bold preaching; meaningful communion; time for contemplation; and a sense of the holy otherness of God. Therefore, church planters are wise to include on their team people with strengths in these areas who will take full responsibility for worship. These people could, in turn, recruit and form their own teams of laypeople who would assist and provide fresh insight.

Creative worship for Boomers might consist of skits, drama, audiovisual presentations, creative dance, and the use of video in preaching. For postmoderns it might consist of the Eucharist, reading of the creeds, times of quiet contemplation, and the celebration of ancient church rituals.

The Practice of Authentic, Holistic Worship

Having a foundation for authentic worship, how might you put this information into practice? This section will provide you with the various steps necessary to implement authentic worship in a newly planted church.

The People Who Worship

The first step is to return to your focus group. Key to how you practice authentic, God-focused worship is the people you choose to reach out to initially—your focus group. Here are some of the questions. Are they Christians or non-Christians? Are they churched or unchurched? Are they a younger or older generation? There is little question that the answers to these questions dictate a number of issues regarding how your church will conduct its worship. For example, if you are targeting unchurched lost people, you'll likely do little worship in that particular service because lost people can't worship God in spirit and truth. If you are targeting a younger generation of believers, you are wise to implement a more contemporary format or possibly a more ancient format if they are postmoderns. If they are an older generation, you are wise to consider the more traditional formats and the great hymns of the faith.

The Number of Services

The next step in establishing a worship time is to determine the number of services that will take place each week. You need to consider how many services you can reasonably expect the people to attend. There are several options.

One meeting. It's biblical and reasonable to expect that believers meet corporately once a week no matter how busy their schedules (Heb. 10:24–25).

Two meetings. If you decide to hold a service to reach lost people, you'll need at least two services or meetings a week. There will be a need to balance the special meeting for lost people with one for believers or else the latter will starve spiritually. Either meeting could take place in a regular service or small-group context.

Three meetings. The maximum is three times per week. With the kinds of schedules people are keeping, asking for three commitments a week may push them to their limit. The old traditional approach, expecting committed people to attend three services a week—Sunday morning and evening and the Wednesday evening prayer meeting (what some refer to as the "three to thrive" approach)—is rapidly disappearing. Willow Creek Community Church attempts to involve people in a Sunday morning or Saturday evening "seeker's service," a new community service on either Wednesday or Thursday evening, and a small group. These expectations are not unreasonable, because they have a highly committed group of believers involved in their ministry. Ultimately, you and your core group must decide what's fair and reasonable, and ask people to commit to it.

The Purpose of the Services

Once you've determined the number of services per week, the next step is to decide what takes place in those services. There are basically three options.

The seeker's service. This is a service designed specifically to reach unchurched lost people, in particular, those who are interested enough that they'll come to a public service if invited by a friend. (Some seekers prefer a small-group setting.) In this approach, there is limited participation on the part of those in the audience. Much of what happens takes place up front among those who are leading and involved in the service.

This service is a vehicle to help those in the church expose their lost friends to a positive presentation of Christianity. While it may occur on the weekend, it may not attempt to be a worship service. That could take place at another time. Some Christians don't understand the purpose of this type of service and will complain that they haven't worshiped—which probably is the case. It's important to explain to them the purpose of the "seeker's service" and invite them to the service for believers.

However, a seeker service may include worship and lots of it. While lost people may not be able to worship God in spirit and truth, they may eventually come to faith through a well-done worship service. The psalmist alludes to this in Psalms 40:3 and 57:9, and Paul does as well in 1 Corinthians 14:23–25.

The nurture service. This is a service specifically designed for believers. This meeting is critical for the church if it attempts to have a separate "seeker's service" because it focuses on worship and a sermon designed to nourish the sheep. It balances the program of the church. A basic mistake on the part of some who attempt to pursue a "seeker's service" is that they pour all their efforts into that service each week but forget or are too exhausted to feed the sheep. The result is that the latter starve spiritually and eventually drift away.

Most unchurched lost people would feel out of place in this service because it's not intended for them. Once they have attended the "seeker's services" and eventually come to faith in Christ, the next step is to involve them in this meeting for purposes of spiritual nurture.

The average traditional church conducts a nurture service each week. The problem is that they have very little to offer unbelievers in this service. Consequently, they aren't reaching any lost people and many have become what some call ingrown "holy huddles" or "cognitive communities."

The seeker friendly/sensitive meeting. This service is designed to reach unchurched lost people and to nourish believers at the same time in one service. Both the worship and the sermon attempt to be "seeker friendly" and to appeal to both groups. For example, the music could be upbeat and contemporary, while the sermon pursues needs and issues from the Bible in a way that is relevant to both groups. This approach has been used by some traditional churches in an attempt to become more relevant and balanced in their approach to reaching people. The obvious problem is maintaining a balance between evangelism and edification.

For some the use of the term *seeker* in relation to the worship services has become a turnoff. This may be due to a bad experience in a contemporary church. In the last church I pastored, we replaced the term *seeker friendly* with *people friendly*.

The Style of Worship

The next decision concerns the style of worship. In particular, much of the focus here is on the music involved in the church's worship. Church planters must understand the importance that music plays in the lives of people—especially young people. And their style of music will deeply impact their worship of the living God. Some important questions need to be worked through in planning and developing the music portion of the worship time:

1. Will the music be ancient, traditional, contemporary, classical, or a combination? Will these musical styles be combined in one service or two or more separate services?
2. What kinds of instruments will be used? Some of the options are the piano, organ, guitar, drums, brass, and synthesizer.
3. Will the songs primarily be hymns, praise songs, choruses, or a combination?
4. Will there be a choir and/or specials?
5. Will the songs be sung from hymnals, from the bulletin or a bulletin insert, or projected on a screen using some type of projector?
6. Will someone lead the music by standing in front of the congregation (a possible distraction) or by playing an instrument? Another option is having several people sing together in front of the church.

The very first question raises the issue of contemporary versus traditional music, whatever those terms mean to your people. The issue of contemporary versus traditional music in church has caused numerous disagreements and a major division between the modern Baby Boomers, the postmodern generations, and the pre-modern Builder generation. Often but not exclusively, the older generations have problems accepting the younger generations' music.

A question might prove helpful. What makes music sacred or secular? Different answers exist in the Christian community. One is the fact that some music was written over two hundred years ago in Europe by people such as Martin Luther and the Wesleys. Another is the notes, melody, beat, or the instruments used in producing the music. A third is the words or lyrics of the song. The first answer is culturally elitist and unbiblical. The second is mere conjecture and leads to legalism. While it may seem a little simplistic, the last answer is the correct answer.

Some attempt to write off a more contemporary style as unbiblical. However, this is true only if it can be demonstrated from Scripture. Actually, the issue is one of personal or generational preference. Only rarely is the issue theological.

It's also helpful to realize that today's traditional music was yesterday's contemporary music, and tomorrow's traditional music is today's contemporary music. For example, when Martin Luther wrote some of the church's great traditional hymns, he was writing contemporary music for his generation. In fact it's said that some of the Wesleys' hymns were penned in a tavern! Consequently, this music concerns issues and struggles Christians were facing in the culture of that day.

Again, the key to answering the questions in the above list concerns the people who make up the focus group of the planted church. The worship and music must be relevant to them, or they will not come.

The Planning for Worship

There are several issues that need to be thought through when planning for worship.

The responsibility for worship. The senior pastor or point person must take the final responsibility for the church's worship. This is true even if there's a worship person on the team. Worship is so vital to the church's life that the senior pastor must see that it's done well.

A worship team. Worship planning involves recruiting a worship team. The team doesn't have to be large. It may consist of only two people. Regardless, planning in general is better accomplished in a team context because several minds are better and more creative and productive than one.

Key to the worship team is the worship director. This may be a talented, gifted layperson who is a part of the core group or congregation. It could be a professional whom you have recruited for the position. If the latter, I have several suggestions. First, when recruiting this person, be sure to get a good recommendation from someone who is known as a good worship director. Second, if possible, observe the individual in another church context. Finding a good worship director is a problem that many church planters face. In most urban areas, a network of these people exists. Contact the worship directors in several churches and ask them for names.

A planning retreat. It's helpful to schedule a planning retreat. The point person or primary communicator should get away for a week or so and plan all of the sermons or a significant portion for the following year.

Once this is accomplished, either the team or the team and the primary communicator should attempt to get away together to plan the worship services around the sermon topics. This could take place once a year over several days or it could take place quarterly for a day or two.

A worship network. Study and network with other churches that share your philosophy of worship. Good leaders are learners in the sense that they never stop learning. In particular, they learn by searching out what others are doing locally and nationally, especially churches that are innovative and open to change. This involvement keeps them on the worship edge.

A worship focus. You'll need to focus the worship service. You may attempt four or five things in a worship service, such as congregational music, special music or event, announcements, and so on. Is there something that ties them all together? If not, will they detract from one another? As much as possible, worship leaders should attempt to focus the service on one theme or central idea. The key to this is the central idea of the sermon.

A worship format. Planning involves formatting the worship service. Each worship service will have a format and may consist of the following:

1. A beginning
2. Announcements
3. Chorus/hymns
4. Congregational greeting
5. Offering
6. Special music
7. Special events (such as drama, a video, baptism, communion, reading of a creed, and so on)
8. Sermon
9. Conclusion

In formatting a service containing these ingredients, you must make a number of decisions. One is how you'll begin the service. It's a good idea to have three or four different ways to begin and end a service. This prevents boredom. Another is how to handle the announcements. Most would like to eliminate them from the worship service but seldom do. Others make them a minute or two before the service begins. Another decision is how to greet each other during the service. Many newer, innovative churches include a congregational greeting time. This has been effective but is hard on introverts, especially unchurched ones.

Evaluation. Good worship planning includes evaluating the worship service. This process helps the worship team grow and get better. It should be done by the worship team and the primary communicator, who is most likely the pastor. It would be wise to include several people from the congregation who have an eye and an ear for good worship. The evaluation should take place weekly and as soon as possible after the worship service. The team should ask, How well did we accomplish our purpose? What did we do and what didn't we do well? How can we do it better next week? In light of what we did this week, what will we do next week?

Presentation. Music in the worship service should be presented in an uninterrupted block of time. It takes time for people to slow down, adjust, and prepare their hearts for worship. People may not be ready to worship until they've sung two, three, or as many as four songs. There should be plenty of singing (six or more songs) in blocks of time. This time can vary from twenty minutes to one or as much as two hours. It's also very important that the transition from one song or hymn to another be smooth or the flow of the service will be interrupted.

Excellence. Good worship strives for excellence! The constant problem that the church faces is that people have become accustomed to technical sophistication in the marketplace, on television, and in the various arts.

On the other hand, the majority of churches in America are small and pride themselves on their family-type atmosphere that says it's permissible to "fly by the seat of your pants." The problem is that over a period of time this attitude breeds carelessness in the preparation and performance of worship. When people visit who are not related to the "family," especially the unchurched, they see this and don't return.

Churches must not pursue perfection, for this is impossible to achieve, but they should attempt to do the very best they can in their worship services. This is because they represent the Savior to a lost and dying world. In this attempt, it's helpful to remember three things. First, something isn't better than nothing. For example, a poor pianist or guitarist isn't better than no pianist or guitarist at all. If they can't play reasonably well, don't use them. Second, do less and do it better. Some people attempt to do too much in a worship service. They try to include too many different events such as a musical special and an audiovisual presentation plus other things. The problem is that the more you attempt, the greater the likelihood that something will go wrong. Finally, rehearsals should be the norm rather than the exception. It's during rehearsals that the bugs are located and exterminated.

Congregational involvement. This relates primarily to the nurture and seeker sensitive services not the seeker's service. If the church has a choir, its role in the service must be minimal. In some traditional churches the ministers of music or the worship people spend 90 percent of their time working with a choir. The result is that the choir does 90 percent of the worship, because the worship leader has no time left to devote to the congregational aspects of worship. If the choir absorbs a lot of the worship leader's time, it's best not to have a choir. Worship must be congregational not choral.

Tension points. An awareness of the various worship tension points will add a dynamic to the worship service that keeps people's attention and facilitates good worship. Sometimes there is a need to establish a balance. Other times the congregation will prefer one end of the continuum over the other. The key is understanding the congregation and their worship needs. The following is a partial list of these tension points:

1. Silence versus sound
2. Solitude versus group participation
3. Traditional versus contemporary style
4. Planned versus spontaneous worship events
5. High-tech versus low-tech
6. Complex versus simple worship techniques
7. Platform versus audience participation
8. Celebration versus reflection
9. Talking versus listening
10. Theme versus no theme
11. Intellectual versus emotional
12. Freedom versus control
13. Formal versus casual
14. Personal versus public
15. Vertical (divine element) versus horizontal (human element)
16. Feminine needs versus masculine needs
17. Familiar versus unfamiliar[5]

The Preaching in Worship

While the other events in the worship service are often underemphasized, the importance of expository preaching can't be overemphasized. People must hear a clear word from God that is relevant to their lives as they attempt to live from day to day. I define expository preaching as the communication of a biblical concept so that people in our contemporary culture understand its truth and apply it to their lives. The following

A Holistic, Authentic Worship   345

material presents several principles that facilitate the excellence and relevance of expository preaching in today's pulpit. These principles assume a working knowledge of preaching in general and sermon construction in particular. It will attempt to build on this knowledge.[6]

Sermons Must Be Interesting Not Boring

One of the biggest complaints from unchurched people, both saved and lost, is that most sermons and preachers are boring. Every church should pass a law that states that it's a crime to bore people with the Bible. The Bible isn't boring—preachers are boring.

There are several factors that create interest in sermons. The minister should strive to say something interesting at the very beginning of the sermon. Preachers can begin with such things as a personal story, a news event, or a statement from a popular celebrity or sports figure. This immediately tells the audience that the speaker is in touch with the real world—the world they live in. Once they've gained this interest, good speakers attempt to maintain it throughout the rest of the sermon with appropriate illustrations and relevant stories.

Another way to create interest is to preach on topics that are important and of interest to the audience not yourself. There's a constant temptation for preachers to address issues that interest them but may not be of interest to their audience. This is often a fatal flaw in those who have recently graduated from school and are relatively new in the pulpit.

Here the Bible provides an instructive example. It's important to note that some books, such as Paul's letters to the Thessalonians, were written to a particular church to answer their questions. Others deal with specific problems, such as Corinthians and the prison epistles. Preachers must realize that most audiences aren't interested in who might be the author of Hebrews, the rationale for supralapsarianism, or the robust economy of the Hittites and the Amalekites. They're interested in themselves and everyday life from Monday through Saturday.

Messages Should Touch Felt Needs

The way to capture people's attention is to address their felt needs—the key to unlocking the closed mind and softening the calloused heart. Then the preacher is able to move to and address an audiences' spiritual needs. Preachers will be able to communicate almost anything if they speak in terms of the audience's needs, aspirations, hopes, and dreams.

Again, various books of the Bible focus on the needs of a particular church. For example, in 1 Corinthians, Paul targets the church's need for information concerning divisions, marriage and divorce, food offered to idols, spiritual gifts, love, and the resurrection of Christ. He specifically mentions needs in Ephesians 4:29. Some in the evangelical community have responded negatively to the emphasis on addressing felt needs in sermons. This seems strange in light of such passages as Ephesians 4:29 and 2 Corinthians 8:14 and 9:12.

Good speakers know where people hurt. If they don't know, they make a point of finding out. They may simply ask or conduct an informal survey in the church or local community. They pay close attention to needs addressed by the local media. Finally, they're aware of the common needs that people have as the result of their humanity.

It's best to present these needs in the introduction of the sermon after the audience's interest has been captured. This tells them that not only will you be interesting but that you understand them and the difficulties of life.

Topical Exposition Is a Valid Form of Preaching

Many evangelical schools train students to preach through a book of the Bible. This is called book exposition. The problem is that some present this as the only way or the best way to preach expository sermons. In fact some seminary graduates feel guilty if they preach a topical sermon. Because those with a liberal perspective preach topical messages, evangelicals feel that anything that uses the term *topical* is wrong and unbiblical.

Topical *expository* sermons are different from topical sermons void of exposition. Actually, there are at least three kinds of expository sermons. One is book exposition, when the preacher takes his congregation through a book of the Bible. A second is biographical exposition that focuses on the life of and learns truth from a biblical character. A third is topical exposition, when the preacher addresses various topics from the Scriptures. Much theological preaching is topical expository preaching.

Actually, there's more evidence in the Scriptures for topical and biographical exposition than book exposition. An example would be all the topical sermons in the book of Acts. Also, the Savior himself used a topical approach, addressing such issues as adultery, greed, money, and hypocrisy. There's no evidence that anyone preached through a book of the Old Testament. This is not to diminish the importance of book exposition but to put the two in proper perspective and to free preachers up to preach topically or biographically from the Bible as well as through a book of the Bible.

A problem with book exposition is that preachers often begin with the text rather than with the audience. They study a particular text and then attempt to apply it to their audience whether or not it applies. For example, some pastors may preach through a particular book of the Bible that deals with issues that neither they nor their audience are currently facing. Consequently, any application comes across as contrived and inauthentic.

An advantage of topical exposition is that it allows preachers to begin with their people. Then they take Bible passages that are relevant and apply them accordingly. Jesus often discerned the needs of people and then addressed them from the Scriptures. One problem with topical preaching, however, is the temptation to take passages out of context and misapply them to the audience's needs.

Preaching Should Balance Both the Practical and the Theological

In general, most people want to know both what the Bible says and how it works. The two must go together! To emphasize one at the expense of the other does injustice to the Scriptures and the preaching process.

Few people are interested in the Bible and theology as ends in themselves. They want to know how these two relate to their lives. While many are interested in what's going to happen at the end of the age, they're even more interested in what's going to happen at the end of the week!

Therefore, sermons that emphasize "how to" are very popular and helpful to laypeople. For example, a series of sermons on Philippians 4 could be entitled: "How to Be Happy in an Unhappy World." The title of a sermon on Romans 12:19–21 might be "How to Right Life's Wrongs." A sermon on divorce could be "Growing through Divorce, Not Just Going through Divorce."[7]

These kinds of sermons are very practical and relevant. They're as heavy on application as on theology. In fact it's most important that preachers realize that the Bible has a lot to say about everyday life and how to live it. Those who remember this truth and preach accordingly will touch lives with Scripture.

Sermons Should Be Simple and Memorable

Two major points are enough for one sermon; it is acceptable to have three points although this may be pushing it. People can easily remember two points, such as a problem-solution approach or a principle-application approach to the text of a sermon. Good preachers realize that the average person in the pew can remember only so much and pay attention for only so long.

One way to help people remember sermons is to tell stories—lots of stories that illustrate biblical principles. This is one of the universal means of communication in many cultures around the world. Everyone loves a story! That's one of the attractions of movies, television, and books. In addition to stories, use lots of illustrations and examples because they'll have a similar effect, especially if they are personal. Be sure to preach from the narrative portions of the Bible. These are very popular today with postmoderns. They prefer narrative because discerning theological concepts in a story context challenges them deeply and authentically.

Messages Should Not Be Too Long

Twenty to thirty minutes is long enough for any sermon. Today's average audience, no matter how great their theological sophistication, probably doesn't hear anything beyond thirty minutes, no matter how important. In some cases, long sermons irritate today's audiences, especially if they're boring and delivered poorly.

A good practice is to study those who make their livelihood by communicating, for example, those in the media. Note how they keep people's attention. Often an hour-long television drama is broken up into numerous segments with different plots and characters. This serves to maintain both the audience's interest and attention.

Language Must Be Clear and Contemporary

Often, in a noble attempt to be true to Scripture, some preachers will use lots of biblical terms, such as "born again," "the glory of God," "repent," "saved," "redemption," "propitiation," and so on. The problem is that these words don't communicate to the average person in the pew and the unchurched guest in particular.

Ordinary people who lived in the first century understood many of these terms because they were used regularly in their culture. For example, the biblical term *redemption* was used for the price paid to purchase or liberate a slave in the local slave market. The Greek of the New Testament was not a special language but was the common (*koine*) Greek world language used from about 300 BC to AD 500.

It is the responsibility of the preacher to contextualize Scripture for today's modern audience. The minister should explain these terms and use contemporary synonyms that convey the same meaning today that they had in the first century. One helpful way to accomplish this is to use a reliable, modern translation of the Bible. Most younger people today struggle with the King James translation of the Bible, simply because they don't understand the language. Does an older generation really believe that young people should or even will learn a different language (King James English) to attend church? (Or is the worship fiasco more about power and control?) Both the New American Standard Bible and the New International Version of the Bible are true to the original text and understandable to the person in the pew. Why not use them?

Sermons Should Be Creative and Positive

Most people appreciate creativity in the church in general and in sermons in particular. Some pastors have sought to be creative by conducting interviews as a part of the sermon. For example, my former pastor was preaching on the topic of homosexuality in Romans 1. Toward the conclusion of the message, he interviewed a converted homosexual! In a sermon on abortion, he interviewed a lady who had experienced an abortion.[8]

A number of preachers are using other creative means such as the mini-drama and video. Videotape could be used to convey an experience or a situation that illustrates visually some point in the sermon. The drama has many uses. It could come before the sermon and present a problem that the sermon then solves, or it could follow the sermon and demonstrate a way in which the sermon could be applied to one's life.

Finally, positive sermons communicate more effectively in the long run than negative sermons. They let people know what you're for rather than what you're against. While there are times when the preacher must address problems in the congregation, he must resist regularly beating his people over the head with the Bible.

The following are two preaching websites that you might find helpful: www.preachingplus.com and www.sermoncentral.com.

A Worship Exercise

1. What is your primary motivation for going to a worship service? What is your response to the worship that takes place in your church? Why?

2. Critique the worship service at your present church in terms of its strengths and weaknesses.

3. Is the worship at your church authentic or inauthentic? Describe the difference.

4. What is your philosophy of worship?

5. Are you an authentic worshiper of Christ? When and how often do you worship?

6. Do you find yourself making some of the preaching errors mentioned at the end of this chapter? Which ones? Is there some person whom you can trust to critique your speaking?

Appendix D

A Biblical, Culturally Relevant Evangelism

Hurricanes can inflict tremendous damage on property and have claimed many people's lives. I know. Having grown up in Florida, I've weathered a few. But fortunately, when a hurricane is coming, various warning signs go up. There are constant weather bulletins, media reports, and special hurricane warning flags that are hoisted to the top of flagpoles.

Today there are numerous warning signs about the dark future of evangelism in this country. One sign comes from western Europe. Western Europe has exerted a great influence on North America in numerous ways, including Christianity. In 1997 Oxford University scholar Dr. Alister E. McGrath, while speaking at Dallas Theological Seminary, noted that England in the eighteenth century was primarily a Christian nation. However, today less than 10 percent claim to be churched. McGrath warned that this was because the church stopped doing evangelism and focused its attention on teaching the Bible and the pastoral care of its members.

In the summer of 1995, I pastored a church in Amsterdam, the Netherlands, where the number of unchurched was around 97.5 percent! The great missionary statesman Donald McGavran stated, "If top priority is not given to effective evangelism by our churches, in two generations the church in America will look much like its counterpart in Europe."[1] While we can't be sure when he said this, I suspect it was two generations ago!

Another warning sign comes from Floyd Bartel. In his book *A New Look at Church Growth*, he wrote: "95% of all Christians in North America will not win one person to Christ in their entire lifetime."[2] Obviously, this is a shocking figure. Sixty-five percent would be high, but 95 percent is frightening!

A third warning sign late in the twentieth century comes from George Barna. In *The Frog in the Kettle*, he wrote: "In the past seven years, the proportion of adults who have accepted Christ as their personal Savior (34%) has not increased."[3] From this he concludes that what American Christians believe about the Bible apparently isn't significant enough to share with others.

A fourth warning comes from Bob Gilliam. In the mid– to late–1990s, Gilliam, a church growth consultant who works with churches from coast to coast, surveyed more than 500 evangelical churches in 40 denominations over a 10-year period, including more than 130,000 church members. His survey revealed that each year the average evangelical church led 1.7 people to Christ for each 100 people in attendance. If you owned an insurance company, and your salespersons sold a total of 1.7 policies per year, you would be out of business in a hurry!

While numerous signs indicate that there's danger ahead if the established church in North America doesn't change its attitude toward evangelism, there's a solution. That solution is church planting. Peter Wagner believes: *"The single most effective evangelistic methodology under heaven is planting new churches."*[4] New churches have the potential to pursue lost people with a passion. A vital church planting principle involves a biblical, culturally relevant evangelism.

A Culturally Relevant Evangelism

Effective evangelism in the twenty-first century is characterized by cultural relevance. A primary reason so little evangelism is taking place in and through evangelical churches is because many don't know how to relate relevantly to the growing number of unchurched lost people in America. There are at least three reasons for this problem.

Christians Don't Know Any Lost People

The first reason is that most people in the church don't know any lost people; they don't have any lost friends.

Most Christians Are Isolated and Insulated from the Lost

The primary problem is that most active Christians have, over a period of time, insulated and thus isolated themselves from lost people.

The fact. Believers know lost people in the sense that they may work next to them or live next door to them, but there are no lost people on their list of friends. They simply don't spend quality time with lost people, especially of the unchurched variety. They don't invite lost people into their homes on a regular basis. They don't consistently spend their leisure time activities with lost people. Most often, when they do things with other people, it's with Christians not unchurched neighbors or workmates.

The exception. The exception is when a lost individual first comes to faith in Christ as Savior. New believers are often so excited about their faith that they make a point of telling the good news of what's taken place in their lives to many of their lost friends. However, they join a church, and, over a period of time, note that others aren't sharing their faith. This is catching! In some churches, these new believers discover that evangelism simply isn't valued. Other important areas are being emphasized, such as social responsibility, physical and spiritual healing, or some program, to the exclusion of evangelism.

The result. Eventually, over a period of time, new believers stop sharing the faith, and other priorities in the church take hold. They isolate themselves from unbelievers and spend all their time with believers. They focus on ministries within the walls of the church. This, in turn, serves to insulate them from the lost as well. Soon they no longer have any lost friends, nor do they want any. They prefer to be around believers only.

The Reasons

There are several reasons why all this takes place.

Christians aren't comfortable around non-Christians. The first has to do with our comfort level. Simply stated, we're not comfortable when we're around lost people, often for what seem to be good reasons. Sometimes they use crude language that we aren't used to, and it has a shocking effect on us. We can add to this list the consumption of alcohol and illicit relationships with the opposite or in some cases the same sex. And the list goes on!

We need to constantly remind ourselves that the Savior spent much of his time with lost people. And they weren't the aseptic religious people of his day, the scribes and the Pharisees, but the sinners and tax collectors (Luke 5:27–32; 15:1–2; 19:1–10).

Christians expect lost people to behave like saved people. Another reason we shun lost people is related somewhat to the first reason. It has to do with our expectations. We expect lost people to behave like saved people. The very fact that we're surprised when a lost person uses a string of expletives says something about our expectations. To expect the lost to act as though they're saved is totally unrealistic and unbiblical! We must not expect lost people to behave like saved people until they've become saved people.

Churches Maintain Culturally Irrelevant Methods

A second reason churches can't relate relevantly to unchurched lost people is because they use evangelistic methods that don't fit people and are generally ineffective with unchurched moderns and postmoderns.

Methods That Don't Fit People

Some churches want their evangelistic outreach to be more effective but aren't sure how to go about it. Therefore, they look to those who have a reputation for excellence in evangelism and are winning people to Christ. Most churches turn to evangelistic parachurch organizations for their evangelistic methods.

On the one hand, this makes a lot of sense. The idea is that if you want to do something well, then study and imitate those who do it well already. Why reinvent the wheel? On the other hand, the problem with looking to the parachurch for its methodology is that the latter most often attracts gifted people, those with the gift of evangelism, those who use primarily one style of evangelism—confrontational evangelism.

The problem in the local church is that only about 5–10 percent have the gift of evangelism and are comfortable with a confrontational approach. A case in point is Coral Ridge Presbyterian Church in Fort Lauderdale, Florida. This church is well-known in Christian circles for its Evangelism Explosion Program. Some of the church's staff travel and conduct Evangelism Explosion seminars around the country. This is an excellent program that uses primarily a confrontational approach, so only about 10 percent of a church's membership will be involved![5]

Methods That Aren't for an Unchurched Generation

Many churches attempt to reach people in *today's* unchurched culture with methods that worked with people in *yesterday's* churched culture. Most of their evangelistic methods are left over from the Harry Truman Generation. The thinking is that if they worked back then, they should still work today and they will still work tomorrow. This would, of course, be true if our culture never changed. But it does change, and these churches haven't thought through the implications of that cultural change on their evangelistic methods.

There are several examples. In general, evangelistic bumper stickers with the words "Jesus Saves" are a turnoff for most unsaved people. They think this is weird. The use of Christian radio and television isn't highly effective either. The problem is the listening and viewing audience. Who watches Christian television and listens to Christian radio? Christians not unbelievers! Handing out gospel tracts isn't as effective as it used to be, unless they are read by "seekers" who are already interested in spiritual matters. Knocking on doors works in blue-collar areas and the inner city but isn't as effective in middle- and upper-income white-collar neighborhoods. Citywide evangelistic crusades aren't attracting people—with the exception of those held by Billy Graham. Lost people will attend a Billy Graham Crusade because he has become an American institution and is a man of high integrity.

Churches Have Missed the Unchurched Culture

A third reason evangelical churches don't know how to relate relevantly to the unchurched generation is because they don't understand the culture. These churches have several false assumptions that need correction.

The Unchurched Aren't Pursuing the Church

Many traditional churches have missed the shift in America from a churched to an unchurched culture. Up until the late 1950s and 1960s, America was predominantly a churched culture. This doesn't mean that much of America was truly born again. But a lot of people, both lost and saved, were in church on Sunday. This was due in part to the large number of churches prevalent in America in those days. Also, there wasn't as much for people to do on Sundays other than go to church. Most towns and cities enforced "blue laws," which kept businesses closed on Sunday. There weren't many events that took place on the Lord's Day to draw people away from attending a church.

Many churches still live and think in terms of those times. While they're aware that some things have changed, they haven't been able to figure it all out. Consequently, they believe that as long as you hang a "welcome" sign out front, lost people will flock to the church. The fact that they aren't has them a little puzzled.

The Unchurched Are Secular Not Judeo-Christian

In the 1950s and 1960s, due to the large number of churches in America, there was a strong Judeo-Christian influence on most institutions and organizations, including public school systems; national, state, and local governments; and the business sector. As the result of a number of decisions by the Supreme Court, this is no longer the case. In fact many of these organizations are prohibited by law from displaying any Christian symbols or sponsoring public prayer and Bible reading.

All of this has affected the typical postmodern person in North America. While some are hostile, many look on Christianity as simply irrelevant to them and the times. Therefore, they've adopted a thoroughly secular mind-set. The older Boomers can remember the old days and what church was like, while their children have little knowledge of Christianity except for that depicted on television and in the movies. We may live in the same neighborhoods, cheer for the same teams, and even speak the same language, but our core beliefs and values are worlds apart.

The Unchurched Are More Concerned about Now Than the Hereafter

Most unchurched people focus on the present not the future. They don't think about eternity because that isn't important. The idea is, to paraphrase one beer commercial, "You only go around once in life, so get all the gusto you can get!" These people struggle with such concepts as delayed gratification. The word *patience* isn't in their vocabulary because it's not found in their dictionary. A 1990s slogan for Burger King advertised, "Have it your way, right away!" People want everything and they want it now—whether it's money, sex, or hamburgers.

The obvious result of all this is that people can't have it all, and they can't have it all now. Therefore, they're extremely frustrated and bear numerous deep, emotional scars. This is reflected in high divorce and suicide rates. This generation populates the offices of psychologists and psychiatrists from Los Angeles to New York.

To reach people today, the American church will have to show the benefits of Christianity in the here-and-now. It will have to demonstrate in life and teaching that Christianity isn't simply some shallow "pie-in-the-sky-by-and-by" approach to life but that it addresses the hard issues, such as who we are, where we have come from, what we are worth, and why we are here.

The Unchurched Are Process Not Event Oriented

In the first half of the twentieth century, evangelism involved a single presentation of the gospel to lost people. Success involved getting them to say yes and pray a sinner's prayer. It was more an event because America at that time was a churched culture where much pre-evangelism had already taken place. Churches didn't have to spend a lot of time discussing the existence of God, the deity of Christ, or the veracity and authority of Scripture. Much of this was already assumed and accepted by the lost. In many cases, they simply needed accurate information regarding how to be saved.

In the 1970s up through the early twenty-first century, all that has changed drastically. With the shift in America from a churched to an unchurched culture and the growing number of first- and now second-generation unchurched lost people, sharing Christ is much more a process than an event. Very little pre-evangelism is taking place. In a post-Christian, postmodern world, people aren't so sure that there is a God. Many believe that Jesus (if they even know who he is—a growing number have never heard of him) was merely a man or at best a prophet and the Bible is just another book. Now the witnessing process must involve a number of "mini-decisions" on the part of those who come to Christ.

It becomes obvious that our methodology, not our message, must be adjusted to allow for all the changes that have taken place in the culture. The people in Christ's church must have patience with the lost and know some of the biblical answers to the hard questions they're asking. Above all, they need to be willing to love and befriend lost people and build long-term relationships with them that have the potential of resulting in their salvation.

A Biblically Based Evangelism

While the methodology of evangelism changes and adjusts to the culture, the biblical principles of evangelism remain the same. Here are some of those principles.

The Principle of Pursuit

The church must pursue lost people, not wait for them to come to it. This principle is found in various passages, such as those on the Great Commission (Matt. 28:19–20; Mark 16:15; Acts 1:8). In particular, it's both emphasized and illustrated by the Savior (Luke 5:27–32; 15:1–31; 19:1–10).

In essence, pursuing lost people is the Great Commission—or at least the first of three steps in carrying out the Great Commission. The problem is that not many churches are doing this. Some go into early "evangelistic retirement," while others are merely attracting Christians from other churches. A church that's not pursuing and reaching lost people isn't a Great Commission church and needs to reconsider its purpose for being here. The church planter's vision must include pursuing and winning lost people.

The Principle of Value

The principle of value says that lost people matter to God. The Savior loves and values them. While this principle is taught throughout the Bible, it's illustrated clearly in Luke 5:27–32; 15:1–31; and 19:1–10. The point is that if the lost matter to God, they should matter to his church.

How can we know if they matter to Christ's church? What's the proof? Those of us in his church will begin to love lost people and pursue them individually and corporately as a church. We will invite them into our homes to meet our families and eat with us. We will attend various events together and be available when they go through difficult times.

The Principle of Relationship

We should spend time with and get to know lost people. This principle is illustrated in such passages as Luke 5:29–32; 15:1–2; 19:7; and Matthew 9:9–13. The idea isn't that we're to be *like* lost people; rather, we're to be *with* lost people. Actually, we're to be different from lost people but in a way that attracts them to Christ. While we can't be with them all the time, we can be with them sufficiently long enough to understand them and how they think. The result is that we learn to relate to them naturally.

Again, the problem is that the longer we're saved, the fewer lost friends we have. The result is that evangelism becomes unnatural (sharing with strangers) rather than natural (sharing with friends). We can apply this principle by committing ourselves to relate to a few lost people on a regular basis, perhaps a lost single person at work, an unchurched couple next door, or an unsaved international student at the local university. The important thing is that we begin to relate to them redemptively.

The Principle of Need

The church can gain the attention of lost people by addressing their felt needs. Scripture doesn't ignore people's needs (Acts 2:45; 2 Cor. 8:19; 9:12; Eph. 4:29; Phil. 4:19). Again, the key to unlocking the closed mind and touching the calloused heart is felt needs. This principle is found throughout the Scriptures. People responded to the Savior because of their felt need for salvation. Jesus regularly met people's physical needs and used this as an opportunity to meet their spiritual needs. Several books of the New Testament were written to address the needs of various local churches.

Lost people will respond to people, sermons, and programs that authentically present biblical solutions to their needs. Some object to this strategy, arguing that we need to start with a just and holy God and not with a lost and depraved sinner. While this may be the case with some lost people, we have to get their attention first. Many aren't interested in God, but they're interested in themselves. As the sign not far from my house proclaims, "It's all about you!" The idea here is to start where they are and patiently take them to where God wants them to be, as the Savior did with the Samaritan woman (John 4).

The Principle of Cultural Adaptation

The church should adapt its practices, not its faith, to the people it's trying to reach. (Another term that we use for adaptation is *contextualization*.) These practices concern cultural things (the world in here)—when the church meets, which translation of the Bible it uses, the instruments used in worship, casual versus formal attire, and so on. Paul teaches this principle in 1 Corinthians 9:19–23 and 10:23–33. It's also demonstrated by Jesus' ministry (see, for example, John 3–4). In practicing cultural adaptation, the church must never change or compromise in any way the clear teaching of Scripture.

We can't expect today's unchurched lost people to come to us on our terms and adjust to the church's unique culture. This simply will not happen. The mature church must be willing to be flexible and put aside its own cultural and individual preferences to reach the lost. For example, if lost people will come to our meetings if we dress informally, then we need to take off our ties! If they will come only on Sunday morning at 11:00 AM, we need to design a special service for them and meet as believers at another time. If they prefer to park close to our church facilities, we must be willing to park farther away and walk.

What are you willing to give up to reach lost people? The Father was willing to give up his Son (John 3:16). The Son was willing to give up his life (Rom. 5:8). Paul was willing to give up his soul (9:3). In light of this, we must ask, What are we willing to give up?

The Principle of Receptivity

The church should pursue receptive lost people, those who *might* be interested in spiritual matters. Unsaved people are at different stages in their view of spiritual concerns. This can be demonstrated by a horizontal continuum, with absolute unbelief on the left side and belief on the right side. Most lost people are located somewhere along this continuum. A biblical example that illustrates this concept is the parable of the sower (Matt. 13:1–9, 18–23). The different soils mentioned represent where various people are along the continuum. Those who are receptive to spiritual matters are somewhere in the middle of the continuum, slowly moving toward belief.

Receptive people also vary in their situations. They could be members of our families or our friends. Some may be experiencing unusual stress as the result of physical disability, financial hardship, or a relationship gone bad.

How can we identify these people? In *The Pastor's Church Growth Handbook*, Charles Arn gives us some help. He writes that unchurched people are most responsive to a change in lifestyle during periods of transition in their lives. A period of transition is a span of time when an individual's normal, everyday behavior patterns are disrupted by some irregular event that causes stress in his or her life. Some examples would be the birth of a child, a marriage, a divorce, or a hospitalization. Those who undergo this kind of transition are even more receptive when irregular events compound themselves over a short period of time. However, the greater the length of time following a period of transition, the less receptive they will be.[6]

The Principle of Responsiveness

The church should not only pursue *receptive* lost people, it must pursue *responsive* lost people, those who are interested in spiritual truth. We would call these people "seekers." There are several biblical examples of this principle. Jesus instructed his twelve disciples to pursue responsive lost people (Matt. 10:11–15; Mark 6:10–11; 12:34; Luke 9:4–6). Paul pursued responsive people (Acts 13:43–52; 18:1–7). Some individuals who were "seekers" were Zacchaeus (Luke 19:1–10), Nicodemus (John 3:1–21), the eunuch from Ethiopia (Acts 8:26), and Cornelius (Acts 10). The point is that these people are strongly moving toward or are very close to faith in Christ. They must be pursued with a passion.

The Principle of Clear Communication

The church must be careful to use language that clearly communicates biblical truth to the lost. The church of Jesus Christ must realize that it belongs to a unique subculture that is different from all other subcultures, even in the same part of the country. One example of this difference is its language. Those in the church speak a "temple language" or what some call "Christianeze." We use terms such as "believer" and "sister" and "brother" that are used in a different way in other subcultures.

We also use such terms as "repent," "righteousness," and "sanctification" in sermons and lessons. These aren't used or understood by those outside the church. Much of this language comes from the New Testament and was commonly used by the average person in the world of the first century. While people understood these terms in the first century, both churched and unchurched people don't understand them today. Therefore, we must be careful to explain their usage and to find equivalent terms from our culture if we're to communicate the biblical message clearly.

The Principle of Multiple Hooks

The church should use as many methods as possible to reach the lost. We see this principle in the Bible as I demonstrate below in the section on the styles of evangelism. When I was in high school, I spent a lot of time hunting and fishing. I soon discovered that if the fish weren't biting, it was a good idea to change my method. For example, early in the morning large mouth bass would often strike at a top-water lure cast next to the grass growing close to the edge of the shoreline. A little later in the day this wasn't effective. Instead, I would stick a hook through an earthworm and drop it into the opening of various submerged stumps to catch perch.

In "fishing for men," it's essential that we keep lots of hooks in the water. Just as it takes all kinds of churches to reach all kinds of people, so it takes all kinds of methods to reach all kinds of people. Different methods work with different people, and some methods change in terms of their effectiveness as the culture changes. If we're open to different methods, we'll reach people with the gospel.

The Principle of Specific, Intentional Prayer

It's essential for the leaders of the church to be intentional in their prayers and to ask God specifically to give his people a genuine desire to reach the lost. In Matthew 9:36 Jesus observes the harassed and helpless condition of the various crowds that approach him, and he feels compassion for them. In verse 37 he turns to his disciples and points out the need for more workers to harvest this large crop of hurting people. In verse 38 he tells them that a solution to this need is to pray and ask God specifically to send out more workers into the harvest field.

Such crowds are found in abundance in every community. The Savior is teaching that there's a need for believers to find and reach them, but just a few people in each church can't possibly do it. There's a need to mobilize the church as a whole. An essential ingredient in mobilizing people for evangelism is intentional, specific prayer on the part of the leaders.

The Principle of Discipleship

The Great Commission demands disciples as well as decisions. There's a general tendency on the part of people to move to one extreme or the other. Some pursue discipleship or some aspect of discipleship, such as teaching, to the exclusion of evangelism. Others pursue evangelism (decisions) to the exclusion of discipleship. Neither accomplishes the Great Commission, although the latter does get people into the kingdom.

The point here is that authentic evangelism pushes past a mere decision and presses for discipleship. In fact a disciple of Christ is a more accurate representation of a true decision for Christ. Conversion is meant to be germinal not terminal, the beginning not the end, of a close relationship with Christ.

Both extremes falsely dichotomize the Great Commission mandate. Scripture clearly separates conversion from discipleship in *presentation.* For example, the two are clearly distinguished theologically in comparing such passages as Ephesians 2:8–9 with Ephesians 2:10. These passages are presenting the theology of salvation. However, Scripture doesn't always dichotomize between the two in *practice* as seen in a descriptive passage such as Acts 14:21–22, where the disciples are seen in action. It's the descriptive passages that cause so much confusion in Christian circles in trying to determine correct doctrine. A case in point is Acts 2:38. The key is to go first to the verses that speak to the doctrine theologically. Then we base what we believe more on theological passages than on descriptive passages.

The Principle of Natural Style

Each Christian has at least one or more natural styles of evangelism.

The Source

Bill Hybels presents this principle in his book *Honest to God?* He got the idea from the Bible! He points out that it takes all kinds and types of Christians to reach all kinds and types of lost people:

> Only a tiny fraction of the unbelievers in this world will be reached by the stereotypical evangelist. The unbelieving world is made up of a variety of people: young and old, rich and poor, educated and uneducated, urban and rural, with different races, personalities, values, political systems, and religious backgrounds. Isn't it obvious it would take more than one style to reach such a diverse population?
>
> That's where we come in. Somewhere in that multifarious group is a person who needs to hear the message of Christ from someone just like

you or me. A person who needs an evangelist of your exact age, career, and level of spiritual understanding, or of my exact personality, background, and interests.[7]

The Styles

Hybels proceeds to list six possible evangelistic styles.[8] The first is the confrontational style demonstrated by Peter with his Pentecost sermon in Acts 2. The second is the intellectual style used by Paul in Acts 17:3. This involves "explaining and proving" that Christ was Messiah. The third is the testimonial style used by the blind man in John 9. Christ had healed him and revolutionized his life. It was all he could talk about! The fourth is the relational style of the demon-possessed person in Mark 5:20. The fifth is the invitational style. It was used by the Samaritan woman in John 4, who, after she spoke with Christ at the well, went and invited her fellow Samaritans in a nearby city to come and listen to him. The sixth is the serving style demonstrated by Dorcas in Acts 9:36. An eclectic approach would involve the use of a combination of these styles.

The Application

Every church with a vision to reach lost people should help people discover their natural evangelistic style(s). This could be a part of the church's lay mobilization process. Evangelism becomes more authentic and natural when people share according to their unique style. Combine this with those who have either natural or spiritual gifts in the area of evangelism, and they'll witness from a position of strength and giftedness. This is a gifts-based, style-shaped evangelism.

The Principle of Natural Prospects

The best and most natural prospects for evangelism are one's family and friends. Tom Wolf, the former senior pastor of the Church on Brady (now called Mosaic) in Los Angeles, California, has developed this principle for the church.[9]

The Examples

There are numerous examples of this principle throughout the New Testament. In Acts 10:24 and 11:14, Cornelius has compassion not only for himself, but his family and "close friends." In Acts 16:14, Lydia comes to faith in Christ, and in verse 15 her family does as well. The same is true of the Philippian jailer and his family in verses 30–34. The pattern repeats itself in the situation of Crispus and his family (Acts 18:8), a royal official and his son (John 4:53), a demon-possessed man and his family (Mark 5:19–20), Zacchaeus' family (Luke 19:9), and the household of Stephanas (1 Cor. 1:16).

It's helpful to understand that a household, as the term was used in both the Old and New Testaments, was much larger than the typical American household of the twentieth century.

> In addition to the men, there were married women and the unmarried daughters, as well as the slaves of both sexes, persons without full citizenship, and "sojourners," or resident foreign workers. If we remember that families had numerous children, and that an Israelite might easily be a father at twenty, a grandfather at forty, and a great-grandfather at sixty, and that the younger brothers of the head of the family, with their descendents, could also belong to a patriarchal family.[10]

Regarding the family in the New Testament, Otto Michel writes, "It is explicitly emphasized that the conversion of a man leads his whole family to the faith; this would include wife, children, servants and relatives living in the house."[11]

The Research

Win Arn demonstrates the importance of the principle of natural prospects in research conducted by the Institute of American Church Growth. The institute asked more than fourteen thousand laypeople: "What or who was responsible for your coming to Christ and your church?" One to 2 percent listed a special need, 2 to 3 percent said they simply walked in and stayed, 5 to 6 percent listed the pastor, visitation was responsible for 1 to 2 percent, 4 to 5 percent listed the Sunday school, an evangelistic crusade was responsible for 1/2 of 1 percent, and 2 to 3 percent listed the church's program. Finally, 75 to 90 percent listed a friend or relative.[12]

The Application

The church must encourage its people to pursue their natural prospects, such as their family, neighbors, and friends, with the gospel. These are people with whom they've already formed important, personal relationships. According to the Scriptures and the survey by the Institute of American Church Growth, this is a natural, biblical form of evangelism that gets lasting results.

The Principle of Grace

Grace is God's unmerited favor toward humankind. He does things for us with "no strings attached." Steve Sjogren has written *Conspiracy of Kindness*, a relevant book on evangelism.[13] The intent of the book is to encourage believers to do various acts of kindness for lost people with "no strings attached." For example, Christians could wash cars, mow lawns, give away Pepsi, clean car windshields, put money in lapsed parking meters, shovel snow, and many other things with no expectation of return. In fact an offer of remuneration is turned down. Christians respond, "We're simply attempting to show the love of Jesus in a practical way." When people ask why, it serves as an invitation to witness to them.

These acts of kindness or grace have a staggering effect on lost people. The unchurched think that all the church is after is their money. This proves them wrong in a positive way, and they, not the Christian, initiate a discussion of the gospel.

The Principle of Community

Close to the principle of grace is the principle of community. It encourages church people to get involved in various ways in their neighborhoods and communities. One of the chief criticisms of the church in the early twenty-first century has been its general lack of involvement in and contribution to its community. As one unchurched, lost person in San Francisco communicated, the church is a pariah; it lives off the community, pays no taxes, and does nothing to help the community.

An exception is Fellowship Bible Church in Little Rock, Arkansas. They are intentionally involved in the Little Rock community. If you were to visit a public school or some other public service organization, they would speak well of this church and what it has accomplished in the city. Its outreach initiatives have impacted Little Rock's public schools, colleges, the police and fire departments, the poor, and the hungry.

Developing a Biblical, Culturally Relevant Strategy for Evangelism

Evangelism is best accomplished through a well-designed strategy that pursues lost people. This should be done with both an individual and a corporate strategy of pursuit. The first involves the individuals in the church, and the second involves the church as a whole.

A Strategy of Individual Pursuit

The church should design a strategy of evangelism for its members that takes into account their unique styles and helps them pursue lost people. The following five-step strategy could serve as a pattern.

Examine One's Relational Community

Every person has a relational community. The idea behind this first step is to encourage the people in the church to examine regularly their relational community, looking for receptive and responsive people who might be interested in and sensitive to spiritual matters. A relational community consists of a minimum of three groups.

The family community. The family community is the various people who are related in some way to the church member. These people would be grandparents, parents, children, aunts, uncles, cousins, and in-laws. While family ties aren't as strong as they used to be in light of the divorce rate and the growing number of single parents, in many places still "blood is thicker than water." These natural ties provide fertile ground for evangelism. A most helpful exercise in discovering receptive and responsive family members is to draw a family tree and use it for prayer purposes.

The neighborhood community. The neighborhood community consists of the neighbors in the immediate vicinity. Often friendships can be developed within this community that are as strong relationally as those between family members. Consequently, the people in our churches must be encouraged to take every opportunity to develop relationships with the people next door. A helpful exercise is to draw a community map with the church member's house in the center.

One problem for a growing number of people in our churches is that they live fairly far from where the church is located. The old parish system, where everyone attended the church in the neighborhood, is long gone. This began to erode with the development of expressways, which allowed people to cover great distances in a short period of time. The result is that some people attend churches that are quite far from where they live. This makes it difficult to invite neighbors to church, because they may not be willing to make the long drive out of their community.

The work community. The work community includes the people that the average church member is in contact with during the week while at work. It often consists of one or two people who may be on the same team and others with whom there's a more distant work relationship. It's helpful for purposes of prayer and spotting responsive people in this community to draw an organizational chart. The problem with inviting these people to church-sponsored events is the same as that for the neighborhood community—distance. The people who make up the work community may live in the opposite direction from where the church is located.

Develop a Focus List

As people in the church routinely examine their various communities, they will begin to discover certain people who might be receptive and responsive to Christianity. These are often individuals who are going through a stressful period in their lives. They may be experiencing illness, the loss of a job, or the loss of a family member. These people could be put on a list in the order of their perceived receptivity to spiritual matters. For the sake of memory and emphasis, we could call this a "focus list."

The Masterplanning Group International has developed a similar idea. They actually sell a card that they call "Ten Most Wanted List." The Group encourages believers to list ten people they most want to see come to Christ. They provide a list of suggestions regarding those who might be on the list and what a person can do to build a relationship with them. Also, the card includes a small tab where all ten names may be listed. This tab can be removed and carried in one's wallet or purse.[14]

Pray for Those on the Focus List

Next, the members are asked to pray daily for those people who are on their focus list. This need not take more than a few minutes of their time and can be accomplished while driving to work or on a lunch break. This serves to help them concentrate on their prayer efforts for the lost and to keep the lost constantly before them.

Most Christians pray to some extent. It may be for a short time daily, or it may be only once a week at the worship service. The point is that they don't spend much time in prayer, so they don't experience a lot of answers to prayer. When people begin to pray, God will begin to answer their prayers. The result is a changed attitude toward prayer, a changed life, and new people populating the kingdom.

Cultivate Relationships with Those on the Focus List

The fourth step in the strategy is to pursue a relationship with the person or persons at the top of the list. If this person is a recent widow, then you could mow her lawn and help with repairs. You could check up on her regularly to see if she has any needs you can meet. If it's the couple next door, invite them over for coffee and dessert. Invite the husband over to watch a football game and eat pizza. Invite him to go along to the local store to buy fertilizer or a hammer and nails.

In particular, people should look for things they enjoy doing, and do them with lost people. If two women enjoy cooking, they can get together and share recipes and cook up a special meal for their husbands. If they both enjoy jogging or a workout, they could jog together or work out together at the local health club. If neighbors enjoy playing board games, invite them over for popcorn and a game of Monopoly.

Discern Their Needs and Look for Times of Receptivity

Finally, as people in the church get to know those in their relational communities, the latter will begin to divulge their felt needs. When a person is hurting in some way, it's difficult to hide it. These are ideal times to talk about spiritual things.

God often uses physical or emotional pain in a lost person's life to get his or her attention and catalyze spiritual interests. Christians need to be alert to these times because they are periods of potential receptivity and response to Christ. And it's at these times that a person in the church could implement evangelism. Using an invitational style, he or she might invite the lost person to a neighborhood Bible study or a special church service for seekers. If it's a confrontational style, this is the time to confront gently. If it's a testimonial style, this is an opportunity to testify concerning all that God has accomplished through Christ.

The church needs to initiate this strategy for individual pursuit at the point of membership. When most people join a church, they're making a commitment to that church. They've decided they want to be a part of the body and are at a point of high commitment. In the membership process, they would be asked to draw up a family tree, a community map, and an organizational chart for work. Next, they could develop a focus list or a Ten Most Wanted List. This would be an excellent start toward implementing the strategy on a personal basis.

A Strategy of Corporate Pursuit

It's imperative that every church with a Great Commission vision develop a corporate strategy for pursuing lost people in general and unchurched lost in particular. This involves two areas.

Develop a Unique Strategy of Evangelism

Not only should individual members be involved in evangelism, but the church as a whole should be involved as well. This is primarily the responsibility of the pastors and their teams who need to design a specific strategy that fits their church and their particular target group in the community.

This strategy is usually reflected in the church's ministries. If you want to know what a church values, examine its ministries. Churches that value social action have numerous programs designed to help various groups in the community, such as the poor, the homeless, and the unborn. Churches that value Bible knowledge have programs that primarily involve a strong teaching ministry. They're marked by Sunday school classes or small groups taught by excellent teachers.

Churches with a Great Commission vision must establish innovative, relevant ministries that balance evangelism and edification. In essence, this process is accomplished by first developing the strategy and then designing the church's ministries around that strategy. The strategy in its simplest form is twofold and consists of evangelism and edification. The next step is to design several ministries to accomplish evangelism and several ministries to accomplish edification.

Churches that God is blessing are balanced in their approach to evangelism and edification. They're both reaching lots of lost people and discipling a significant portion of them. And each of them has developed a strategy on which their ministries are based.

Encourage and Help People in Their Personal Evangelism Efforts

A corporate strategy that balances evangelism and edification encourages the people in a church or beginning core group to share their faith individually. This needs to be reinforced by other efforts as well. People will need constant encouragement from the pulpit. Pastors who value evangelism will communicate this in their sermons. The church will need to sponsor evangelistic classes that help people discover their evangelism styles and share their faith. The church could encourage the leaders of small groups to take their people through this training. Also, small groups could be created specifically for the purpose of reaching lost people.

An Evangelism Exercise

1. Do you have any lost friends? How much time do you spend with lost people, not including those you work with or members of your family? If you spend little time with lost people, then list some of the reasons.

2. Why are so few Christians and churches reaching lost people today? Do you know of any exceptions?

3. Using the biblical principles of evangelism listed in this chapter as a checklist, which are characteristic of your evangelism efforts and those of your church?

4. Draw a map of your neighborhood with the houses or apartments that immediately surround your house or apartment. Place people's names on it appropriately and use this as a means to pray for opportunities to relate to them. Do the same for your relatives using a family tree, and for people at work using an organizational chart.

5. What were the circumstances surrounding your coming to faith in Christ? Did they involve a relationship with a friend or relative? If so, what does this tell you about the effectiveness of friendship evangelism?

Appendix E

A Robust Network of Small Groups

Over the past twenty to thirty years much ink has been spilled concerning the gap between the Baby Boom Generation and the Harry Truman Generation. Yet the biggest gap the Boomer Generation feels is within itself. The Baby Boom Generation has been described as "a relationally vacuous generation struggling in their ability to form lasting relationships."[1] As Paula Rinehart writes in *Christianity Today*, "Their lonely statistics speak for themselves. They are 500 times more likely to be single than their parents were, and even half of those who marry will probably divorce."[2]

One reason for this problem according to Michael Morris, an Episcopal priest, can be found in the Boomers' desire to lead a life of anonymity. He writes, "Most live in their own isolated boxes in the suburbs, a thousand miles away from family, in communities in which they feel no roots. . . . They are plagued by loneliness—yet driven by demanding jobs and competing family needs. Underneath all that activity is a deep longing for a connection with God that seems real and intimate."[3]

The Boomer and postmodern generations don't share a lot in common. However, they both crave authentic relationships with people at an intimate level.

Churches with a Great Commission vision often grow big in a hurry. On the one hand, this is exciting because lost people are accepting Christ and populating the kingdom. On the other hand, for those (the Boomers and postmoderns) who prize honesty and disclosure on an intimate level, this growth doesn't seem so good. Will the church of Jesus Christ have to choose between one or the other? Or is it possible to have the best of both worlds?

Here church planting provides some help. A vital church planting principle concerns a robust network of small groups. This principle can be summed up in these words: The bigger we get the smaller we get. To accomplish a Great Commission vision, churches must not only reach lost people but also develop a robust network of small groups. One must be balanced by the other for healthy church life. There are several considerations that can help church planters initiate such a program in the new church. The first three provide the rationale for the program; the others provide help in organizing and starting it.

Small Groups Are Biblical

Small groups were an integral part of the early church and vital to its life.

The Size of the Early Church

The various churches in the book of Acts were large in comparison to the typical North American church. For example, the church in Jerusalem began in an upper room with about 120 people (Acts 1:12–15). In response to the preaching of Peter it grew almost immediately to 3,120 members (2:41). Acts 2:47 tells us that the church *continued* to grow (Luke uses the Greek imperfect tense, which indicates continuous action). Then Peter preached a second sermon and the number of men alone grew to be about 5,000 (4:4).

The early church and the apostles underwent great persecution. As a result the apostles were scattered into other areas such as Judea and Samaria (8:1). Ultimately, God used this persecution to spread the gospel according to his plan, stated in Acts 1:8. The result is that the apostles and Paul, in particular, planted churches in Judea, Samaria, Asia Minor, and Greece. Many of these churches, beginning with the Jerusalem church, grew into large, citywide congregations (Acts 2:41, 47; 4:4; 5:14; 6:1, 7; 9:31, 35, 42; 11:21, 24, 26; 14:1, 21; 16:5; 17:4, 12; 18:8, 10; 19:26; 21:20). However, these larger city churches were made up of smaller house churches (Acts 2:46; 5:42; 12:12–17; 20:20; Rom. 16:3–5, 14–15; 1 Cor. 16:19) that likely had some affinity with today's small-group meetings.

The Structure of the Early Church

The large size of the churches in Acts presented some obvious problems in terms of ministry.

The Problem

A conservative estimate of the size of the Jerusalem church alone was twenty to twenty-five thousand people. It could have been much larger and so could some of the other city churches that were planted later. How was the church to minister to and care for all these people?

The apostles and elders solved this problem by structuring the churches around both large and small groups. According to Acts 3 the Jerusalem church met as a city church in a large area in the temple (Solomon's Colonnade), and Acts 2:46 indicates that they also met in homes (house churches). Acts 5:42 says that the church continued to meet "in the temple courts and from house to house." Finally, in Acts 20:20, Paul says that he taught in Ephesus "publicly and from house to house."

Large-Group Meetings

It would appear that the large city-church meetings were used primarily for three purposes.

Evangelism. Large-group meetings were used for evangelism (Acts 4:4; 5:42). Solomon's Colonnade in the temple (Acts 3:11) was a large area where a number of people could gather, as indicated by the response to Peter's sermon in Acts 4:4. Apparently, the church moved into the area at a certain time, used it temporarily, and then moved on. With persecution, these meetings may have occurred infrequently or not at all.

Preaching. A second purpose of large-group meetings was for preaching (20:20). The text gives no clues as to where this preaching took place.

Teaching. Teaching was also accomplished in the large-group meetings. Acts 5:42 suggests that such meetings were tied closely to evangelism and the fact that Jesus was the Messiah. This teaching was public and consisted of anything that was helpful to the church (20:20).

Small-Group Meetings

The small-group meetings or house churches had a variety of purposes, all of which contributed strongly to developing a vital sense of community.

Provision. According to Acts 2:44–45, small-group meetings served to meet people's material needs. Acts 4:32–37 indicates that people were willing to sell their possessions to provide for those who for various reasons had nothing.

Communion and worship. These meetings also served as a place where Christians broke bread (2:46), which could be a reference to communion, and worshiped (v. 47).

Evangelism. In Acts 5:42 Luke indicates that a purpose for small-group meetings was evangelism.

Prayer. In Acts 12:12 Peter escapes from prison and interrupts a prayer meeting that was taking place in a group.

Encouragement. In Acts 16:40 we see that Paul used small groups for encouraging other believers. These meetings, of which there were probably many, took place primarily in people's homes.

The Purpose of Small Groups

The one major, all-encompassing purpose for small groups is the transformation of a person's life through biblical community. The broad sweep of the Scriptures indicates that God's people are to be constantly changing and growing more and more like him (Lev. 20:7; Col. 1:28–29; 1 Peter 1:15–16). This process is commonly referred to in theology and the Bible as sanctification. But there's some confusion as to how this takes place in the context of the local church.

An Assumption

Most people assume that life change takes place as the result of the pastor's preaching ministry in the church. Certainly, a major purpose for preaching is to encourage the transformation of a person's life. The problem in many churches, however, is that this is either the primary or the only vehicle for implementing life change. I call these pulpit-driven churches.

The reason this is a problem is because preaching is only one of many ways to facilitate life change and it's not necessarily the best way. There are at least four reasons that this is true. First, we discovered in chapter 2 that church attendance in general and attendance of the worship service in particular are down. And those who do attend don't attend every week. Second, the average attender forgets 90–95 percent of what he or she hears within seventy-two hours. Third, people may make a decision in response to a sermon but rarely a commitment. What's the difference? A decision is short-term in effect, while a commitment is long-term. Finally, if the church is sermon-dependent, then the preacher better be a good communicator. Average or mediocre won't do!

Pause for a moment and join me in an experiment. Think about how long you've been a Christian. Let's assume ten years. Next, attempt to calculate the number of sermons you've heard during the period of time you've been a Christian. If you've attended a traditional church where the pastor preaches three times a week, you'll discover that you've heard a lot of sermons over the years! Let's assume only one sermon a week for twelve months a year, which comes to forty-eight sermons a year. If we multiply this times ten years, we come up with 480 sermons. Are you surprised?

Now here's the question: How many of those sermons have had a major impact on your life? When I've conducted this experiment with students in a seminary classroom or with people in a local church setting, the answer is usually somewhere between one and ten. Most, however, remember fewer than five significant sermons.

Another question is: Did you come to faith in Christ as the result of hearing an evangelistic sermon or the witness of one or two individuals? While some Christians could answer that it was a combination of the two, statistics indicate that 75–90 percent of people come to faith in Christ through a significant relationship with another person. It would seem that the sermon doesn't have the life-changing qualities that so many today take for granted.

Some important variables exist. First, the ability of a sermon to affect a Christian's life will vary according to the giftedness and capabilities of the person in the pulpit as well as the receptivity of the listener. This will range from high impact to little or no impact. Another variable is the fact that consistent exposure to sermons can and usually does have a cumulative effect. While we may not think they're affecting our lives, because we can't recall very many that have, the Spirit has been using bits and pieces of various sermons over the years to bring about some life transformation.

You might assume from what I've just said that I don't like preaching or think that it's very important. Nothing could be further from the truth—I teach preaching at Dallas Seminary. It's imperative that we preach God's Word from our pulpits. However, we must not be sermon-driven, that is, expecting preaching to carry the church and win the day. That's rare and not what the New Testament is all about. Healthy, biblically functioning churches in the first century appear to have sought to balance the teaching and preaching of the Scriptures with fellowship, prayer, worship, evangelism, and community (Acts 2:42–47).

The Reality

The reality is that life change takes place most often as the result of a significant relationship with either an individual or a small number of individuals in community. Let's conduct a second experiment. The chances are good that if you're reading this book, you've committed your life to service and ministry for Christ. This may have happened only once for you or it could have happened several times over the years since you've become a Christian. Now consider the circumstances surrounding your commitment to Christ. The question is, was it the influence of the life of one or a few significant people in your life? Most people indicate that this, indeed, was the case.

Let's conduct one last experiment. Take a moment and recall the circumstances surrounding the time when you accepted Christ. Was it the result of the witness of one or two significant people in your life? When I've conducted this experiment, in most cases the answer has been yes. Again, this is confirmed by Win Arn's survey and the various passages presented in appendix D.

The obvious conclusion is that, if churches expect their people to grow spiritually and mature in Christ, they'll need to provide ways to facilitate that growth. One of the primary means that God has used since the days of the early church to accomplish growth is some type of small-group ministry. Therefore, churches that take seriously the Great Commission mandate will have a robust network of small groups.

The Advantages of Small Groups

Small Groups Aren't Limited by Facilities

Most churches, no matter where they're located, struggle at some point with their facilities. Planted churches usually experience problems with locating adequate temporary facilities. It's not easy to find the kind of place that will accommodate all the ministries of a new church, including such things as a nursery, classroom space, and adequate parking. Another factor is the cleanliness of these facilities.

Even when a church has purchased or constructed its own building, there continue to be problems. There are the usual problems with maintaining the existing facilities, which all churches face. A significant number of churches today are losing people and becoming smaller. They meet in facilities that have become too large. Some churches are growing and struggle with where to put all their people. Most likely, the planted church will have to face the latter situation.

A decided advantage of a robust network of small groups is that the new church doesn't have to worry about locating and renting additional facilities. They can meet just about anywhere at a wide variety of times. For example, they can meet in someone's office, a home, or even outdoors in good weather. They have the option of meeting in the same place, or they can vary the location of the meeting from time to time.

Small Groups Are Geographically Expandable

Not only are small-group ministries not limited by facilities, they're not limited by location. While they can meet where the primary congregational meetings take place, they don't have to. They're geographically expandable. They can meet just about anywhere they want. In fact one way to reach your neighbors is to locate an evangelistic small-group ministry at your house and invite the people next door.

Geographically expandable small groups also facilitate the planting of branch churches. Small groups that are located at some distance from the church could provide potential future sites for the planting of other churches in those areas of the town or city. While most churches begin with a single core group, which itself is a small group, another strategy is to plant a church by starting several small groups and bringing them together once or twice a week for evangelism and worship.

Small Groups Promote Biblical Community

It's difficult for people who meet in large groups to get to know one another. These kinds of meetings are designed to facilitate corporate evangelism, preaching, and teaching, not the development of biblical community.

Authentic biblical community is what takes place when Christians implement the biblical imperatives and exhortations that affect how they relate to one another. This is seen in the "one another" passages of the Bible. Fifty-nine times the Bible exhorts believers to minister in some way to one another. Twenty-one times (one-third) they exhort us to love one another. Others that fall somewhere under the capstone of love are the following:

"Be at peace with each other" (Mark 9:50).
"Be devoted to one another" (Rom. 12:10).
"Honor one another" (Rom. 12:10).
"Accept one another" (Rom. 15:7).
"Have equal concern for each other" (1 Cor. 12:25).
"Serve one another in love" (Gal. 5:13).
"Be kind and compassionate to one another" (Eph. 4:32).

"Consider others better than yourselves" (Phil. 2:3).

"Admonish one another" (Col. 3:16).

"Encourage one another daily" (Heb. 3:13).

"Each one should use whatever gift he has to serve others" (1 Peter 4:10).

These and other exhortations are all elements of biblical community that are realized best in a small-group context. This was true of the ministry of Christ in the first century as he worked with the Twelve to change the world. It was also true of the church (Acts 2:46; 5:42; 8:1–3; Rom. 16:5; 1 Cor. 16:19). And it is true of Christ's disciples and his church in the twenty-first century.

Small Groups Encourage Lay Ministry

Repeatedly and in various ways, Scripture promotes lay ministry in the local church. One way is through the exercise of spiritual gifts (1 Corinthians 12–14). Another is by equipping laypeople for ministry (Ephesians 4). A third is the ministry of believer-priests (1 Peter 2; Revelation 5).

There are numerous commands and exhortations in the New Testament regarding lay ministry. The "one another" passages encourage believers to do things to or for each other. For example, in 1 Thessalonians 4:10, Paul tells the church to "love each other" and in 1 Thessalonians 5:11 to "encourage each other."

The question is, how do we implement these commands and "one another" passages in the church? Most people note them mentally and attempt to apply them when possible. Small-group meetings and ministries provide an ideal community in which these may be implemented and consciously pursued.

Small Groups Aren't Limited by Finances

The cost for operating most churches ranges from minimal to exorbitant, depending on the size of the church and its buildings. The rule is simple: the larger the church, the greater the operating costs. These expenses include such things as the purchase and maintenance of facilities and vehicles and the provision of staff salaries.

While the cost of operating most churches is significant, the cost of conducting a small-group ministry is minimal if any. The leader is usually a layperson who isn't paid. Neither are there any vehicles or facility expenses. In fact it's possible to conduct small-group ministries without incurring any costs whatsoever. In many cases, small groups charge the participants for supplies or for coffee and donuts.

Small Groups Decentralize Pastoral Care

In the traditional cultural model, the pastor is expected to provide pastoral care for the people in the congregation. In fact this is where we get the title "pastor." This model works as long as the church has fewer than one hundred members. Once a church begins to grow beyond this figure, pastoral care needs to involve more than one person.

Many of the early churches were megachurches. How did they solve the problem of pastoral care? Evidently, they used a different model. Much pastoral care took place in and through small-group communities. Two examples of this are found in Acts 2:44–45 and 4:32–37. In essence, those in the various house meetings took care of their own. It is imperative that, as a planted church begins to grow, it establish small groups. Otherwise, there will be a breakdown in the pastoral care component of the church, which could have tragic results (see Acts 6).

Small Groups Facilitate Leadership Training

One of the reasons 80–85 percent of the churches in America are plateaued or in decline is because of a lack of adequate leadership. One solution to this problem is the small-group ministry. Small groups can be used as proving grounds and incubators for training new leadership in the church.

One of the problems in the training of leaders is that much of it takes place in a classroom. Rarely do people have the opportunity to actually lead until they've completed the class or even have a degree from a school. The best leadership training takes place in actual life. Indeed, the proof of the proverbial pudding is what happens when the prospective leader is placed in charge of a group. This kind of training can best be accomplished in the local church through its small-group ministries. Those who have proved their leadership abilities could adopt intern or apprentice leaders for whom they take responsibility. When they believe the new leader is ready, the group could split and the new leader take the new group.

Small Groups Promote the Assimilation Process

One of the problems many churches face in terms of growth is how to keep people from slipping out the back door of the church. This involves what church growth people call the assimilation process. Often one of the major reasons people leave a church is because they're searching for significant relationships that the church doesn't provide. In time they look elsewhere.

Participation in a small group should be a requirement for membership in the church. When people join a church, it is usually at a high commitment point in their lives. They're willing to make commitments that they might not make at another time. Once they put down some roots in the group, they become assimilated and aren't likely to leave the church unless some other problem should surface. Usually, the longer they're in the group, the more committed they become to the small-group concept and the more they become assimilated in the broader church community.

The Organization of Small Groups

There are several ways a small group can be organized.

Small Groups Can Be Organized according to Geography

One way to organize a small-group program is on the basis of geography—where people live in the community. People who live in the same area of the community come together at some central location and form a small group. Once the group is established, other people in the area are invited to join as well. As new people join the church, they're assigned to a small group on the basis of where they live in the community. As people move to new areas or new people come into the church from those areas, new groups are formed there as well. This also has the potential to facilitate church plants in those communities.

While this is a viable option for the church, most groups don't organize according to geography. In fact most organize on the basis of affinity. People, no matter where they live in the town or city, are attracted to one another on the basis of such things as age, occupation, common interests, and needs.

Small Groups Can Be Organized according to People's Schedules

The large-group meetings of the church occur at certain designated times that are deemed best for the entire church or for a specific target group. The traditional meeting time has been on Sunday morning at 11:00 AM. As the culture has changed and the "blue laws" in many areas of the country have been eliminated, this may no longer be the best time for every church. Yet most older churchgoers set 11:00 AM aside in their minds, because the church has been meeting at this time for so long. For them, this is the "Lord's Day." As mentioned earlier in this book, some churches are so intent on reaching lost people, they've given 11:00 AM over to their focus group for a seeker's service. They hold a believer's service at another time.

Unlike the large-group meetings of the church, the small-group meetings aren't limited to a specific time of the day or week. They can meet once or twice a month or even weekly. And they can meet at practically any time during the day. The determining factor is the time schedules of the participants—when they can all meet. This flexibility allows people who are on difficult work schedules to meet with others during the week, even though they may work all day Sunday or on Sunday mornings.

Small Groups Can Be Organized around Common Interests

The large-group meetings of the church usually have a specific purpose for meeting. It could be for evangelism, worship, preaching, or teaching. Large-group meetings may be targeted at believers, unbelievers, or both. These purposes usually remain consistent throughout the life of the church. While change may and should take place, it often remains within these purposes and not beyond them.

The small-group ministry of the church can be used for these same purposes and for other purposes as well. Many ministries are organized around people's common interests. These interests consist of such things as prayer, outreach, family, singles, support, caring, and Bible study. Some ministries consist of focus group ministries, which attempt to reach specific peoples, such as the cults, the elderly, the poor, or international students, with the gospel.

Small Groups Can Be Organized around Dependence Problems

For years the church of Jesus Christ has all but ignored some major social problems. These problems include addictions, codependency, eating disorders, sexual abuse, depression, dysfunctional families, and pornography.

A large-group meeting can address these problems only in a sermon or forum approach, which at best deals with the problem at a distance. The small-group ministry of a church can focus specifically on one of these problems and deal with it more directly as well as provide support for those experiencing it. Today more and more churches are moving in this direction, much to the delight of churchgoers and those outside the church. The group may or may not provide some kind of therapy. Wisely most groups avoid therapy and are there more for support.

Small Groups Can Be Organized for Specific Ministry Tasks

Some churches organize their small-group ministries with a wide variety of options. In some situations various groups may come into existence on their own for specific purposes determined by those who make up the group, such as MOPS or a men's Bible study, or they may be dictated by the church.

Another option for a church is to use its small groups for specific ministry tasks either within or outside the church itself. These might consist of such tasks as outreach, worship, teaching, building and grounds maintenance, drama, or children's ministries.

The Basic Ingredients of Robust Small Groups

Lyman Coleman and the people who are a part of Serendipity have established themselves as leaders in the field of small groups. Their work in this area has performed a great service for the church at large. They have determined three basic ingredients for small groups and point out that these must be kept in balance in any small group if it is to remain healthy and accomplish its purpose.

Bible Study/Nurture

The first ingredient—which Coleman calls the "basic building block of an effective small group"—is Bible study for the purpose of spiritual nurture. These Bible studies can focus on any number of areas or issues. In reality, the choices are unlimited. But there's more involved than Bible study. Any healthy small group is based in some way on the nurturing and instructive qualities of Scripture, not on the opinions of those people who make up the group. However, Coleman says, "'Too much of a good thing' can lead to spiritual indigestion."[4] For example, if the church is already strong in teaching the Scriptures (during the worship service or in Sunday school), it must not make a small group simply another Bible study.

Group Building/Support

The second ingredient concerns building the group. This involves developing group trust. The group must strive to become a trusting community if it seeks to develop biblical community. According to Serendipity, group building involves a fourfold process. History giving requires that group members tell their personal "stories" (roots, spiritual journey, and dreams) to the group. Dallas Seminary uses life maps in spiritual formation groups as one means for accomplishing this purpose. Gift awareness and affirmation involve sharing gifts and receiving affirmation from others regarding them. Goal setting concerns asking what each group member needs to do or why that person is in the group. Fellowship and building depth in ministry consist of caring and accountability.[5]

Mission/Task

Bible study and group building aren't enough by themselves. Serendipity believes there's one more ingredient that is necessary—the mission or task of the group. Essentially, this mission is ministry to others: "The most natural form of outreach is to reach out to others who have a similar need for support and bring them into the group. But a group that concentrates exclusively on ministry (like most committees in the church) often ends up with burnout."[6]

Determining the Role of Small Groups

What is the role of small groups in the overall ministry of the church? Will it be a church *of* small groups or a church *with* small groups? What's the difference? In the former, small groups are the primary ministry of the church. While the church will have a worship service with preaching, the primary emphasis is on the small-groups ministry. Everyone is encouraged to involve themselves in a group. Carl George and Ralph Neighbour are strong advocates of this emphasis.

In a church with small groups, however, the groups are just another ministry of the church. They are valued on the same level as a Sunday school program, Awana, and any other program.

Determining the Purpose of Small Groups

What is the purpose for the small groups within the larger ministry of the church? How do they fit in? There are at least three purposes, each of which has its advantages.

To Minister to the Needs of the Church

Small groups can meet the basic, general needs of the church that can't be met in a large-group setting. This is an eclectic approach and might include a wide variety of such needs. For example, small groups can serve as a means for assimilating new members into the church; they can be used for mobilizing the laity for ministry; they are vital to developing future lay leadership and potential staff leadership; and they provide an excellent vehicle for communication between the staff and the larger church body. Other examples of needs are pastoral care, fellowship, support, community, and accountability.

To Balance the Ministry of the Church

Another purpose of a small-group program is to balance the other ministries of the church. Churches may find that their large-group meetings don't cover all their ministry bases, leaving a vital base uncovered. Consequently, small groups are designed and implemented to cover that base. For example, some churches may have only one large-group meeting a week and use it for either evangelism or edification. In these churches, the small-group ministry is established to provide the other missing ingredient. If the large-group meeting focuses on evangelism, the small group focuses on edification (or vice versa).

When I pastored Northwood Community Church in Dallas, we used our small-groups ministry to balance our other ministries. We provided a large-group meeting on Sunday as a "people-friendly" event where we not only worshiped but preached biblical messages that addressed the needs of both the believer and the unbeliever. Prior to this service, we provided a Sunday school program for all ages that focused on in-depth Bible study. We developed our small-group ministry to provide biblical community that included pastoral care. These components were not found in our other ministries.

To Perform the Pastoral Care of the Church

A third approach to small-group ministries is to use them to provide for the basic needs of people on a pastoral care basis. This is often a function of small groups in larger churches. As noted earlier, it's not possible for the senior pastor of a large church to provide the pastoral care for all the people in a large church.

Consequently, small groups are established and function as mini-churches to provide this pastoral care component. The key factor in this approach is that the leader of the group and/or others in the group must be able to shepherd and minister to people's needs much as the pastor would. In effect, they all function as lay pastors of small flocks within the church itself. Therefore, it's critical that churches that adopt this approach recruit and thoroughly train their mini-church pastors since they play such a vital role in each small group.

The Leadership for Small Groups

Good leadership is critical to the success of any small-group program. There are three questions that must be answered in establishing well-led small groups.

Who Are the Leaders?

While the pastoral staff may want to lead a small group to remain in touch with the people in the church, the leadership of the small groups must be the responsibility of the lay leadership within the church. God raises up gifted and capable lay leaders to function in these capacities. This is the concept behind the analogy of the church and the human body in 1 Corinthians 12–14. This provides for the best use of lay leaders in contrast to sitting on church boards that meet once a month to administer the affairs of the church.

Initially, in a planted church, the core group may be small and the pastor will lead it. As it grows and splits into other small groups, qualified laypeople should assume leadership responsibility. Eventually, the pastor will shepherd and train these lay leaders in a small-group context of their own.

Where Will They Come From?

Small-group leaders must be recruited. The key in the planted church is to recruit qualified people to lead the initial small groups. It's very important that planted churches start a small-group program as soon as possible. If there are no qualified leaders, they must delay beginning the church. While these qualifications vary from church to church and depend on the purposes of the groups, the initial qualifications could be those found for elders and deacons (see 1 Tim. 3:1–13; Titus 1:5–9) or those listed in Acts 6:2–5. These qualifications serve only as a starting point and are probably too strict for many who would lead a community.

Once the initial small-group leaders have been selected, it will become their responsibility in conference with the pastor to recruit and train other apprentice leaders to assume the leadership of future small groups. As the initial small groups grow and divide into other small groups, the recruited leaders will lead the new groups. Another option is for them to recruit their own small groups from the people who make up the growing congregation.

How Will They Be Trained?

One of the problems numerous small-group ministries experience is either poor small-group leadership or constant turnover of leaders. The solution to this problem is regular leadership training. The fault in so many ministries is that we recruit willing and capable small-group leaders, train them initially for the position, and then promptly abandon them. There are several ways in which this training can be accomplished.

The Apprentice/Intern Model

The first model involves an apprenticeship or intern program. The leaders of the small groups take responsibility for this training. The idea is that experienced leaders recruit apprentice or intern leaders from the congregation at large, their own small group, or other small groups and give them on-the-job training.

The 6+6+6 Model

Another approach is the 6+6+6 Leadership Training Model developed by Serendipity. This plan begins with an initial six-week program for those who wish to serve as leaders. A pilot group is led by a trainer who uses a six-week course from the Serendipity New Testament. During the second six weeks the potential leaders practice teaching and are evaluated by the trainer and the other potential leaders. This, in turn, is followed by one more six-week period during which those in the pilot group start their own groups. The trainer continues to supervise these leaders but not as closely as before. The trainer meets with them once a week as a group to answer questions and to deal with specific problems. A church could follow a similar approach, substituting its own curriculum for the six-week course from the Serendipity New Testament.

The Metachurch Model

A third approach is the metachurch model developed by Carl George in his excellent book *Prepare Your Church for the Future* (Revell). This model includes the apprentice/intern approach above and is led by a pastor or staff person who meets at least once a month with the leaders and provides continual training in VHS. The V stands for vision and relates to vision casting. The leader or pastor attempts to keep the vision before the leaders. The H stands for huddling and involves nurturing the souls of the leaders. The S is for skills and concerns the continual development of established skills and the acquisition of new skills needed for ministry in the groups.

The Organization of a Small-Group Ministry

Every ministry in a church must be organized if it is to function and minister efficiently. The organization of the small-group ministry in the church must help leaders assume responsibility for a manageable number of people.

An Organizational Model

An excellent model for this organization is found in Exodus 18. At the beginning of the chapter, Moses attempts to counsel and advise approximately two million Israelites on a one-on-one basis. His father-in-law, Jethro, wisely advises Moses to select other capable men from among the people "and appoint them as officials over thousands, hundreds, fifties, and tens." They are to bring only the most difficult cases to Moses. The result is twofold: an emotionally healthy Moses and a satisfied ministry constituency. This model provides an excellent example for organization in today's church in general and small groups in particular.

The Application of the Model

Large Churches

Most large churches, which are still growing, probably have already implemented this model or something similar to it. If a church has grown very quickly over a short period of time into a large but poorly organized ministry, it could benefit immensely by adopting this organizational model.

New Churches

This is an ideal model for the planted church as well. A new church could adopt it at the very beginning and continue to use it for the life of the church.

Even if the church becomes a megachurch, the model simply expands with the growth of the church.

Implementation

To implement this organizational model, the church will need to determine the ideal size of its small groups. Each group should be led by a lay pastor. Someone will need to take responsibility for these groups and their lay leaders as they begin to grow and divide. This could be a person on the team who is a specialist in small groups and one or two other areas. It could also be a gifted layperson. This person would be the primary leader and could work with and cultivate the lay leaders of each group.

Once there are five groups of from seven to twelve people, this leader should be replaced by a second leader who begins to cultivate other groups of seven to twelve people with lay leaders until they too reach five groups and the process repeats itself. These five groups are similar to Moses' groups of fifty. Eventually, as the program grows, the primary leader will build a network of leaders, who, in turn, develop other leaders. In this manner, it's possible for the primary leader to lead hundreds, and maybe even thousands, depending on the growth of the church.[7]

Developing a Small-Group Ministry

The church planter and the team will need to develop a small-group ministry for the new church. There are eight steps in this process.

1. The Role Step

The church planter and the team must decide how big a role the small-groups program will play in the overall ministry of the church. Will it be a church *of* small groups or a church *with* small groups? That is, will small groups be the primary thrust of the church or just one of many ministries of the church?

2. The Purpose Step

The team must decide the purpose for small groups in the church. Will small groups be used to meet some of the general needs of the church that can't be met through the large-group meetings? Another option is to use small groups to balance or complement the other major ministries in the church. Small groups can also be used as the primary means for pastoral care.

3. The Organization Step

The next step will be to decide who will be responsible for the small-groups ministry. There are several options. It could be the pastor of the church. Ultimately, the pastor is responsible for the ministry regardless of whether or not someone else has direct responsibility. One of the team members could oversee the small-groups ministry. Or a part-time professional person who isn't a part of the ministry team but has some time available and the skills and abilities to work with the ministry could do the job. Another option is a layperson in the church who has the gifts and capabilities to handle the program.

4. The Participation Step

This step involves a decision on the part of the team as to how many people in the church they desire to see involved in the small-groups ministry. What is the numerical goal? What is the desired percentage of involvement? This could range anywhere from 25 percent to 125 percent if it's to be a church *of* small groups.

This decision is important for two reasons. First, it will demonstrate how committed the leadership of the church is to the small-group concept. For example, a numerical goal of 125 percent congregational involvement doesn't seem very realistic. However, the use of this figure in sermons and conversation communicates to the flock a strong pastoral commitment to the program. Second, it will determine how strongly the pastoral team emphasizes the ministry. Any ministry of the church that has more than a 50 percent rate of congregational involvement should and will be strongly emphasized by the team.

5. The Recruitment Step

It's not possible to begin and maintain a small-group ministry without people. Recruitment means locating people and getting them involved. The only limit on the various ways to recruit participants is the imagination and creativity of those leading the ministry. The point is that there are all kinds of ways to interest and implement people in small groups.

Perhaps one of the best ways to recruit people is through satisfied customers—lay leaders and other participants who are already involved in a group and are delighted with its ministry in their lives. People who are both ministering and being ministered to are excited people who make great recruiters. They want to tell others what's happened in their lives so that these people can benefit as well.

Another way to recruit people is through advertising. This involves such things as a clever note in the church bulletin, a special bulletin insert, a verbal announcement, a well-done skit, and posters strategically placed on the walls of the facility. These catch people's attention and "grab" their interest.

There are other recruiting methods as well. The church could require involvement in a small group as a condition for membership. It could set up an attractive small-groups booth in a highly visible place, such as the lobby or at the main entrance to the sanctuary or the church building.

6. The Training Step

The sixth step involves determining how the lay leaders will be trained. Several methods have already been mentioned. One is the apprentice or intern model. Another is Serendipity's 6+6+6 model. And a third is the metachurch VHS model that includes the apprentice/intern model. The church could develop its own training process unique to its people.

7. The Administrative Step

The small group, not those who are setting up the ministry, takes this step. The group will need to decide such administrative matters as are necessary to accomplish the purpose of the ministry. These consist of when the group will meet, how long they'll meet, where they'll meet, how they will maintain confidentiality, and any attendance requirements.

The group needs to deal with three other important issues as well. First, the group will need to select a host or hostess. The leader cannot be expected to lead the group and be the host at the same time. The second issue involves childcare. The group will need to determine how they'll care for young children during the time the community meets. While this latter point may seem trivial, the issue of finding good childcare can hamstring the entire small-group ministry of a church! Third, the group will need to decide for how long they plan to meet as a group. I suggest they covenant for nine months (for example, September through May). After nine months people would have the option to move to another group. If the group decides to continue meeting, they can recovenant for longer.

The role of those responsible for setting up the ministry is to make sure that these administrative matters are accomplished and to provide any assistance necessary to help the groups make these decisions. They might ask that all the groups agree to sign a covenant in which the above administrative matters are written down for purposes of accountability.

8. The Evaluation Step

Constant evaluation is necessary if the ministry is to improve and make necessary corrections. A number of decisions need to be made here.

Who?

First, who will evaluate and who will be evaluated? All those who are involved in some sort of leadership role should be evaluated. They, in turn, must also be involved in evaluating others. The pastor or the ministry team could evaluate the leader of the small-groups program. The leader of the ministry could evaluate the lay leaders (or vice versa). The lay leaders could evaluate their apprentices.

When?

Another decision involves when this evaluation takes place. The pastor's evaluation of the group leader could take place quarterly. The group leader's evaluation of the lay leaders could be on a quarterly basis as well. Lay leaders need to evaluate their apprentices weekly or whenever they lead the group.

What?

A third decision would concern the criteria for evaluation. They should be kept as short and simple as possible. They could involve such questions as: What am I not doing well? What am I doing well? How can I do it better next time?

A Small-Group Exercise

1. What were the circumstances surrounding your coming to faith in Christ? Did it involve a relationship with one or a few people or was it in the context of a large group such as a worship service? Is the same true of your commitment to minister for Christ whether as a professional or layperson?

2. Have you ever been involved in a small-group ministry? If yes, was this a part of a church or parachurch ministry? How many churches are you aware of that have a robust network of small groups?

3. What were some of the advantages and disadvantages of any of the ministries you may have been involved in? How might this information help you in planning a ministry for a planted church?

4. Are you personally convinced of the need for a small-group ministry in the planted church? Why? If you're convinced, how strong is your commitment to this ministry (weak, strong, very strong)?

5. What effect does age have on a person's commitment to a small-groups ministry? Do small groups appeal more to those of the postmodern and Baby Boom Generations or the Harry Truman Generation? What might this tell you about planning a small-groups ministry for a planted church?

Appendix F

Personal Ministry Core Values Audit

Using the scale below, circle the number that best expresses to what extent the following values are important to you (actual values). Work your way through the list quickly, going with your first impression.

1 = not important
2 = somewhat important
3 = important
4 = most important

1. **Communication**: Preaching and teaching God's word to people   1 2 3 4
2. **Family**: People immediately related to one another by marriage or birth   1 2 3 4
3. **Bible knowledge**: A familiarity with the truths of the Scriptures   1 2 3 4
4. **World missions**: Spreading the gospel of Christ around the globe   1 2 3 4
5. **Community**: Caring about and addressing the needs of others   1 2 3 4
6. **Encouragement**: Giving hope to people who need hope   1 2 3 4
7. **Giving**: Providing a portion of one's finances to support the ministry   1 2 3 4
8. **Fellowship**: Relating to and enjoying one another   1 2 3 4
9. **Leadership**: A person's ability to influence others to pursue God's mission for his or her organization   1 2 3 4
10. **Cultural relevance**: Communicating truth in a way that people who aren't like us can understand   1 2 3 4
11. **Prayer**: Communicating with God   1 2 3 4

12. **Excellence**: Maintaining the highest of ministry standards that   1 2 3 4
    bring glory to God

13. **Evangelism**: Telling others the good news about Christ   1 2 3 4

14. **Team ministry**: A group of people ministering together   1 2 3 4

15. **Creativity**: Coming up with new ideas and ways of doing ministry   1 2 3 4

16. **Worship**: Attributing worth to God   1 2 3 4

17. **Status quo**: A preference for the way things are now   1 2 3 4

18. **Cooperation**: The act of working together in the service of the   1 2 3 4
    Savior

19. **Lost people**: People who are non-Christians and may not attend   1 2 3 4
    church (unchurched)

20. **Mobilized congregation**: Christians who are actively serving in   1 2 3 4
    the ministries of their church

21. **Tradition**: The customary ways or the "tried and true"   1 2 3 4

22. **Obedience**: A willingness to do what God or others ask   1 2 3 4

23. **Innovation**: Making changes that promote the ministry as it   1 2 3 4
    serves Christ

24. **Initiative**: The willingness to take the first step or make the first   1 2 3 4
    move in a ministry situation

25. **Other values**:

What will be really unique about this church that will attract people and likely differentiate it from other churches in the community? What value(s) is/are driving this?

Note all the values that you rated with a 3 or 4 and any that surfaced in the answer above. Rank these according to prioroty. The first six are your core values.

1.

2.

3.

4.

5.

6.

Appendix G

Understanding Postmodernism

While philosophical and cultural modernism is still alive and well in Europe and North America, postmodernism seems to be slowly taking over—especially with the younger generations. Thus church starters need to understand postmodernism and how to minister to the many who have embraced it. The following is from *Church Next*, chapter 5 of the book I wrote with Michael Malphurs. While it is written to churches in general, you may easily apply this information to church planting.

The term *postmodernism* isn't commonly understood among the members of most churches. If you listen carefully at the next congregational meeting or board meeting, chances are good that you won't hear it mentioned. Of course, the same is true for the grocery store where you shop, the office where you work, and the post office where you mail your letters. However, you will see the concept being discussed and debated in books on theology and philosophy, and you'll hear it discussed on college and seminary campuses. A growing number of people are adopting a postmodernist perspective, and the worldview known as postmodernism is having and will continue to have a profound effect on the United States and the American church. If the church is to make a comeback as a vital cultural force, it will need to do more than target the younger and the current generations and develop a theology of change. It will also need to understand what is invading and capturing the minds, hearts, and souls of young people and what the church can do about it.

Postmodernism isn't simply a philosophical concept tossed around by intellectuals in the ivory towers of some remote university or seminary campuses. Postmodernism is profoundly affecting the thinking of the Buster and the Bridger generations, not only in our schools, but also inside our churches.

So, what is postmodernism? From where did it come? Who are the postmodernists? What do they believe? And how can Christ's church reach postmodernists effectively and minister to our emerging postmodernist society?

The purpose of this chapter is not to be theologically deep or overly philosophical. Rather, it is to answer these basic questions and give an overview of postmodernism, to familiarize churches and their leaders with this pervasive worldview.

Understanding the Postmodern Context

A good teacher will tell you not to take ideas out of context. If you do, you can make ideas say whatever you want them to. So in order to gain a fair understanding of postmodernism, we must look at it in its context, both historical and philosophical.

The Historical Context

Postmodernism is primarily a product of Western civilization, which traces its roots back to ancient Rome (to 500), and extending up through the Middle Ages (500–1400), the Renaissance (1350–1650), the Reformation (1517–1648), the Enlightenment (1689–1789), Modernism (1789–1989), and culminating in Postmodernism, which began to take shape around 1919 and continues up to the present. Each phase in the development of Western civilization contributed in some way to postmodernism, but modernism has had the greatest and most direct impact.

Postmodernism is a reaction to the modernist worldview and stands in stark contrast to modernism in many ways (table 1). The age of modernism corresponds historically with the Industrial Revolution, whereas postmodernism has accelerated through the Information Revolution with information technology leading the way. Under modernism, America experienced a deep sense of nationalism. Postmodernism and the Internet, however, have moved younger Americans toward a greater sense of globalism. Modernism bought heavily into Descartes' concept of man's autonomous self, whereas postmodernism emphasizes community. Each view holds to a different authority. Modernism's authority is reason; postmodernism's authority is experience. Modernism has an optimistic view of life; postmodernism began with a pessimistic view that seems to be shifting back toward optimism.

Other differences exist as well. Modernism assumes that man is basically good; postmodernism assumes that man is essentially bad. Modernism presupposes a natural world in which nothing exists outside of nature; postmodernism views the world supernaturally and believes in a world outside of nature. Modernists are skeptical about spiritual things; postmodernists believe in and are deeply interested in spiritual things, but not necessarily the spiritual things of the Bible. Modernists prefer a logical, didactic approach to literature such as the Bible; postmodernists love stories and therefore prefer biblical narrative. In fact, postmodernists view reality as a system of overlapping narratives, and they not only want to hear your story but also want to tell you theirs. The modernists' heroes are the scientists and the educators; the postmodernists' heroes are the poets and the artists, those who communicate creatively. Modernists believe that truth is out there somewhere and that we can discover it through the scientific method; postmodernists believe that truth is within us (our truth is what is true to us), and thus we create our own truth. Modernists believe in noncontradiction (i.e., that ideas shouldn't contradict each other); postmodernists have no problems with contradictions (seeing them as simply overlapping narratives). Finally, modernists believe that there's one overarching metanarrative (a story or truth into which all truth fits); postmodernists believe in many metanarratives or many different "true truths."

Table I
The Modernist/Postmodernist Clash

Modernism	Postmodernism
Industrial Revolution	Information Revolution
Nationalism	Globalism
Authority: reason (Descartes)	Authority: experience
Optimism	Pessimism
Man is good	Man is bad
Natural world	Supernatural world
Skeptical	Spiritual
Didactic	Narrative
Scientists, educators	Artists, poets
Noncontradiction	Contradiction
Discover truth (scientific method)	Create truth
Metanarrative	Metanarratives

The Philosophical Context

The philosophical context of Western civilization is the various world-views that have bridged and affected these civilizations. I define a dominant worldview as a set of beliefs about the most important issues in life that help a significant number of people, such as an entire civilization, make sense of their world. A dominant worldview includes beliefs about such concepts as God, the world, truth, reality, morality, and humanity.

Western civilization has experienced four dominant worldviews (table 2), and each was generally a reaction to its predecessor. Theism was the dominant Western worldview from the Middle Ages up to the end of the seventeenth century. Deism had a limited impact that affected Western culture from the late seventeenth through the eighteenth centuries. Modernism or philosophical naturalism prevailed beginning in the eighteenth century up through 1989 (the fall of the Berlin Wall) and is still the dominant worldview in the West. Postmodernism or philosophical supernaturalism[1] most likely began in 1919 with Arthur Eddington's expedition that established Einstein's Theory of Relativity. And postmodernism is becoming a dominant worldview in America.[2]

Table 2
Western Worldviews

Theism

Deism

Modernism
(Naturalism)

Postmodernism
(Supernaturalism)

As a worldview, modernism seems to have fallen on hard times. It hasn't passed the test of experience. Horrified by such events as the Holocaust and terrified by crime and the threat of nuclear war, postmodernists have observed correctly that science hasn't solved all of the world's problems as promised and that humans are evil far beyond what a good education can repair. And the modernist emphasis on rational thought that purportedly routed the Bible and its miracles has left them cold.

Although modernism is still strong in America even among the younger generations, postmodernism seems gradually to be capturing the allegiance of many younger Americans. Postmodern advocates argue that no one universal story (metanarrative) or universal truth can hold for all time because truth isn't objective, it's subjective, depending on who is speaking and who is listening. Instead, many truths (metanarratives) exist because truth is relative to various individuals, their cultures, and their individual circumstances. Truth for one person isn't automatically truth for another person, contrary to the modernist perspective.

Postmodernists have also challenged and deconstructed literature, history, and even religion, meaning that they reject everything that people have believed about their stories, heroes, and even God. "Diversity" and "tolerance" are in fashion, whereas traditional authority and moral pronouncements are out.

Not everyone agrees, however, that postmodernism is now the reigning worldview. Some people believe that the postmodernist party is already over. You can only thumb your nose at the rules for so long; ultimately people want rules by which to live. Critics argue that modernism was about construction whereas postmodernism is all about deconstruction, and no worldview can survive such a negative, cynical approach to life that tears down without reconstructing. For example, Sally Morgenthaler writes, "Postmodernism is no foundation for a fulfilled, rewarding life. Postmodernism is a response to something, but it is not a solution in and of itself. It is a commentary, not a text, and people, everybody, needs a text to live by. They need a narrative to live within which can give their lives meaning."[3]

Although all of this has yet to play out, we've already noted in chapter 4 that the Bridger generation is typically much more optimistic than the Buster generation, a generation that reacted strongly (and negatively) to the older, optimistic Boomer generation. Perhaps postmodernism as a worldview is waning; however, it has made such an impact on American life and Christianity that the church must not take it lightly. Worldviews die a slow death. Thus it's doubtful that any church that ignores postmodernism will be effective at reaching Busters and Bridgers.

Postmodernist Pegs

Because postmodernism is a worldview, anyone—regardless of age or generation—can be a postmodernist. All one has to do is embrace a postmodernist perspective in how he or she understands and relates to the world. However, few Boomers, and even fewer Builders, have adopted postmodernism, because they have been so completely immersed in modernism. Although elements of postmodernism have been around since 1919, it did not begin to exert itself fully until the second half of the twentieth century. Consequently, postmodernism is more characteristic of the younger generations such as the Busters and Bridgers. However, we must be careful not to blanket these two generations with a postmodernist label. Not all Busters and Bridgers are postmodernists. As we've discovered, modernism is still alive and well in the lives of America's youth.

What is important to grasp, however, is the spiritual state of these two younger generations. Whether they're modern or postmodern thinkers, they're not doing well spiritually. This is a serious concern when you consider that they're the two predominant generations in America and now outnumber the Boomers and Builders combined. George Barna has warned that two-thirds of the younger generations shun all organized religion. And Thom Rainer has warned that only 4 percent of the Bridgers understand the gospel and have accepted Christ, even if they are churched. Clearly this is the church's challenge in the twenty-first century, to continue to pursue these new generations while continuing to reach out to Builders and Boomers.

As we examine briefly what postmodernists believe, we must remember that postmodernism is a mind-set that helps them to understand and relate to the world. What they believe affects how they think and react when they consider the claims of Christ or any other religion or spiritual movement (e.g., Islam, New Age). We'll look briefly at nine tenets, or postmodern pegs, on which most postmodernists would hang their caps.

There Is No Absolute Truth

Postmodernists believe that truth is relative. What is true in one situation or culture isn't necessarily true in another setting or culture. Therefore, Christ must be wrong when he claims in John 14:6 that he is the way, the truth, and the life, and that no one can come to the Father except through him. The obvious problem is that what Jesus said is an absolute and absolutes are not allowed. Of course, the view that there are no absolutes is itself an absolute statement that contradicts and disproves the postmodernists' own premise. The problem, however, is that postmodernists reject the law of noncontradiction. Thus they have no problem holding mutually contradictory positions.

Reality Is in the Mind of the Beholder

Postmodernists believe that reality is what is real to them or to me or to you; hence, reality is in the mind of the beholder. What is real to me might not be real to you—but that's okay. Neither of us is wrong; actually, we can both be right—for ourselves. Christianity might be real to me but not to you. However, as a Christian, I would be wrong to push my beliefs on you.

Intuition and Feelings Are Okay

Intuition and feelings are valid means to discover reality. Reason and logic no longer reign supreme. Humanity is basically bad, and that affects our capacity to reason. Consequently, reason is no more valid than one's feelings or intuition as a means for interpreting reality. It was okay for Jesus to resort to reason when he encountered doubting Thomas in John 20:24–29 and asked him to touch the nail marks in his hands and the wound in his side. However, from a postmodernist perspective, to appeal to Thomas's intuition and feelings about what had happened would have been just as valid an approach.

Science and Education Prove Nothing

Science, education, history, and other logic-based disciplines no longer have a corner on the market of truth, because these disciplines attempt to discover truth using primarily the scientific method. We, however, are able to create our own truths, because truth is whatever you or I decide it is. Consequently, Christ was wrong when in John 8:31–32 he said that his objective, propositional teaching was key to the Jews' knowing truth.

Culture Molds Our Minds

Culture largely affects what people think and do. It has so invaded and molded their thinking that they're unable to think independently apart from their culture; therefore, truth is relative to one's culture. This means that all lifestyles, religions, and worldviews are culture-based; therefore, no one view is more valid than any other view—they simply differ based on cultural concepts. Thus, Christians have no business judging other cultures, and Christian missionaries have no business going to other cultures to persuade them to adopt the "objective truths" of Christian culture. However, if we follow this line of reasoning, we would have to conclude that Hitler must have been right (within his own cultural understanding), and racism in America is okay, too, because truth is relative to one's culture.

The Glass Is Half Empty

Postmodernists are pessimists. Their glass is half empty. They believe that we must view the future with pessimism and cynicism because we're digressing, not progressing, as a society. Disciplines such as science and education have failed to deliver on their promises—to conquer diseases and to educate people—and thus have failed to make this world a better place. We aren't any better off today than we were in the past. For example, we still have as many criminals as we did in the past. The only difference is that they're healthier and better educated now. As is the case with some of the other tenets of postmodernism, there is some truth here. Modernism hasn't delivered on its promises because it has no power to change sinners into saints. Only the Holy Spirit can accomplish this feat through the absolute, objective truth of the gospel.

Tolerance and Acceptance Rule

We must never criticize or seek to correct other people's views or moral choices; rather, we should treat them with tolerance and acceptance. To do otherwise is to commit the sin of intolerance. The terms *tolerance* and *acceptance* are postmodern buzzwords that appear repeatedly in their writings. In short, it's inappropriate to tell other people that they're wrong. To hold that one's beliefs are true not only for oneself but also for others is bigoted and narrow-minded. The problem for postmodernists, however, is that they take this position only so far. They don't show tolerance or acceptance for views—such as Christianity—that differ with their own.

Justice for the Marginalized

We must do justice to the claims of the marginalized—those who historically have not been heard, such as women, gays, lesbians, non–Northern Europeans, and others. We must listen to these people. Their claims and ideas deserve the same kind of historical and philosophical attention that we give to those of mainstream America. Again, much here is true. However, just because a marginalized people haven't been heard or given due attention doesn't mean that what they're saying is true.

Metanarratives Are Essentially Power Plays

At the heart of every truth claim is a story, or metanarrative (absolute truth), that enhances one group but marginalizes another. Consequently, what is really taking place in America is an attempt by one group to impose its metanarrative on another group. This, in effect, is a philosophical or political power play to subjugate others—most often the marginalized—in the guise of absolute truth.

Postmodern Players

In football, when a team is performing poorly, the coach will do practically anything at halftime to motivate his team. He might jump up on a bench and shout, "Okay, who wants to win this game? Who are my players?" The church has also experienced a difficult first half, and it, too, needs to know who wants to win this game. Who'll be its players?

We have one final goal for this chapter. We must probe what kind of church Christ will use to reach the postmodern world. I predict that successful churches will come in all shapes, sizes, and colors, because it takes a diverse church to reach a diverse society. However, I believe that along with other general functions—such as people mobilization, leadership development, and other activities—the church must accomplish the following tasks in particular.

A Church That Teaches and Lives the Bible

In order to capture the postmodernists' attention, the church must teach and live the Bible. Regardless of the generation, there can be no substitute for the communication of God's Word. However, it's imperative that pastors teach and preach from the narrative portions (such as the Gospels, Acts, and much of the Old Testament) as well as from the Epistles. The tendency in the modern context is to teach more from the didactic portions (such as the New Testament Epistles) because of the prevailing modernist emphasis on reason and logic. However, postmodernists love narrative and also want God's truth in the context of a story (metanarrative), and that fits very well with the biblical narrative genre. After all, the gospel is a metanarrative. This doesn't mean, of course, that the church avoids didactic literature or any of the other genres found in the Bible. God has chosen a rich diversity of genres in which to record his Word.

Postmodernists are looking for Christians who live the Bible as well as listen to it or read it. In other words, Christians must "walk their talk" or sit down and be quiet. This is what some people refer to as incarnational Christianity. Postmodernists aren't interested in the typical apologetics that were persuasive with the modern generations. *Evidence That Demands a Verdict* doesn't cut it with them. Incarnational Christians are the primary Bible that lost, unchurched postmodernists will read. If they don't see the reality of Christ displayed there, in the lives of Christians, they won't bother opening a leather-bound Bible. Far too many young people have joined the ranks of the unchurched because they've attended churches where the older, established generations have become complacent doing church a particular way. This well-meaning establishment is reluctant or afraid to change the ways in which they've always done things because they might lose control. The tragedy is that many of these Christians have sat under good Bible teaching for thirty or forty years, but they've not applied much of it to their lives. The result is that they've run off and marginalized their young people.

A Church That Is Proactive in Evangelism

I'm somewhat troubled by a new church in Dallas that seeks to minister to lost postmodernists. The *Dallas Morning News* featured a story about this church and quoted the pastor as saying that "conversion is downplayed in favor of community." In light of the New Testament teaching in general and the Great Commission in particular, this statement alarms me. Although I'm for new paradigm churches, those churches must function biblically. Scripture provides the final say about how we do church, what we can and can't do. As we saw in chapter 4, although the Bible gives us much freedom in the forms that our churches take, it does require certain functions. Community is important, but not at the expense of conversion. Perhaps that pastor's idea is that authentic community enhances conversion, but he doesn't say that.

The church that reaches postmodernists must be proactive and "play up," not downplay, the gospel and the importance of conversion. The obvious reason is that conversion makes the difference between heaven and hell and whether one exists in the kingdom of light or the kingdom of darkness. And it's the gospel that leads to conversion.

Although the Bible is about more than just the gospel, the gospel is certainly central, and the Bible has a lot to say about it. Postmodernists need to know that the gospel is a metanarrative (story) that doesn't oppress or marginalize people. In fact, the gospel is the metanarrative that tells the truth, the story of how Jesus was "marginalized" on behalf of all who are the marginalized. (Whether poor or oppressed, we've all been marginalized by the ravages of sin.) Although the use of the term marginalized doesn't begin to capture what the Savior experienced on the cross, it does communicate in a way that is consistent with a postmodernist worldview—and thinking postmodernists will recognize this.

The church of the twenty-first century must be missional. And the Savior made it clear in Mark 16:15 and Matthew 28:19–20 that his church's mission includes the conversion of lost people and the making of disciples. We discussed in chapter 2 that the American church is not only struggling in evangelism but is also not winning the younger generations—especially the Bridgers—to faith in Christ. America has become a mission field. Consequently, a missionary mind-set that focuses on conversion must be near the top of the "to-do list" for any church that seeks to reach postmodernists.

A Church That's Creative in Worship

When we worship, we attribute extreme worth to our God, who is a most creative God. Because those with a postmodern mind-set tend to be culturally creative, churches that seek to reach postmodernists will attribute extreme worth to a creative God in creative ways. For example, the church must find creative ways to include the use of such media as painting, music, film, film clips, poetry, drama, dance, and other creative art forms. In its creativeness, the church will pursue new, contemporary worship forms, revive historic worship forms, and combine the old with the new.

Creative Christians won't be content to limit themselves only to traditional forms of worship. They'll constantly be exploring new and different ways to worship God. They might include a corporate reading, painting, creative dance, film clips that highlight some aspect of the sermon, and other forms that haven't even been thought of yet. (Some churches are already using creative dance and film clips in their worship.) They'll not be content with old music forms alone. This is too confining of worship. They will constantly be writing new music to aid the church in expressing the wonders of our marvelous God.

At the same time, some new paradigm churches have returned, and will continue to return, to worship forms of the past. Churches that are currently reaching out to busters often depend heavily on sixth-century liturgy, monastic images, and recitation of a creed or response to a catechism as part of their worship. These activities often take place in a setting with a plethora of candles, and communion is served every week.

Some churches that reach postmodernists will merge the old with the new. They might mix the liturgy, the Nicene Creed, and a corporate reading with Christian alternative rock. They might blend the neoclassical with a touch of Celtic. They could combine a little bit of Christian rock, Christian jazz, or Christian rap with ancient texts and prayers.

As occurred in the past, these churches will worship in a variety of locations. They'll use such contexts as an inner city storefront, a nightclub, a fitness center, or a facility that belongs to an older church. Regardless of the form or the location, the object will be to divert the worshipers' attention away from the particular form or location to focus on our awesome God.

A Church That Is Authentic

A characteristic of postmodernists is their strong desire for authenticity. The church that reaches postmodernists will pursue authenticity. This isn't exactly new. The Boomer generation also appreciates churches that practice authenticity.

About ten years ago, I worked as a consultant with a church whose board consisted of Boomers and Builders. My assignment was to assist and advise them in their pursuit of a new pastor. While we were discussing the characteristics of a good pastor for their church, one of the Builder members strongly expressed that he wanted a pastor who didn't talk about his shortcomings and failures from the pulpit. He asked, "How can we follow a pastor who doesn't have it all together?"

Before he could finish, one of the Boomer members interrupted him angrily and stated, "That's exactly what we need, a pastor who's willing to admit publicly that he doesn't have it all together!" That's authenticity.

Nothing has changed with the younger generations. The problem is that most of them struggle to define authenticity. Mark Driscoll writes, "Authenticity is when your inside matches your outside, one person said. It is two parts integrity and one part self-disclosure. It is not soul-letting without a tourniquet, but a willingness to share from one's faith experience for the benefit of others is required."[4] Driscoll is correct. Authenticity includes the willingness to disclose publicly your shortcomings as well as your successes. Some young people would say that it's "being real."

The twenty-first-century church can display authenticity in a number of contexts. One must be the pulpit. Preaching pastors must have the freedom to verbalize their shortcomings and vulnerabilities. There must be a willingness to share from their faith experience that includes defeats as well as victories. Most congregations know that pastors are frail human beings, but they do need to hear them admit it from time to time. Even more important, many congregants consider themselves pilgrims who want to learn from pilgrim pastors who are a little farther along in their spiritual journeys and have bled some along the way.

The church that pursues authenticity would also be wise to have an active small-group ministry. Authenticity is developed and nurtured in the context of community. *Community*, as I'm using the term here, means a gathering of believers. Most Christians desire to build deep relationships with a small group of other, like-minded believers. This is especially a characteristic of and most important to the Busters and the Bridgers. However, this kind of community demands authenticity. People fellowship and relate best with one another when they can talk about their shortcomings and struggles with others who will listen and give comfort.

A Church That Values Community

Some of the more seeker-oriented Boomer churches value anonymity, because they realized that many seekers from the Builder and Boomer generations preferred to be left alone to consider the claims of Christ without having to stand and introduce themselves or interact with the people sitting near them. So these churches created a style of service where these people could come and participate at their own discretion.

Busters and Bridgers might prefer anonymity when they first make contact with a church. However, they are ultimately more interested in being part of a community of believers. Busters and Bridgers are two generations that highly value community, and the term often punctuates their conversations about the ideal church.

The type of community they desire most is biblical community, which is what occurs when believers practice the "one another" passages that are sprinkled throughout the New Testament. These passages exhort Christians to pray for one another, encourage one another, confront one another, care for one another, and engage in numerous other "one another" ministries. At the core of biblical community is a commitment to share who they are and relate at length and in-depth with one another. Acts 2:42–47 and Acts 4:32–35 provide us with a first-century snapshot of biblical community. It includes such events as spending time together, sharing and holding possessions in common, providing for one another's needs, and other ministries. For today's young person, getting to know

God often involves getting to know the people of God first. And community is the way they can get to know the people of God best.

The church that reaches postmodernists in the twenty-first century will develop new structures that encourage community. Many churches have already developed small-group ministries with the intent to cultivate biblical community. As we train church planters, we ask them, "Will your future churches be faith communities with small groups, or a community of small groups?" In other words, "Will your ministries include small groups, or will your ministries consist primarily of small groups?" Churches with small-groups programs include community, but churches of small groups are community.

A Church That Uses Technology

Over the last twenty years or so, America has experienced a technological explosion. Technology that wasn't around five to ten years ago is now part of our everyday lives. It's common to see people on the street with a cell phone mounted on their hip or plastered to their ear. Churches that reach postmodernists won't hesitate to use technology in their ministry.

The problem up till now is that the church has been hesitant at best to incorporate technology. Lyle Schaller, who is of the Builder generation, tells how difficult it was for the church to embrace the telephone when it first became available. And he shares humorously how some people greeted the church's move to adopt indoor plumbing with the following words: "We're not going to do that in the house of God are we?" One wonders how long it took the church to adopt the printing press when it first became available in the middle of the fourteenth century. In order to reach postmodernists effectively, the church must look at the available technology and ask how it can be used creatively for the cause of Christ.

Our particular concern in this book is the use of the Internet and related technology to advance the mission of the church. If, as I mentioned earlier, as many as three out of four Americans go online, the Internet has clearly become a mainstream activity that should be utilized by the church. A report by the Pew Internet and American Life Project indicates that, in 2001, 25 percent of people used the Internet for religious purposes (up from 21 percent in 2000), an increase that equates to nineteen or twenty million people. The report states, "For comparison's sake, it is interesting to note that more people have gotten religious or spiritual information online than have gambled online, used Web auction sites, traded stocks online, placed phone calls on the Internet, done online banking, or used Internet-based dating services."[5]

We believe that Americans are just beginning to warm to the idea of using the Internet for religious purposes. Therefore, a primary challenge for the church early in the twenty-first century will be to harness the Internet and use it powerfully for the cause of Christ.

Notes

Introduction

1. Lyle E. Schaller, *44 Questions for Church Planters* (Nashville: Abingdon, 1991), 78.
2. Win Arn, *The Pastor's Manual for Effective Ministry* (Monrovia, CA: Church Growth, 1988), 16.
3. George Gallup Jr, *The Unchurched American—10 Years Later* (Princeton, NJ: Princeton Religion Research Center, 1988), 2.
4. George Barna, "Number of Unchurched Adults Has Doubled Since 1991," Barna Research, online: www.barna.org (May 4, 2004).
5. Kennon L. Callahan, *Effective Church Leadership* (San Francisco: Harper and Row, 1990), 13.
6. Cited in Ed Stetzer, *Planting New Churches in a Postmodern Age* (Nashville: Broadman and Holman, 2003), 4, 11.
7. C. Peter Wagner, *Church Planting for a Greater Harvest* (Ventura, CA: Regal, 1990), 11.
8. Unfortunately, most of this criticism has come from well-meaning Christians.

Chapter 1 What Are We Talking About?

1. Wagner, *Church Planting for a Greater Harvest*, 11.
2. George Barna, *The Frog in the Kettle* (Ventura, CA: Regal, 1990), 115.

Chapter 2 Do We Need Another Church?

1. Arn, *The Pastor's Manual for Effective Ministry*, 41.
2. Ibid., 43.
3. Carl S. Dudley and David A. Roozen, *Faith Communities Today: A Report on Religion in the United States Today*, Hartford Institute for Religion Research, Hartford Seminary, online: fact.hartsem.edu (March 2001), 10.
4. Randy Frazee with Lyle E. Schaller, *The Comeback Congregation* (Nashville: Abingdon, 1995), 11.
5. Benton Johnson, Dean R. Hoge, and Donald A. Luidens, "Mainline Churches: The Real Reason for Decline," *First Things* (March 1993), 13.
6. Constant H. Jacquet Jr, ed., *Yearbook of American and Canadian Churches, 1988* (Nashville: Abingdon, 1989), 261; compared with Eileen W. Lindner, ed., *Yearbook of American and Canadian Churches, 2001* (Nashville: Abingdon, 2001), 353.

7. "Missions Memo," *Missions USA* (July-Aug. 1988), 2.

8. Linda Lawson, "SBC '98 Stats Reveal First Drop since 1926," in *Facts and Trends* (Nashville, TN: LifeWay Christian Resources, 1998), 3. You can observe this firsthand by going to the American Religious Data Service Archieve (http://www.thearda.com). Once you are there click on the Interactive Maps and Reports and then survey any of the counties listed under Membership Reports by Counties.

9. Scott Thumma, "Megachurches Cluster in Bible Belt, Study Shows," *Faith Communities Today (FACT)*, The Hartford Institute for Religion Research (Dec. 6, 2001), 1.

10. Wagner, *Church Planting for a Greater Harvest*, 14, 16.

11. Jackson W. Carroll, Douglas W. Johnson, and Martin E. Marty, *Religion in America: 1950 to the Present* (San Francisco, CA: Harper and Row, 1979), 16.

12. Ibid.

13. Dean M. Kelley, *Why Conservative Churches Are Growing: A Study in the Sociology of Religion* (New York: Harper and Row, 1972).

14. Tom W. Smith, "Are Conservative Churches Growing?" at www.icpsr.umich.edu (Jan. 1991). Note that Smith uses the terms *conservative* and *fundamental* interchangeably.

15. "Church Attendance," Barna Research, at www.barna.org (Dec. 3, 2001).

16. "Worship Attendance Falls to Pre-September 11 Levels," *Dallas Morning News*, Dec. 1, 2001, 5G.

17. Barna, "Number of Unchurched Adults Has Nearly Doubled."

18. "Gallup Poll Topic: A–Z," The Gallup Organization, at www.gallup.com (Dec. 13, 2001).

19. "U.S. Attendance at Services Down in Poll," *Dallas Morning News*, May 28, 1994, 43A.

20. Cathy L. Grossman and Anthony DeBarros, "Still One Nation under God," *USA Today*, Dec. 24, 2001, 2D.

21. C. Kirk Hadaway, Penny L. Marler, Mark Chaves, "What the Polls Don't Show: A Closer Look at U.S. Church Attendance," *American Sociological Review* (Dec. 1993).

22. *Dallas Morning News*, Aug. 14, 1995, 16A.

23. Frazee, *The Comeback Congregation*, 39.

24. C. Kirk Hadaway and P. L. Marler, "Did You Really Go to Church This Week? Behind the Poll Data," *Religion Online* at www.religion-online.org (Dec. 10, 2001), 3.

25. "Church Attendance," *Barna Research* at www.barna.org (Oct. 15, 1999).

26. Thomas Reeves, *The Empty Church* (New York: Simon and Schuster, 1996), 61.

27. Jacquet, ed., *Yearbook of American and Canadian Churches, 1988*, 262; compared with Lindner, ed., *Yearbook of American and Canadian Churches, 2001*, 348, 352.

28. *Dallas Morning News*, February 16, 2002, 1G.

29. Jacquet, ed., *Yearbook of American and Canadian Churches, 1988*, 262; compared with Lindner, ed., *Yearbook of American and Canadian Churches, 2001*, 348, 352.

30. Ihsan Bagby, Paul M. Paul, Bryan T. Frochle, "A Report from the Mosque Study Project," *The Mosque in America: A National Portrait* (April 26, 2001), 3; online at www.cair-net.org/mosquereport/.

31. Marcy E. Mullins, "A Measure of Faith," *USA Today*, Dec. 24, 2001, 4D.

32. Thom S. Rainer, "Shattering Myths about the Unchurched," *Southern Baptist Journal of Theology* 5, no. 1 (spring 2001): 47.

33. "Schaller Says SBC Must Decide about New Church Starts," *Biblical Recorder* (June 15, 1991), 8.

34. Stetzer, *Planting New Churches in a Postmodern Age*, 4, 11.

35. Wagner, *Church Planting for a Greater Harvest*, 7.

36. Ibid., 11.
37. Win Arn, "Church Growth and Church Age Are Related," *The Win Arn Growth Report* 1, no. 21.
38. Schaller, *44 Questions for Church Planters*, 22.
39. Ibid., 22–23.
40. Bruce McNicol, "Churches Die with Dignity," *Christianity Today* (Jan. 14, 1991), 69.
41. C. Wayne Zunkel, *Growing the Small Church* (Elgin, IL: David C. Cook, 1982), 48.

Chapter 3 How Do You Make Ends Meet?

1. Dallas Willard, *The Spirit of the Disciplines* (San Francisco: Harper and Row, 1988), 130–31.
2. In planning and raising funds, most often the Savior allows church planters to raise most but not all of their support. While the entire process is a faith venture, he wants them to step out in faith and trust him for the remaining necessary support.
3. This concept will be developed further in chapter 8 of this book. However, it's treated in depth in Aubrey Malphurs, *Developing a Vision for Ministry in the Twenty-first Century*, 2nd ed. (Grand Rapids: Baker Books, 1999).
4. Much of the following information was developed by my friend and former student Clayton Hayes.

Chapter 4 What You Don't Know Might Hurt You!

1. Barna, *Frog in the Kettle*, 115.
2. Some Bible colleges such as Moody and Multnomah continue to remain strong in evangelism. In fact, the president of Multnomah, Joe Aldrich, has written two excellent works on evangelism: *Life-Style Evangelism* and *Gentle Persuasion*, both published by Multnomah Press.
3. Calvin Guy, "Theological Foundations," in *Church Growth and Christian Mission*, ed. Donald A. McGavran (William Carey Library, 1976 reprint), 44.
4. See Lyle E. Schaller, "Megachurch!" *Christianity Today* (March 5, 1990), 22–23.
5. "Church Growth Fine Tunes Its Formulas," *Christianity Today* (June 24, 1991), 47.
6. Barna, *Frog in the Kettle*, 136–37.
7. Carroll, Jackson, and Marty, *Religion in America*, 16.
8. I have written a book on hermeneutics for pastors and the church that explores this and other issues of what the church can and can't do. *Doing Church* (Grand Rapids: Kregel, 1999).
9. I deal briefly with this important topic in chapter 9 of *Developing a Vision for Ministry in the Twenty-first Century* (Grand Rapids: Baker Books, 1992).
10. Quoted in James M. Kouzes and Barry Z. Posner, *The Leadership Challenge* (San Francisco: Jossey-Bass, 1987), 137–38.

Chapter 5 Are You a Church Planter?

1. Here I'm using the term *soul*, as Genesis 2:7 does, of man as a complete whole, a total being, including both the material and immaterial aspects of his being. According to Scripture, man *has* a soul but also *is* a soul.

2. The idea of using the term *limitations* rather than *weaknesses* is the suggestion of Dr. William Lawrence, who is the executive director of the Center for Christian Leadership at Dallas Theological Seminary.

3. Charles C. Ryrie, *The Holy Spirit* (Chicago: Moody, 1965), 83.

4. This material on gift-mix and gift-cluster is heavily influenced by Robert Clinton's *The Making of a Leader* (Colorado Springs: NavPress, 1988).

5. Ibid., 92.

6. The Keirsey Temperament Sorter can be ordered from Prometheus Nemesis Book Company, Box 2748, Del Mar, CA 92014.

7. For more information, contact Mr. Paul Williams at PO Box 9, East Islip, NY 11730-0009.

8. Roy M. Oswald and Otto Kroeger, *Personality Type and Religious Leadership* (Washington, DC: Alban Institute, 1988), 30.

9. Ibid., 35.

10. Ibid., 38.

11. Ibid.

12. Ibid., 69.

13. Ibid., 68.

14. Ibid., 69.

15. Ibid., 41.

16. Ibid., 81.

17. Ibid., 40–41.

18. Arnell ArnTessoni, *Gentle Plantings* (The Church Planter's Network, 2001). You may obtain a copy by writing the author at PO Box 924, Concordville, PA 19331, or calling her at (866) 447-5268.

19. "The 'Johnny Appleseeds' of Church Planting," *Leadership* (spring 1984), 126.

20. Ibid.

21. Ibid., 127.

22. Ibid.

Chapter 6 Leading with Sustained Excellence

1. I provide an expanded definition of a leader and leadership in Aubrey Malphurs, *Being Leaders: The Nature of Authentic Christian Leadership* (Grand Rapids: Baker Books, 2003).

2. Bill Hybels, *Too Busy Not to Pray* (Downers Grove: InterVarsity, 1988).

3. Dallas Willard, *The Spirit of the Disciplines* (San Francisco: Harper and Row, 1988).

4. Charles R. Swindoll, *Leadership: Influence That Inspires* (Waco, TX: Word, 1985), 19–20.

5. Ibid., 20.

6. In fact, as I was writing this section, I received a phone call from one of my former students pastoring in the Dallas area who is struggling with this very situation.

7. C. Peter Wagner, *Leading Your Church to Growth* (Ventura, CA: Regal, 1984), 74.

8. Lyle E. Schaller, *Effective Church Planting* (Nashville: Abingdon, 1979), 162, quoted in Wagner, *Leading Your Church to Growth*, 75.

9. Larry Osborne, *The Unity Factor* (Carol Stream, IL: Word, 1989), 67.

10. Ibid., 67–68.

11. Robert G. Gromacki, *Called to Be Saints: An Exposition of 1 Corinthians* (Grand Rapids: Baker Books, 1977), 134.

12. F. F. Bruce, *The Book of Acts* (Grand Rapids: Eerdmans, 1977), 43.

13. Ibid., 429.

14. Lyle Schaller estimates that one-fourth of all Protestant churches in America average fewer than thirty-five in the morning worship service and at least half average fewer than seventy-five. See Lyle Schaller, *Growing Plans* (Nashville: Abingdon, 1983), 18.

15. According to Acts 2:47, the church experienced significant growth after the 3,000 of Peter's first sermon were added and before the 5,000 of the second sermon. In verse 47 Luke chooses the imperfect indicative, which expresses continuous action in the past. Therefore, the passage could read, "And the Lord kept on adding to their number daily."

16. R. C. H. Lenski, *The Interpretation of the Acts of the Apostles* (Minneapolis: Augsburg, 1934), 239.

17. Lyle Schaller, "Trends in Pastoral Care," *Leadership Journal* (winter 1990), 26.

18. Wagner, *Leading Your Church to Growth*, 119.

19. Ibid., 119–20.

20. Gene Getz, "Sharpening the Pastor's Focus," *Leadership* (summer 1985), 13–14.

Chapter 7 We Want to Have a Baby

1. This analogy is not original with me. For example, Bob Logan and Jeff Rast use it in *Starting a Church That Keeps on Growing* (Pasadena, CA: Charles E. Fuller Institute of Evangelism and Church Growth, 1986). In this work they give credit for this analogy to Don Stewart.

2. Actually these steps and those of the five other church planting stages are crucial not only to church planting but to pastoring healthy churches and those in desperate need of renewal. Consequently, those ministering in these situations would profit from reading this book as well as church planters.

3. Peter Wagner has done some excellent work in this area. He includes a small section on prayer in *Church Planting for a Greater Harvest*, 49.

4. For an in-depth coverage of the values concept and several examples of credos, see Aubrey Malphurs, *Values-Driven Leadership*, 2nd ed. (Grand Rapids: Baker Books, 2004).

5. For an in-depth treatment of the missions concept, see Aubrey Malphurs, *Developing a Dynamic Mission for Your Ministry* (Grand Rapids: Kregel, 1998).

6. For an in-depth treatment of vision, see Aubrey Malphurs, *Developing a Vision for Ministry in the Twenty-first Century*, 2nd ed. (Grand Rapids: Baker Books, 1999).

7. This section focuses on the organizational vision. Actually church planters and anyone in ministry should have two kinds of vision. One is a personal ministry vision, derived from their divine design. This concept was developed in chapter 5. The other is an organizational vision, which is the vision for the ministry or, in this case, the planted church. The same is true for values and mission.

8. I would like to give credit to my friend and former student Mike Baer for his thinking regarding this definition.

9. There is a further explanation of this and an example of what it will look like in chapter 4 of Aubrey Malphurs, *Developing a Vision for Ministry in the Twenty-first Century*.

Chapter 8 We're Going to Have a Baby!

1. Kenneth H. Sidney, "Church Growth Fine Tunes Its Formulas," *Christianity Today* (June 24, 1991), 47.

2. Barna, *Frog in the Kettle*, 146.

3. Arnold Mitchell, *The Nine American Lifestyles* (New York: Warner, 1983).

4. Tex Sample, *U.S. Lifestyles and Mainline Churches* (Louisville, KY: Westminster/John Knox Press, 1990).

5. The Percept Group Inc. at www.percept1.com.

6. C. Peter Wagner, *Your Church Can Grow* (Ventura, CA: Regal, 1976), 96.

7. Roger S. Greenway and Timothy M. Monsma, *Cities: Missions' New Frontiers* (Grand Rapids: Baker Books, 2000), 67.

8. Roger S. Greenway, *Apostles to the City* (Grand Rapids: Baker Books, 1978), 11.

9. Michael E. Gerber, *The E-Myth* (New York: Harper-Collins, 1986), 92.

10. William H. Frey, "Three Americas: The Rising Significance of Regions," *APA Journal* 68, no. 4 (autumn 2002): 349–55.

11. For more information on these times and on how to reach the community through mailers, advertising, and so on, read Robert C. Screen, "Effective Communication to Your Community," in *The Pastor's Church Growth Handbook*, ed. Win Arn (Pasadena, CA: Church Growth, 1979), 206–20.

12. Pastor Keith Stewart used the direct mail method and planted and pastors Springcreek Community Church in Garland, Texas.

13. Ezra Earl Jones, *Strategies for New Churches* (San Francisco: Harper and Row, 1976), 92.

14. James F. Engel and H. Wilbert Norton, *What's Gone Wrong with the Harvest?* (Grand Rapids: Zondervan, 1975), 45.

15. Lyle E. Schaller, "Southern Baptists Face Two Choices for Future," *Biblical Recorder* (April 27, 1991), 8.

16. *Performax "DiSC" Profiles Trainer's Transparency Masters Manual* (Performax Systems International, 1987).

17. Oswald and Kroeger, *Personality Type and Religious Leadership*, 122.

18. Stetzer, *Planting New Churches in a Postmodern Age*, 68.

19. Schaller, "Southern Baptists," 8.

20. Keri Kent, "Adopting a Team Strategy," *Willow Creek* (Sept.–Oct. 1991), 9.

21. Stetzer, *Planting New Churches in a Postmodern Age*, 96–100.

22. The steps that make up the conception stage are the steps leaders take when they do strategic planning. I have written *Advanced Strategic Planning* (Baker), which includes a much more in-depth treatment of these steps.

Chapter 9 Childbirth Classes

1. It's possible that a core group could be different from a launch group. The former may consist of those who have caught a vision for the new work and plan to be an integral part of it. The latter, however, might consist of the core group and/or people from a supporting church or churches that desire to aid in the birthing of the church but don't plan to be a part of it long term. Some have referred to the latter as a "swat team." Regardless, I use the two terms in this book synonymously.

2. I would like to give credit to Robert Salstrom for these general questions, not the details. He is a graduate of Dallas Seminary and the former director of Alumni Affairs who has encouraged a number of seminarians to pursue church planting.

3. Some have challenged the seeker concept (popularized by Willow Creek Community Church near Chicago) on theological grounds. They argue simply that a lost person (seeker) can't seek after God (Rom. 3:11). However, they seem to miss Acts 17:27, which indicates that people can seek God. These two passages appear to contradict. I believe that man, in

and of himself, can't seek after God. However, I believe that what we can imply from Acts 17:27 is that God the Holy Spirit begins to pursue people and enables them to seek after him. There are also several biblical examples that support the seeker concept: Nicodemus (John 3:1–21), Zacchaeus (Luke 19:1–9), the Ethiopian Eunuch (Acts 8:26–39), and Cornelius (Acts 10).

Chapter 10 It's a Baby!

1. Wagner, *Church Planting for a Greater Harvest*, 97–98.
2. Donald J. MacNair, *The Birth, Care, and Feeding of a Local Church* (Grand Rapids: Baker Books, 1971).
3. Ibid., x, 22.
4. Wagner, *Church Planting for a Greater Harvest*, 119–20.
5. Ibid., 120.
6. Ibid.
7. Paul W. Powell, *Go-Givers in a Go-Getter World* (Nashville: Broadman, 1986), 59.
8. Ibid.
9. Jones, *Strategies for New Churches*, 82.
10. Schaller, *44 Questions for Church Planters*, 60.
11. Ibid.
12. Ibid., 62.
13. Lyle Schaller also recognizes this problem and refers to it as the "Second Sunday Syndrome" in *44 Questions for Church Planters*, 92–94. I strongly recommend that you look at his solutions to this problem as well as my own.
14. Stetzer, *Planting New Churches in a Postmodern Age*, 98.
15. George Thomasson, *The Church Blueprint* (Columbus, GA: Brentwood Christian Press, 2002), 120.
16. Steve Sjogren, *Conspiracy of Kindness* (Ann Arbor, MI: Vine Books, 1993).

Chapter 11 Feed Them and They Grow!

1. In this chapter, I'll quote a lot of material from Peter Wagner, Lyle Schaller, and Win Arn. I consider these men to be experts in the field of church growth.
2. Wagner, *Leading Your Church to Growth*, 89.
3. Schaller, *Growing Plans*, 85.
4. Wagner, *Your Church Can Grow*, chap. 3.
5. Wagner, *Leading Your Church to Growth*, 97.
6. You may want to turn back to chapter 5 and briefly review the section on the *Personal Profile*.
7. I have taken many of these characteristics from the interpretation section of Ken R. Voges, *Biblical Personal Profile* (Minneapolis: Performax Systems International, 1985), 7.
8. You may want to review the section on the MBTI in chapter 5.
9. I say more about this model and how it developed historically from a biblical-theological perspective in Aubrey Malphurs, *Being Leaders* (Baker Books, 2003).
10. Wagner, *Leading Your Church to Growth*, 59.
11. Lyle E. Schaller, *The Small Church Is Different* (New York: Abingdon, 1982), 53–54.
12. Christian A. Schwarz, *Natural Church Development: A Guide to Eight Essential Qualities of Healthy Churches* (Carol Stream, IL: ChurchSmart Resources, 1996).

13. Schaller, *Growing Plans*, 115.
14. Ibid., 116.
15. Joel Arthur Barker, *Discovering the Future* (St. Paul, MN: ILI Press, 1985), 32.
16. Wagner, *Leading Your Church to Growth*, 213.
17. Wagner, *Your Church Can Grow*, 77.
18. Ibid.
19. Similar programs are available from Network Ministries International (www.bruce bugbee.com).
20. Arn, "The Characteristics of an 'Incorporated Member,'" in *The Pastor's Manual for Effective Ministry*, 79.
21. Ibid., 7.
22. Schwarz, *Natural Church Development*, 32.
23. Ibid.
24. Ibid., 33.
25. Surprisingly, an exception here is the recent seminary graduate. Most seminaries don't spend much time with practical ministry but focus more on theology and biblical studies. Many seem to think—incorrectly—that the practical aspects can be learned later. In these situations, seminarians should try to gain as much practical experience and knowledge as possible through their field education programs. If this doesn't work, then they should pursue an internship after they graduate before going into ministry.

Chapter 12 I'm No Longer a Kid!

1. Win Arn, *The Church Growth Handbook* (Monrovia, CA: Church Growth, 1990), 10–11.
2. John Carver, *Boards That Make a Difference* (San Francisco: Jossey-Bass, 1997).
3. Schaller, *Growing Plans*, 151.
4. Win Arn, "Average Driving Time to Church," *The Win Arn Growth Report* 1, no. 20, 1.

Chapter 13 Let's Have a Baby

1. Wagner, *Your Church Can Grow*, 96.
2. I have written *Advanced Strategic Planning* and *Pouring New Wine into Old Wineskins* (both published by Baker Books) to address why and how to revitalize churches.
3. Sherri Brown, "The Search for Saddleback Sam," *Mission USA* (July–Aug. 1988), 17.
4. Kent, "Adopting a Team Strategy," 9.
5. Ibid.
6. Dean Merrill, "Mothering a New Church," *Leadership* (winter 1985), 103.
7. Ibid., 102.
8. Ibid., 103.
9. Ibid., 104.
10. Ibid., 103.
11. Wagner, *Church Planting for a Greater Harvest*, 119–20.
12. Merrill, "Mothering a New Church," 105.
13. Ibid.
14. Ibid., 100.

15. Ibid.
16. Ibid.
17. Ibid.
18. Ibid.
19. Ibid.

Appendix A A Well-Mobilized Lay Army

1. Bill Hybels, *Honest to God?* (Grand Rapids: Zondervan, 1990), 107–8.
2. Peter F. Drucker, *Managing the Non-Profit Organization* (New York: HarperBusiness, 1990), 145.
3. Howard G. Hendricks, *Say It with Love* (Wheaton, IL: Victor, 1972), 113–14.
4. Frank Tillapaugh, *Unleashing the Church* (Ventura, CA: Regal, 1982), 20.
5. Robert S. McGee, *The Search for Significance* (Houston, TX: Rapha, 1990), 15.
6. I first heard this term and the concept from my friend Bruce Bugbee, who was one of the pastors at Willow Creek Community Church in South Barrington, Illinois.
7. There aren't many assessment programs available. I highly recommend Network Ministries International—the ministry that Bruce Bugbee leads. Contact him about such programs (www.brucebugbee.com).
8. I've adopted several ideas for this process from Bruce Bugbee and the *Networking* program that he designed for Willow Creek Community Church.
9. The latter term, minister of involvement, is the title my pastor, Steve Stroope, used at Lakepointe Church, located in the suburbs of Dallas.
10. This approach is illustrated in Tillapaugh, *Unleashing the Church*, 168–80, 188–97.

Appendix B A Culturally Relevant Ministry

1. Source unknown.
2. Barna, *Frog in the Kettle*, 49.
3. Donald C. Posterski, *Reinventing Evangelism* (Downers Grove, IL: InterVarsity, 1989), 28.
4. Tom Peters, *Thriving on Chaos* (New York: Harper and Row, 1988), 183.
5. The exact source of this survey is unknown. Some credit Bill Hybels, pastor of Willow Creek Community Church. Others credit Rick Warren, pastor of Saddleback Valley Community Church.
6. Donald A. McGavran, *Understanding Church Growth* (Grand Rapids: Eerdmans, 1970), 223.
7. See Aubrey Malphurs, *Doing Church* (Grand Rapids: Kregel, 1999).

Appendix C A Holistic, Authentic Worship

1. Ronald Allen and Gordon Borror, *Worship* (Portland, OR: Multnomah, 1982), 67–68.
2. Ibid., 9.
3. Barry Liesch, *People in the Presence of God* (Grand Rapids: Zondervan, 1988), xi.
4. Allen and Borror, *Worship*, 16.

5. A number of these worship tension points are taken from a cassette tape by Doug Murren entitled "Developing Dynamic Worship Services," a part of *The Pastor's Update Monthly Cassette Program* published by the Charles E. Fuller Institute of Evangelism and Church Growth.

6. Excellent texts on preaching are Haddon W. Robinson, *Biblical Preaching* 2nd ed. (Grand Rapids: Baker Academic, 2001), and Ramesh Richard, *Scripture Sculpture* (Grand Rapids: Baker Books, 1995). Both books will be very helpful for anyone who has not had a course in homiletics or who needs some review in the field.

7. This is the title of a sermon used by my friend Keith Stewart, who pastors Springcreek Community Church in Garland, Texas.

8. This is Dr. Bill Counts, who pastors Fellowship Bible Church of Park Cities, Dallas, Texas.

Appendix D A Biblical, Culturally Relevant Evangelism

1. Exact source unknown.

2. Floyd Bartel, *A New Look at Church Growth* (Newton, KS: Faith and Life, 1987), 59.

3. Barna, *Frog in the Kettle*, 115.

4. Wagner, *Church Planting for a Greater Harvest*, 11.

5. Wagner, *Your Church Can Grow*, 86.

6. W. Charles Arn, "How to Find Receptive People," in *The Pastor's Church Growth Handbook*, 142–43.

7. Hybels, *Honest to God?*, 126.

8. Ibid., 126–32.

9. Tom Wolf, "The Biblical Pattern of Effective Evangelism," in *The Pastor's Church Growth Handbook*, 110–16.

10. Hans Walter Wolff, *Anthropology of the Old Testament* (Philadelphia: Fortress, 1974), 214–15.

11. *Theological Dictionary of the New Testament*, ed. Gerhard Kittel and Gerhard Friedrich; trans. and ed. Geoffrey W. Bromiley, s.v. "oikos," by Otto Michel (1967), 5:130.

12. Win Arn and Charles Arn, *The Master's Plan for Making Disciples* (Pasadena, CA: Church Growth, 1982), 43.

13. Steve Sjogren, *Conspiracy of Kindness* (Ann Arbor, MI.: Servant, 1993).

14. This list can be ordered from the Masterplanning Group International, Box 952499, Lake Mary, FL 32795.

Appendix E A Robust Network of Small Groups

1. Paula Rinehart, "The Pivotal Generation," *Christianity Today* (Oct. 6, 1989), 24.

2. Ibid.

3. Ibid.

4. Lyman Coleman and Marty Scales, *Serendipity Training Manual for Groups* (Littleton, CO: Serendipity House, 1989), 7.

5. Ibid., 9.

6. Ibid., 7.

7. Bob Logan has an excellent section that develops this concept in *Beyond Church Growth* (Grand Rapids: Revell, 1989), 133–35.

Appendix G Understanding Postmodernism

1. I don't use supernaturalism here in the sense that Christianity uses it. I'm using it in contrast to philosophical naturalism's idea that nothing exists outside the natural order of this material universe—that this material universe is the sum total of reality. Whereas, postmodernism believes that something does exist beyond the material universe—hence there exists a spiritual dimension in addition to the material dimension.

2. Paul Johnson, *Modern Times: The World from the Twenties to the Nineties* (New York: HarperCollins, 1991), 1–4.

3. Sally Morgenthaler, "Is Post-modernism Passé?" *Rev.* (Sept./Oct. 2001), 700.

4. "Warrior, Chief, Medicine Man," *Leadership* (fall 2000), 54.

5. Lee Rainie, *CyberFaith: How Americans Pursue Religion Online*, Pew Internet and American Life Project, online at www.pewinternet.org/ (Dec. 23, 2001), 2.

Index

Aubrey Malphurs is a professor of pastoral ministries at Dallas Seminary and the president of The Malphurs Group. He is available for consultation on various topics related to leadership, vision, church planting, and church renewal. Those wishing to contact him for consulting or speaking engagements may do so through The Malphurs Group, 7916 Briar Brook Court, Dallas, TX 75218; 214-841-3777; aubrey@malphursgroup.com; www.malphursgroup.com.

THEMALPHURSGROUP
ENVISION TOMORROW TODAY

Aubrey Malphurs, Ph.D.

President
The Malphurs Group

Professor
Dallas Theological Seminary

Let us serve you!
We offer training and consulting services such as:

- Strategic planning
- Church refocusing
- Church planting

- Values discovery
- Personal leadership coaching

Visit our Web site! Features include:

- Books
- Seminars
- Newsletters

- Events
- Resources
- and more...

aubrey@malphursgroup.com • www.malphursgroup.com

For more info: 214.841.3777
7916 Briar Brook Court • Dallas, Texas 75218

Made in the USA
Lexington, KY
17 March 2014